JESUS

JESUS

*A New Understanding
of God's Son*

Joseph F. Girzone

DOUBLEDAY

NEW YORK LONDON TORONTO SYDNEY AUCKLAND

ⅅⅅ
DOUBLEDAY

Copyright © 2009 by Joseph F. Girzone

Map previously appeared in *The New Jerusalem Bible* published by
Doubleday Religion, a division of Random House, Inc.

Library of Congress Cataloging-in-Publication Data
Girzone, Joseph F.
Jesus: a new understanding of God's son / Joseph F. Girzone.—
1st ed.
1. Jesus Christ—Biography. I. Title.
BT301.3.G57 2009
232.9'01—dc22
[B]   2009015424

ISBN 978-0-385-52815-3

Printed in the United States of America

10 9 8 7 6 5 4 3 2 1

First Edition

CONTENTS

PREFACE

When I first began to write and give talks about Jesus, a very pious priest shocked me one day by asking me the question, "How can you possibly talk about Jesus for an hour and a half?" This was the average length of my talks as I traveled from country to country trying in my own simple way to evangelize. I always thought that evangelizing meant talking about Jesus so people could know him and fall in love with him. As I had admired this priest since my childhood, I was taken aback by his remark.

When I asked him why he should be so surprised, he said, "We were not taught about Jesus in the seminary. We had good Scripture courses and theology courses, and courses in canon law and liturgy and so many other subjects, but other than the course on Christology, which merely studied the history of the development of the earliest Christians' understanding about Jesus, we really never learned anything in depth about Jesus, about how he thinks and how he feels and what his values are concerning so many issues in life. So, I don't think I could talk about him in any depth for more than five minutes."

I never forgot that, and from then on I kept looking every place I went and in every denomination, and it was the same. Protestants were enamored with the Scriptures, especially the letters of Saint Paul, and with Old Testament morality, while Catholics were enamored with the Church as the only teaching authority established by Jesus. One old German lady sized up the situation precisely during a talk one night when she said, "The way I size up Christianity is like this: The Catholics worship the Church, the Protestants worship the Bible, and there are darn few who ever get to know Jesus Christ." And that is what has happened to Christianity. The Church and the Bible have become the message. And that is not the way it should be. Jesus is the message. The Church and the Bible are the medium of the message. The New Testament has value because it was authorized by those given authority by Jesus himself to teach. When we evangelize, we are supposed to preach Jesus as the message. But instead we preach the medium and have made the medium the message. The most graphic example of how true this is happened when I gave a two-hour talk on Jesus one day at a Southern Baptist university in Alabama. When I finished the talk, a number of professors approached me and said, "You will never know what you did by coming here."

"What did I do?" I asked them.

"You gave us Jesus."

"What do you mean, I gave you Jesus? You people are experts in the Scriptures."

"We may have studied Scripture all our lives, and may be considered experts, but you made us realize we never got to know Jesus. You gave us a flesh-and-blood Jesus who has lifted burdens from our hearts and healed wounds we have carried all our lives. And we want to thank you."

I was deeply touched by the humility of these scholarly people who could say to a Roman Catholic priest that he'd introduced them to the real Jesus for the first time after they had studied Scripture all their lives. Unfortunately, the theologian who invited me was asked to leave a short time later for having invited me. It is because of this experience and others like it that I have spent whatever has been left of my life and energy trying to learn even more about Jesus so I could gather all these insights together and put them into writing, so others might have the benefit of whatever I may have learned over these final years of thoughtful and prayerful reflection.

Each of the gospel writers, Matthew, Mark, Luke, and John, relayed his account of Jesus' life for different audiences and different cultures. As a result, they emphasized different aspects of Jesus' life and teachings. Trying to understand the various messages and reconcile their various approaches has given rise to lively discussions among Scripture scholars. What I have done for almost fifty years is read constantly the differing interpretations—and meditate prayerfully—the gospels' scenes in an attempt to enter into Jesus' mind and heart as he lived those scenes.

While these reflections are formatted into chapters, they were originally delivered as a series of talks on Jesus' life over a period of three and a half years. As I set these talks to manuscript, I tried to make my thoughts flow more smoothly so the readers could more easily meditate on each new insight as it presents itself. I hope and pray these reflections will accomplish what was intended: to draw us all into a deeper understanding of the God-Man who came among us to become one of us and offer his life for us as our Savior.

Joseph F. Girzone

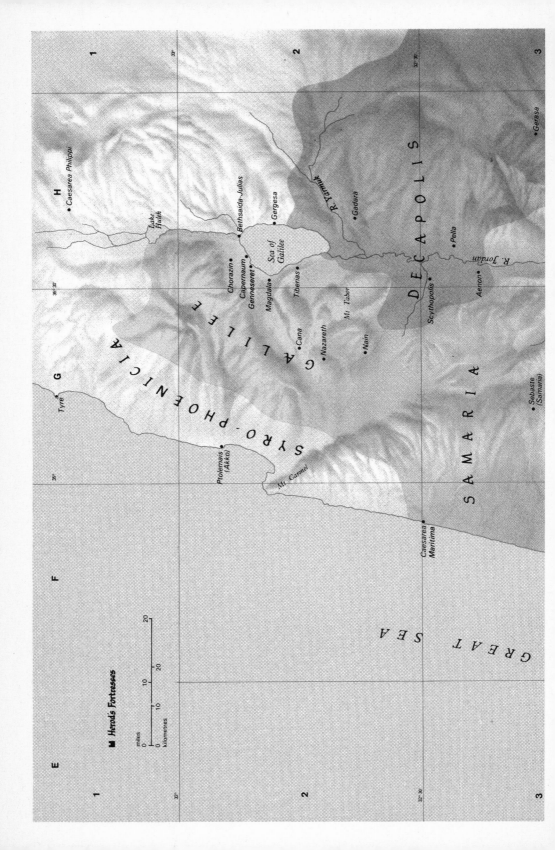

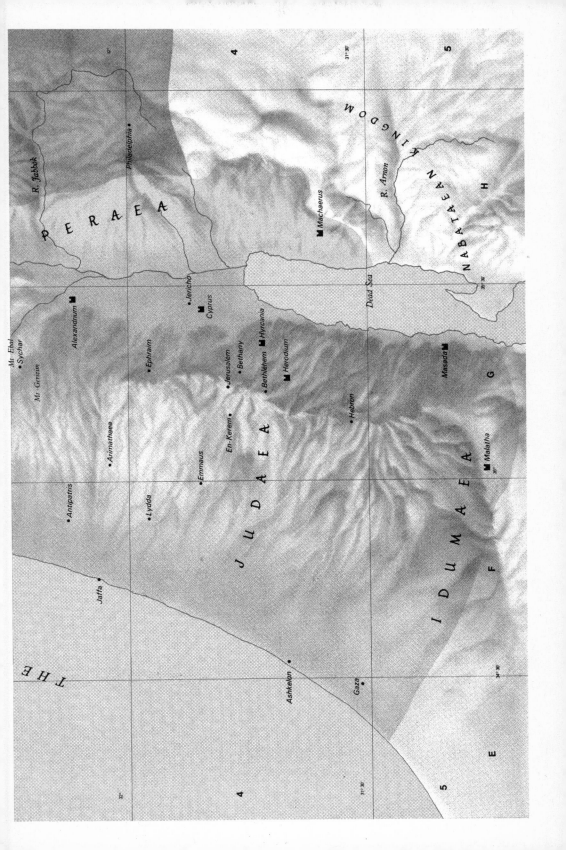

JESUS

HEROD, THE MAD KING

I t is necessary to understand the type of life people lived in Jesus' day before we even begin to study Jesus' life and the situations and conditions that affected his outlook and reactions to various peoples he would encounter. The territories of Galilee, Samaria, Judea, and Idumea made up the land of the Israelites. In the time of David the land extended as far as Damascus, and into other lands across the Jordan River. Under David's reign there was only one kingdom. Shortly after his death, the kingdom was divided into the kingdom of Israel, which included Galilee and Samaria, and the kingdom of Judea. In the time just before the birth of Jesus, however, the situation was further confused by being broken up into various jurisdictions. A very wealthy and powerfully connected Idumean, who contributed supplies and money to the Roman generals needing local support, managed to convince the Roman emperor to install one of his sons as governor of Galilee. The son was Herod, one of the most brilliant, but also one of the most ruthless, rulers of his time.

After losing his governorship because of his cruelty, Herod schemed to get back into the good graces of Rome. Eventually, he won the support of the Roman general Mark Antony, who convinced the emperor Octavian to persuade the Roman senate to confirm Herod as king of Judea.

After the decree was issued making Herod king of Judea, he went to Judea to take over his kingdom. Judea was a thin strip of land that extended from Jericho and the Dead Sea, north to Mount Hermon, which is in present-day Lebanon. It also included Lake Huleh, the cold-water lake that fed the Jordan River, which extends all the way south to the Dead Sea.

The northern part of the kingdom called Galilee was rich in farmland and fruit and olive orchards, and produced wheat and barley and other grains. There were also extensive forests that provided lumber for construction. Herod took personal possession of all this land and its resources and rented it out to the inhabitants, from whom he collected high rents. It did not take long before Herod became a very wealthy king. He also benefited from the mines, principally the copper mines, in southern Judea. Shortly after becoming king, he undertook the construction of a vast network of buildings: palaces, fortifications, public baths after the style in Rome, and monuments to the Roman emperors, including vast amphitheaters for plays and other dramatic shows that rivaled in grandeur and splendor the impressive buildings in Rome itself.

As great a genius as Herod was in many ways, he also suffered from a pathological insecurity. Suspecting that others were plotting against him, he had hundreds of people executed on the slightest suspicions. To his Jewish subjects, he did the unthinkable when he dispossessed the high priestly family of their sacred positions and appointed as chief priests his own friends from Idumea, men who were not even priests, much less Israelites. He also eliminated the wealthy and highly influential Sadducees from their positions as members of the Sanhedrin, who ruled Jerusalem. He promoted the Sadducees' bitter enemies, the Pharisees, to fill the vacancies, inflaming a political rivalry among them that would last for decades. The Sadducees were well educated, mostly by Greek teachers who instilled in their students a deep love of Greek culture and pagan philosophy. The Pharisees, on the other hand, were totally dedicated to preserving the religious laws and customs and traditions of their ancestors. The bitter animosity between these two groups would last until the destruction of Jerusalem in 70 A.D. One of the few times they were to become allies was when they needed each other's help to destroy Jesus. Even their best and sharpest minds could not outwit Jesus' by themselves.

Herod kept control of his kingdom by keeping his enemies in constant conflict with one another. His own family, however, was to become his undoing. He was insanely suspicious of everyone, and powerful members of his family could exploit that flaw for their own advantage. His ten wives were a constant cause of trouble, each one hoping that her offspring would be heir to his wealth and power. His Jewish-born wife, Mariamne, together with her mother, overstepped her bounds when they schemed to have Mariamne's brother made high priest. He was at least a Jew and not a pagan. A short time later the brother was drowned in a family pool, without doubt under Herod's orders. Then, Mariamne's grandfather, who had previously been in power, was assassinated. And finally, Herod had his beloved Mariamne put to death, which he much regretted afterward.

Intrigue in Herod's family never stopped. His wives were continually scheming, poisoning Herod's mind against one another's sons. It is hard to count the number of family members Herod had murdered to protect his throne. By the time Jesus was born, he had killed off practically every potential heir to his kingdom. After the assassination of Antipater, his son by his first wife, a Jewess, Emperor Octavian made the remark, "It is better to be one of Herod's pigs than one of his sons."

As Herod grew older he became more prey than ever to suspicions fostered intentionally by his own inner family circle, whose plotting never ended. It took its toll on him, as he was rapidly deteriorating mentally as well as physically.

By the time rumors began to surface that the coming of the long-awaited Messiah was imminent, he was totally consumed with fear of plots on his life and on his throne. The insane king was in no mood to deal with an avenging king the Judeans had been expecting for almost two thousand years.

2

THE MESSIAH HAS ARRIVED

It had been prophesied that Yahweh's anointed Savior would be born in Bethlehem, in Judea. In exile Daniel had prophesied, though in a veiled way, that he would be born 490 years from the ending of the Babylonian exile, which was quite accurate. (Dn. 9:24) He would also be a descendant of King David. He would be born of a virgin, as interpreted by Hebrew scholars. (Is. 7:14) His name would be Emmanu-el, "God living among us." He would be called Prince of Peace, Wonder-Counselor, and Father-of-the-World-to-Come, among other epic titles. (Is. 9:5) He would also destroy Israel's enemies, establish a reign that would last for a thousand years, and extend Israel's power and influence throughout the whole world, fulfilling Yahweh's ancient promise to Abraham that he would be the father of many nations.

And this is how it began. One day, according to Saint Luke's Gospel,

In the sixth month the angel Gabriel was sent from God to a town of Galilee called Nazareth, to a virgin engaged to a man named Joseph, who was from the house of David. The virgin's name was Mary. When the angel appeared, he greeted her with the words, "Hail, full of grace, the Lord is with you. Blessed are you among women." When she noticed his presence, she was troubled by his words, and wondered at the meaning of such a greeting.

The angel said to her, "Do not be afraid, Mary, you have found favor with God. And, listen to what I tell you. You are to conceive in your womb and give birth to a son, and you will name him Jesus. He shall be great and shall be called the Son of the Most High; and the Lord God will give him the throne of David his father, and he shall be king over the house of Jacob forever. His kingdom will be forever."

Mary said to the angel, "How will this happen since I do not know man?"

The angel said to her, "The Holy Spirit will come upon you and the power of the Most High will overshadow you, and the Holy One to be born of you will be called the Son of God. And, listen to this, Elizabeth, your kinswoman, also has conceived a son in her old age, and she who was considered sterile is now in her sixth month, for nothing is impossible to God." (Lk. 1:26–37)

This mentioning of the Holy Spirit is a new revelation involving the nature of God. It is the first time the Holy Spirit is mentioned in Scripture as a person. Mary, who told this to Luke, certainly could not have invented this new concept involving the nature of God. She merely related to Luke what she had experienced at the angel's visit.

Mary said to the angel, "Behold the handmaid of the Lord. May it be done to me according to your word." And the angel departed from her. (Lk. 1:38)

Saint Augustine said in commenting on this event that the salvation of the human race hung on Mary's consent to God's proposal. There is an extraordinary delicacy on the part of God in sending the angel, and not just an angel, but an archangel. The mission of the angel was to propose to Mary, and ask if she would consent to become the mother of God's Son. That is stunning. It also manifests the sensitivity of God toward the free will He has given to us. Adam and Eve were given free will so they could freely choose to love God. They chose their own independence instead. And their descendants waited for millions of years for God to give us another chance. Now Mary was asked to make another decision that would also affect the destiny of the human race. She was asked if she would consent to become the mother of the Savior, to be the vehicle of our salvation. Fortunately for us her response was "yes," and thus we were given another chance. In becoming the mother of God's Son, she became our mother also, since we are the adopted brothers and sisters of Jesus, who shares his life with us in baptism. We are her children not by a mere adoption but because we have Jesus' life within us. In saying "yes" to God, and consenting to bring our Savior into the world, she has given us a gift for which we could never possibly express adequate gratitude. The awesome greeting of the archangel expressed the lofty position to which God raised this humble young girl. Never has a messenger from God saluted anyone with such sublime praise, as the archangel Gabriel did Mary. It is not the Church who has raised Mary to her awesome position in the drama of our salvation. It is God Himself who so honored her, as was expressed in the archangel's greeting.

No one knows the time of the year when this took place. The introduction to the angel's visit said the sixth month, but does that refer to Elizabeth's sixth month of pregnancy, which Luke's gospel mentioned previously, or the sixth month of the year? Whenever it was, Mary almost immediately left to visit her cousin Elizabeth in the hill country down in Judea, in a town named Hebron, not far from Jerusalem. When Mary entered Elizabeth and Zachary's house, she greeted her cousin. When Elizabeth heard Mary's greeting, the baby leaped in his mother's womb. Elizabeth, filled with the Holy Spirit, broke out into loud praise: "Blessed are you among women, and blessed is the fruit of your womb! And who am I that the mother of my Lord should honor me with a visit? For, behold, the moment the sound of your greeting came to my ears, the baby in my womb leaped for joy. And blessed is she who believed, for the things promised her by the Lord will be accomplished." (Jn. 1:42–45) This is interesting from so many aspects. Elizabeth and Zachary are Mary's relatives, apparently close relatives, as the angel knew that the families were on very intimate terms when he revealed to Mary her cousin's pregnancy. And Mary left almost immediately to visit her cousin and stayed with her until Elizabeth's baby was born three months later. It is also interesting that although Mary was herself pregnant only a couple of weeks at most, Elizabeth, under the inspiration of the Holy Spirit, recognized that the two- or three-week-old fetus that Mary was carrying in her womb was God's Son.

Another interesting detail concerns Zachary. He was a priest—not just an ordinary priest of lower rank like the Levites, but a member of the elite aristocratic priests who served in the Temple and who shared in all the wealth that was due the Temple priests. This is interesting when you think of how Zachary and Elizabeth's son turns out later on, when we will see him wandering in the desert-like hills of Judea dressed in the skin taken from a camel's carcass and living on locusts and wild honey. One cannot but wonder about his relationship with his relatives in his young adult years after the death of his parents, as he was wandering the countryside as a Nazarite, with uncut hair and a long unkempt beard, an object of scorn and ridicule by religious officials. The relatives knew from his infancy that he was destined by God for something special, but for this? Only his cousin Jesus would recognize him later on for what he was, "the greatest prophet born of woman," in spite of his appearance.

When Mary returned to Nazareth three months into her pregnancy, to the more perceptive and inquisitive among the townsfolk, her pregnancy must have shown. Joseph was shattered, but being a kind and caring person, he could not find it in himself to destroy her by publicly divorcing her. While he considered divorcing her quietly, an angel appeared to him and told him the story of God's plan, and that he should not worry about taking Mary into his home, because the child to be born of her would be the Son of God, and should be called Jesus. On the surface, the story is hard to believe, but as Franz Werfel wrote in the beginning of his novel The Song of Bernadette, "for those who have faith, no explanation is necessary. For those without faith, no explanation is possible." One can only wonder what Mary and Joseph endured from the townsfolk. Ancient Jewish writings still carry the old tales down to the present time.

At that time a decree went out from Caesar Augustus that a census should be taken up throughout the whole Roman world. This was during the reign of Cyrinus, governor of the Roman province of Syria. Each person had to go to his own town, the town of his ancestors, and register. Since Bethlehem was the town of Joseph's ancestors, the house of David, he and Mary eventually had to leave Nazareth and make the long trip to Bethlehem in Judea, a trip of almost a hundred miles. So, joining up with a caravan on its way to Jerusalem, they began their long trek.

Late one afternoon the young couple was finally approaching the village of Bethlehem. As they entered the village, hoping to see some relatives they might know, they were surprised to find only strangers. Mary, still in her teens, was about to have her child. Joseph was anxious to find a fitting place for his wife to give birth. Asking everyone along the village streets if there was any available shelter for the baby to be born in, they could find no place at all in town, since the town was being invaded by strangers who had come for the registration.

After losing hope of finding a place, the couple approached a caravansary outside of town, a primitive version of a motel with stalls for animals on the first floor, and a long row of rooms on the second floor extending along the three sides of a courtyard below. The manager was considerate enough to show concern for the young couple's plight, as the place was filled with animals and crude travelers, which was no place for a young mother to have a baby. He told them of a cave in the hillside down along the sheep path. Thanking the man, the couple lit a lantern the man had given to them and started down the hillside.

They found the cave not very far at all from the village. It was not much of a shelter, but it would provide protection from the elements, and at least some privacy. Helping his wife dismount from the donkey, Joseph led her to one of the sawed-off tree trunks the shepherds must have used for chairs.

"Joseph," the woman called to her husband as he was tethering the donkey to a pole near the entrance to the cave, "I think my time has come. That long ride has moved the baby along."

"Just a minute, Mary, and I will have everything ready." Moving nervously, Joseph spread out on the cold floor of the cave the mats they would be using for beds, and the other things needed for the baby's birth. He then tried to make his wife as comfortable as possible.

Many details had been prophesied about this child's life and death and even about his birth. One of the most striking prophecies concerned the manner of his birth. "A virgin shall conceive and bear a son, and shall name him Emmanuel." (Is. 7:14) It says *maiden* in the Bible, but the Hebrew scholars in Alexandria, Egypt, responsible for the Septuagint translation of the Bible into Greek, translated the Hebrew word *alma* as *parthenos*, which in English means *virgin*. The precise details of the child's birth were never revealed. Mary later on revealed many of the incidents leading up to the birth of the child, and the dramatic events that took place afterward. But the intimate details of the birth itself she kept between herself and God. However, from the earliest times the Fathers of the Church considered Mary forever a virgin, one of the Fathers describing the coming of the child as like a ray of light passing through a window without shattering the glass.

Though it was a sacred time filled with such divine mysteries that only the two of them could share, it must have been a lonely night. Bethlehem would have been filled with relatives, some no doubt from Galilee, who may have already brought with them some of the local gossip about the couple. It does seem strange, considering how important hospitality was to the Israelites, that no one could find room for them, especially seeing that their baby was about to be born. I suppose even then, at this most sacred moment, when the Light of the World entered our midst, the mark of the cross was beginning to cast its fearful shadow.

But nothing could destroy the couple's sense of destiny that Yahweh had chosen Mary, and indeed her spouse, as well, for a sacred mission. It was their destiny to bring a very special Son of God into the world, even though neither of them could fully realize the implications of those words of the angel Gabriel.

There was not much time to rest that evening, as they were about to have visitors. Not far away, a group of shepherds tending their sheep were surprised when an angel appeared to them and told them of the birth of the Messiah, the Savior of their people, and that they would find the infant and his mother in a cave not far away. As the angels left singing the praises of God, and offering a blessing of peace upon the world, the shepherds hurried to find the child. (Lk. 2:8–20)

It could not but be a shock to find the newborn Messiah in a cold and smelly cave, with two weary parents, not nobly dressed. But, they were shepherds, and they were used to seeing goodness and nobility in the lowest of people. Perhaps others more highly born would find it difficult, if not impossible, to recognize divinity in such shameful surroundings and with such poor-looking parents, but these humble shepherds had no problem at all. Their hearts were ecstatic that they had been chosen by Yahweh Himself to welcome the newborn Messiah. Their joy was beyond measure, and after offering their simple gifts, whose value was more in the love they expressed than in the gifts themselves, they humbly took their leave.

When the shepherds left they could not restrain themselves from running through the village telling everyone they met that the Messiah had just been born, and that they had been told by angels, and had seen him with their very own eyes. Obviously, no one believed them, thinking they were just simpletons, ignorant shepherds who had probably had too much to drink, for there is no record of anyone else from the village visiting the cave that night or even shortly afterward. The Gospel writers mention only the shepherds, obviously the only ones whom God invited and wanted to witness this important historical event.

If, as seems likely, the little family stayed in Bethlehem or in the neighborhood, Joseph would have had to find work. For a person with his skills, if he'd brought his tools with him from Nazareth, he should have had no problem getting small jobs around town. There are always people needing a carpenter or a handyman to fix a thousand things around the house and in the yard. Cartwheels were constantly breaking. Hinges on doors needed frequent attention. Plows and shovels and other tools needed regular repairs. There was enough work in the neighborhood for this humble couple to earn a simple living for whatever time they might have to spend there to fulfill for the child all that was required by the Law.

3

VISITORS FROM FAR-OFF LANDS AND THE FLIGHT INTO EGYPT

It is not known how long the family stayed in the cave on the hillside. Was it for a few days until they found lodging? Did they return to Nazareth after they fulfilled their legal obligation to register? Did they find distant relatives in Bethlehem who welcomed them into their home? There is no way of telling. A newly born son had to be circumcised eight days after birth. Where did the circumcision of the baby take place? Saint Luke says the baby was circumcised eight days after his birth, and he was given the name Jesus. Luke then mentions his presentation in the Temple, followed by the ritual of his mother's purification, which had to be performed forty days after childbirth, also in the Temple in Jerusalem. Bethlehem was only five or six miles from Jerusalem and its Temple. They would hardly have gone back to Galilee only to come back down a short time later for the ceremonies that had to be performed at the Temple.

It was at that occasion that the saintly old man Simeon, "prompted by the Holy Spirit," as Saint Luke writes, went up to the Temple, and when the parents brought in the child Jesus, Simeon took him in his arms and praised God, as he burst out in grateful prayer: "Now, Lord, you can let your servant die in peace, just as you had promised, because my eyes have seen the salvation which you have prepared for all the nations to see, a light for the pagans to see, and the glory of your people Israel."

Mary and Joseph, in awe over what was happening, could only wonder what it all meant. Then, giving the baby back to his mother, the old man prophesied, "This child is destined for the rise and fall of many in Israel, and as an enigma that will be rejected; and your own soul a sword will pierce, as the evil in people's hearts becomes manifest."

At the same time, an old lady, a prophetess by the name of Anna, came upon the scene and began to prophesy, praising God and telling everyone in earshot that the Holy One of Israel had come for the deliverance of Jerusalem. (Lk. 2:21–40)

Quietly, Mary and Joseph left with the child. Saint Luke writes that when all had been done to satisfy the Law, the family returned to Nazareth. Since he mentions no other incidents occurring in Bethlehem, it would make sense for him to have them go back up home to Nazareth, though he was bypassing a number of intervening years. So, it is most likely they did not go back to Nazareth after the presentation in the Temple.

Saint Matthew fills in those years with a few fascinating events. One is the coming of the Magi, and the flight into Egypt. He tells the story of the Magi, or wise men, or minor kings, coming from the East to visit the newborn king of the Jews. He writes that they found the child and his mother in Bethlehem, and *in a house.* This interesting story is related by Matthew:

After Jesus had been born at Bethlehem in Judea, during the reign of King Herod, some wise men came to Jerusalem from the East. "Where is the infant king of the Jews?" they asked. "We saw his star as it rose and have come to pay him homage." When King Herod heard this he was deeply troubled, as was the whole of Jerusalem. He called together the chief priests and the scribes of the people and enquired of them where the Christ was to be born. "At Bethlehem in Judea," they told him, for this is what the prophet wrote: "And you, Bethlehem, in the land of Judea, are by no means the least among the leaders of Judah, for from you will come the leader who will shepherd my people Israel."

Then Herod summoned the wise men to visit with him privately. After asking them the exact date when the star had appeared, he sent them on to Bethlehem: "Go and find out all about the child and when you have found him, let me know so that I too may go and pay him homage." Having listened to what the king had told them, they continued on their journey. And they then saw the star that they had seen on its rising. It went forward and stopped over the place where the child was. The sight of the star filled them with gladness, and going into the house, they found the child with his mother Mary. Falling down on their knees, they did him homage. Then, opening their treasures, they offered him gifts of gold, frankincense, and myrrh. But, they were warned in a dream not to return to Herod, so they returned to their own country by another route. (Mt. 2:1–12)

Some Scripture scholars and historians have ridiculed this story, saying that the Gospel writers put it in the story to make it look like an ancient prophecy was being fulfilled, the prophecy being that the Messiah's star would appear in the East and that wise men would come and pay him homage.

The scholars held that there was no corroborating evidence to back up the story and, for that reason alone, concluded that the story was not credible. However, evidence has recently been unearthed that throws more light on the subject. A group of archaeologists working on a dig in a remote part of present-day Iran made a remarkable discovery. Locals working for the scientists dug up a cache of ancient gold coins with a crowned head on the face, and the inscription, "King Caspar." This is interesting, as it has always been a tradition that there were three kings, or wise men, from the East who came to visit the Holy Family. The traditional names of the three persons were Caspar, Melchior, and Balthazar.

After Constantine became the Roman emperor in 306 A.D., his mother, Helena, who had become a Christian, went to Palestine and hired a team of locals to help her find objects associated with Jesus' life and death. The workers had found a number of crosses. One had nail holes on the cross bar and on the lower part of the upright beam. What is significant if the story is true is that a number of miraculous occurrences, including healings, were associated with that particular cross, which led Helena to conclude that that cross was the one on which Jesus had been crucified. Whether that was true or not, the news of the finding was so sensational that it spread all throughout the area, and as far as Persia. A short time later the king of Persia, knowing the emperor's mother was interested in items associated with Jesus, and wishing to honor her, sent courtiers to Palestine with a gift. It was a cask containing the funeral remains of King Caspar, obviously indicating the Persian king's belief in the local Persian tradition that Caspar was one of the kings who went to pay respects to the newborn king of the Judeans. Helena brought those remains with her when she went back to Italy, and presented them to the bishop of Milan, where she had previously been baptized. This is another example of how, little by little, pieces of the Biblical puzzle are being put together as archaeologists unearth valuable evidence, giving credence to events in the New Testament that had previously been thought to be unhistorical or unbelievable.

No sooner had the Magi left, than an angel appeared to Joseph in a dream, telling him, "Rise, take the child and his mother, and flee into Egypt, and remain there until I tell you, for Herod will search for the child to destroy him." Joseph immediately rose, took the child and his mother by night, and departed for Egypt. They remained there until the death of Herod some three or four years later. Meanwhile, in Bethlehem, Herod's troops wreaked havoc among the residents. Going from house to house, they methodically killed every male child two years old or younger, based on Herod's calculations from what the Magi had told him. No one knows how many babies were slaughtered. Estimates range from fewer than a hundred to much larger figures. Bethlehem was not a large village. However, since people were going there to register for the census, the number could have been considerable if outsiders coming to register brought babies with them. Even then, how many would have had babies under two years old? It seems there is no way to resolve the question. (Mt. 2:13–16)

Mary, Joseph, and Jesus' lonely, frightening journey into Egypt is intriguing. How did they travel in a dark desert? Was there a bright moon to partially light the way? Did they travel alone? Most probably, at least when they started out. It is possible that along the way they met up with a caravan already on its way into Egypt. They would have joined the caravan for protection and also for the security of the caravan leader's knowledge of the route. We know nothing about their time in Egypt nor their whereabouts in that country from the Gospels. To know that would be fascinating, and we cannot but wish that Mary later on would have told Saint Luke about their stay in Egypt, as he is the one who relates so many details about Mary and young Jesus. All we know about those three or four years in that country is from stories passed on from the earliest Christian communities formed later on by Saint Mark, who brought the Gospel to Egypt. Churches and shrines scattered throughout Egypt, marking the places where Mary and Joseph traveled or spent time, tell stories about the Holy Family's stay in those places. Whether these stories are founded on fact or ancient legend remains to be determined. Coptic Christians have written about this journey of the Holy Family, and this information is available on the Internet for those interested in learning more about this very intriguing subject.

Although there were large colonies of Israelites living in Egypt, especially in and around Alexandria, Mary and Joseph would have had to find them. As time went on they most certainly found some of their country folk here and there, who became not only friends but customers, as well. They would not have felt so alone when they went to worship knowing that others worshiping with them had only recently come from one of the towns in Judea or Galilee. And after a short time there, it would have been easy to fit into the social life of their fellow Israelites and participate in family gatherings and simple parties. And although they certainly must have missed home and all their neighbors, it might have been a good thing for them to distance themselves from gossiping neighbors who could cause much pain just by their loose talk and scathing rumors.

The ancient stories of Mary and Joseph and Jesus being in different places in Egypt may not be far from reality if Joseph had to travel from one village to another as friends and relatives referred him to do jobs in different villages. It seems quite possible that he had a considerable circle of customers, which would necessitate traveling from place to place. The presence of large numbers of Israelites would have assured that their stay in Egypt was not unpleasant, although homesickness and a feeling of being displaced and maybe even hunted by Herod's spies could have been most stressful. In time their stay there ended, with the news of Herod's death.

4

RETURNING HOME FROM EXILE

How long was the Holy Family's stay in Egypt? We don't know exactly, but it was at least until the death of Herod, which took place perhaps four years after their departure for Egypt. Matthew's Gospel records the message of the angel:

After Herod's death, an angel of the Lord appeared in a dream to Joseph in Egypt, and said, "Get up, take the child and his mother and go back to the land of Israel, for those who wanted to kill the child are dead." So, Joseph got up, and taking the child and his mother with him, went back to the land of Israel. But, on learning that Archelaus had succeeded his father Herod as ruler of Judea, he was afraid to go there, and being warned in a dream, he left for the region of Galilee. There he settled in a town called Nazareth, thus fulfilling what was spoken through the prophets: "He will be called a Nazarene." (Mt. 2:19–23)

One can only wonder what kind of reception greeted the family on their return to Nazareth. Such a long absence would have caused all kinds of rumors. That baby, about whom there was so much talk, had come home not as a baby, but as a six- or seven-year-old boy, a bright lad, most probably with thoughtful brown eyes, and a winsome smile, and features very much like his mother's, since he had only his mother's genes. Relatives and kindly neighbors welcomed the family warmly. Others who previously had had an attitude about them hardly changed. Time would either open their eyes and soften their hearts, or would harden their hearts even more. The mystery about how that child came about in the beginning would not disappear all at once. The long separation may have helped some to feel differently about Mary and Joseph and the child, whatever their feelings may have been previously. The family's return, however, after the long absence, would have made them immediate celebrities, especially when they began to share their experiences of that faraway country and all that had happened to them there, and about neighbors' relatives living in various places in Egypt. And other questions were put to them, like whatever possessed them to go, of all places, to Egypt, and were they there in Bethlehem when Herod's soldiers slaughtered all those innocent babies?

And, you wonder, what was their response? Could they really tell the whole story? And did they tell about the visit of the shepherds and about those important strangers from the East who had followed a star and come all the way across the desert from Persia to visit the baby? Surely they kept all those stories to themselves. That mystery was only between them and the Almighty. It was not for them to share the secret plans of God with anyone. Yahweh would reveal those special events to whom He wished, and in His own good time. In the meantime, that special family would live a life just like everyone else in the town, keeping God's mystery hidden in their hearts.

While we don't know much about the Holy Family's life in Nazareth, there were many things they had to do in common with other people in those days. There was a common well in Nazareth, and someone had to go each day with large vessels to fill them and cart them back home. Women used to gather at the wells and share stories and personal happenings with one another. It gave the women a few minutes to meet with their friends and relax. So, perhaps, it was Mary who went to draw the water each day. If young Jesus was a thoughtful boy, it is easy to imagine him offering to do the chore, as the water jars were not light.

People in Nazareth, as in other places in Galilee, usually rented four or five acres of land from the king, who already had assumed ownership of all the land. The king of Galilee at this time was Herod Antipas, a rather mild and moderate ruler, though he was the one who would in time behead John the Baptizer, at the demand of his wife Herodias, even though in his heart of hearts he had great respect for John. On these pieces of land rented from the king, a family could grow all the food they needed. A section of the land would be reserved for olive trees and another section for fruit trees, for figs and dates, and a third section consisting of the vineyard, providing grapes for the table and for the making of wine, which was an important part of family life. A large piece of the land would be reserved for grains, wheat and barley, and for vegetables, which would have been part of the family's staple diet.

Many families at that time lived in small compounds surrounded by a wall. Inside the wall was a courtyard with three or four units built into three of the walls. The living quarters were small and simple, often not more than one or two rooms raised above the courtyard floor. Most families had at least a few animals—some chickens, a few sheep and goats, and perhaps a donkey. In compounds like this the animals would wander around loose or be tied to a place along the courtyard wall. In the compound there might be a number of large ovens for baking, which would be shared by all the families. Compounds were usually inhabited by larger families, with grandparents and aunts and uncles and cousins all living together in the small homes. There was no clear identification among the children. They were all one extended family, so for all practical purposes they were all brothers and sisters to one another. There were no toilets. Washing and other physical necessities were taken care of somewhere in the courtyard, as there were no baths or showers or toilet facilities in the living quarters.

The large room providing the living space was used for sleeping and eating and, in bad weather, cooking. Furniture was rare. Beds were for the well-to-do. Most of the poorer people just spread a mat on the floor and slept on that. If they had blankets or a pillow, they were fortunate; a cloak would do just as well. The table was low-lying, perhaps sixteen or eighteen inches high, so the tabletop was only that much off the floor. Individuals reclined on mats as they sat around the table, eating food with their hands. Usually food was served from a common pot, and individuals would pick their portion out of the pot and eat it, using their fingers as fork and spoon. Little Jesus certainly was not brought up with the same delicacy that we are today, even the poorest of us in our wealthy countries.

Children were expected to help out with the chores. Mothers could not do everything. They already had enough to keep them busy day and night, as they did not only the cooking and baking of bread and pastry, but were also expected to make the clothes and buy what fabrics they needed at neighborhood shops. They often did their own spinning and weaving and made the fabric for the tunics, cloaks, and mantles with their blue fringes, veils, and prayer shawls. Sandals and other footwear could be bought from the lower-class priests, the Levites, who had a monopoly on the leather market. That was their income, as the aristocratic Temple priests cut them out of their rightful share of the Temple money offerings and the animal sacrifices. But these Levites were nonetheless wealthy, as everyone needed leather goods.

The families who lived in compounds often worked together, helping one another. Many people, however, did not live in compounds. Small families, and families with no close relatives, for the most part lived in small one- or two-room cottages, with part of the house serving as living quarters and part as workshop and showroom for the father's business, where he would make articles of his craft and offer them for sale right out of the shop. Some craftsmen, such as woodworkers and those who worked with iron, had to travel and work at the customers' property, though they would still spend time at their shop making what they could there before bringing the work to be finished at the customer's house. A craftsman might do most of the work for a door at his workshop and then bring the almost-finished product to the customer and fit it in place on the site, together with the latches and either leather or iron hinges, which he might have made at his forge in the workshop. Jesus probably learned to do these things quite early: first by watching, then gradually, when he could be a help to his father rather than a distraction, by assisting Joseph in making simple articles that might be components for more complex items.

Since Joseph was a master craftsman, he had to know how to do iron-work and how to run a forge so that he could make finished products for his customers. And since mostly everyone in Galilee was a farmer of one sort or another, Joseph was kept busy making plows and shovels and winnowing forks, and rakes, and wooden pitchforks, and hammers, and a whole array of tools needed at home and for the small farms and orchards. Wheels would have been an important commodity, and Jesus must have been a big help to his father, as repairing wheels and making new ones was not the kind of work that could be postponed. Wheels were always a necessity.

Although there may have been craftsmen who specialized in making boats, it is possible that Jesus and his father had a customer now and then who might want not a big fishing boat, but a small boat for travel to local villages, and might have contracted with Joseph for such an item. That might have taken a little ingenuity, but being locally made, it would save the customer the trouble of having to travel to Capernaum and take a chance with a stranger who might or might not be a good craftsman.

Galilee was a busy place, with its mixture of Romans and Greeks and other Gentiles from across the nearby borders and even from distant lands, travelers who had stopped on their way to Egypt, or who came and mingled with the Galileans for trade and business.

5

The Boy Jesus at Twelve Years Old

There is a small synagogue in Nazareth today that the inhabitants say was there in the time of Jesus. That, however, is doubtful. Not much of what was there in the time of Jesus exists today. But when you visit that little synagogue, you cannot but feel that it might well have been the synagogue Jesus worshiped in two thousand years ago. If my memory serves me correctly, the inside of the building is not more than twenty-five feet wide and maybe forty feet long, with a slightly raised platform at the far end of the room and stone benches in two tiers facing one another on both sides of the room. The women would have sat on one side and the men on the opposite side. They were not supposed to sit together. It is a very simple and unpretentious place, but then Nazareth was an unpretentious village with a very small number of inhabitants. Later on, on hearing that Jesus, who might possibly be the Messiah, came from Nazareth, Nathaniel would comment, "What good can come out of that place?" People, especially the Jews, or more properly called, the Judeans, had little more than contempt for the people from that area. Many of the riots in the territory were started by easily agitated Galileans.

In visiting that little synagogue with my mother and father, hoping it was authentic, my mind wandered across the centuries, and I tried to imagine what experiences Jesus had in that place, if that indeed was where he worshiped. Even if it was not, wherever he did worship would not have been much different, so I tried to imagine what it was like for him.

I doubt if it was the custom to bring children to worship. It was, it seems, a man's responsibility to worship. Women would have also gone. There would be a service on Friday evening after sunset, which was really Saturday for the Jews, since the day began after sunset on the evening before. For a prayer service to take place there had to be a minyan, or ten men, at least, or the service was not official. I have the feeling that even as a young child Jesus pestered his father to take him along. I am sure Joseph eventually gave in.

What would Jesus have experienced at the synagogue? When I was teaching my high school students, I used to take them to the local orthodox synagogue in Pottsville, Pennsylvania, every Friday night for the service. The synagogue service today is exactly the same as what Jesus would have experienced in his day at Nazareth. So the students got a taste of some of the experiences that Jesus would have had as a young boy. Interestingly, Christian church services follow pretty much the same format and content as the Jewish synagogue services. The part added later on that made the service Christian was the Eucharistic part, or second part of the service. So in the Mass today, you have the scriptural part containing readings from the Jewish Scriptures as well as readings from the New Testament, and after that instructional part, the heart of the Christian service from apostolic times, the Eucharist. What Jesus experienced is basically what we have in the first part of our Sunday liturgy, the Liturgy of the Word.

Although we know nothing for sure of the young years of Jesus, there are clues that at least outwardly he was just like any other boy in the neighborhood. When later on rumor comes back to Nazareth that Jesus is preaching, the fact that the townsfolk were shocked indicates that nothing like this had happened in his life in Nazareth. Certainly he did not have a bad reputation, but he did not seem in any way extraordinary, just a normal young village boy. What his parents saw of him around the house was different. They had to have seen glimmerings of rare gifts and talents manifesting themselves as he was slowly becoming aware of himself and beginning to understand his unique relationship with his "Father in heaven," although they could not have completely known what it meant when he would use that term.

The story about the family's visit to the Temple when Jesus was twelve years old indicates that Jesus was becoming more aware of who he was.

When Jesus was twelve years old, his parents, as was their custom, took him to the Temple in Jerusalem to celebrate the Passover. When the feast was over, and they were returning, the boy Jesus remained in Jerusalem, but they did not know it, thinking that he was in the caravan. They had come a day's journey before it occurred to them to look for him among their relatives and acquaintances. Not finding him, they returned to Jerusalem to continue the search.

Finally, after three days they found him in the Temple, sitting among the scholars, both listening to them and asking them questions. And all those who were listening to him were amazed at his understanding and his answers. And when his parents saw him, they were astonished, and his mother said to him, "Why have you done this to us? Your father and I have been so upset looking for you everywhere."

He said to them, "Why were you looking for me? Did you not know that I must be about my Father's work?"

They did not understand a word of what he had said to them. But, he went down with them and after arriving at Nazareth, he was subject to them. His mother kept all these things in her heart. And Jesus advanced in wisdom and age and grace before God and man. (Lk. 2:41–52)

You can sit and ponder what Mary and Joseph must have gone through during those three horrendous days. Losing an ordinary child is one of the most terrifying experiences parents can go through. The panic, the guilt they must have felt, and God did not even comfort them by assuring them that His son was all right, that there was no need to worry. No, this was something they were going to have to work out for themselves as they agonized over it. You can only imagine the nightmares that went through their minds. Did someone kidnap him? Did he get lost and was he in a caravan headed for a foreign country, with some unreliable people telling him that they would make sure he got home? The anguish must have been horrendous.

It makes me smile when I see Mary scolding young Jesus for what he had done and the worry he had caused her and Joseph. She, like so many mothers, seems to have been the disciplinarian, while Joseph remained in the background. But, then, that is only one incident. Under ordinary circumstances things might have been different.

Why did Jesus stay behind? He should have been sensitive to his parents' worry. It is easy to assume that, but teenagers can be most inconsiderate without even realizing it. They are trying to act grown up, and they are preoccupied with that. The effect this might have on anyone else may never cross their mind. Probably Jesus was no different. Now that he was twelve years old and legally an adult, with responsibilities under the Law, he felt ready to shoulder what he was beginning to feel was his greatest responsibility, to be concerned about his Father's interests here on earth. He could not wait to begin that work, even though he may not have fully understood his relationship with his Father in heaven. He still was drawn to share with others his love of his Father.

It is strange when God calls someone to do His work. Often the person knows it from infancy. When I was two years old, my father took me to church on Sunday mornings. When I saw a man dressed in a long black robe standing out in front of church, I asked my father, "What's that?" He told me, "That's a priest." I said, "That's what I'm going to be when I get big." It was not that I was attracted to it, but I just knew that that was what I was supposed to be. And when I was twelve years old I found out that I could go into the seminary at fourteen. Even at that age I used to talk to older people about God. I don't know why. I just could not wait to start doing a priest's work. When I became fourteen, I told my parents I was going into the seminary. I know they were shocked, and even though I'd talked about it, for a fourteen-year-old to decide he was leaving home for the seminary was not quite ordinary. Somewhat bewildered, I am sure, my mother and father discussed it, but not much was said to me about it. And that September I entered the seminary, almost a hundred miles from home. It is not hard for me to understand that Jesus could not wait until he was an adult to begin his Father's work. To have to wait that long when he knew he was destined for the work would have been unbearable. So, in his overpowering enthusiasm, even though he was just a boy, he felt he had to get started in some way.

Then try to imagine the boy Jesus in this room, this colonnaded section of the court, with the Temple scholars, those experts in the Law and the Scriptures, much more sophisticated and cultured than the traveling scribes. Not many other scribes or Pharisees could shock these highly elite scholars, but they were amazed at the wisdom and the questions and answers of this little boy. They must have been impressed, because if a little boy were to enter a room with lawyers or doctors and start talking about law or about serious medical matters, he would soon be asked to just listen. But these scholars were impressed enough to let Jesus speak and then give ear to his understanding of difficult matters of the Law and the Scriptures.

And when his parents finally heard his voice coming from somewhere in the vicinity, they followed the voice. As they approached where Jesus was, it is not hard to imagine them just listening to what he was saying and discussing with those learned men. They themselves could not but be impressed. And noticing that the scholars were willing to listen to this boy, it is not likely that Mary and Joseph would have interrupted. They would have waited until there was a lull in the discussion, then courteously made their presence known and told the scholars that they had been looking for their son and they had to start on their long journey home.

It is easy to imagine these learned men telling Mary and Joseph that they had a remarkable son and would like him someday to be enrolled in their classes in the Temple, since he already had such potential for understanding and interpreting the Scriptures and the Law.

It would have been with mixed feelings of pride and bewilderment that Mary and Joseph took their precocious son and started back home, hoping they could find another caravan going that way, so they would not be alone on the dangerous highway, threatened by bandits and highwaymen all along the route. The whole time, Mary must have kept wondering about all the things the angel had said to her so long ago, and what Elizabeth had meant when she greeted her with the words, "Who am I that the mother of my Lord should come to visit me?" And what Simeon had said when he told her that "this child is destined for the rise and fall of many in Israel," and that "your own soul a sword will pierce that the thoughts of many may be revealed." All that Saint Luke says about Mary's reaction to the Temple incident and what followed was that "she kept all these things in her heart," and pondered and pondered over them.

6

WHAT DID THE TOWNSFOLK SEE IN JESUS?

We know nothing about the events in the childhood and boyhood of Jesus. All it says in Scripture is that "he grew in wisdom and age and grace before God and his neighbors." But we can deduce some characteristics about his personality and his understanding of himself as a boy, and also about his understanding of holiness, from what we see later in his life and his response to life around him. We can also deduce certain things about him from his neighbors' comments later on.

When Jesus left Judea after his forty-day retreat and returned to Galilee, he did a little preaching and may have healed a few people. Word reached the townsfolk in Nazareth that people who had heard him were quite impressed. The townsfolk were shocked, and the talk started. "Where did he get all this from? Isn't this the carpenter, the son of Joseph, whose family we all know?" This comment shows that they did not consider him particularly holy. He was just one of them and did not stand out in their estimation as being the kind of person who would be out preaching religion. That one simple comment reveals a lot. In the eyes of the townsfolk he was just an ordinary young man. He was their village craftsman who took over his father's business after his father died, so he could support his mother and, perhaps, other relatives who were part of the family.

Knowing who he really was, we cannot help but ask ourselves how he could have kept his divinity and his holiness hidden for all those years. How could the people who had seen him and mingled with him and his family each day not get some glimpse of his rare goodness? How could God live in a little village for thirty years and not be seen as a person of extraordinary holiness? The only answer could be that his understanding of holiness was entirely different from the people's perception of a holy person. In those days and even in our own day, the common perception of a holy person is one who keeps all the religious laws and prohibitions. The more observant the person, the more holy he or she is considered. In the Jewish religion that was quite an accomplishment, because there were not just ten commandments like people think, but 613 commandments, and 365 prohibitions, and a further 365 lesser prohibitions. The scribes and Pharisees had a reputation for being fastidious in their observance of these regulations.

Jesus, however, seems not to have had a reputation for the faithful observance of all these injunctions, most probably because he knew most of them were man-made with very little, if any, relevance to people's lives. This would explain why the townsfolk were shocked when he started traveling around, talking about God and healing people.

So, what did people see in Jesus, then? Apparently just a very ordinary young boy and young man, conscientious about his job as a master craftsman, a person with a light heart and a caring spirit, and possessed of deep insight, with a mind as sharp as a razor; also a person who was courageous and afraid of nothing, and possessed of sensitive emotions, and yet who from hard work was strong and manly. He could readily see the incongruities in human situations and with his keen sense of humor would laugh quite spontaneously when something funny occurred. He also would have had a far-seeing vision of life and life's purpose for all of us. In short, I think what people must have seen in Jesus was a person who was deeply in love with life and everything alive, from God down to the simplest little creature, and with none of the hang-ups so many of us humans have; thus a perfectly balanced personality, and a person who was fun to be with. To Jesus that would have been holiness, a very real and personal kind of holiness, and certainly not the sanctimonious and scrupulous kind that was obsessed with rules and regulations, and with a self-centered pursuit of personal perfection all day long.

Later on we see Jesus showing great compassion for the sick and the blind and for orphans and widows, which makes one wonder about his personal concerns as a young boy for the poor orphaned children in his neighborhood, and for widows who had little means of support after the death of their husbands. One might also wonder if the brothers and sisters of Jesus mentioned in the Gospel were not orphaned children whom Jesus befriended and then invited to his home after pressuring his parents to take them into the family as his brothers and sisters. Even as a child he would have had that deep concern for hurting people that he manifested later on as the Good Shepherd who cared for "the bruised and hurting sheep." He would have had that same concern for the homeless who had no parents and no home, and for old folks who were hungry and had no one to care for them, and for other unfortunate people. It is not difficult to imagine him seeking out these people, bringing them food, and doing chores for them.

Even though Isaiah said that there was nothing beautiful about the suffering Messiah, it is hard to believe that he was not a perfect specimen of our humanity. Perhaps in his suffering and after his lashing during the Passion, he certainly was no one whom his enemies would have considered a man of esteem, but during the ordinary part of his life there had to be something beautiful about him. He was the Son of God in the real sense of the word and perfection itself. Why would his heavenly Father make him ugly? It does not make sense. Also, since he received his genetic makeup solely from his mother, that would seem to indicate a certain refinement and emotional sensitivity in his personality, and when you put that together with a certain physical toughness that shows in the grueling routine of long treks from Galilee to Judea and back while speaking to huge crowds all along the way, you can see a beautifully balanced personality, a strong and virile human being, quite thin from daily exercise, and with a delicate emotional sensitivity, a most attractive combination in any person. It is easy to see why people were so strongly attracted to him later on.

7

Two Cousins Meet

Mary's whole life was centered on her son. She was, by God's plan, destined to be his mother. She was truly created for him. He was her whole life. Now he was leaving to begin his Father's work full time. Mothers have a very painful time when a child leaves for college or, worse, goes off to war. Mary had been told by a prophet that her son would have a difficult divine mission and would be the focus of many people's hatred. Now he was leaving to launch that mission. She was beginning to feel the pain of that sword that Simeon had prophesied in the Temple many years earlier. There was nothing that she could do or say that could change things. He had to do his Father's will.

The Gospels do not say, but one wonders: Did she go with him or did he go alone? Later on we see her with him every place he goes, but this first time, maybe not. All the Gospel stories have Jesus appearing at the Jordan, where his cousin John was baptizing. Had they ever met?

Mary seems to have been close to John's mother, Elizabeth, as she wasted no time in making that long trip to Hebron and spent three months assisting Elizabeth in the last months of her pregnancy. The Gospels never mention whether Mary and Joseph went the few extra miles to their home in Hebron when they went on their frequent trips to Jerusalem for the important feasts. Perhaps they visited Elizabeth and Zachary in Hebron during the years they lived in Bethlehem. Then one wonders how long Elizabeth and Zachary lived after the birth of John. They were already old when John was born.

Zachary was a priest, a Temple priest, which is interesting. He belonged to the priestly aristocracy of Jerusalem, and they shared in the lucrative offerings of the people and also the Temple sacrifices, and he and his wife were in some way related to Mary, seemingly rather closely. (Lk. 1:5–25) It is possible that Mary may have lived with Elizabeth and Zachary when she was a young girl, attending classes taught by the Temple priests and scribes, a common custom for the families of Temple priests.

Did Jesus and John ever meet when they were children? There is no way of knowing. The first time Jesus appeared at the Jordan, where John was preaching and baptizing, John did not recognize him, though the next time when Jesus entered the water and asked John to baptize him, John was shocked and remarked that Jesus should be baptizing *him*. It is possible that they'd met as young boys but had not seen each other recently, so John did not recognize Jesus immediately.

And when you imagine John, the son of a prestigious Temple priest, and himself by birth a priest, dressed in a camel-hair garment and dieting on locusts and wild honey, you wonder how long he had been living that way. Being a member of the priestly aristocracy of Jerusalem, John could have had a comfortable job taking his father's place among the Temple priests. But that was not to be. John was someone very special in God's plan of human redemption and salvation, and he had to have had a sense of what he was supposed to do, especially after his parents died. There certainly were relatives in the area who would have willingly cared for him, but that was not to be, either. Scripture does not say when his parents died, but he was probably a teenager when that happened.

When a person has a mission that he or she knows they are destined for, they often spend much time by themselves, not realizing that God is communing with them. They are just drawn to quiet aloneness. Seeing how comfortable John felt living like a hermit later on, it is not difficult to imagine him, especially after the death of his parents, living like a Nazirite, like Samson of centuries gone by, a man dedicated to Yahweh, and also like Samson not cutting his hair, but letting it grow naturally. For food, well, what was there in the Judean hills? He could have trapped animals, and designed snares for birds, but no, he did not do that. Was his sensitive soul reluctant to take the life of those little creatures of God wandering so freely? He contented himself with eating locusts and wild honey, washed down with water from a spring, and never touching any strong drink. In the wilderness no one sold clothes, so naturally he was pressed to make his own, out of animal skins, skins from the abandoned carcass of a camel he had found along a trail. In his younger years as a teenager, it is easy to imagine John, already possibly orphaned, wandering the hills and just being alone with God, living like a hermit, without his more refined parents to pressure him to be more presentable as a member of a highly respected priestly family. He could feel free to live like a Nazirite, a particular Nazirite, called by Yahweh to a life of special service. He knew he was chosen to prepare the way for the Messiah, whose appearance was imminent. His mother and father must have told him that his cousin, Jesus, was the Messiah, and that it was John's responsibility to prepare the people to embrace him and follow him when he came.

For whatever time John spent in the wilderness of Judea, it must have been most difficult. He would have lived in caves on the side of the hills, or he may have visited the people at Qumram, the Essenes, who were a Jewish sect dedicated to preparing themselves for the coming of the Messiah. They even had a chair reserved for the Messiah at the head of the table in the dining room of their impressive compound not far from the shores of the Dead Sea. But most probably he spent much of the time alone, communing with Yahweh, who was the only one who could prepare him and instruct him about his mission and how he should conduct it.

Being called and dedicated to a special ministry is never easy, because it separates the person from everyone else. It is the preparation that sets the person apart, as voices and special lights coming from unseen places must be received in the lonely quiet of solitude. John's life had to be one of frightening solitude as he lived those days with God in the wilderness, just like Moses lived in painful solitude, living with his guilt over having killed an Egyptian soldier, as Yahweh was preparing him for his work as the savior of his people and the great lawgiver of civilization.

Gaunt and wild-looking, John appears at the crossing of the Jordan River, at the spot where travelers would be coming from Moab and Transjordan, and others would be going back that way. It was a busy spot, a place where John could receive the greatest exposure to launch his ministry. And what a strange image he presented: A priest with a prestigious family background was now a wild-looking hermit dressed in outlandish garb and unshaven, with hair that had not been cut in months. He certainly did not live for the things of this world. Outward appearance meant nothing to him. He was obsessed with his mission and he knew it was his only reason for being there and for being on this earth. When that mission was finished, then Yahweh would dispose of him as He willed. But for now it made no difference how he looked. He might look like a wild man, a madman, as the Pharisees called him, but no one could doubt his authenticity. His family roots were too respectable for their home atmosphere not to be refined, visited by the more respected persons in the local priestly society. John had to have absorbed that refinement, but a refinement of spirit and emotion, which has little to do with refined outward appearance.

When I was growing up, there were twelve kids in our household, plus our parents. My father made sure our mother and the children had good, substantial food to eat, good meat frequently, as my father was a meat cutter. For his supper, he would have a bowl of vegetable soup made with a meat bone he had brought home from the store. We were all nicely dressed, except my father. He would not allow my mother to use the money for new clothes for himself. He always wore worn clothes. I will never forget his overcoat. The pocket on the right side was so badly torn, it just hung there, beyond fixing. His crumpled fedora had a hole in the front of it where he always picked it up. And yet, as poor as he decided to be, he was a man of refinement and sensitivity. I will never forget one snowy Saturday morning. He took me up to the store to help him. On the way we picked up special cuts of meat at the packinghouse for his very discriminating customers, who were waiting for him outside the store. When my father got out of the truck, and I saw him walking through the snow, with his torn coat and crumpled hat and his shoes covered with burlap because his sensitive feet could not bear overshoes, I was so ashamed. An elegantly dressed judge, standing at the store entrance with the other members of my father's fan club, commented as my father approached, "That's quite an outfit you're wearing today, Peter." The men all smiled, and my father, not the slightest bit embarrassed, joked back, "Yes, judge, you have to have dignity." They all knew that what he was really saying was, "Real dignity is what we are inside." Realization of so many things often comes late, and as I grew older I became very proud of my father, knowing that his life was really beautiful. In spite of his appearance he had real dignity, and refinement. I could see that also in John the Baptizer. Sincere people saw him as a prophet, a man called by God to bring His people to repentance and reunite them with their Maker. The religious snobs, the scribes and Pharisees, saw him as a madman and a fanatic. Jesus, reflecting God's understanding, would later say, "There is no prophet greater than John the Baptizer," and referred to John as the prophet Elijah come back to prepare the way for the coming of the Messiah. (Lk. 7:24–28)

On the occasion of Jesus' first visit to John's place of preaching, nothing significant seems to have taken place, but on the second visit, Jesus got in line with the other penitents. When it was Jesus' turn to be baptized, John looked at him, recognized him, and remarked in shock, "It is you who should be baptizing me, rather than me baptizing you."

Jesus did not want a big scene, so he quietly told John, "Let it be so for now that all justice might be fulfilled." John did not understand, because he knew who Jesus was and was aware he had nothing to repent of. What John probably did not understand was why Jesus felt he should be baptized. That was an important moment for Jesus. He was not confessing his own sins. He had no sins. He was standing there in the water in solidarity with all of humanity from the beginning of time till the end of time, standing there in our place, taking upon himself the sins of us all, and asking his Father to accept and forgive us, that "all justice might be fulfilled." It was a most important moment in our redemption when Jesus took upon himself the burden of our sins, thus balancing the scales of justice with his divine innocence, thereby fulfilling what justice required. This commitment of Jesus reached its fulfillment with the ultimate sacrifice of himself in his Passion, Death, and Resurrection.

As Jesus was emerging from the stream, an opening appeared in the sky, and the Spirit of God in the form of a dove hovered over him and a voice spoke from above: "This is my Son, my beloved. My favor rests on him." (Lk. 3:21–22; Mt. 3:13–17; Mk. 1:9–11)

8
_____

JESUS' FORTY-DAY RETREAT TO PREPARE FOR HIS MISSION

How many people make a forty-day retreat in preparation for some important part of their life? How many engaged couples would consider making a forty-day retreat to prepare for the most important decision of their life? If there is anyone we would have thought was prepared to begin his ministry, it was Jesus. Yet, the Gospel says that Jesus was "driven by the Spirit into the desert to be tempted by the devil." That is the way St. Matthew's Gospel describes the event, but Jesus really went into the Judean wilderness, those rocky cliffs overlooking the ancient city of Jericho some five or six miles in the distance, for the purpose of praying and conversing with his Father before beginning the work of our redemption. He fasted for forty days, and at the end was hungry. Then Satan came and tempted him.

When Christianity began to spread throughout the Middle East, it was not long before individuals decided they wanted to leave the world and spend their lives in the desert praying and fasting. Fasting was supposed to sharpen the faculties and prepare the soul for communing with God. Fasting can be a good form of self-discipline. Giving in to everything we want can undermine our strength of will. Fasting can help control our desires, and help build strong character. This practice spread in time all throughout the East and also in the West. Eventually there were monasteries of monks and nuns dotting every region of the Roman Empire. Some were extremely strict and dedicated completely to prayer and fasting. Others prayed, fasted, and then reached out to the local communities, sharing what they had learned from God with the townsfolk who were willing to listen. They also reached out to the poor.

The forty days in the desert was a preparation for Jesus' reaching out to the world to offer it salvation. Desert prayer and contemplation is never self-centered in its vision. It is an immolation of a person's life as a plea to God for troubled humanity. Some may consider a life spent in prayer as a waste of time, and I have heard some preachers say that about monks and nuns, but it is because they set little value on a life spent with God, as an offering of their lives to God completely. It is not a self-centered life. It is a life of offering glory and thanksgiving to God for His goodness, and calling down blessings and graces for struggling human beings.

Jesus' forty days in the desert had to be a beautiful time for him to commune with his Father and the Holy Spirit, asking for guidance and strength. He knew that he would be battling not just difficult humans, but would be besieged continually by the powers of hell as Satan marshaled all his forces to frustrate and try to defeat his work of redemption. And you can look at the whole Gospel story in that light, as one continual struggle between Jesus and Satan for the control of souls. That struggle will culminate in the Garden of Gethsemane, when Jesus will make the ominous comment to the apostles, "This is the hour of the power of darkness." We will see later what Jesus meant by those words.

At the end of the forty days, Jesus was hungry. Then Satan closed in on him: "You must be hungry. Your fast is over. Your retreat is ended. It is a long distance up that dusty mountain road to Jerusalem. Look at those stones over there. Don't they look like loaves of bread? Why don't you take one of them and turn it into bread so you will have strength for your journey—after all, your fast is over?"

A simple enough temptation, and it was not to do something evil; it was just a suggestion, as if Satan was showing concern for Jesus. But Jesus knew Satan only too well, and knew Satan's real purpose, which was to find out if Jesus was the promised Messiah, the one come to destroy Satan's kingdom on earth. For Jesus to work a miracle would be a good indication, but Jesus would not give him that satisfaction. "It is not on bread alone that man lives, but on every word that comes from the mouth of God."

Then the devil took him in spirit up to the pinnacle of the Temple and said to him, "You know, if you are the Messiah, you could jump off of here and nothing would happen to you, because it says in Scripture that God has given his angels guard over you so that you won't even stub your toe against a stone. So, jump! Nothing will happen."

But Scripture also says, "You shall not tempt the Lord your God."

Then, the devil took Jesus, in vivid imagination, to the top of a very high mountain, and showed him all the kingdoms of the earth, and said to him, "These kingdoms are all mine, you know. If you are the Messiah, you have come to win these people back to your Father, but you know as well as I do that people won't listen to you. So, I'll make a deal with you. Kneel down just once and worship me, just once, and I will relinquish my power over all these people, and they will all be yours. And your mission will be accomplished in one simple stroke."

"It is also written, 'The Lord your God shall you worship and Him alone shall you adore.' "

Then Satan left Jesus.

They were clever temptations, and although they may not seem to us very appealing, they were real, and Jesus felt their power, because he knew his mission was going to be difficult and that many would turn their backs on him, especially the religious leaders. If Satan could be trusted, it was not a bad deal he was offering, but, then, Jesus knew that Satan was a liar. He'd had too many dealings with him over eons of time. Besides, there was no way he would have worshiped Satan. And if he did, it would show Satan that he was only a human, and not the Messiah. And Satan would have been relieved. All Satan really wanted from the encounter was to find out if Jesus was the Messiah. At the end he knew nothing more than when he started. Rather than revealing anything of himself, Jesus used Scripture quotes as his cover, which revealed nothing, other than that Jesus was observing the Law.

The Gospel then merely says that Satan departed from him until an opportune time. Angels came and ministered to Jesus. The information for this whole episode with Satan must have been relayed to the apostles by Jesus himself. (Lk. 4:1–13)

Realizing who Jesus is, it is difficult for us to see how Jesus could be tempted. Yet, he became one of us of set purpose so he could learn to understand how we live and what we go through in our experiences here on earth. Were these temptations of Jesus real temptations? They had to be if Jesus was not just putting on an act. Remember, Jesus chose to lay aside everything that was special about himself so that he could live like us and get to know us. As Saint Paul wrote, "Jesus did not think his divinity something that he had to cling to, but became like us in all things, except sin." The temptations were real enough. Just because Jesus would not give in to the temptations does not mean that he could not feel the emotional appeal of what Satan was offering him. Realizing that Jesus will be our judge one day, it is comforting to know that he could feel the power of human temptations, and in his understanding of what we experience, he can show pity on us for the times we have fallen.

9

JESUS' FIRST DISCIPLES, PASSOVER, AND THE JOURNEY BACK TO GALILEE

It seems that when Jesus left the place of retreat, he returned to the area where John was still preaching and baptizing. While walking casually along the banks of the Jordan, John noticed him and, looking intently at him, called out, "There is the Lamb of God that takes away the sins of the world. He is the one I spoke of when I said there is one coming after me, who is greater than I because he existed before me. I did not know him myself, yet it was to reveal him to Israel that I came baptizing with water. I have seen him and I am the witness that he is the Chosen One of God." (Jn. 1:29–34)

That statement is filled with so much to meditate on. The Lamb of God. What depth of comprehension did John have of Jesus? What did he mean when he shouted out for the whole crowd to hear, "There is the Lamb of God?" What did he mean? Did he understand the significance of what he was saying, or was Yahweh speaking through him, like the time when the Heavenly Father spoke through Simon, when he spoke out without understanding, "You are the Christ, the Son of the Living God?" John certainly wasn't talking about Jesus' gentle nature. That would have had no meaning for this rough crowd. The Lamb of God was the very special Lamb foretold by Isaiah that Yahweh was sending down to become the sacrifice for the atonement of human sin. In Judaism, the Paschal Lamb was the animal used at Passover as the official sacrifice of the Hebrew Covenant to atone for sin. An animal's blood cannot possibly atone for human evil; this lamb was only a symbol, a prefiguring of the true Lamb, whom the Father would send to adequately atone for all the sins of the human race from Adam to the last living person at the end of time. Did John know what he was announcing? Most probably he did. His mother knew under the inspiration of the Holy Spirit that Mary was the mother of the Lord when she came to visit her. "Who am I that the mother of my Lord should come to visit me?" It is easy to imagine she told John the whole story when he got old enough to understand.

Two disciples had been standing there with John. When they heard John say these things they immediately started to follow Jesus. Noticing that they were following him, Jesus turned and asked them what they wanted. "Where do you live, Rabbi?" "Come and see," Jesus replied. They then spent the rest of the day with him. One of the disciples was Andrew, the brother of Simon. In response to their question as to where he lived, where did he take them? He had no house in Judea, unless he had relatives who are not mentioned anywhere. Mary, Martha, and Lazarus became friends later on. Maybe all he had to show them was where he camped out, in a quiet, isolated spot on the bank of the Jordan. They seemed to have parted as night fell, because on the following day they got together again.

On the following day, Andrew brought his brother Simon to meet Jesus. Jesus looked at Simon and said to him, "You are Simon, son of John. You will be called Cephas, which means 'Rock.'" That was the name Jesus gave to Simon. I don't know why we don't call him Rock. There was no such name as Peter in those days. *Peter* comes from the Greek word *petra*, which means *rock*, but Petra wasn't what Jesus called him. The translation of the Hebrew and the Greek should have carried through and ended as Rock, not Peter.

The next day, as Jesus was considering going to Galilee, he met Philip, who was from Bethsaida, the same town where Simon and Andrew lived. He said to Philip, "Come, follow me!" Philip was the one who found Nathaniel, and Nathaniel, when told about Jesus, whom they thought might be the Messiah, commented, "What of any importance could come out of Nazareth?" But when he met Jesus he was impressed, especially when Jesus told him that he knew what he was doing under the fig tree when Philip came to call him. Whatever it was that Jesus knew shocked Nathaniel, and he spoke out: "Rabbi, you are the Christ, the Son of the living God; you are the king of Israel."

It is impossible to know where all this took place, because Simon and Andrew had a fishing business, and you cannot help but wonder what this little group of Galileans was doing way down in Judea. Of course, it was the celebration of the Passover, and they may have all come south to Judea in the same caravan. Apparently they all knew one another and were rather friendly. Surely they were fans of John and probably spent time in Judea listening to John whenever they could take leave of their business and trek down to Judea to spend a few days with John. (Jn. 1:35–51) It seems they all made the trip back to Galilee together.

It is confusing trying to follow the events in the Gospels, because the writers had no intention of putting everything in place as it happened. It seems that Jesus went first back to Nazareth, and if he made the trip with his new friends, they probably separated when they reached Galilee, with Jesus going to Nazareth, the others continuing on their way to Bethsaida, or Capernaum.

It seems logical that we next see Jesus in Nazareth. Filled with the Spirit from his retreat in the desert, he began to preach in the neighborhood where he grew up and had worked as a craftsman, while his new comrades were spreading his name all over the neighborhoods of Capernaum and Bethsaida. Having already become a celebrity of sorts, he was invited to speak on the following Sabbath at the village synagogue in Nazareth.

The attendant handed him the scroll of the Prophet Isaiah. Jesus unrolled it and began to read,

"The Spirit of the Lord is upon me, for he has anointed me.
He has sent me to bring the good news to the poor,

To proclaim liberty to captives,
Sight to the blind, freedom to the downtrodden,
And to announce the time of salvation."

Rolling up the scroll, he handed it back to the attendant and sat down.

The whole congregation sat there with eyes fixed on him, wondering what he was going to say, this carpenter, and what he could possibly know about religion. Looking across the crowded room, he saw the looks on their faces. There was no friendly welcoming smile. I always wondered why Jesus began the talk the way he did that day. It sounded as if he was insulting them. But, now, after speaking for so many years to crowds of every type, I've learned to pick up messages the audience sends me. It is written all over their faces. For the most part the messages are positive. Occasionally, I feel hostility. Jesus saw hostility and envy and resentment on their faces that day. He also saw hearts open and willing to listen. He knew these people. He'd lived with them most of his life. He knew the cynics. He knew the gentle, kind-hearted folk. He knew the self-serving politicians and the self-appointed judges in the village. He knew the ones who never had anything good to say about anybody. Their faces betrayed their thoughts, and the messages they sent. His opening words responded to those messages.

He began by telling the people that the prophecy he had just read was being fulfilled right then and there in their very sight. Those with open minds and open hearts were deeply moved by what he was saying to them. He had honored them by revealing to them that he was the long-awaited Messiah. Then, responding to the cynics, he said, "No doubt you will say to me, 'Physician, heal yourself! Do here in your own town, the things we heard you have been doing in Capernaum.' But, I tell you, no prophet is without honor except in his own country." And he went on to tell them that in the days of the prophet Elijah, there were many widows in Israel, but to none of those were the prophets sent, but only to the pagan woman of Zarephath, in Sidon. And there were many lepers in Israel in those days, but to none of those were the prophets sent, but only to Naaman, the Syrian general, who was cured of his leprosy. The prophets could work no miracle in Israel, because the people had no faith.

The good people in the synagogue that day were glad he'd said that. They knew well the cynical attitude of many of their neighbors, and they were happy he'd brought it out into the open. The rest of the crowd were furious. They rose up in a body and physically dragged him from the platform and out of the synagogue to the brow of the hill on which the town was built, intending to throw him down the steep incline, but he passed out of their midst and left the village, never again to return. (Lk. 4:16–30)

I am sure his mother was there that day, and maybe some others of the family, all so proud of him until that last moment. "Simeon, the old priest, was right," Mary must have thought. "He will be an object of rejection and contradiction." And she would have remembered the rest of his prophecy to her: "And your own heart a sword will pierce as the meanness in people's hearts is laid bare."

As he walked away from the town, this place of so many happy memories, and not-so-happy experiences, it must have been with a heavy heart. There were many good people there, ordinary people, not evil, but in the course of time, they drifted away from God and from those things that are important for life in the Spirit. Faith can grow faint and can die if it is not nourished. Without faith Jesus' hands were tied. It is faith that opens the floodgates of God's mercy and compassion, and makes possible wonders of all sorts. These people had long since lost that contact with the things of God. With that kind of mentality, Jesus was, as were the prophets of old, nothing more than a magic man who could do healing tricks of some sort and please the audience. Jesus was not about tricks or magic, and he was powerless in the presence of such cynicism. He was being honest with these people whom he knew only too well.

And yet, his family had to live with these people. Mary's heart must have been broken. She would have been so proud that he would be speaking to all the neighbors, never thinking that the outcome would be so tragic. What had happened? What had gone on beneath the surface that she'd missed? What did her son see in those people that she missed? Where was he now?

Did Jesus go back home to comfort his mother? Not likely. The people were too filled with hate. Worse things could happen. The Gospel merely states that he left the town. What was it in those people that had been festering for so long that it could so quickly turn to violence? What was it that Jesus saw in their hearts that prompted him to say what he did and ignite the fuse for such an explosion? He knew what was in their hearts, and it was a mixture of already hateful, unhealthy feelings about him that had lain suppressed and seething for many years. Like a doctor lancing a boil or an abscess, he had exposed the poison, and their hatred spewed forth with a vengeance.

Rejection is never easy. It is always painful and leaves scars that are long in healing. Jesus' rejection was just another human experience that made it possible for him to further understand the difficulty of being human. He would always understand the pain and damage that rejection does to people without the inner strength that he had to get past it. He could from then on understand the various strange reactions of people to their own experiences of rejection, by parents, by friends, by loved ones, by colleagues, by society. Jesus' tragic experiences again taught him a lot about human pain. His sensitivity toward lepers who were ruthlessly rejected not only by society in general, but often by parents and loved ones, was due to his own painful experiences of rejection. His own rejection made it possible for him to feel particularly close to those who have been rejected, and to seek them out and befriend them, like Levi, the tax collector, and the Samaritan woman at the well, and Zacchaeus, the chief tax collector in Jericho.

10

JESUS' CALL TO HIS DISCIPLES; THE WEDDING FEAST AT CANA

It seems that after Jesus left Nazareth he went to Capernaum, a good day's walk. Imagine, if you can, the thoughts and the pain he carried with him. His talk at Nazareth was the first talk after his forty-day retreat to prepare for his ministry. What a miserable failure! Unless what he accomplished there was what he wanted to accomplish. Perhaps, it was to hold a mirror up to those in his hometown who had long turned their backs on God. But if that was not what he intended, then he could have walked away with a sense of failure.

Rejection is always painful. I will never forget the first talk I gave when Sister Dorothy had come to work with me. We were invited to come to Atlanta, Georgia. We were so excited. Dorothy had been talking about Jesus and using the Joshua books at Western Michigan University for thirteen years to introduce the students and the parishioners to Jesus. Over three thousand students came to Mass on weekends as a result. This talk at a parish in Atlanta would have been our first experience together, and her *first* talk in our series around the country. I wanted it to be a happy time for her. But, it was not to be. So many things went wrong. The priests at the parish were enthusiastic, but the chancery office delayed in giving the parish permission for us to speak there until it was too late for any advertising. A priest in the chancery had wanted all kinds of credentials, which we supplied, but still no approval was forthcoming. The only other time when credentials were demanded and a copy of my talk demanded beforehand was from a Baptist church in Birmingham, Alabama. Cornelia Wallace, Governor Wallace's wife, who was arranging for the talk, was so ashamed, she called me up and told me it was an insult to put me through this kind of treatment, so she refused to ask for what they demanded, and canceled the request.

I never expected anything like that from Catholic officials. However, the priests at the parish decided to go ahead with the talk, and although there was not as large a crowd as they would have liked if they could have advertised, those whom God wanted to be there, were there, as well as some others.

I was the first one to speak, and Dorothy was to follow. It did not take long before individuals started to walk out in protest, although they did not leave completely. They walked to the back pews and sat down, and listened intently. It was obviously planned by a group of parishioners who had determined to stage their protest in dramatic fashion. Fortunately, Sister Dorothy's talk on Jesus' teaching on forgiveness touched people's hearts and later a little child came up to her and threw her arms around her and, crying, thanked her for what she had said about forgiveness. Her talk had brought peace to the girl's troubled heart. She had not spoken to her father in a long time, and felt so bad, and she said she was going to tell him she was sorry. That little girl was with the group that had come to protest, I was told. When the mother saw her daughter talking to Dorothy, she finally came over to her and apologized to Dorothy for their rude treatment.

When I read about Jesus' experience at Nazareth, I am reminded of how painful it is to be rejected, and it made me realize how much more painful it must have been for him. People could easily find fault with me over any number of shortcomings, but Jesus, goodness itself, had come to share the good news from God that people had been waiting for for thousands of years, and was treated that way. It had to be devastating.

Capernaum was a different story. It was a big city, with a large synagogue built by a wealthy Roman military officer who was kindly disposed toward the Jewish religion. It was also a bustling business center, with considerable pagan influence due to the large number of Greek-speaking people who were residing there, as well as a large Roman garrison. But, importantly for Jesus, his new friends were living there, the ones he had recently met at John's gathering at the Jordan down in Judea.

Now that Nazareth could not be the base for his ministry, Jesus had to find a place to center his ministry. Nazareth would have been ideal, since he knew so many people there, and he could have developed a solid core of disciples. But now he had to start from nothing, nothing but a few friends whom he had just met days earlier, almost a hundred miles away from home.

Walking along the shore in Capernaum, where fishermen were tending their boats and repairing their nets, Jesus watched them, curious about these rugged, boisterous, big-hearted men who, in their rough, good-natured manner, joked with one another as they continued their work.

Farther along the shore he saw others whom he recognized. They were Simon and Andrew, and nearby, two other men working in their father's boat. Their names were James and John, the sons of Zebedee, who had already heard of Jesus from Simon and Andrew. Jesus stopped briefly and called to Simon and Andrew and, looking over at James and John, called to them also, telling them, "Come! Come follow me!" (Lk. 5:1–11; Mt. 4:18–22; Mk. 1:16–20)

Whatever it was that Jesus had said to them previously, and whatever

James and John had been told about him by the others, they were ready, and they left everything and followed Jesus.

Remains of an ancient synagogue built by the Roman officer in charge of the area still stands not far from the shore of the Sea of Galilee. While spending time there, Jesus was invited to speak at the Sabbath service. Word about him had spread around the area, and curiosity brought crowds to see him. In the packed sanctuary, a disturbed man burst out in the middle of Jesus' talk, "Jesus of Nazareth, have you come to destroy us? We know who you are, the Holy One of God."

"Be quiet and come out of him!" Jesus ordered. After convulsing the man, the evil spirits obeyed Jesus' command and came out of him. The people were filled with astonishment and were saying to one another, "What teaching, and what power! Even the evil spirits leave when he commands them." (Mk. 1:21–28; Lk. 4:31–37) And word spread throughout the whole countryside about this new preacher who had recently come to their area, and who had strange powers to heal and to drive out devils. But his powers were nothing like those of the Pharisees, who just recited their rituals. "This man talks to the demons as if he knows them and gives commands to them and they grovel before him and obey him. They are afraid of him. And he is such a humble man, and does not judge anyone. He seems to understand the pain in people's lives and how difficult life is. He shows a rare warmth and love for each person he meets, and people enjoy just being in his presence. Even little children run up to him and hug him, something they never do to strangers, especially men." These were the thoughts and the images the people had of him.

When Jesus left the synagogue, he went with Simon and his companions to Simon's house, where they found Simon's mother-in-law sick with a high fever. They asked him if he would do something to help her. He bent over and touched her, and the fever left her immediately. And she right away got up and began to wait on them. Hopefully, that was not the reason they'd asked him to help her! Perhaps it was. It seems they had invited Jesus over to relax and spend the afternoon enjoying refreshments and getting acquainted with their family and neighbors. So they may well have had an ulterior motive in asking Jesus to cure her. And again they were proud of their new friend, and healing the sick lady was a nice way of showing him off to the family. So very human! (Mk. 1:29–31)

It could not have been long after that incident that Jesus left for a wedding in Cana, a distance of about fifteen miles from Capernaum. Jesus felt that he should be there even if he was going to be late. When he arrived he was indeed late, three days late. With him were his newfound friends, who had also been invited. The newlyweds may have been relatives of Jesus and Mary, because we see Mary working behind the scenes and feeling comfortable enough to take charge if something needed to be done, as she was the one who noticed that the wine was running short. So, when Jesus arrived, she immediately approached him with the comment, "Son, they have run out of wine."

"How does that concern us? What do you expect me to do? My time has not yet come." This was not the time appointed by his Father. Interesting! He knew she was hinting for him to do something. It would have been a terrible embarrassment to the family to have run out of wine after only three days, when the party was supposed to last for another five days. People prepared for those weddings long in advance, practically as soon as the child was born, like we today might prepare for a son or daughter to enter college. The father would start making a separate batch of wine that year and every year afterward to prepare for the eight-day wedding party, maybe sixteen years down the line. He had to make sure there would be enough to satisfy the thirst of a whole village for eight days.

Whatever else was said between Mary and her son, she understood him to have agreed to do something. She went to the waiters and told them to do whatever he told them. Think about this situation, and ask yourself, "Why would she be dropping him a hint unless she knew he could do something? And how would she know that he could do something unless she had seen him doing interesting things around the house?" The exchange between the two shows a delicate intimacy between them. Only Mary knew he could do something. And Jesus knew she was asking for a miracle, and at a time not appointed by his Father. The waiters went to Jesus and asked him what he wanted them to do. "You see those big stone water jars?"

"Yes."

"Fill them up."

Six stone water jars capable of holding 25 to 30 gallons each, a total of between a 150 and 180 gallons. These jars of water were to be used for ceremonial washings whenever anyone incurred legal impurity, which was many times a day. This shows what Jesus felt about ceremonial washings.

"Now take some to the headwaiter," he said, and they did. The headwaiter scolded them: "Usually people serve the best wine first, then when people cannot tell the difference, they serve a lesser quality. But you have saved the best until last." (Jn. 2:1–12)

We have always looked upon this wedding party as Jesus' way of consecrating marriage, and elevating marriage to the level of a sacrament. But there are also many other messages in this incident that Jesus may have felt were important for us to understand.

This wedding party turned out to be, even if it was not the time appointed by his Father, the inauguration of his sacred mission of redemption. And he began it during a very earthly celebration at which he gave the bride and groom a wonderful wedding present, an extra 150 to 180 gallons of the best wine, and this after they had already finished a huge supply. It is not hard to visualize the situation—the guests had been partying for three days and had already finished off so much wine. It is hard not to imagine that some were boisterous and not too delicate in their behavior.

It is comforting to see Jesus so relaxed and having a good time at a party, even when some guests may have had too much to drink and were acting silly or boisterous. And it was not that people just stayed at the party for eight days straight. People still had to work, even though they did not have a forty-hour work week in those days. They would go back to work for a couple of hours, then return to the party later on and enjoy the fun and the refreshments for a while longer. And this went on for eight days. It was all quite casual. The scene shows a side of Mary that we might not ordinarily think of. She is not upset by all the drinking. She is more concerned about the bride and groom being embarrassed for having run out of wine when there were still five days left of the party. People would have remembered that and brought it up to them for the rest of their lives. So, Mary saved them that embarrassment.

It is so good to see Jesus having a good time at a party. It seems he enjoyed parties. We see him going to more parties as time goes on. He really enjoyed being human, which is strange, because we do not enjoy being human. We are embarrassed at being human. God forbid that anyone ever see us men cry. Of course, women cry a lot. They cry when they are sad, they cry when they are happy, and as one woman told me one day, "We don't need a reason to cry, we just enjoy crying." That is hard for men to understand, but crying is probably a lot healthier. It is a built-in release valve for stress. Men might be better off if we were not embarrassed to cry. We look upon it as a sign of weakness. Jesus was not ashamed to cry. We see him crying on a number occasions.

And as the wedding party continued, and especially if the couple were relatives of Jesus and Mary, it is not hard to imagine some of Jesus' cousins going up to him and grabbing him by the hand and dancing with him in the Jewish equivalent of a jig or a polka, and Jesus really enjoying it. Why not? There is nothing wrong with it. I have seen very saintly monks dance, and they were good at it; one was especially good at those squatting, kicking Russian dances. It would be a heartwarming experience to see Jesus dancing and having a good time. Is that not what he was all about, "like us in all things but sin," as Saint Paul wrote?

And no one can draw the conclusion from what Jesus did that he had a casual attitude toward excessive drinking. That would be ridiculous. His concern, as was his mother's, was for the newlyweds. That would have been a very humiliating experience for them, and both Mary and Jesus manifested a sensitive compassion toward the family.

Also, something that has been overlooked is the fact that Jesus worked this, his first public miracle, because his mother asked him, even though "the time had not yet come," the time appointed by his Father. What a powerful example from Scripture for Mary's intercession with her son. And is it not also interesting that this event became the official inauguration of Jesus' mission as the Messiah? And look at how he celebrates it, by providing over a hundred gallons of wine to an unfortunate couple at a wedding party. Saint John sums up the event with the simple statement, "And this was the first sign given by Jesus. And it was given at Cana in Galilee. He let his glory be seen and his disciples believed in him." (Jn. 2:11)

There are many healthy messages that can be gleaned from that event, messages that throw a new light on our image of Jesus, who had come down to earth to teach us how to live. Perhaps God is more realistic than we are on what it means to be human. I am sure not everybody at that party was perfectly sober. Of all the hundreds of wedding receptions I have attended, I cannot remember one where there were not at least a few who were obviously drunk. Could it be that we take ourselves too seriously and have unrealistic ideas of what it really means to be a good human being? That certainly does not mean that we should be too easy on ourselves and find excuses to be careless in ways that threaten our relationship with God, or harm ourselves or offend others. But seeing Jesus enjoying himself is good for us. It helps us to understand that he enjoys being one of us and can understand us.

It was not until Jesus took upon himself a human nature with a human body and a human soul, with all that that implies, that God could feel what we feel, and experience what we experience through our senses. This may come as a surprise for many who think that God knows all things. And God does know all things, but human beings experience life and learn new things through our five senses. That is a very imperfect way of learning. Not until Jesus became one of us could he learn the way we learn, and in learning, grow in knowledge, because as God he did not have the bodily senses and nervous system that we have. Once he had our human body he could experience what we experience, and so learn new things as they presented themselves. As Saint Luke says in his Gospel, as the family was returning from the Temple, "He went back with them to Nazareth and was subject to them, and grew in wisdom and age and grace before God and man." (Lk. 2:41–52)

It is his intimate knowledge of our nature, which he learned from his own experiences, that made it possible for Jesus to have such compassion for us. Being one of us, he could feel our sadness, our joy, our hope, and our feelings of depression and sense of failure. He could share our dreams, and know the distress that comes from shattered dreams and broken hearts.

At the end of the party at Cana, Saint John writes, Jesus went down to Capernaum with his mother and his kinsfolk and stayed there a few days. (Jn. 2:11)

11

The New Disciples

J esus spent much of his time at Capernaum. It was becoming his new home, even though he told a man who wanted to be his follower that the Son of Man had nowhere to lay his head. Since being told he was unwanted in his hometown of Nazareth, Jesus had no home. Did he stay at Simon's house, or at the home of one of the other disciples? Or did he sleep up in the hills? The Gospels do say on a number of occasions that he went up into the hills to pray, often spending the whole night in prayer. It is not likely that he slept in the hills every night, especially on cold, rainy nights. Most probably he stayed at Simon's house. It was conveniently located very near where he spent much of his time preaching to the crowds in Capernaum, and when people with sick relatives and friends were looking for him, they seemed to know they could find him at Simon's house. There he seemed to hold many of his smaller sessions, until the crowds got too big. It was while he was at Simon's house that a small group, frustrated that they could not get their crippled relative to Jesus for healing, climbed up on the roof and took the tiles off the roof and lowered the fellow down with ropes, practically plopping him right into Jesus' lap.

Jesus seemed to feel quite at ease in Simon's company. There are some people who are so outgoing and full of fun and friendly banter, they make you feel at home immediately. Simon was clearly one of those people. Jesus could always have fun with Simon. He was rugged and affectionate, and Jesus could be totally relaxed with him and with his family. James and John, although they also were close to Jesus, seemed to belong to a family that was more proper in their manners and perhaps more highly strung than Simon and his family. James and John, we will see, could be very excitable. Simon was blunt with Jesus, and Jesus was just as blunt with him. It is a sign of a real friendship when two people can be perfectly up-front and say to each other just what is on their minds and not be offended. Those kinds of relationships are fun, and healthy.

Jesus often stayed at Simon's house the whole day and even slept there, at least for a good part of the night. Jesus was an early riser, and at Simon's house he felt comfortable enough to get up early in the morning, walk down to the seashore, and meet people or go up into the hills behind the town to spend time in prayer with his Father in heaven.

If Jesus went out early to walk along the seashore, his manner was always casual. Being warm and friendly, it is easy to see Jesus striking up a conversation with a stranger walking along the beach. And as they talked, other townsfolk gathered out of curiosity, and Jesus talked to them as well, about how close God is to his children here on earth. He might say very casually, "Your Father in heaven is never very far away. In fact, the kingdom of heaven is right in our midst." Strange talk, curious talk, fascinating, in fact—not the kind of talk they would hear from the scribes or Pharisees. It was as if this man was intimate with God and knew what he was talking about. He sounded like a prophet.

Then as the crowd began to grow, Jesus spotted Simon walking toward his boat. Going over, with the crowd following him, he stepped into Simon's boat and told him to shove off a bit so he could talk to the crowd from off the shore. It was safer. It is not difficult to imagine the conversation. New people drifting in to listen were curious as to what was going on. And they yelled out the question, "Who are you? Aren't you the one they threw out of Nazareth?"

"I tell you, no prophet is without honor except in his hometown. But, you are fortunate, because you are now my family and my neighbors."

"But, what are you about? What is your business?"

"My business is to do the will of my heavenly Father. And His will is for me to bring you the good news of the coming of the kingdom. The kingdom of God is near at hand. You have waited since the time of Abraham for the coming of the kingdom, and now it has arrived."

"Who are you? What do you say for yourself? Why should we listen to you?"

"I have come to fulfill what the prophets promised. I have come to bring you good news, to give sight to the blind, to announce freedom to those in captivity, and to announce that the time of salvation has come."

"Are you the Anointed One?"

"What do you see? You have eyes to see. Do not look and refuse to see.

What is it you see? What has been taking place in your midst these past few days? You have seen and you have heard what others have seen and heard. These things speak for themselves. And it is not just the signs that speak. It is my Father who speaks through the signs, giving testimony as to who I am. He is my witness."

And they had either already seen the miracles he had performed or had heard from others the awesome healings that had been worked through him. That testimony should speak loudly enough. They should need no further testimony that he had been sent by Yahweh.

With nothing more to say, but giving the crowd enough to think about, Jesus turned to Simon and told him to cast the nets into the sea. They immediately hauled in a huge catch of fish that almost sank the boat. Simon was so shocked he fell on his knees and impulsively told Jesus, "Leave me, Lord, for I am a sinful man." In the boat with the others were James and John, who were partners with Simon. Jesus, seeing how frightened they were at this display of power, told them, "Do not be afraid. From now on you will be fishers of men." When they had brought their boats to land, they arranged for the fish to be shipped to market, then left all and followed Jesus. (Lk. 5:1–11)

Shortly afterward Jesus wandered toward the main street, where he came across a tax collector sitting in his booth. He had walked by this way on other occasions and had nodded and smiled at the tax collector, and had stopped to talk to him, as well. The two were not unfamiliar with each other. As he passed this time, Jesus could see that the man had a generous heart and was ready to make a commitment. When Jesus approached the booth, the publican looked up at him, and as he did, he caught Jesus' eye.

Jesus smiled and said to him, "Come, follow me!" (Mk. 2:13–17)

And the tax collector, Levi was his name, closed his booth and left immediately to follow Jesus. He could not wait to go home and spread the word, and also contact all his colleagues, informing them that he was throwing a retirement party for himself, and that they were all invited. These men were always ready for a party. It was obvious one of them could whip up what was needed for a party in a matter of minutes, as they had the means to keep their larders well stocked. And this was going to be one great party, and that new rabbi, the one that got kicked out of Nazareth a few weeks ago, would also be there. The publicans for miles around were invited, and they never missed a party. They were the only ones who would come to a tax collector's house for a party anyway. The publicans were the most hated people in town, in every town. It is interesting to see how comfortable this new rabbi was in the presence of such a group.

It was not long after the party started, and after a few cups of wine, that the event came to life. These men had no inhibitions. They had no high image to protect. They knew people hated them, and so they just acted themselves, and they turned out to be a fun-loving group, and quite loud. Some wandering Pharisees heard the noise down the street and decided to walk past the house to see the cause of all the excitement. As they walked slowly past the house they could see from the street the whole scene through the large open window on the front of the house. There inside was the crowd of publicans and in the place of honor that new rabbi from Nazareth, with this crowd of sinners. "Look at what a great time he is having. He is some rabbi! First, for some reason or other he was kicked out of his hometown; even they didn't want him. Now he comes here and takes up with all these criminals. Look in there! See how the wine is flowing. And he is supposed to be a religious teacher, a miracle worker. It is going to be interesting to see where this is all going to lead—the rabbi and his band of holy tax collectors." In self-righteous glee, and shaking their heads in holy disapproval, they continued their walk.

Jesus spotted the band of Pharisees as they took their time walking past. The image of Jesus at a big bash for a retiring tax collector would stay in their memories for a long time, as they spread the word far and wide. The subject would eventually come up again, in a verbal clash that Jesus would have later on with another group of Pharisees in Judea. His reputation as a drunk, a glutton, and a partygoer would spread like feathers in the wind throughout Galilee and Judea, among self-styled holy people.

But there are important messages in this scene at Levi's party. Who of us would ever visualize God attending a party thrown by a sinner, and not just attending, but the guest of honor and surrounded by such a loud, boisterous crowd? Then, thinking about it, you soon come to realize that after all, he had come to offer redemption to sinners, and what better group to start with than the most despised people in Palestine, collaborators with the Roman occupation forces, hired to collect taxes from their fellow countrymen, and none too honest in their assessment and collection methods? How many good people were in Roman jails because they could not afford the outrageous demands of these despicable people? It is not hard to understand why the Pharisees were shocked at Jesus' enjoying the company of such people. Good people today are shocked when priests hear confessions and give the last rites to people who had been members of the Mafia. They would be just as shocked at Jesus caring for such sinners. The tax collectors were not much different. They were really extortionists. The parable of the workers who all received the same pay even though some worked longer than others reflects the same generous mentality of the Master. Those who came late were still rewarded.

It is not mentioned in the Gospels how many tax collectors at Levi's party were won over by Jesus that day, but he had been popular with those people ever since and all during his ministry. They were generally tough, hardened businessmen. It is not easy, however, to understand why they were so easily won over to him, unless it was because he always found a good word to say about them, like the time he told the parable about the Pharisee and the publican who went to the Temple to pray, and how God found the Pharisee's prayer unacceptable and the publican's humility and repentance pleasing. That story must have spread like wildfire among not just the Pharisees, but the publicans, as well, so when they met him personally, they already liked him and were open to whatever he had to say.

When I was working in parishes, I enjoyed meeting the rather rough men whom I found out had just as rough reputations in the community. I met them sometimes at wakes for their parents or close friends, who also may not have had the best of reputations. They were so shocked to see a priest spending time with their families on these sad occasions that their attitudes toward the Church changed completely. They then invited me to meet their friends, who were just as shocked that a priest enjoyed being a friend of theirs. It made all the difference in the world. From that point on they would do anything for me. The whole parish was shocked when they saw all these fellows going to Mass every Sunday.

The people I really had a problem with and found it almost impossible to love were crooked judges and ruthless prosecutors who took delight in their reputations for condemning people to the harshest prison sentences, especially when the convictions were based on concocted evidence. They were invariably good church people. One very prominent judge, who was a faithful churchgoer, and who had the reputation for being the hanging judge, always impressed me as being the closest I had come to meeting a Pharisee, totally dedicated to the law, and to the strictest punishment for violation of the law, and seemingly without compassion. One day my own lawyer, who grew up with one of these judges, was defending a client. The judge was about to give the fellow a long prison sentence, when the lawyer asked for a private consultation with the judge. All he said to him was, "Judge, how you can possibly be so hard on this kid when you and I and the rest of us did a lot worse. Remember the day when—"

The judge cut him off. "Counselor, don't remind me of that," he said, his face beet red. He did relent in the sentence he was going to impose, and the fellow got off with a reasonable sentence and a stiff warning.

Jesus saw goodness deep down in everyone's heart and had the genius to bring out that goodness. Whoever would have thought that Levi the tax collector would be the author of the inspired Gospel according to Matthew, the new name Jesus gave him?

12

Jesus Expands His Ministry in Galilee

Jesus often started his day by the busy shore at Capernaum. It was a bustling center of activity, as fishermen were continually coming and going, some arriving from their all-night fishing trips, and others starting out to catch their share for the next day's market, and still others repairing their nets or patching up the leaks in their boats. Since people lived on fish, even eating fish for breakfast, there had to be a steady supply to satisfy the large local population. Jesus enjoyed sitting by the shore, watching all the activity as he learned more and more about what it was like to be human and the way humans made their living and transacted their business deals, and how they talked to one another. It shows in his parables later on. Jesus' depth of knowledge about businesspeople and their financial dealings he learned not only from his own work with his foster father, but from watching the shrewd fishermen as they haggled with the local women who were always demanding better deals. More than once the thought crossed his mind that it was too bad people were not as shrewd and prudent in their pursuit of spiritual treasures as they were in protecting their material possessions.

On another day as he was standing on the beach watching the fishermen readying their boats for the day's fishing trip, he saw others of Simon's group, who were not with Simon and James and John previously. One of them was Andrew. To these he also called out, "Come, follow me, and I will make you fishers of men."

Surprisingly, they brought their boat to shore, put away their nets, and left to follow Jesus. What was the appeal that could cause these rugged fishermen, whose livelihood depended on their hard work, to leave everything and follow this man who only a short time before was a total stranger? And as they walked along the shore together, they came across their colleagues, James and John, Zebedee's sons whom Jesus had called the day before, and they joined their friends as they walked down the street. They were young fellows still working in their father's fishing business. One wonders what happened to their business when they left and followed Jesus. James and John's father, Zebedee, obviously had to keep running the business, probably with mixed emotions about Jesus. The hired hands hopefully were loyal and trustworthy.

We should not look upon these fishermen as just private fisherman catching fish for themselves and their families. They were running big businesses with not just one or two boats but with a number of good-sized vessels. There was enough business for a fleet of fishermen, since the population of the whole area lived on fish, not just the local Galileans. The constant demand kept prices high and the profit margin considerable. So when these men walked away from their boats it was at considerable cost, and loss of income. Of course, they would not have just left their fishing vessels there to float near the shore. They would have told their more trusted hired help to take care of the business until they returned, which they did on numerous occasions when they were traveling with Jesus.

What was it that inspired these hardened businessmen to leave all in an instant to follow a man they hardly knew? Was it excitement over the prospect of an adventurous life with a popular wonderworker? Were the stunning miracles he worked indicative of Messianic powers, and did joining up with him offer the prospect of a promising future? Was it the thought that they could finally be free from the daily pressure of their very demanding business, and the tedious job of keeping their boats and equipment in top condition to cope with the violent storms from the northern mountains that created havoc on the lake, often destroying many a vessel?

There must have been more enticement than mere adventure or even the thought of freedom from work. These men were not children. They were responsible men with families and partners in family-run businesses. They must have seen something in this new teacher who spoke with a power and charisma that touched their hearts, and even more deeply, their souls. This was not just an ordinary man. It was a man who had some kind of powerful, indefinable connection with the Almighty. He was not a rabble-rouser, or a ruffian. There was class and sensitivity in this man. He was capable of really leading the people without resorting to armed revolt. What he said made a lot of sense, and the signs he performed showed that Yahweh was with him. He was a man with a purpose, and with the powers he had, he could go far. So, these men felt honored when they were invited to follow Jesus.

Each day was a new epiphany, a manifestation of another facet of their new leader's life. His message was like his cousin John's message, "Repent, the kingdom of God is near!" This message and elaboration on that theme he preached in the synagogues all throughout Galilee and began to heal all who came to him, from whatever infirmity they suffered, and from those possessed he drove out the evil spirits. And as his fame spread even into Syria and Phoenicia, people came from all around to be healed and to listen to his dream of the kingdom. At the same time, Jesus was learning. He was learning new things every day about people, the pain they suffered, the complicated sicknesses under which they labored, the mental disorders and unremitting depression, the debilitating paralysis, and the hopelessness that was so much a part of their lives. And he reached out and cured them all. In his extraordinarily sensitive soul he could feel their pain, and how they suffered from the harshness of life. We will see Mark later on in his Gospel expressing that anguish of Jesus: "He felt sorry for the people. 'They are like sheep without a shepherd.' " (Mk. 6:34)

One day, after seeing the frightful conditions that oppressed so many people, Jesus' heart felt their anguish and their pain. He went up on the mountainside and, sitting down and directing the huge crowd to sit on the grass all around him, he spoke to them in words they'd never heard before. "Blessed are the poor in spirit, for the kingdom of heaven is theirs."

What a strange thing to say to these people, many of whom had hardly enough money to buy food! "What is he talking about? We are blessed? We are lucky? How can he say such a thing? What does he mean?" He obviously meant it to be a word of comfort. How could that be comforting?

What Jesus said may not seem to make sense when poverty is so frightening to those who have lost everything, but I learned from my own experience that, in spite of the paradox involved, Jesus was right. When I retired I had nothing. I measured what I could eat. I saved seeds from a tomato so I could grow tomato plants in a little piece of land outside the bungalow a kindly undertaker made available to me. I grew corn from an ear of corn I had. I grew lettuce, and a few other vegetables. I had no money for clothes or shoes. And I saved money to make sure I could pay my medical insurance when it came due. My car had over two hundred thousand miles on it and a hole hidden somewhere near a rear tire, which would squirt me in the back of the head when I drove through a puddle of water.

I don't see how anyone could be much poorer, and yet, they were the happiest days of my life. I had never felt closer to God than I did in those days. I really knew what Jesus meant when he said that "the kingdom of God is within you." I was happy being poor, happier and freer than I had ever been, and closer to God then, because I knew how much I needed Him, and it was a joy knowing that He was taking care of me, though I still had the difficult feeling that He was keeping His distance from me. I still knew He was protecting me and I was happy. I knew what Jesus meant when he told those poor people, "Blessed are the poor in spirit, for the kingdom of heaven is theirs." I had all that I needed.

I took long walks in the morning to lower my blood pressure. My heart thrilled as I drank in the beauty of the sun, and the pure blue sky and the hills and the fields and the wild flowers and the goats and sheep and cows, and horses and all the other farm animals as I walked past the farms. If I legally possessed them I could not have enjoyed them as much. I would have been shackled to them. I enjoyed all of nature in total freedom. Possessing them would have stripped me of enjoying their beauty. One day I reached to catch a butterfly, but stopped, and thought, "I love it because it's free. If I capture it I will lose what I love in this beautiful creature, its freedom." I loved the songs of the birds and thought how nice it might be to have a songbird in the house, but then I realized that what I loved about the birds was their freedom. My possessing them would have destroyed what I loved about them. Jesus was so right: It takes very little to survive; to live comfortably maybe not, but to survive and enjoy the fruits of having little does not take much. I experienced the kingdom of heaven within me.

And Jesus continued in his words of comfort to the crowd: "Blessed are the sorrowful, for they shall be comforted." Again, this is impossible to understand unless a person understands what Jesus meant. He was continually trying to encourage people to develop an intimacy with their Father in heaven. With that in mind, what he was telling the people made sense. When you are in deep sadness from some tragedy or from some inner pain, throw yourself into the arms of your heavenly Father and He will comfort you, and that comfort will be unimaginably sweet. That did not make sense to me until I had experienced a horrible tragedy. No human could comfort me, and I took long walks up into the hills, resting in the knowledge that God was near as I walked along. I cannot begin to explain the peacefulness and the comfort I found after a while, knowing that God was my companion, and with Him in my heart and all around me, what more did I need? My pain did not go away, but it eased, knowing that in some mysterious way, God was sharing my pain, so I was not suffering alone. And even Jesus had to practice what he was preaching to the people that day. When he was undergoing painful experiences in his ministry from the hateful things the religious leaders did to him daily, and the sense of failure he was experiencing from the people's rejection of his message, he would reach out to his Father. At those times he would retire to the hills at night and pour his heart out to his Father, and from Him receive the comfort of his Father's love and strength. So, when he spoke like he did to the people, it was not an empty religious placebo that he made up on the spur of the moment. He was sharing his own experience of the awesome, all-embracing love that comes from God if only we are willing to open our hearts to him, and let God hold us close.

"Blessed are the meek, for they shall inherit the earth." We don't see in our world the meek inheriting anything. It is the arrogant and the greedy who take what they want and ferociously fight off any possible threat. It was the same in Jesus' day. People do not change. What Jesus said about the meek and the gentle, however, is valid. A little story may help. A religious sister, member of an order that cared for the poor, wanted so much to build a school for poor children. A very wealthy man who was hostile to everything the Church stood for lived in the neighborhood and owned a piece of property that was in a most convenient location for a school. The nun one day got the courage to approach the man and tried to explain her dream to him, hoping that he would donate the piece of land on which to build the school. He was totally unsympathetic and even insulting in the way he treated her. After telling her that he was very busy, he ushered her to the door. The nun tried to be gracious, but the most she could do was to promise that since he was a neighbor she and her sisters would pray for him each day at Mass. That meant nothing to him. Anyone who has dealings with sisters knows that they do not easily give up. Weeks went by, months went by, years went by. The nuns continued their prayers and sent the man and his family greetings at holiday times and at other times during the year, each time assuring him and his family of their prayers. They tried to be gracious neighbors in every way they could, even though there was never a response. The nuns meant nothing to him. If anything, they were like pests. Their goodness made him feel uncomfortable

After a number of years the man, who had grown quite old, called the nuns and asked if the sisters in charge would come over to his house. They had a very nice visit, and the man ended by pouring his heart out to them, telling them that he had been very sick, and the doctor had told him that he was dying and was lucky to have lived as long as he had. He told the sisters that he was sorry for having been such a rude neighbor and that he had done much soul-searching during his illness, and decided that he would be very proud to see a school built for poor children through a generous gift that he intended to offer to the nuns. Not only did he donate the land, but he also made money available to build the school and subsidize the children's education. There are so many stories similar to this one, which bear out dramatically Jesus' words, "Blessed are the meek, for they shall inherit the earth."

The people in India wanted for centuries to be free. They tried everything: war, violence, terrorism tactics; nothing worked. Mahatma Gandhi decided to take Jesus seriously. He started a peace movement in India, which spread all throughout country. The movement grew and pressure mounted, and after many years, the British government finally relented and gave the Indian people their freedom, and turned the country over to them. "Blessed are the meek, for they shall inherit the earth."

When Pope John Paul II was an archbishop in Poland, and the Communists ruled the country with an iron fist, he held the people in tight control spiritually, insisting that they be strong and pray for peace and for their freedom. He quietly and steadfastly resisted government control of the Church and preached constantly that people were created to be free, telling them at the same time that they must never resort to violence to obtain their freedom. In time he was elected pope, and from the Vatican he still guided his Polish flock with a steady hand, insisting on their freedom and warning against violence. At the right time, he encouraged trade unions in Poland to go on strike all across the country. He had inside information that the Warsaw Pact forces would not invade Poland because they knew the Polish troops would never turn against their own people. Within a matter of weeks, the Polish Communist government fell, and the Soviet Union itself came unglued and disintegrated, without one shot being fired or one person killed. Whoever would have thought that the dreaded Communist threat to take over the world would become so easily and peacefully dismantled without a horrible war, and without one shot being fired? Later on, in a column entitled "My Partner the Pope," President Mikhail Gorbachev wrote in an Italian newspaper that he could never have accomplished what he did in freeing the Soviet nations without the help of John Paul II. For the most part we do not take Jesus seriously, and even today we insist on solving problems by resorting to war, which never works. We end up with more problems than before the war, and live with the horrible human destruction for generations. When an advisor told Joseph Stalin to be careful of the Vatican, he scoffed and said,

"How many divisions does the pope have?" Hardly fifty years later the whole Communist empire collapsed because of the holiness and prayers of a peace-loving pope and his loyal followers. "Blessed are the meek, for they shall inherit the earth."

There is no logic to Jesus' beatitudes, as these sayings of Jesus are called, unless we understand where Jesus is coming from. Jesus knows how much God is concerned about our lives, and all he wants is for us to let Him into our lives so He can help us. When we do, there is no limit to His power, and the help He can give us. Jesus knows that, and his beatitudes start out from the premise that with God all things are possible, as we have just seen.

"Blessed are those who hunger and thirst for righteousness, for they shall be satisfied." The word *righteousness* could also mean "holiness" or "fulfillment of justice." It is not easy to understand completely what Jesus had in mind, but if you look at Jesus' own life, you can see how each of these blessings mirrors a different facet of his own personality. Jesus certainly hungered for righteousness, for just treatment of everyone, for personal holiness in the fulfillment of his Father's will. How was this hunger met in his life? First of all, he always had the peace that came from his assurance that as difficult and painful as his life was, he was doing his Father's will to make righteousness and goodness flourish in the world. On a daily basis, Jesus may not have had the satisfaction that his struggle for righteousness was taking hold in people's hearts, and that struggle became even more intense and frightening with each passing day. In the end, on the cross, he could cry out triumphantly, "It is finished. I have accomplished the mission for which I was sent." He had been victorious. He had won the battle with Satan and the powers of hell. He lived to see the victory of righteousness and justice, and the redemption of the world from evil. His hunger for justice, for righteousness, for holiness was fully satisfied. But we can never expect that promise to be immediate. That one demands great patience and long suffering. But in the end there will always be victory.

That hungry pursuit of holiness and righteousness on our part may be no more immediately satisfying in our lives than it was in Jesus' life. The pursuit of goodness never ends, and although in the daily skirmishes we may become discouraged because we are not victorious, in the major, ultimate battle for righteousness, we have the assurance that the outcome of that battle will never be in doubt. That outcome will be total vindication. So, the daily struggle may be painful, and at times terrifying, for it will haunt us each day as we forge our way through this life, but there is a comforting satisfaction in knowing we are doing what God wants of us. The obstacles to righteousness sometimes may be too great, too many, too unrelenting in their brutal battering of our frailty to give us much peace or assurance of victory. That may come briefly and at rare moments. For many of us it will come only toward the end of our earthly struggle. The ultimate satisfaction will come most assuredly when Jesus finally welcomes us home as victors in the challenge to follow behind him on earth's battlefield. What Jesus does is assure us of the total support of his powerful grace as the nourishment we need in our daily *striving* for righteousness. Sometimes some people have the satisfaction during their lifetime of unexpected vindication of their difficult struggle for righteousness, but that is rare. But when it does occur it is sweet.

"Blessed are the merciful, for they shall receive mercy." This is one that I think Jesus could even smile at as he thought it over. No one ever showed more mercy than he did. Yet, no one was ever treated as mercilessly as he was treated by those whose honor and loyal allegiance he had a right to expect. So, I am sure he knew we would have a difficult time understanding this one unless we had reached a point where we could see things through his rare point of view. Superficially, people who are merciful often become victims of their own mercy as mean or vicious people see their goodness as weakness and cannot resist exploiting that goodness. So, in trying to understand this blessing we have to go far beneath the surface of our lives and of Jesus' life, and search for those things that prompted Jesus to speak this blessing.

Who showed mercy in Jesus' day? Not the Romans, not the chief priests, not the Levites, not the Pharisees; we do not even see the apostles showing mercy, which does not mean that they did not, but we do not see them in situations where they show mercy, except later, after Jesus had left. Often they were impatient with Jesus for being so merciful. We rarely see anyone showing mercy in the Gospels other than Jesus. However, we do see Jesus praising certain prostitutes for their charity and mercy and love toward people in need. And they themselves were never shown mercy by anyone, only contempt.

So, when is a merciful person the recipient of mercy? That is the great question, and Jesus knew that. When was Jesus ever shown mercy? I cannot think of one incident in the Gospels where anyone every showed mercy to Jesus. Maybe once, when he said from the cross, "I thirst," and the Roman soldier gave him a sponge soaked in sour wine to ease his thirst and his pain. Where did Jesus go when he needed understanding and someone who could comfort him? Up in the hills to be alone with his Father.

There are some people whose lives are so removed from ordinary life around them that they find it difficult if not impossible to find anyone who could understand them even if they could share their pain and their anguish. So, like Jesus, the only place they can go is to the mountain to be with the Father and with Jesus, and Holy Spirit. That is why when reading these blessings, or beatitudes, it is important to see them through Jesus' eyes. I know a young person who always showed extraordinary understanding and mercy toward troubled people, and went out of his way to help them, often to his own detriment. When he was once in trouble, it was clear the judge had a hardened attitude toward the young man, and showed him no mercy. The young fellow had high principles and found it difficult to compromise or even plea-bargain to protect himself, which the judge looked upon as arrogance. Jesus was only too aware of situations like this, so when he spoke this blessing he knew full well that the merciful person may not find mercy in this life, but will, however, be assured of mercy at the time when mercy is most needed, when he stands before the final tribunal, when Jesus himself will show mercy to those who faithfully tried to follow him by being merciful toward others, often at great cost to themselves.

"Blessed are the pure in heart, they shall see God." There are many meanings to the word *pure* in the Scriptures. In our day, purity refers almost completely, in people's minds, to chastity, even to chastity in our thoughts. In the Scriptures, purity refers to singleness of purpose, singleness of focus, simplicity of intention, or a certain innocence of spirit. Purity could be expressed most simply by describing a person as innocent and uncontaminated by the corruption of the world around us. Again, place yourself in Jesus' way of looking at life. He sees into the hearts of everyone. Most people are ravished by the enticements of material possessions and personal prestige, trapped in the mesh of worldly worries, or enamored of the exciting things the world has to offer. On a rare occasion Jesus finds a person whose heart is still unsullied by the attractions and cares of the world, who still, like a little child, has preserved his or her childlike innocence and trust in God. The innocence of little children touched Jesus' heart and prompted his comment that "it is for such as these that the kingdom of heaven exists." He even warned his apostles that "Unless you become like little children, you shall not enter the kingdom of heaven." (Lk. 18:15–17)

I have seen families living near me, Mexican families, with very little in material goods, who ate the most simple of meals, growing what they could in their little gardens, and buying whatever other food they needed, and living very simply and happily. They radiated goodness and peacefulness that was the admiration of their neighbors because they had so little of the things that others thought were necessary for happiness and contentment. These people were content with what little they had. They needed nothing more, and in their meager possessions they always had enough to share with neighbors who had even less. In church their piety was the inspiration of the whole community. People loved to watch how intently they prayed, and one could easily see that they were deeply moved by the mystery that was taking place at the altar. Watching them receive the Eucharist was a lesson in humility and devotion. Knowing these people was a constant and inspiring reminder of the beatitude, "Blessed are the pure of heart, they shall see God."

Not all the beatitudes will be fulfilled in this life. Jesus always had a view that extended into the life hereafter, and there are certain blessings that come only after this life is ended.

"Blessed are the peacemakers, they will be called the children of God." What a beautiful tribute from the lips of God Himself for people who try to restore peace upon the earth, and bring peace into the lives of others. Jesus is saying in effect that because they are peacemakers they are so like God that even the Father could look upon them as His special children.

We have seen over the years so many good people who have sacrificed their lives and suffered much to bring peace to our troubled world and into their local communities. There are so many peace movements and men and women who dedicate their lives trying to prepare the world for peace, but the world never seems to be ready for peace. Peace has to be the fruit of people's willingness to forgive evil done to them. That is the essential condition for peace. Peace is a gift from God, but God cannot force peace upon our lives, and as long as we insist on refusing to forgive our enemies, and refuse to talk to them, and insist that war is the only way to peace, there can never be peace. We ourselves are the greatest obstacle to our own peace and to the peace of others. Our attitudes are in such contradiction to what Jesus demanded that we can never expect to receive the gift of peace. As Christians we should be experts in knowing what Jesus demands of us if we are to receive his gifts. But we are so deaf and so blind. It is not more and more troops that are needed to bring peace, but the need to forgive one another and begin to heal wounds, and to honestly face up to the reality of our own evil that has generated hatred in others. As long as people are blind to the evil they have committed, and refuse to reach out to those they have violated, and as long as they refuse to forgive injuries, it makes no difference how many battles we win, or how many troops we commit to battle; peace will never come. Winning a war does not bring peace. The hatred generated in war seethes like molten lava until it can erupt in a future war.

Even though so much abuse is heaped upon people who work for the United Nations, especially the Secretaries General, they are really doing the work of God. They try at the cost of great personal sacrifice to themselves and to their families, and the ridicule and scorn of vulgar and boorish politicians, to rise above the petty values and selfish ambitions of the leaders of nations. For the benefit of humanity they try to function at a level beyond the moral reach of lesser people. Trying to inspire petty, self-serving politicians to think nobly is fruitless. As a result they become the object of scorn from those whose lives and actions continually disrupt their endeavors for peace and harmony. These people deserve not the abuse they often receive from mean-spirited leaders of some nations, but the honor and respect of all of us for their selfless dedication to the most difficult work of bringing peace to a world filled with hate and unforgiveness, and cynicism, and, too often, paranoia.

The same phenomenon occurred in the case of Pope Pius XII. Here was a saintly priest and brilliant Vatican diplomat who dedicated his whole life to peace, and when he was elected pope in 1939, it was at one of the most difficult times in history. He had worked as the secretary of state for the previous pope, Pius XI, and had been the instrument of his efforts at restoring peace among belligerent nations. Then when Pius XI died, he continued the work on his own. While millions of Jews and Christians were being murdered, knowing he could not openly oppose a madman, he shrewdly set up a network of churches and monasteries and convents and chanceries throughout Europe to hide and protect the Jews. And this was at a time when the rest of the world, even relatives of the victims, stood by and did little or nothing. Yet, dishonest historians tried to discredit all the good that he had done, and paint him as a coward and a Nazi collaborator. Fortunately, of late, reputable historians are uncovering the rich evidence that through the efforts of Pope Pius XII approximately 850,000 Jews were saved from the death camps, and this holy man's reputation is finally being vindicated. "Blessed are the peacemakers, they will be called the children of God."

"Blessed are those persecuted for their pursuit of righteousness; theirs is the kingdom of heaven." All through history there are stories about brave souls, men and women, who had the courage and perseverance to endure suffering and unbelievable torture and death for their loyalty to God and for what is right, as God himself is the witness and promises that "this day you will be with me in paradise."

As I offer Mass each morning and read the biographical sketch of the saint or saints of the day, I feel so humbled when I read about the terrible sufferings they endured for their loyalty to God. Some had their skin torn off, others were crucified, others hung, drawn, and quartered while still alive just for being a priest, others had their arms and legs torn off and were then left to die, all done by people who called themselves reformers. Yes, I feel so humbled because I know I would never have the courage or the bravery to endure such torment. I suppose God gives faithful souls the grace necessary to endure such martyrdom, just as he is the source of whatever strength and goodness we may already possess. But the witness of these brave souls is a constant source of inspiration. That is why it is unfortunate that our children are not taught about these heroes of the faith, so they can have inspiring role models of loyalty to God, rather than the dubious role models they have today, sports figures often addicted to steroids or other drugs, and other criminal heroes on television. When certain Christian reformers ridiculed the honoring of saints, and forced them out of Christian education, they did something that filled Satan with glee, knowing that he could then supply his own role models. Now look at what our children have instead: role models who are on drugs or on steroids, as the whole family sits for hours in awe and veneration at their performance. These are the heroes and role models parents admire and display to their children. Fortunately, there are a rare few among these television and sports heroes and heroines who rise above the pack, and whose lives are exemplary of all that is good and decent and beautiful. But we don't hear much about them or their lives and the inspiration they are to their own children.

And finally, "Blessed are you when people abuse you and persecute you and speak all kinds of wicked things against you unjustly because of your faith in me. In fact, rejoice and be glad, for your reward in heaven will be great, for so they treated the prophets before you." (Mt. 5:1–12)

13

JESUS EXPANDS ON HIS TEACHING

The beatitudes, or blessings, that Jesus delivered to his followers, and especially to his closest disciples, were a stunning new teaching, not just the expression of opinions like the teaching of the scribes and Pharisees. Now Jesus discusses the sublime importance of what he is teaching, and goes even deeper into what his good news will mean to the whole world, and how it should be understood relative to the traditional teachings of the Law and the prophets.

He tells the apostles the importance of their ministry to the world when they go out to spread his message far and wide. "You are the salt of the earth, but if the salt becomes tasteless, what can restore its tang? It is good for nothing but to be thrown out for people to walk all over. You are also the light of the world. A city built on a hilltop cannot be hidden. No one lights a lamp and then puts it under a container. They put it on a lamp stand where it can give light to all in the house. In the same way, your light must shine before people, so that, seeing your good works, they can give praise to your Father in heaven." (Mt. 5:13–16)

Jesus had not yet sent his apostles out on their own to teach, but was impressing upon them the paramount importance of the mission he would one day commit to them, and for which they were now in training. It was the highly critical position they would occupy in the future of the world, to teach and make clear the all-important revelation that he was now teaching them. Whether the apostles even understood what he meant is far from clear, judging how dense they could be when Jesus revealed to them things that were new and unfamiliar. It sounded nice how important they were going to be one day, but they had no idea what it all meant. Still, they had to know and Jesus had to tell them. One day it would all become clear to them, after Jesus left and the Holy Spirit came upon them, and they found themselves responsible for the kingdom that Jesus turned over to them.

Knowing how conservative the Galileans were and how tenacious they were in holding on to the old ways, he realized his teaching was disturbing to them, and difficult for them to digest. They and all their ancestors were thoroughly indoctrinated in matters of the Law and the prophets. There was no room for contrary beliefs, or for the slightest shifting away from the rigid teachings impressed on them since childhood. What Jesus was teaching and, even more upsetting, his casual attitude toward the Sabbath rest were shocking. He knew his disciples were having a difficult time with it, although they did not have the nerve to confront him on the issue. So, Jesus brought it up.

> Do not think I have come to abolish the Law or the prophets. I have not come to abolish them but to fulfill them. Till heaven and earth pass away, not one jot or tittle of the Law will be done away with until it is all fulfilled. And anyone who breaks even the least of the commandments, and teaches others to do so, will be considered least in the kingdom of heaven. And the one who keeps them and teaches them will be considered great in the kingdom of heaven. (Mt. 5:17–20)

Now, let us take a look at what Jesus just said. He had not come to destroy the Law and the prophets but to fulfill them. And not one stroke of the Law will be done away with until it is all fulfilled. What he said is so clear, but I wonder if the apostles grasped it at the time. We know that Jesus came to fulfill all that was said of him by the prophets, or all that prefigured him in the Law. Here he clearly stated his mission, to fulfill all that was said of him in their Scriptures. So, by his coming to fulfill all that was said of him, there was no more need for the Law with its 613 commandments, and its 365 prohibitions, and 365 lesser prohibitions, which constituted the Law. Saint Paul later on states that Jesus came to free us from the unbearable burden of the Law, which no human being could possibly carry, or to quote Saint Paul precisely, "Christ redeemed us from the curse of the Law . . ." (Gal. 3:13) and in another place, "For Christ Jesus is our peace, he who . . . broke down the dividing wall of enmity, through his flesh, abolishing the Law with its commandments and legal claims, that he might create in himself a new person." (Eph. 2:13–15)

Jesus did not abrogate the moral code, or morality itself. In fact, he raises our moral responsibilities to a much more sublime level. The very next thing he says to the apostles is, "I tell you, if your holiness does not exceed that of the scribes and Pharisees, you will never enter the kingdom of heaven." How could this be, since the scribes and Pharisees had the impeccable reputation for their perfect observance of the Law? So, it is not the observance of the letter of the Law that Jesus is talking about. He knows that all Law concerns our relationship with God and with one another, and our treatment of God's creation. Jesus' concern is not for the Law itself, but for the rights and the reverence due to God, and for the honor and respect due to God's children, all of which is the substance of the Law. And he goes on to talk about anger, and revenge, and hatred of others, and refusal to forgive others, and nurturing lust in our hearts, and planning evil undertakings, of which Jesus knew many of the scribes and Pharisees were guilty, though they boasted of their meticulous observance of the Law, which dealt with external actions.

To God it is not the Law that is sacred, but the human soul. So, the Law means nothing if the heart and soul of a human being is polluted by willfully entertaining evil thoughts and desires, and evil plotting against the interests of God and our fellow human beings. If our souls, the temples of God's presence, are contaminated with filth, what value does the mere external observance of the letter of the Law have in God's eyes?

And then Jesus launches into a realm that is so sublime in its moral demand that even today, most Christians totally ignore it as impractical or nonsensical.

> You have heard it said, "An eye for an eye, and a tooth for a tooth," but I say to you, offer the wicked no resistance. On the contrary, if anyone strikes you on the right cheek, offer him the left as well. If a man takes you to court for your tunic, give him your cloak as well. And if anyone orders you to go one mile, go two miles with him. Give to anyone who asks, and if anyone wants to borrow from you, do not turn him away.
>
> You have heard how it was said, "Love your neighbor, and hate your enemy," but I say to you, "Love your enemy, pray for those who persecute you." In this way, you will be the children of your Father in heaven, for He lets the sun rise on the bad as well as the good, His rain to fall on honest and dishonest alike. For if you love those who love you, what credit is that to you? Even tax extortionists do as much. And if you greet your brothers, are you doing anything out of the ordinary? Even the pagans do as much. You must be as perfect as your heavenly Father is perfect. (Mt. 5:38–48)

This is what Jesus is substituting in place of the Law. He states it in another way on another occasion, when the issue is brought up by a lawyer as to which is the greatest commandment of the Law, not an honest question but a neat trap, as there were so many complex laws. Jesus cuts through them all and goes to the heart of the Law: "The first commandment is 'Love the Lord your God with all your heart, with your entire mind, with all your soul, and with all your strength.' The second is like it, 'Love your neighbor as you love yourself.' On these two is based the whole Law and the prophets."

Then the lawyer, embarrassed at the laserlike precision of Jesus' insight, tried to justify his question: "Well, that is my problem, sir. Who is my neighbor?" And Jesus told the story of the Good Samaritan.

> A man was going down the hill from Jerusalem to Jericho and he fell among thieves. They stripped him, robbed him, beat him, and left him lying there half dead. A priest went down the road, saw him lying

there, and passed by on the opposite side of the road. A Levite, a priest of lower rank, was going the same way. He saw the man lying there half dead, and he passed him by on the opposite side of the road. Then a stranger came down the road and saw the fellow lying there, and felt sorry for him. He got down from his horse, took out a flask of oil and wine, cleaned out his wounds, and put him on his own beast and brought him down to an inn, and took care of him. The next day, he took out two denarii and gave them to the innkeeper, and told him, "Take care of him, and if I owe you anything more, I will repay you on my return journey." And that man was a Samaritan. Now, which one showed himself neighbor to that poor wretch? (Lk. 10:25–37)

The lawyer, now totally embarrassed, had a difficult time answering, first of all because Judeans hate Samaritans, and after two priests callously walked right past, a Samaritan, of all people, helped the fellow. Jesus then asked the question, "Who showed himself neighbor to the poor wretch?" The lawyer merely muttered, "The one who showed him compassion." No way could he get himself to say, "The Samaritan."

But, Jesus' remark in the beginning, "Love is the basis for the whole Law and the prophets," is so incisive. If you love properly, there is no need for written commandments. Commandments are a substitute for people who have never learned how to love, and have to be told how to treat God and one another. Saint Augustine was so impressed with the simplicity of Jesus' reduction of the complex body of commandments to one charge for his disciples that he refused to allow the catechists in his diocese to teach the Ten Commandments, saying they were statements of the Jewish Law which, as Saint Paul said, Jesus abrogated. He told them to teach Jesus' law of love to those preparing for entrance into the Church, and how to love properly. When the catechists, however, insisted they could not teach morality without using the Commandments, he eventually allowed them to use the Commandments, but not in their negative form. They should express them in a positive way: "If you really love God, this is the way you will treat Him; if you really love your neighbors these are the ways you will treat them." And when Jesus said earlier that his disciples "should be perfect as your heavenly Father is perfect," he did not mean in the keeping of Commandments, because the heavenly Father is beyond Commandments. He meant his disciples should imitate the unselfish perfection of God's love. We should be perfect in the way we love, and in the way we express that love. And Jesus showed us how we should express that love. Jesus loved everything alive, from God down to the simplest creature. He had reverence for everything his Father created. This was the model of love he set for all of us, a love and respect that included, not just our fellow human beings, but everything his Father fashioned, the land, the sea, the forest and the plants, the animals, and even inanimate creatures.

When it came to intimacy with God, however, there was something special in Jesus' attitude. He spoke quite freely about his Father in heaven, but when he communicated with his Father, it was intimate and private. In fact, as time went on, we see the apostles wondering why Jesus did not pray with them when they spent quiet time together on those long trips from Galilee down to Judea. One of the apostles broached the subject when they were probably sitting around a campfire in an olive grove one night. He asked Jesus point blank, "How come you do not teach us how to pray, the way John taught his disciples how to pray?" Jesus' response is rather surprising.

When you pray, do not pray like the scribes and Pharisees, who love to stand at the street corners and pray loudly for people to hear. I tell you they already have their reward. When you pray, go to your room and lock your door and pray to your heavenly Father in secret, and your heavenly Father, who knows what is secret, will hear you. And when you pray, do not prattle on like the pagans. They think that by the mere multiplicity of words they will get a hearing. Do not pray like that. Your heavenly Father already knows what you need before you even ask him. When you pray, pray like this: 'Our Father, who are in heaven, may your name be forever held in honor, may your kingdom come, may your will be done here on earth as it is in heaven. Give us today our daily bread, and forgive us our debts as we are willing to forgive others' debts to us. And do not put us to the test, and protect us from the evil one.' (Lk. 11:1–4)

Jesus seems always to be showing a concern for what is inside of us. I so often have the eerie feeling that when Jesus looks at us, it is as if he sees with x-ray vision deep into our souls and wants us to realize that it is the life that is deep within us that is the real world in God's eyes. It is important that God see goodness and holiness and love and forgiveness within us. The externals of our life are symptoms of the life within, and they indicate a healthy soul or a soul that is sick and diseased. This is why it is so important to Jesus that we be not judgmental of our neighbor's sins. Jesus is telling us, in effect, that "What I see in your own soul is precisely what you hate and condemn in your neighbor's soul, so I give you fair warning that you may be liable to the same judgment and condemnation before my heavenly Father that you so readily pass on others."

Jesus' concern about our inner life is jarring, because he talks as if there is a whole other world inside us, the world where God lives, and the world where the most important activity of our lives plays out its drama. That world consists of our dreams, our hopes and aspirations, our ambitions, our visions of ourselves and our relations with others, and our decisions as to how we treat others and use others. And most important of all, it is where God and our heavenly friends fit into our life. That is an entirely different world from the world outside ourselves. It is the world that is most real to God even though we may not even be aware of its existence other than on those rare occasions when we may do a little soul searching and for a short while become aware of things happening inside of us. The world inside us may be just as vast as the universe outside our senses. It makes one think of the vastness of space. For centuries we have been exploring that outer universe. Now as we analyze the molecular and atomic and subatomic composition of matter, we are becoming aware of a whole new universe on the opposite side of tiny matter. The world inside our souls may be similar in its dimensions. It is a heaven where God dwells. "My Father and I will come and live within you," Jesus promised.

Then Jesus goes on to tell us not to spend our energy on pursuing material things. They are of less importance than the life inside us. Love of money can become like a trap that ensnares the soul and become an addiction. It can lead to the corruption of the human spirit, and it tears our souls away from God. It is impossible to be in love with money and in love with God. Love of money makes the thought of God repulsive.

Nor should we worry about what we need in our lives. Jesus seems to be only too aware of our fears and anxieties, and brings up the subject.

Do not worry about your life and what you are to eat, or about your body, and what you are to wear. Your life is more important than food, and the body is more important than clothing. Look at the birds of the air; they do not sow nor reap, nor do they gather into barns. Your heavenly Father feeds them. Are you not worth much more than they? And what you are to wear; look at the flowers in the field. They do not spin or spend time working. Yet, I assure you, Solomon in all his glory was not dressed in such splendor as one of those. Now, if your heavenly Father clothes the grass in the fields which springs up today and dies tomorrow, will he not take much more care of you, oh, you of little faith?

So, do not worry, or do not say, "What are we to eat or what are we to drink, or what are we to wear?" Your heavenly Father knows you need these things, so pursue the kingdom of God and his righteousness, and all these other things will be added to you besides. And do not worry about tomorrow. Tomorrow will take care of itself. Each day's trouble is enough for that day. (Mt. 6:25–34)

It is interesting the way Jesus' mind works. He tells his followers not to worry, yet he knows they cannot avoid it, so then he tells his followers to be tenacious in their prayers.

Ask, and you will receive; search and you will find; knock and the door will be opened to you. For the one who asks will receive; the one who searches will always find; the one who knocks will always have the door opened for him. Is there one among you who would hand his son a stone when he asks for bread? Or would hand him a snake when he asks for a fish? If then, evil as you are, you know how to give good gifts to your children, how much more your heavenly Father will give good gifts to those who ask Him. (Lk. 11:9–13)

Jesus knows that his Father is not always going to jump when people want something. After all, he is not everybody's personal genie. He is the Creator of the universe and we are only His creatures, so Jesus is delicate in telling us to approach his Father with humility, and not be demanding, though he does strongly encourage us to be persistent. The only time Jesus praised the manner in which a person asked for a favor was when the Roman centurion felt he was unworthy to ask Jesus himself and asked an elder in the local synagogue to intercede for him with Jesus. And even as Jesus was approaching the centurion's house, the official said, "No, no, Lord. I am not worthy that you come into my house. Only say the word and my servant will be healed." Jesus then remarked, "I have not found such faith in all of Israel." It was the humble faith of the man that impressed Jesus, so humble he felt unworthy to ask Jesus himself and asked another more worthy to intercede for him. Jesus is telling us that that is the kind of humble faith we should have when we approach the Father in prayer. He knows that many people do not approach his Father with humility, and when He does not answer the way they like they become impatient and annoyed because He does not give them what they demand. And that is not the attitude we should have. We are the creatures; He is the Lord. If anything, we should pray for what we need to be better servants out of gratitude for His having created us and given us life and so much more, especially the daily miracles in each of our lives that we are not even aware of.

Then Jesus goes on to give us a very graphic portrait of the kind of followers he knows will join his community. He is very much aware that there are followers who take very lightly their responsibilities as disciples. "Oh, yes, we are his followers. We were baptized. We worship occasionally, and are nice to people, but it's a hard life if you take it seriously." His response comes in the form of a warning, "Enter by the narrow gate, since the road that leads to perdition is wide and spacious, and there are many who take that road. It is a narrow gate and a hard road that leads to life, and there are only a few who find it." (Mt. 7:13–14) Is he saying that only a few are going to be saved? That is certainly not what he is saying, but he is warning all of us that we should not be too easy on ourselves, but should make every effort to reach out to others and reflect God's love in our lives. That is the essence of true holiness. It takes a lifetime to progress along that road, but if we do not give up, we will find that gradually the road we are following has become narrower and narrower as our lives become more focused on what we should be like and we are less and less inclined to follow the distractions. So, we eventually find ourselves on the narrow road to the kingdom without even realizing it.

Jesus is also aware that not all teachers who go by his name can be trusted. They are like the false prophets of the Old Testament. They preach things that people like to hear, and please people so they can draw in more members. People are made to feel comfortable with the way they are living. They depart from the strong teaching of Jesus and lead the people into the wilderness away from Jesus' true family. "Beware of false prophets who come to you in sheep's clothing, but underneath are ravenous wolves. You will be able to tell them by their fruits. You do not pick grapes from thorns or figs from thistles. A healthy tree produces good fruit, an infected tree produces infected fruit." (Mt. 7:15–20) A careful discerning person will understand how far they have departed from the truths that Jesus taught and the early Christians cherished. The infected fruit may be pleasant to people's taste, so it is hard to recognize as infected, but its effects become obvious as those flocks break down into other splinter groups, as they drift farther and farther from the original Body of Christ. Those who set themselves up as teachers are like the false prophets of old. We don't appoint ourselves as ministers of God's word. We are appointed through the method Jesus established. He set up the process by which his apostles are called until the end of time. They first chose Matthias to fill the vacancy left by Judas. Shortly after they all received the Holy Spirit, and immediately began to go out into the street and preach the Word of God. Later on we see Paul choosing Timothy to become an apostle to succeed him as bishop of Ephesus, and passing on to him the power and authority to preach the Gospel. People cannot make themselves apostles. When they do, their message is often pleasant to listen to, but they subtly lead the sheep astray, far from Jesus' flock, far from what Jesus gave us—the spotless Bride of the Lamb, come down from heaven, radiant with the glory of God, and established on the twelve foundation stones engraved with the names of the twelve apostles. (Rev. 21:9–14) As a result the people do not know what they believe or even what they are supposed to believe as loyal disciples of Jesus. They become satisfied just hearing pleasing words, and not the solid doctrine that Saint Paul insisted on. Jesus' flock has to be identifiable for its loyalty to all that Jesus taught, for its strong message, and for its internal unity and universality of belief.

Then Jesus goes on to mention other types of disciples who will eventually be recognizable among his followers—those who will talk about him, and indulge in sensational practices, but who for many reasons have made themselves unrecognizable as his followers. It is a rare example of how Jesus looks deep down into the hearts of his followers and sees those who have remained faithful to him. "It is not those who say, 'Lord, Lord,' who will enter the kingdom of heaven, but the person who does the will of my Father in heaven. When the day comes, many will say to me, 'Lord, Lord, did we not prophesy in your name, cast out demons in your name, work many miracles in your name?' Then I shall tell them, 'I do not know you, away from me, you evil people.' " It seems on the surface rather strange that Jesus should speak like that. After all, were these people not doing good things, prophesying in his name, working miracles in his name, and doing other good things? What Jesus sees in them, however, is not devotion to him, but their personal enjoyment of religious practices while they have little or no interest in Jesus himself, or in those things that were so important to Jesus. They are thus identified with the scribes and Pharisees, who were totally dedicated to their religion, but whose hearts were far from God. So Jesus recognizes them as total strangers. On another occasion we will see Jesus excoriating the Pharisees for wandering throughout the world to make one convert, yet when they finally do, they turn that person more into a child of hell than even themselves. It is such a real insight, because religions have so many people like that. They fight for the purity of religion, but in their personal lives they are abusive of their families, vindictive toward their enemies, hateful of people who are different from themselves, have little interest in or love for the poor and begrudge them even a small share in the good things that they themselves enjoy. They totally lack compassion for sinners and demand the meanest punishment for their sins, until someone in their family is caught in crime, then they demand compassion and understanding, which they had always denied to others. They think nothing while pursuing political office of destroying opponents' reputations and families while they boast of their Christian principles, rejecting in their abysmal ignorance all those things that Jesus held dear, like love and compassion, and forgiveness and understanding of others, and Jesus' unique principle of justice that is compassionate.

Jesus then describes a true follower, and in the process also describes the community of his true followers. "Therefore, everyone who listens to these words of mine and makes them part of his life will be like a sensible man who built his house on solid rock. The rains came, the floods rose, violent winds blew against that house, and it did not fall. It was founded on solid rock. But, everyone who hears these words of mine and does not make them part of his life will be like a stupid man who built his house on sand. The rains came, the floods rose, violent winds blew against that house, and it fell. And what a fall it had!" (Mt. 7:21–27)

True followers are those who practice all the things that Jesus taught. Their lives are focused on God and, as an expression of their love of God, reflect the beauty and goodness of God to all whom they meet. They are loyal followers of Jesus, not just calling his name all day long, but being living images of who he is, as their lives become more and more a living replica of what the Jews saw when Jesus came walking down the street in their village. They are known by their gentleness of spirit and their nobility of soul, rising above the pettiness of life, and never taking offense at the meanness of others, but always forgiving, and not finding violent conflict a solution for differences, but relentless in trying to work for peace. They are easily identified by their caring and concern for those less fortunate than themselves, and by their willingness to enrich others' lives by their own bigness of spirit.

That long discourse on discipleship revealed an extraordinary insight into the prophetic mind of Jesus, and stunned the people with the power of its authority. He was so different from their scribes and Pharisees, who merely dabbled in opinions, boringly backing them up with endless Scripture quotes.

This extended talk that Jesus gave was probably like an afternoon retreat. Outside of Capernaum was a small mountain, as it is called in the Gospels. It is more like a good-sized hill in our way of thinking, with a hundred- or two-hundred-foot rise from the Sea of Galilee, and a perfect place for Jesus to lead the crowds as they gathered around him. It is a beautiful, serene setting, overlooking the sea, which is over eight miles across. It must have been in Jesus' day a very quiet, relaxed atmosphere, with no motors or engines whirring or horns blasting, so that every word that Jesus spoke could be easily heard. It may have also been a picnic setting, as the people nibbled on whatever snacks they brought with them as Jesus talked. When Jesus finished speaking, the crowd picked up their belongings and started back down the hillside for home. Some may have stayed afterward to talk to Jesus and ask for guidance and help with family problems. Imagine having Jesus right there to talk to him and get his personal advice on what to do. Did they realize how lucky they were?

14

JESUS IS MET BY ANOTHER LARGE CROWD

After delivering an hour-long lecture, especially to a large crowd, an ordinary person would be tired and need a rest. As Jesus descended the mountainside, he was confronted by another crowd, a large crowd, as Matthew's Gospel records. A leper came up to him and, bowing down low in front of him, said, "Sir, if you want to, you have the power to cure me."

"It is my will," Jesus said, and stretching out his hand, *he touched the leper*, saying as he did so, "Be cured." And the man was immediately cured of the leprosy.

That is a very moving scene and one that must have startled the people, causing loud drawn breaths. Lepers were forbidden to appear in populated places. Their hideous disease was considered by most people to be highly contagious, so once they were declared diseased, they were banished from family and village, and from all human contact. They had to go out into deserted places and join the companionship of other lepers, who were also exiled forever from society. Jesus stunned the crowd by approaching the leper. In a gesture of affection he rested his hand on the man and cured him. He then strictly told the man not to tell anyone what had happened, and directed him to go show himself to the priest and make the offering prescribed by Moses as evidence to them of his cure.

Jesus then went to Simon's house, where he found Simon's mother-in-law with a fever. He touched her hand, the fever left her, and she got up and waited on him. This seems to be a different occasion from the previous time Simon's mother-in-law had a fever, although it could be another evangelist's description of the same event. The details are different. In the course of the evening people came from all around with their sick and the possessed. Jesus drove out the evil spirits by a mere command, with no long ritual, and he cured the sick, thus fulfilling all that was said of the Messiah by Isaiah: "He took away our sicknesses and took our diseases upon himself." (Isa. 53:4)

A scribe had been watching all that Jesus was doing and was impressed. He walked up to Jesus and told him, "Master, I will follow you wherever you go." That was quite a commitment coming from a scribe who, as a master of the Law, was jeopardizing his standing in the religious community by doing this. Jesus tells the scribe there is little he can offer him, as "The son of man has nowhere even to lay his head." It is assumed that the scribe continued to follow him. Another man wanted to follow Jesus, but wanted first to go home and bury his father. "Follow me, and let the dead bury their dead." The dead, of course, were those who had not received or who refused to receive the new life that Jesus was offering to them. (Mt. 8:18–22)

As there was no escape from the pressing crowd, Jesus got into the boat, with his disciples following him, and started for the opposite shore. Suddenly a storm overtook the boat, while Jesus was asleep in the shelter. The storm was so violent that the waves kept breaking over the boat, threatening to capsize it. Afraid they were going to drown, the disciples woke Jesus. "Save us, save us, Lord! We are going to drown." Jesus woke up and, still half asleep, pulled himself up enough to look over the side of the boat. Seeing the raging storm, he yelled out, "Calm down, calm down," which it did immediately. Jesus complained to the apostles for waking him up and for their lack of faith, and probably just fell back down to continue his sleep. All the paintings of the scene show Jesus standing up. How could he be standing up with the boat being tossed around by the violent wind? The apostles then muttered among themselves as if Jesus was out of earshot, "What kind of man is this, that even the wind and the sea obey him?" This may indicate that he did go back to sleep. If the apostles had to wake him, he had to be extremely exhausted to sleep so soundly during such a violent storm. (Mt. 8:23–27)

They then arrived at the opposite shore, at Gadara, where they were met by two men possessed by demons, extraordinarily fierce demons whom people in the neighborhood were so frightened of that they shunned the place. The possessed men just stood there shouting at Jesus, "What do you want with us, Son of God? Have you come here to torture us before the time?" By now, word of Jesus' identity had been passed around among Satan's cohorts, as these strange demons already knew him. They also had been expecting some kind of confrontation with him at some time in the future, and were fearful that this might be the time, a time that was unexpected. One can tell they were afraid and were cowering in his presence. They knew he would not tolerate their evil presence. They asked him if he was going to cast them out, not to send them back to the lower regions, but into a herd of pigs browsing nearby. "Go then," he told them, and they entered the herd of pigs, which then rushed headlong over the nearby cliff and perished in the water. The swineherd ran off into the town and told the whole story. The whole town then went out to meet Jesus and, obviously frightened of his powers, begged him to leave their neighborhood. (Mt. 8:28–34)

As graphic as is this Gospel story, there are still people today who do not believe there is a devil or Satan. Even some clergy do not believe there are devils. I suppose it is a difficult concept to accept, real beings dedicated to evil. In reading the Gospel stories about Jesus' confrontations with Satan, some of the possessed persons do appear to have nothing more than what we would call today symptoms of psychological problems, or emotional disturbances, or epilepsy. Jesus would have known the difference. On occasion, he indicated some were the work of the devil, though it is possible that others could have been serious psychological or medical conditions.

But that Satan is real is not fantasy. One night when I was writing the manuscript for *Joshua and the City,* I got a telephone call from a faraway country. I had been writing about Joshua having a confrontation with Satan while I was walking down a street in New York City. As Joshua was passing a certain house, he suddenly became nauseated, and he commented to his companions, "Satan is in that house." He went into the house and was confronted by members of a Satanic cult. In the manuscript, I was describing the devious ways Satan tries to undermine the moral fiber of our civilization. It was at that point that my telephone rang.

It was one-thirty in the morning, and I was wondering who would be calling me at that hour. It was a man, a stranger from a faraway country. He started telling me about his girlfriend, who had a multiple personality disorder, and that her psychiatrist had been treating her for three personalities. I do not know how the caller knew me, or how he got my phone number, but he went on to tell me that the night before, while he was working on the computer, putting an accompaniment to some music, he heard a deep, guttural voice coming out of his girlfriend's bedroom. He went in and she was sound asleep, yet this strange, ugly voice was coming out of her: "You think there are three of us, don't you? There are not three of us. There are five of us."

The man then asked me for advice as to what it meant and what he should do. We talked for about half an hour, then, after thanking me, he said good-bye and hung up. I went back to my manuscript, and the thought then occurred to me that that telephone call was meant for me, with a message from Satan. And it was a warning not to continue writing what I was writing about the devil or I would pay a terrible price for it. I was afraid to continue, but I knew now I had to. So, I did. I finished the manuscript a few weeks later and sent it to my publisher. The day he received it, my phone rang at one-thirty in the morning, and the person on the other end told me that my godchild, whom I loved dearly, had just been killed in an automobile accident. I cannot describe the terror I felt. I have never hurt so much in all my life as I did at that moment. And the man who called asked if I would tell the boy's parents before the state police arrived to break the news to them. Although I knew God would never give Satan the power to hurt someone, to kill someone, I had to have assurance that my godson was okay. That reassurance came at seven-thirty, later in the morning, when a priest called from Australia. A voice had told him to call me. He told me he knew something terrible had happened and he was supposed to tell me that God was trying to give me a sign that my godson was at peace and was with God. The sign turned out to be that a beautiful star magnolia tree that my godson and his girlfriend had planted the year before had just bloomed. It bloomed for the first time that day, two months out of season. It bloomed again the day my godson was buried. So, having experiences like this and others similar, it is very difficult not to believe that evil is real, and that Satan is also very real.

When Jesus was rudely invited to leave the land of the Gadarenes, after their difficult voyage to get there, he and the apostles embarked and sailed back across the lake, where some people spotted them, and a crowd again began to gather, bringing with them more sick people, one of them a paralyzed man stretched out on a mat. As weary as Jesus was after all the excitement and the fifteen-mile water crossing, he was touched by the faith of the people and said to the paralyzed man, "Courage, my child, your sins are forgiven."

At this some scribes standing nearby heard what he had said, and con-cluded, "He is blaspheming."

Knowing their thoughts, Jesus said to them, "Which is easier to say, 'Your sins are forgiven,' or 'Get up and walk?' But to prove to you that the Son of Man has authority on earth to forgive sins,"—then he said to the paralytic, "Get up, pick up your bed and go home!" And the man got up and went home. And a feeling of awe came over the crowd, and they praised God for having given such power to men. (Mt. 9:1–8)

These few hours of following Jesus as he goes about his ministry of teaching and healing shows how chaotic life was becoming for him. Had he not felt such pity for troubled people, and just preached his message of salvation, he could have gone about his daily schedule in an orderly and stress-free manner, with time to relax and socialize and be with friends. But that was not to be. He was God come down to live among his hu-man family. His overwhelming compassion for these people would not allow him to walk past them when he could see how painfully they were suffering. So, what started out as a distraction from his teaching in the beginning became a major part of his ministry. Each day was from then on filled with healing from morning till night. He never seems to have become tired of all this healing, although it was without doubt a major distraction from his teaching ministry, and a most taxing part of his min-istry, as power went out from him each time he healed someone. His pa-tience with each person is remarkable. Each person he treats like a friend, with tenderness and caring, even though hardly any of the thousands he cured, or from whom he cast out demons, ever thanked him for saving their lives. But that is the way God is. It is difficult for us to understand that God, and in this case, Jesus, does not look for our thanks, though he seems overjoyed when he receives it. He works his miracles of mercy nonetheless. He knows us all only too well: quick to ask for favors, slow to offer thanks.

People, however, were also quick to find in him what they considered flaws, like the time when a group who had previously been John's followers complained to him for not encouraging fasting. "Fast," he says. "How can people fast when the bridegroom is with them? That's the time to celebrate. But, you can be sure, when the bridegroom leaves, they will fast then. People do not use a piece of new cloth to patch an old cloak. If you do, the patch will shrink and pull away from the cloth and the hole will be bigger than ever. And again, people do not put new wine into old wine skins. If they do the new wine will expand and burst the skins and both will be lost. People put new wine into new wine skins and both are preserved."

It took me a long time to realize fully what Jesus was driving at when he talked about the patch and the wine. He could have spoken those words when asked about fasting, or it may have been said to the apostles on another occasion. Whatever the occasion, the lesson was the same. The apostles and all the people in Jesus' day were brought up in strict and rigorous observance of the religious laws. Jesus' entirely new teaching was a culture shock. His disciples loved their religion, as traditional and encrusted as it was with ancient and outdated customs. But they also loved their new teacher. As a result they were continually trying to fit Jesus' teachings into the framework of what they had been taught all their lives. It was difficult, if not impossible. Jesus knew they were trying to do this, and I think he told this little analogy to help them to understand, so they would not keep trying to reconcile his new teachings with the tired old ways they had been taught. Once they realized that it was a whole new world Jesus was leading them into, then they could relax and just bask in the sunshine of his divine wisdom. That would take a long time.

Jesus' ministry in Galilee and the neighboring region was intense. He could not just have a casual gathering of only a few people. His reputation had spread fast, especially his reputation for healing, and the fact that he never turned anyone down who requested healing assured him of huge crowds. Without the advanced medical procedures and medicines we have today, disease and physical and emotional maladies were rampant.

Once the people found a healer who could really heal, there was no letup in the crowds who came flocking to Jesus. He tried to keep hidden his power to raise the dead, but once word spread that he could even raise the dead, there was no way he could control the crowds. So, one day a local official came to Jesus and, very humbly bowing down to him, told him his daughter had just died, but could he come and lay his hand on her so she could be well again. They had already heard that when Jesus healed, he often did it by laying his hand on the person, so the man asked Jesus to lay his hand on his daughter. As he was on his way to the official's house, a woman in the crowd following him had been bleeding continually for twelve years. She thought that if she could only touch the tassel of his cloak, she would be healed. So she did. Jesus felt the healing power leave him. He turned and, looking at the woman, told her, "Courage, woman, your faith has healed you." From that moment, the woman was healed.

When Jesus arrived at the official's house, and saw the mourners in the girl's room making a scene with their dirges and professional wailing, he had them leave the dead girl's room, telling them that the girl was not dead, but only asleep. They left the room ridiculing him. Entering the room, Jesus walked to the bedside. He took the girl by the hand, and she got out of bed and stood up. Word about the incident spread throughout the whole area. (Mt. 9:18–26)

Jesus left and continued on his way, hoping to go to Simon's house, but two blind men followed him, shouting out, "Jesus, Son of David, have pity on us." When he reached the house, he turned and said to the blind men, "Do you believe that I can do this?" They said, "Sir, we do." Then Jesus touched their eyes and said, "Your faith has earned your healing, may it be done as you wish." Their sight immediately returned and he strictly ordered them to tell no one, but when they left they spread the story everywhere they went. (Mt. 9:27–31) Again, Jesus touched their eyes. It is all so personal. Each person is special.

Before Jesus could enter the house, a man who could not speak approached him, begging Jesus to cure him. He was possessed by a devil who was dumb. When Jesus cast out the devil, the dumb man spoke, to the amazement of the crowd, who said that nothing like this had ever happened in Israel. The Pharisees, however, were annoyed and countered with their own opinions: "This man casts out devils by the power of Satan himself, the prince of devils." (Mt. 9:32–34)

After spending the night at Simon's place, Jesus rose before sunrise, as was his custom, and went up into the hills to spend the best time of the day with his heavenly Father. It did not take long for Peter and the others to go looking for him. Finding him, they left the area with him and began making the rounds of the towns and villages, preaching the kingdom of God as they went along. It was more casual, with space and time between villages for Jesus to continue his teaching of the apostles.

But no matter where he went, the great part of his ministry was in healing. The demands were endless.

How much can a man take? Is the Gospel writer exaggerating? Probably not. Sickness and disease were rampant in those days, as they had no cures, and few people lived to our idea of old age. Old age for them was perhaps forty or fifty. Seventy was ancient, though many did make it to that age. It is understandable that when people found a healer with Jesus' awesome power, they would come not just by themselves but in caravans with all their sick family members and friends. And Jesus was so generous with his time and the sharing of his gifts, he never turned anyone away. The gatherings must have been chaotic. Every now and then in the Gospels you see the apostles becoming annoyed at the pressure, but Jesus seems always to maintain an amazing serenity in the midst of the noise and confusion.

It strikes me for the first time after all these years that Jesus never did a mass healing. Each healing seems to have been special for that person. He wanted to meet each one, and wanted them to know that each one was special and was loved. Each was physically touched by the hand of God, in a personal mark of affection. It shows so powerfully how every individual is special to God, whether it be the daughter of the local synagogue official, or the servant of the Roman centurion, or lepers with their hideously rotting bodies, with no identifiable faces. Even when he healed a leper, it was with a gentle healing touch. What a beautiful God! No wonder no one was afraid of Jesus. They all benefited from the depths of his divine love, except for the scribes and Pharisees, who were suspect of his love. In spite of the massive number of authentic healings he performed each day, they hated Jesus so much, they could only ridicule the healings that his love generated as emanating from Satan himself. Yet it is this strong love in Jesus' soul that was the cause of salvation for all of us, now and way back then. And when people looked into Jesus' eyes, they saw none of the searing criticism they were used to from the self-righteous and ever-suspicious cynics who saw evil lurking everywhere, even in Jesus' goodness. The look the people saw in Jesus' eyes told them, "I know you, and I know what you did yesterday, and before, and I see all that is in your heart, and I love you, and want you to be my friend." Each person saw that look in Jesus' eyes and was immediately drawn to him. Those who followed that call from Jesus eventually changed their lives, as he inspired them to the holiness God intended for each of them.

15

JESUS IN JERUSALEM, AND THE CURE AT THE POOL OF BETHZATHA

It is difficult to place the time of this visit of Jesus to Judea, but it was possibly for the Festival of Pentecost, or the Festival of Weeks. This was one of the three important festivals celebrated in Jerusalem, and the happiest and most joyful of them all. It was celebrated seven weeks after the Passover Festival. It was also called Pentecost, which was the fiftieth day after Passover. All adult males were required to travel to Jerusalem for this festival, and the people would gather at the Temple and make offerings in thanksgiving for the wheat harvest that had just been taken in. It is also considered the time when Yahweh gave the tablets of the Law to Moses on Mount Sinai, a time when their ancestors lived in tents. Although this festival and Jesus' attendance at it are not mentioned in the Gospels of Mark, Matthew, and Luke, John mentions Jesus going to Jerusalem for a festival, but does not mention which festival. He immediately relates the story that occurred at the Pool of Bethzatha, the Sheep Pool, which was enclosed within five porticoes, or walkways between rows of columns supporting the roof. The place was the object of great veneration among the Judeans, and among Israelites in general, as it was long rumored that miraculous cures took place there. It was said that whenever an angel came and stirred up the water of the pool, the first one to reach the pool was cured.

> As Jesus walked among the crippled and the suffering he came across a man who had been ill for thirty-eight years. Knowing the plight of the man, Jesus asked him if he would like to be cured. "I have no one to take me to the pool," the man complained. "Every time the pool is stirred up, I try to reach the pool, but someone always reaches the pool ahead of me." Then Jesus told him, "Get up, pick up your mat and walk!" The man did so and began to walk away. (Jn. 5:7–9)

It happened to be the Sabbath, and when Temple officials saw the man carrying his mat, they told him that he was violating the Sabbath rest. "But, the man who cured me told me to pick up my mat and walk."

"Who is he?" the officials asked him. The man had no idea who it was who had cured him, as Jesus casually walked away and disappeared among the crowd.

A short time later, Jesus met the man in the Temple and said to him, "Now you are well again. Be sure that you sin no more lest something worse happens to you." Usually Jesus did not associate sin with a person's illness, but this time he did, which might indicate that whatever illness the man had may have been caused by some behavior that brought on his illness, or he may have been involved in some shady situation that resulted in a crippling injury.

The man went back to tell the officials that it was Jesus who had cured him. They then went out looking for him, and when they found him, they immediately confronted him because of his contempt for the Sabbath. It was because Jesus did things like this on the Sabbath that the officials began to persecute him. Jesus told them, "My Father continues His work, and so do I." This was a subtle way of saying, "If I work, it is the Father who is working through me, so if you want to find fault, find fault with Yahweh, as He is the One Who works through me." This made them even more furious, because Jesus was saying that as God's Son, He was equal to God. It made them more intent than ever to kill him.

Jesus then went on to explain to the officials,

The Son can do only what he sees the Father doing, as the Son does nothing on His own. Whatever He sees the Father doing, the Son also does. The Father loves the Son, and shows him everything He is doing, and He will show him even greater things than these, works that will surprise you. Then, as the Father raises the dead and gives them life, so the Son gives life to whomever he chooses, for the Father judges no one. He leaves all judgment up to the Son, so that all may honor the Son as they honor the Father. Whoever honors the Son honors the Father. Whoever refuses to honor the Son refuses to honor the Father who sent him. (Jn. 5:1–47)

Jesus goes on, trying in every possible way to show the Temple officials that he is doing the work of God, using evidence from the Scriptures themselves, from Moses, and the prophets, that especially testify to the authenticity of the Son's mission and message. But, even more importantly, the things the Son does, the miracles, the healings, the raising from the dead, and the giving of sight to the blind, are all graphic evidence that God is trying to tell them something, that the Son is the one He has sent, warning them to accept His Son if they want to avoid harsh judgment in times to come. In effect, He is saying to them, trying to make them understand, "You accept others with less credible certification. The certification the Father gives on behalf of the Son is stunning by comparison, and yet you refuse to accept that endorsement. You even refuse to accept the endorsement of Moses, who spoke about the Son and the things that he would do." Moses, then, will be the one who will accuse them. "You have been prepared for the Son's coming, yet now that he has come *you blind yourselves* as to who he really is."

That is always a danger, even for Christians—not that we blind ourselves to Jesus as the Savior, but we can blind ourselves to what he really teaches, and what he really stands for, because it threatens our deeply seated beliefs and actions that are often foreign to his thinking. In so blinding ourselves to Jesus' living model of holiness, our lives become a denial of all that he is, and yet we still consider ourselves loyal Christians while judging others as radical. Jesus says to forgive; we only too easily ignore that teaching and quietly consider it unreal. Jesus says to forgive your enemies and pray for them. We will never forgive them, or talk to them, much less pray for them, even if our national good can benefit from dialogue with them. Jesus says that we should care for the poor, whom we will always have with us; we deny that there are any authentic poor, only lazy drunks or addicts, thus protecting our money from the obligation of charitable giving. Jesus says that we should share our gifts and talents with the community and with those who have little; we bury our talents and hoard what God has given to us, so we can pass His gifts on to our families. Jesus says we should show mercy, yet Christian judges and prosecutors vie with one another for the reputation of being the most merciless toward sinners, to assure their election or reelection. Jesus says we should be honest in public life; we replace that with the motto, "Get them before they get you," saying that in order to succeed we must divorce business and politics from morality. And when parishioners see these people coming up so piously to read the Bible at services in their church or to receive the Eucharist, it is often enough to turn weak people away from their church. And even decent people have a difficult time believing in Jesus' command not to judge others if we do not want God to judge us. Jesus also told the apostles that whoever wants to be the greatest among them must be willing to be the servant of all the rest, and that they should not be like the powerful people of this world, lording their authority over their subjects. Yet so many ordained as modern-day apostles enjoy the titles of lord and prince and are insensitive in the exercise of authority, often ignoring the needs of hurting people, refusing them compassion and protection because it might jeopardize their own political ambitions.

Jesus apparently did not stay long in Judea. It was too dangerous, and staying there could only disrupt his ministry, though the time he did spend there was fruitful and there were many people who were impressed with his teaching and accepted him and were baptized. After this brief ministry, Jesus left for Galilee, where there was still much work to be done.

16

JESUS SEES INTO THE HUMAN SOUL

Every place he went, Jesus was moved by the large crowds who gathered to welcome him. When we give talks to large gatherings, we see faces, unknown, unfamiliar faces and nothing more. Some may be smiling, some serious, but other than that, nothing more. When Jesus looked across a crowd, he saw no strangers, no strange faces, and not just faces. He saw immediately into the heart of each one. He saw their pain, the fearsome anxiety that was sucking whatever joy and pleasure they could have had in life. He saw the crushing pressures of life's daily problems. He remarked to the apostles, "I feel so sorry for the people. They are like sheep without a shepherd." It was an expression of what Isaiah foretold about the Messiah: "He took upon himself the pain and anguish of us all, and carried in his heart the burden of our sins." It is this pain that Jesus felt that made him realize how real his cousin John's words were at the Jordan, when he said, "Look, there is the Lamb of God, who takes upon himself our sins and is sacrificed for us." (Jn. 1:15–16)

What added to Jesus' pain was the rude way the people were so often treated by their religious leaders, who had no compassion for the heavy burdens they carried and added still more burdens to their lives. When they could not carry them, the religious officials expelled them from the Temple and the synagogue as unworthy. Jesus then described himself as the Good Shepherd sent to care for his Father's sheep, wandering aimlessly in dangerous places and not knowing where to go. The Good Shepherd loves the sheep and goes out in search of the lost, the troubled, the bruised, and the hurting sheep. When he finds them, he picks them up, places them on his shoulders, and carries them back home. (Jn. 10:1–18, Lk. 15:4–7) And we know he is not talking about sheep, but about sinners. Pharisees expel them, glad to see them go, so they might have fewer people but better quality, and God goes out looking for them, hoping they have not been too badly damaged. Strange how God goes out to find and embrace sinners, yet we tell them they are not worthy to be embraced by God. They have to keep their distance, not realizing that they need his embrace all the more, precisely because they *are* sinners and may be not strong enough to make the decision to do better when we want them to. So, we deny them approval to communion while the others go to receive Jesus' loving embrace. Sometimes, I think we as religious leaders missed the message of the Good Shepherd. But why not? Hardly any seminary, Catholic or Protestant, teaches any in-depth courses on Jesus other than Christology, which merely traces the history of the development of the doctrine about Jesus. Without in-depth studies of the behavior and feelings of Jesus, how could we be expected to understand in any depth the thinking and feelings of the Good Shepherd? There are still so many otherwise good clergy who insist that sinners should not be embraced by Jesus in the Eucharist. If the Good Shepherd chooses to go out and embrace sinners, who are we to tell them they are not worthy to let Jesus take them into his love and embrace them? I never want it on my conscience when I go before God that He should have to ask me why I turned sinners away from Him, telling them they were not worthy. I will never forget my godson, Joe Della Ratta, who, when he was in the depths of cocaine addiction, in the depths of sin, some might say, found a church that was open during the day in the dangerous Harlem district of New York. It was not far from Juilliard, where he was studying at the time, and he sat before the Blessed Sacrament for two and three hours pouring his heart out to Jesus. And this he did every day, begging for strength. He was closer to God then than at any other time in his life. He literally clung to Jesus, at a time when some clergy would say he was cut off from God because of his sins. Ever since he had fallen in love with Jesus at three years old, he had never lost that intimacy with him, and never gave up Mass and the Eucharist. In the end he was finally freed of the horrible addiction, and had the most beautiful experiences of God's presence, which seemed to be genuine mystical experiences, just three days before God took him home.

From what we have all read in school about the pagan gods and the gods of other peoples, it is hard to believe that a god could be concerned about his human creatures to the point where he feels their pain and is anxious about each one. Such solicitude is hard for us to comprehend, though just thinking about it is so healing for us, knowing that Jesus understands us and unlike humans feels no need to be cruelly judgmental. It is almost as if he tells us, "What father would strike a crippled child because he keeps falling when he tries to walk? Or what mother would punish a blind child because she trips over things and falls?" We clergy have a lot to learn about damaged and crippled sinners.

Mercy is another motif that weaves its way all through Jesus' messages. It is mercy God wants, mercy and justice, but justice tempered with mercy. What did Jesus mean by that concept?

The Pharisees really could not be considered evil in the ordinary sense of the word. Far from it. They prided themselves on being scrupulous observers of the Law to the point of fanaticism. The Law was black and white. There were no gray areas. Either you are doing what the Law says, or you are breaking the Law. There were no exceptions, although they made many exceptions for themselves, even when it meant preempting the Divine Law for their own convenience.

The reason why Jesus brings the concept of people into the framework of law is to show God's underlying reason for the Law. The purpose of the Law is to benefit people, not to force people into the observance of laws that have no relevance to their lives. It is to help them in the peaceful and secure living of their lives, and in the proper way of doing things so that everyone benefits. So, laws cannot be so rigid in their application that it frustrates the purpose of the Law. This the Pharisees could never understand. As a result they were not only rigid, but ruthless in their enforcement of the Law. No matter what excuse a person might have for breaking a law, it was rarely justified, or condoned. The offender was punished severely, regardless of how it affected their life or the condition of their family. The punishment was applied without mercy. Jesus faulted the Pharisees because they were devoid of compassion.

This attitude of Jesus presents a very interesting situation. One might think that God would be pleased that these religious leaders were so zealous in the enforcement of the Law. Instead, he was furious with their merciless attitude toward people, who were already overburdened in their lives. Who would have ever thought that God would be upset with people insisting on the strict observance of His Law?

But that is not quite the issue. It is not God's Law that the Pharisees are passionate about. It is the Law in general, most of them concocted by scribes in the course of centuries, many having nothing whatsoever to do with bettering people's lives, but making their lives more and more miserable by the incessant creation of new laws. As Jesus said of them one day, "The scribes and Pharisees occupy the chair of Moses, so do what they tell you and listen to them. But do not imitate them, because they do not practice what they preach. They pile up heavy burdens and lay them on people's shoulders and lift not one finger to lighten those burdens." (Mt. 23:1–5)

He is telling the scribes and Pharisees that they do not know God. God is not enamored with the Law. It is His children He cares about. He is telling them they got the whole thing wrong. It is people who are important. *They* are God's concern. *They* are the object of God's love, not the Law. The Law is for people; it is their shield. So, when you are discussing laws and their violation, you must consider the people first and what is good for them. That is the way God looks at these issues. That is why God is always concerned about His hurting children, and how difficult their lives are. And it is mercy that is needed in the application and enforcement of laws. When clergy put the demands of the Law first, and cause more pain and damage to the sheep, they are following the ways of the scribes and Pharisees, not the way of the Good Shepherd.

Unfortunately, the number of these clergy is rapidly increasing. So many of the older priests would rather take on heavier burdens themselves than have many of the younger priests work with them, because they have little or no feeling for the sheep. I sometimes get the impression the Vatican officials are totally unaware of what is happening. They think these priests are models of correctness because they wear their button-down cassocks and appear so pious on the surface, but so often they show little love or compassion for the painful plight of the hurting sheep, and like the scribes and Pharisees, they drive more and more people away from the Church and into fundamentalist communities. And their comment when you mention this to them is merely, "The Church is better off without them. There may be fewer members but better quality." Can you imagine the Good Shepherd saying that?

What is it that the Good Shepherd does say? "Be compassionate as your heavenly Father is compassionate. Do not judge and you will not be judged. Do not condemn and you will not be condemned. Pardon and you will be pardoned. Give and it will be given to you, in full measure, pressed down, shaken together, and running over will it be given to you, because the amount you measure out will be measured out to you." (Lk. 6:36–38)

On another Sabbath he went into a synagogue and began to teach. There was in the room a man with a shriveled hand. The Pharisees were watching him to see if he would heal on the Sabbath, hoping he would so they could use it against him. Knowing their thoughts, he said to the man with the shriveled hand, "Stand up, and come out here in front of everyone." The man came up and stood there. Then Jesus said to the Pharisees, "Is it lawful to do good on the Sabbath, or evil on the Sabbath, to save a life or let it be destroyed? Who among you, if he had one sheep and it fell into a hole on a Sabbath, would not lift it out? Now a human being is much more precious than a sheep, so it is permissible then to do good on the Sabbath."

Looking around at them all, he then told the man with the shriveled hand, "Stretch out your hand!" He did so and his hand became normal. The Pharisees then went out and began to plot against Jesus. (Mt. 12:9–14)

It was about this time that Jesus went into the hills to pray, spending the whole day communing with God. When the following day came, he called together his disciples and from the group, he picked twelve. Those whom he picked, he called apostles, meaning those who are sent on a mission. They were Simon, whom he named Rock; Andrew, Simon's brother; James; John; Philip; Bartholomew; Matthew; Thomas; James, the son of Alphaeus; Simon, called the Zealot; Judas (Thaddeus), the son of James; and Judas, who was to betray him. (Lk. 6:12–16; Mk. 3:13–19; Mt. 10:1–10)

He then went home again [probably to Simon's house], and as soon as he appeared a huge crowd began to gather so there was not even time to eat a meal. When his relatives heard of this they went to rescue him, for they were convinced he was going out of his mind. When his mother and his brothers arrived, they sent word for him to come with them. A crowd seated around him told him, "Your mother and your brothers are outside asking for you."

He said to them, "Who are my mother and my brothers?" Looking around at those seated in the circle, he said, "These are my mother and my brothers. Whoever does the will of God is my brother, my sister, and my mother." (Mk. 3:20–21; Mt. 12:46–50; Mk. 3:31–35)

In speaking like this he was not demeaning his mother, for she was the foremost in the observance of God's will. He was merely pointing out the importance of the new relationships he was establishing with those who were willing be faithful to God by welcoming His Son into their hearts, something his mother had done all her life.

As Jesus' reputation spread, so concern about him among the religious authorities also spread. Now we begin to see not just local Pharisees and local Levites among the crowds who come to listen to him, but the aristocratic Pharisees and scribes from Jerusalem. They came not to learn from him, but to gather information for the authorities in Jerusalem. On one occasion,

The people brought to Jesus a blind man who was also possessed by an evil spirit that made him dumb. Jesus cured him and the man began to see and to speak. The people were amazed and remarked, "Could this not be the Son of David [the title used in referring to the Messiah who was to come]?" But, the scribes and Pharisees were saying, "He is possessed by Beelzebul, the prince of devils, and it is by the prince of devils that he drives out demons."

Jesus, summoning them, spoke to them in parables. "How can Satan drive out Satan? If a kingdom is divided against itself, it cannot last. And if a household is divided against itself, it will fall apart. If Satan is divided against himself, then he cannot endure. That is the end of him. No one can enter a strong man's house and plunder his property unless he first disarms the strong man. In truth, anyone who is not with me is against me, and anyone who does not gather with me causes many souls to be lost. I tell you in serious warning, sins and blasphemies people utter will be forgiven them, and whoever blasphemes against the Son of Man will be forgiven, but whoever blasphemes against the Holy

Spirit will never be forgiven, but is guilty of a sin that will never end, because they refuse to acknowledge and accept the one who brings them God's forgiveness and life." For they said, "He has an evil spirit." (Mt. 12:22–32)

This is one of the most powerful confrontations Jesus has had with the religious officials. When he saw this group of scribes and Pharisees from Jerusalem, dressed more elegantly than the more common traveling scribes, and looking every bit the aristocrats of the religious establishment, he knew immediately what they were up to. They had not come to learn. He knew they had been informed by their local spies that he already had a vast following, and that the control he had over the people could be dangerous, and the reason for his great influence was his power to heal all kinds of diseases. The blind see; the crippled walk; there are rumors he has even brought dead people back to life, one of whom was said to be the daughter of the president of the synagogue. Jesus knew these men came to discredit him in the eyes of the people. He knew them well, for they immediately started by ridiculing him, and attributing his powers to Satan himself. It is interesting; they did not deny the reality of what they witnessed. They had seen it with their own eyes. They could not deny it happened without being laughed at by the people who'd also witnessed, not only this stunning miracle, but the many more they had seen with their own eyes. It is interesting, though, to watch how Jesus handled the situation. He called aside the group from Jerusalem and conversed with them in a very professional manner. To paraphrase his words: "Now let us consider what you have said, that I cast out demons by the power of Satan. Does it really make sense that Satan would be in league against his own agents, starting a war against his own followers? It would be nonsense for him to wage war among his own followers." But then he went on to give them a stern warning for their own good. They were treading on dangerous ground by attributing his power to Satan when it really came from the Divine Spirit, for, "in doing this you all calling God evil, the very One from whom you need forgiveness for your sins, thus cutting yourself off from eternal salvation." Fair warning, and something they should really ponder.

But Jesus did not stop there. The disciples of the Pharisees also were known to exorcise people possessed by demons. So, Jesus asked them, "If it is by the power of Satan that I cast out demons, by whom do your disciples cast them out? Let them be your judges. But, if it is by the Spirit of God that I cast out devils, then the kingdom of God has come upon you. So, make up your minds: either the tree is good, and if it is good, its fruit is good; or the tree is evil, and then the fruit is rotten, for the tree is known by its fruit." (Lk. 11:14–26)

Then, his whole tone changed. Jesus could see they had not the slightest intention of opening their hearts to God's redeeming grace, and that they were no better than the devil he had driven out of the man, because they were doing the work of the devil by undermining the very mission of the Messiah. "You brood of vipers! How can I expect you to speak honestly and say good things, when you are evil? For out of the abundance of the heart the mouth speaks. The good man from his treasure trove of good brings out good; the evil man from his evil treasure brings out evil. I tell you, on the day of judgment men will make an account of every careless word they speak, for by your words you will be condemned." (Mt. 12:34–37)

Then Jesus went back to his commentary on Satan. "Furthermore, when an unclean spirit goes out of a man, he wanders about in waterless places, seeking rest. Not finding it, he then says to himself, 'I am going back to my house from which I came forth.' He goes back, finds it swept and adorned, and unoccupied. Then he leaves to bring back with him seven other spirits more evil than himself. They go into the house and establish themselves. And the last state of the man is worse than the first. Such will be the case for this generation, for it is truly evil." (Lk. 12:24–26)

Jesus hit hard this time, and it must have made the Pharisees more furious than ever. They knew that he was talking about Israel, and their history of embracing pagan gods, and how, in so doing, they invited the demons into their lives. In time, thanks to the prophets, especially Elijah, the devils were for the most part driven out, but after they left, they were soon devastated by their own misery and decided to go back to Israel. It had been swept clean of demons, and they found it clean and in good order. So they went out and got reinforcements, and came back stronger than ever. They knew he was accusing them of allowing Satan back into

Israel, and themselves being the agents of Satan in trying to destroy their Messiah.

But it did not end there. Some scribes and Pharisees pressured him again: "We would like to see your credentials, a sign that you are authorized to speak and do the things you do."

Now Jesus lashed back at them. "An evil and faithless generation demands a sign. The only sign you will be given is the sign of Jonah. As Jonah was in the belly of the whale for three days, so the Son of Man will be in the belly of the earth for three days and three nights. On the Day of Judgment the men of Nineveh will rise up and bear witness against this generation for its condemnation. For, when Jonah preached to them, they repented. And I tell you, something greater than Jonah is here. And on Judgment Day, the Queen of the South will appear and give evidence against this generation to condemn it, because she came from the ends of the earth to listen to the wisdom of Solomon, and yet there is something greater than Solomon here." (Lk. 11:29–31)

Though the scribes and Pharisees remained unmoved by his words, the crowd standing by was thrilled because of the power of his speech, and because he knew what he was talking about, as if it was truth coming directly from God Himself.

When Jesus finished speaking with them, he left and went back to Simon's house to rest. Later in the day he walked down to the water and sat beside the sea, just to watch the water and spend time with his thoughts. But for Jesus to enjoy such luxury was not to be. Word soon spread that he was down at the seashore, and a crowd began to gather. It ended up not being just a few curious neighbors but turned out to be a big crowd. Jesus had to get into one of the boats moored there so he would not be crushed by the press of so many people.

Sitting in the boat, he began to teach the people many things, apparently some of the things he had been thinking about before, while he was sitting by himself looking across the water. The thoughts he shared were about the various ways people accepted his messages.

A sower went out to sow. As he sowed, some seeds fell along the path, and the birds came and ate it. Other seeds fell on rocky ground, and having little soil, they sprang up fast, and having no roots, they were scorched by the sun and dried up. Other seeds fell among thorn bushes. The thorns grew up and choked them. Still other seeds fell on good soil and brought forth grains, some a hundredfold, some sixty, some thirty. Those who are listening should take heed. (Mt. 13:4–9)

The parable seems simple enough, but it was beyond the grasp even of those closest to Jesus. Some of the disciples had drifted into the crowd as Jesus was speaking and did not understand what he was driving at. So, they asked him why he spoke to the people in such a roundabout way. And he answered them, "To you it has been given to know the secrets of the kingdom of heaven, but to them it has not been given. To him who has much more will be given, so he will have abundance. From him who has not, even what he thinks he has will be taken from him. This is why I speak to them in parables, because seeing they do not see and hearing they do not hear, nor do they understand."

It is not that Jesus does not want the people to see and understand, but they are the ones who make themselves blind and deaf to Jesus' teachings. With them, really, what Isaiah prophesied is fulfilled: "Yes, you shall hear but not understand, and yes, you shall see but not perceive. This people's heart has grown dull, and their ears thick, and their eyes covered, lest they perceive with their eyes and hear with their ears, and understand with their heart, and turn to me so I could heal them." They conveniently closed their minds to what he was teaching. "But, blessed are your eyes, for they see, and your ears, for they hear. And let me impress upon you, many prophets longed to see what you see, and did not see it, and to hear what you hear, and did not hear it." (Mt. 13:10–16)

Then Jesus went on to explain the parable of the sower and the seed, which he had just spoken to the people. Does it give us a key to what he had been pondering as he sat on the shore deep in thought? He had to analyze what was on the minds of those who came to him in such vast numbers. After many years of speaking to large groups, a speaker can usually sense the various responses to the messages he is sharing with them. Jesus was even more aware of what was in the hearts of those who came to his gatherings. He describes them all in this parable. The people, like the various kinds of soil receiving the seed, receive the Word of God in various ways. Those who are educated beyond their intelligence see the Word as overly simplistic, and of no value to them in where they are at in their lives. There is no depth, so they fail to see beneath the surface of the Word. They are like the ground along the path, which has no depth where the seed can take root. There are others who listen to the Word and like what they hear, but are afraid of making a commitment to the Word because it will mean a change that will complicate their lives, and maybe cause them pain or loss. They are like the rocky ground, incapable of supporting long-term growth. The seedling eventually dies. Then there are others who hear the Word, like what they hear, but are too enamored of the things of the world, which they find more enjoyable. They follow the Word for a while, but in time it becomes boring, as it distracts them from the addiction to material interests, and they eventually lose interest in the Word. They are like the ground overgrown with thorns that choke the seed. Then, finally, there are those who hear the Word, fall in love with what they hear, and make a lifelong commitment to the Word and nurture it. The Word thrives in their hearts and transforms their lives. They are like the ground with good, fertile soil, which welcomes the seed and provides what it needs to thrive.

Jesus was beginning to realize how difficult it was for people to understand, accept, and embrace his teachings. The treasure he had to share with them was so simple, and the rewards were so great for those who would open their hearts to receive what he wanted so much to give them, he couldn't understand why they were having such a difficult time with it. He had been spending a lot of thought trying to make sense out of it. And the people's difficulty accepting and embracing his messages was not the only problem troubling him. He was beginning also to notice that as a growing number of people accepted his message, another strange thing was happening. Among these good people grew an ever more powerful group of people who were distorting what he was trying to teach. They confused his new followers. He verbalized this in another parable, about a farmer who planted good seed in his field. While the farmhands were sleeping, an enemy came and sowed weeds among the wheat, then left. In time all the seeds grew, and the grain began to appear, but also the weeds. The workers were troubled, because they knew they had planted good seed. They immediately told the owner, who knew an enemy had done this evil deed. "What shall we do?" the servants asked. "Let them grow. If we try to separate the weeds from the wheat we will destroy the whole crop. When harvest time comes, we will have the reapers gather the weeds first, and burn them. Then they can collect the wheat and put it in the barn." (Mt. 13:24–30)

This group that was accepting his message and taking it to their hearts was developing into a sizable community of believers, and Jesus could see his new kingdom taking shape. It was not the kind of kingdom the people were expecting, and they were trying to understand why Jesus did not come out clearly and state precisely who he was and that he had come to set up the kingdom. Jesus knew what they were expecting, and they wanted an answer. Jesus did not want to disillusion them or deceive them. He wanted them to appreciate the true value of the kingdom he was proposing to them, so he described it in terms they could understand. The kingdom of heaven is like a tiny mustard seed, so small it seems insignificant. But when it grows, it spreads its branches in all directions and becomes home for all the birds of the air that come and nest in it. The mustard plant then provides shelter and space for all kinds of birds, and a place where they can have the companionship of others of their kind.

I never realized this before, but outside Joshua House in upstate New York, there is a large lilac bush. Lately, I have been shocked at how many different kinds of birds rest in that bush all day long. There are juncos, sparrows, blue jays, blackbirds, chickadees, cardinals, robins, bluebirds, goldfinches, purple finches, black-crested titmice, grackles, wrens, and even hummingbirds, and often many kinds at the same time. What attracts them in such numbers and varieties? The answer is very simple: the three bird feeders hanging above the front porch. They come for the seed, and they stay for the shelter. But what is significant is Jesus' vision of the surprising number of birds that would come to the mustard bush. The mustard bush he talks about must be different from the mustard bushes we see today. The one he mentions had to be a very large shrub for all kinds of birds to flock to it and shelter in it. What impressed Jesus were the numbers and also the variety. That is probably one of the reasons he used the example. Jesus' mind is not like our tiny minds. When Jesus talked about the kingdom of heaven, his vision was global and transcendent of time. When he saw the mustard bush filled with birds of every variety, it quickly reminded him of the kingdom spread throughout the world, with people of every description and race all gathered together in the one global family, attracted by the food it offered, the Living Bread, the Eucharist. His Church would in time embrace the whole world, not just particular nations, or a particular type of people, or a particular nationality. He had come to bring salvation to the whole human race, and it is the mark of his kingdom that it is precisely that, a global community embracing all peoples and all cultures. As beautiful as that is, it is also the reason that the Church is so difficult to guide, because of the wide spectrum of cultural differences, which make even the slightest change in customs or rituals difficult for everyone to accept. What is miraculous is that such vast and varied peoples can all be one in belief, and even to a great extent one in worship throughout the world. But that is precisely what Jesus wanted and what Jesus prayed for, that his family would all be one: one in worship, one in belief, and one in their concern for one another, as different as they are.

There is also an interconnecting logic between this parable and the parable of the yeast in the dough. "The kingdom of heaven is like leaven which a woman mixed into three measures of flour till it had all risen." What does it mean? Simply the presence of the new kingdom of heaven which Jesus is founding will act like yeast in a batch of dough. The yeast is the community of his disciples. The dough is the wider community, spread throughout the whole world, with a vast variety of peoples and cultures symbolized by the vast variety of birds that find shelter in the mustard shrub, which is the Church. The presence of the Spirit working in the Church will cause the whole worldwide community to rise to a higher level of existence, to a higher level of culture. A society inspired by the Spirit of God working in the Church must be radically different from a society without Jesus, but that depends on how sincere Jesus' followers are in embracing his message and making his presence burst into life throughout society.

Jesus did send his apostles and Peter into the whole world to teach and to preach his good news of salvation. He also said he would be with them until the end of time. He also promised to send the Holy Spirit to guide them in their teaching, by bringing back to their minds all the things that he himself had taught them. The Spirit would be with them as their teacher until the end of time, so they could understand more fully what Jesus was expecting of them, and to guarantee that his message would be taught in its integrity to each generation until the end of time.

That part I could always understand. It seemed more preventative than positive guidance. Preventative in that the Holy Spirit would prevent

Peter and the apostles and their successors from teaching anything contrary to what Jesus taught. I could also see how the Holy Spirit had been working on the minds of the early Fathers of the Church, and the later Doctors of the Church, in their development and understanding of what Jesus' teachings all meant. Their teachings were profound as they probed deeper and deeper into the meaning of Jesus himself and also his message of salvation. Each of the Fathers and great theologians through the centuries expanded our understanding of Jesus and his message. It is like each one contributed a new thought, a new insight, like a new piece of a puzzle, until the image on the puzzle was finally emerging as a beautiful portrait. After two thousand years of the Holy Spirit's guidance, we are two thousand years more advanced in our understanding of Jesus than what was written two thousand years ago in an entirely different age and culture. That guidance the Church calls tradition. To reject those two thousand years of the Spirit's guidance and teaching, and just use the Bible as the sole guide, has no justification. It is rejecting the Holy Spirit, which Jesus promised to guide his Church, and the continued presence of Peter and the apostles in each generation until the end of time. When we say in the Creed that we believe in the apostolic Church, we are professing our acceptance of duly consecrated successors of the apostles, like Timothy and Barnabas, having the same authority and power as the apostles, and all those who succeed the apostles in future generations.

What I never fully realized, however, was how the Holy Spirit used the yeast to cause the dough to rise in society during the long history of the Church. I never realized this until recently, when I read a book that told very vividly how the Holy Spirit worked in the Church, inspiring it to elevate the whole of civilization. Thomas E. Woods, the historian who wrote *How the Catholic Church Built Western Civilization*, did a massive amount of research into the work of the Church throughout Western Europe from the Dark Ages to the Age of Enlightenment. In the so-called Dark Ages, when the Church had to work with the hordes of barbarians then living in the midst of the dying Roman Empire, the Church still accomplished wonders, contrary to what historians had written about the Church for centuries. When Charlemagne, the Frankish Holy Roman Emperor, was converted and ruled the empire, he worked with the Church to establish schools all throughout Europe to teach all the children, including the poor. This was in 800 A.D. At the same time, bishops established schools of higher learning as part of their cathedral complex. One of the most famous of such schools was the Cathedral school at Chartres in France. Also during the Dark Ages, which historians have considered as the death of a civilization, the pipe organ and polyphonic music were invented, the violin was created, and three-dimensional painting developed, rather than the flat two-dimensional painting that had been in vogue for so many centuries. A monk developed a way of writing down music on parchment or its equivalent in those days, so musicians could play music although they had never heard it. During those centuries the Benedictine monks and nuns flourished, and by the eleventh century they had over 37,000 monasteries, with huge tracts of land that they cleared from swamps and jungle-like forests and developed into farms, providing work for the millions of poor people wandering the streets and the countryside of Europe and the British Isles. The monasteries became vast factories, inventing and manufacturing an almost unlimited array of products by the use of machines driven by water power. This gave rise to the development of fundamental economic principles as early as the thirteenth century.

By the late eleventh century the monks and other learned people had developed enough understanding of geometry and engineering to have the tools needed to design the massive cathedrals which were being built all throughout Europe. Shortly after, the bishops and monks developed the concept of the university as an institution of higher learning, where theology, philosophy, science (called natural philosophy then), mathematics, art, music, medicine, law, and other subjects could be taught. These universities were established all throughout the Church, with tens of thousands of the poor, as well as the children of the well-placed in society, being educated by the thirteenth century. One of the most significant developments flowing from theology was the recognition of the inalienable rights of God's children. Human rights extended not just to baptized Catholics but to all human beings. Human rights did not come from the king or the government but directly from God, and no earthly power could violate those rights. People accused of crimes had a God-given right to a trial based upon facts, and not upon the outcome of trial by ordeal. With all these institutions of higher learning so firmly established, the stage was set for the burst of learning and culture that was soon to take place throughout the whole Western world, making it far more advanced than the rest of the world, a phenomenon which has lasted even to the present time. Hospitals and orphanages were built to care for the sick and needy and for orphans wandering the streets. This was stunning proof of the power of the Holy Spirit causing the Church to become the leaven in the dough of society to create a whole new civilization based upon the ideas preached in seed form by Jesus himself. That little parable of Jesus comparing the kingdom of God to yeast in the dough has had a profound effect on our civilization ever since, which has made Christian civilization a unique phenomenon in the history of the human race.

17

THE PARABLES LOOK FAR INTO THE FUTURE

Jesus' parables are a powerful mark of his genius, as he uses his knowledge of the past as well as of future events to give vast dimension to these apparently simple stories. He knows full well what a paradoxical phenomenon the kingdom of God is, and the effect it will have on people's lives far into the future. He has no illusions as to what will happen once it takes hold of people. He tries to tell people that it is a precious treasure, comparing it on one occasion to a man who came across a treasure hidden in a field. The man quickly covered it up and, full of joy, went, sold all he had, and purchased that field. On another occasion he compared the kingdom of heaven to a man who was interested in fine pearls. One day he found a pearl of exquisite quality. He went and sold all he had and bought that pearl. Jesus realized that the whole world is looking for that rich treasure, which is intimacy with God, personal peace, and inner happiness, as well as salvation and life after death. Once people realize that the things of the world cannot bring happiness or peace, they are ready to give anything to obtain that treasure. One day they stumble onto the kingdom of God through fortuitous circumstances and, realizing the kingdom's potential to fill their heart's greatest desire, they are willing to make any sacrifice to possess it.

But Jesus is not under any delusions. He knows full well that one day the kingdom of God will be filled with all kinds of people, many good souls as well as many sinners, and those who bring disgrace upon the kingdom. That does not make the kingdom less precious. It is still the treasure Jesus gave us, and he tries to tell us that he realizes that there will be those who bring shame upon the kingdom. He foretold the havoc that selfish, ambitious, and evil people would create in the kingdom. He one day compared the Church to a catch of fish. The fisherman draws in his catch, drags it up on shore, then begins sorting the fish. There are good healthy fish, and some sick and rotten. The fisherman puts the good fish into pails and readies them for market. The others he throws away. That is the human side of the kingdom that is not easy to cope with, and demands constant discipline and perseverance of all of us to remain in the kingdom. It is never an excuse to leave the kingdom and start our own.

Working and living with unlikable people is not easy, but it is a small price to pay for what we receive from belonging to the kingdom. There will always be problems living in the kingdom, but no matter how bad they get, they do not justify leaving the kingdom, because it is still the living presence of Jesus in our lives. It is the family that Jesus established to be here until the end of time. It is still guided by the apostles under the Holy Spirit's inspiration, which Jesus guaranteed. If the Church is doing its job, it will *always* be full of sinners, and if it is full of sinners, it is bound to be a dysfunctional family. And if it is a dysfunctional family, it is going to be very difficult to live in. But it is still Jesus' family, and each person must find his or her place in the family. Bruised feelings and disagreements are part of family life, and mature disciples will resolve whatever issues trouble them. If we realize the importance of living in the kingdom, walking away is not an option. It is walking away from Jesus. It is hard to imagine the early Christians walking away from Jesus' family of disciples because there was a Judas among his apostles. They would have realized they were departing from Jesus. Starting a new family without Jesus and expecting him to go along with them would have made no sense. He promised to be always with his family until the end of time. His will was that his followers stay united as one family. "That they all may be one, Father, as you and I are one, that they may be one in us, so that the world may believe that you have sent me." Fragmenting his family by starting other families destroys the clear witness of Jesus' mission, confuses the world, and dishonors the will of God. Jesus may be close to individuals born into these situations, but is it something that pleases him, when his expressed will insisted that his family stay together?

As a finale to this set of fascinating descriptions of what people can expect of the kingdom of heaven on earth, Jesus asked the apostles if they understood what he was saying through these parables. They said, "Yes." But, seeing how limited their understanding was of other things that Jesus said, it is doubtful they even grasped the meaning of these parables in any depth. But Jesus let it pass, and then, referring to the apostles as the scribes of the future kingdom of heaven, he gave them some serious direction: "Every scribe who has been trained for the kingdom of heaven is like a householder who brings out of his storehouse both the old and the new." This was a solid peace of advice, and it was not applicable only to what the apostles were expected to do when it came their turn to be the teachers of world. They had to blend what was of value in what they had been taught about the Law and the prophets with the new and exciting teachings of Jesus, which was the fulfillment of the hopes and dreams of the children of the Covenant.

18

THE SIGNS, MIRACLES; APPROVAL FROM YAHWEH

While in Capernaum, a large crowd heard about Jesus' presence and gathered around him, as he walked along the seashore.

An official of the synagogue, named Jairus, came to Jesus, and falling down at his feet, begged him, saying, "My little daughter is at the point of death. Come and lay your hands on her so that she may be made well, and live." And he went with him. The crowd followed him and surrounded him on every side. (Mk. 5:21–24) [This incident is similar to another, but as there are different details we will continue with this story.] . . .

A messenger arrived from the official's house saying that the little girl was dead. "Why trouble the Teacher any further?" Ignoring what they said, Jesus said to the official, "Do not fear, only believe." And he allowed no one to follow him except Peter, James, and John, the brother of James. When they came to the synagogue official's house, he saw all the commotion, and people weeping and wailing uncontrollably. And when he had entered he said to them, "Why all the commotion and the crying? The child is not dead; she is asleep." And they laughed at him. Asking them all to leave, he took the child's father and mother and those who were with him and went to where the child was. Taking her by the hand, he said to her, "Talitha, cumi," which means, "Little girl, arise." Immediately the girl got up and walked. She was twelve years old. They were immediately overcome with awe. And he strictly charged them that no one should know about this, then told them to give the girl something to eat. (Mk. 5:35–43)

Jesus then left Capernaum and began a tour of the cities and villages, teaching in their synagogues and preaching the Gospel of the kingdom, and healing every disease and sickness. When he saw the throngs that followed him, he had pity on them, because they looked so weary and helpless, like sheep without a shepherd. Then he said to his disciples, "The harvest indeed is ripe and plentiful, but the laborers are few. Pray the Lord of the harvest to send laborers into his harvest." He called the twelve disciples together and gave them authority over unclean spirits, to cast them out, and to heal every disease and illness. These twelve Jesus sent out, and directed them, "Do not go among the Gentiles, and enter no Samaritan town, but go to the lost sheep of the house of Israel, and preach as you go, saying, 'The kingdom of heaven is at hand.' Heal the sick, raise the dead, cleanse lepers, and cast out devils. You received without pay; give without pay. Take no gold nor silver, no copper in your belts, no bag for your journey, nor two tunics, no sandals nor a staff, for the laborer is entitled to support."

Jesus then gave them other pointed advice. "Now, realize, I am sending you out as sheep in the midst of wolves; so be wise as serpents, but innocent as doves.

"It is not going to be easy. Watch out for people! They will deliver you up to councils and whip you in their synagogues, and you will be dragged before governors and kings for my sake, to bear testimony before them and the Gentiles. When they deliver you up, do not worry about what you are to say, for it will be given to you in that hour what you are to say. It will not be you who speak, but the Spirit of your Father speaking through you." (Mt. 10:1–20)

Reading these counsels and admonitions is not very impressive until you realize that Jesus is speaking not about things that will happen locally and will continue to happen, but about what will take place in the distant future, when they will find themselves in foreign lands, and among strange people who will find their teachings bizarre. He tells them they are not to worry; that the Holy Spirit will be with them wherever they go, and will guide them and prompt them as to what they are to say. And he tells them not to be shocked when they find out that families will turn on their own who accept the Gospel message, and turn them in to be put to death. And he warns them that they should not be afraid of what men will do to them. They can only kill the body, but cannot touch your soul. Fear only the One who can destroy both body and soul in hell. But he tells them they will be rewarded for their dedication in acknowledging him before others, and he promises to reward them by acknowledging them before his Father in heaven.

Jesus further advises the apostles that, although it may appear that he came to cause conflict on the earth because of people's reaction to his message, he really came to bring peace, and it is people's unwillingness to open their hearts to the good news that causes the conflict, and all the evils that will follow. They should be aware of these things beforehand so that when they happen they will not be taken by surprise.

Thinking about these chats that Jesus had with the disciples, you try to picture the setting. They had embarked on a tour of the towns and villages. During the day there was no privacy for such extended, serious conversations between Jesus and the friends. They had to occur at times when they were alone, probably at night after the townsfolk went home with their families. Having no motels or inns, Jesus and his disciples had to find shelter for the night. Usually it was a grove of olive trees or an orchard, or any sheltered place, where they would light a campfire and gather around and listen to Jesus as they reclined on the ground munching on whatever light provisions they might have brought with them or whatever people might have given them during the day, like a flask of wine and bread, perhaps some fruit, and cheese, maybe some already cooked fish. Picture them sitting around the fire on a chilly evening, watching the flames as they listened to Jesus give them instructions for the future, or practical lessons for their life. These were intimate moments, times when they really got to know one another and could share their feelings about the people and their reactions to Jesus' message that particular day.

"Lord, do you think the people are really sincere in accepting your teachings, or are they here just for the healings? You know, these are not easy people to deal with. They bargain hard. We know them from our business, and you work for every copper you get out of them. They don't impress me as being interested in anything spiritual." I am sure one of the twelve asked Jesus that question and made that observation more than once.

Jesus listened patiently and, with an agreeing smile, finally responded, "I have no illusions about why they come. Their ancestors gave Moses a miserable forty years. My Father did Moses a favor when he forbade him to enter the Promised Land with them when they arrived. Moses was at first hurt, but when he realized what my Father had done, he was shocked at my Father's humor. 'I'll be free at last,' he realized. That had to be the happiest day of his life, finally being free of the overwhelming responsibility of caring for all those complaining people for all those years. I know what is in the people's hearts. They crave relief from the harshness of life. I know their lives are not easy. You do not see the rich people in the crowds. They are content with their lives and are as yet unconscious of the emptiness within. I realize there are many people who come for healing, but they stay because they have found what they craved all their lives and did not know it, intimacy with God. Look at their faces! You can see the peace that comes over them when I tell them about their Father in heaven, and about how my Father loves them and cares for them, even though they do not look upon themselves as lovable. They never knew that God really cares for them and is deeply involved in their lives, and watches over them like a doting mother. I know they first came for the healing, but when they return the next day, it is not for the healing of their bodies, but for the healing of their souls. They are truly like lost sheep, wandering about confused, not knowing what to do, or where to go. To you they are strangers. To me, I have known them from before they were born. They are my Father's beloved children, and I came to save them, and gather them together into one family, as my Father commanded."

Though the apostles may have had misgivings about the sincerity of the huge crowds who followed Jesus, there are still beautiful scenes expressive of those grand family gatherings that took place on at least two occasions, when the people who had come to spend time with Jesus and hear him speak were asked to sit in groups of fifty or more. Then from a few loaves of bread and a couple of fish, Jesus fed those crowds of roughly ten thousand people, with food enough for leftovers to take home with them. What an awesome picture of a Jesus family picnic! That is the kind of kingdom of God Jesus dreamed of, where we are all one, in spite of our failings and sins and irritating ways, but still struggling together to make the family more attuned to Jesus' ideal. Unity is critical and indispensable if we are going to be loyal to Jesus, and we all have a responsibility to work toward that unity.

A number of years ago, I was surprised by a phone call from the Catholic chaplain at Baylor University, a Southern Baptist institution in Waco, Texas. We had not known each other, but he was excited to tell me about something that had happened at the university that he felt was nothing short of miraculous. The officials at the university had read the Joshua book, *The Shepherd*, and were deeply affected by Jesus' insistence on unity among his followers. Out of obedience to Jesus they wanted to take a small step toward that unity, so they called in the campus ministers, including the Baptist minister, and said that from now on, it would be the policy of the university that, even though it is a Southern Baptist university, chaplains would work together as a team, and do programs together to show their unity, rather than work separately, showing their differences. Someone, somewhere in Texas, was responding to Jesus' plea for unity. That must have made Jesus happy. And it must have taken great courage to take that step. Another incident also happened in Texas.

Bishop Grahmann, the Catholic bishop of Dallas-Fort Worth, talked to bishops of other denominations in the area, and asked if they could see their way clear to working with him as a team. How beautiful! He told me many years ago how much fun it was and how well they worked together, and all they were accomplishing. And there are many others who try in so many different ways, not just by talking and endless dialoguing, but by actually doing things together, developing the habit of thinking together and working together with their people, getting them used to working together as a family, trying honestly to respond to Jesus' prayer, "Father, that they may be one, even as you and I are one, that the world may believe that you have sent me."

The two episodes in the Gospels of Jesus' picnics with the vast crowds of followers were not things to be accepted lightly by the political officials in Galilee. The picnics were intimate, with the people enjoying their food, gratuitously given to them by Jesus through some supernatural power, and Jesus walking among the small groups as they asked him questions and made small talk with him. One could tell that these people were not there just for that one occasion. They had been coming back to him on a regular basis, whenever he would appear in their neighborhood, sometimes daily. The people, who had been strangers, many of them from the neighboring pagan cities, were now bonding. Judeans, Galileans, and other Israelites, Gentiles, Syrians, Philistines, Canaanites, Romans, people from Herod's court, were getting to know one another and sharing a meal at a family picnic, and none of it according to the Law. They were, without realizing it, becoming a family. Revolutionaries could only dream of having that effect on vast multitudes. With Jesus it was spontaneous. The political officials had to take notice. It was not just Galileans, but people from all over. The gatherings were growing and spreading to other places. Jesus' hold over them was electric. Where would it end?

It is interesting that Herod, who was always aware of large public gatherings in his territory, took no action against Jesus, whose popularity was growing steadily. He allowed Jesus to continue his ministry. Of course, the king had spies monitoring every move Jesus made, and every word he said. But, apparently, the spies had nothing negative to report, and some of them even became Jesus' disciples, like members of Chuza's family, who were palace insiders. Jesus' reported activities caused Herod sleepless nights, nonetheless, because his guilt over murdering John the Baptizer was stirring up nightmares and attacks of conscience. He was beginning to see in Jesus John come back to life again and haunting him. He was finding it difficult to decide what he should do. As Luke writes, "Herod came to learn of all that was happening, and he was divided by what was being said by some and what was being said by others. For some said, 'John has risen from the dead.' But others, 'Elijah has appeared.' And still others, 'One of the ancient prophets has come back to life.' As for Herod, he said, 'John! I had him beheaded. But, who then is this man of whom I have heard such things spoken?' And he sought to see him." (Mk. 6:14–16)

The tetrarch was confused, tortured in conscience because he knew he had done an evil act in killing John, whom he secretly revered. Now this new phenomenon, who was he? Herod could ill afford to make another tragic mistake by taking strong action against Jesus. He let him be, although under continual surveillance. Herod's loyal sycophants, the Herodians, continually gathered material critical of Jesus, and secretly met with the Pharisees and Sadducees, plotting ways to undermine and trap Jesus. The scribes and Pharisees on their own were more of a nuisance to Jesus than was Herod. But, later on, in league openly with the Herodians, they were more of a threat. Herod himself, for his part, stayed aloof of the situation, while his loyalists, knowing the Pharisees hated him, were only too willing to cozy up to them and quietly undermine Jesus' ministry.

If Herod Antipas was on civil terms with his brother Herod Philip, who was the tetrarch of the neighboring region of Trachonitis, he would have had knowledge of Jesus' whereabouts and doings while Jesus was wandering and preaching in that part of the territory. It seems Jesus left Herod Antipas' territory when he heard of the arrest and execution of John the Baptizer. Herod Philip had no complaints about Jesus, either, and saw no threat in his being in his country. In fact, Jesus did not stay there for very long, since it was not properly in Israelite country, and his mission was to the children of Israel, and not to the Gentiles.

A while back, when John was in prison, a group of his disciples had come to visit him and told him the latest gossip about that new teacher,

Jesus, and that he was preaching a doctrine different from what John had taught them. They wanted to know what John thought of this Jesus. John knew from a revelation the true identity of Jesus and could have told his followers what he knew of Jesus, but he wanted them to learn for themselves. And yet it is possible that John, locked in the darkness of his prison cell in the Machaerus fortress on the eastern shore of the Dead Sea, was having his own doubts as to Jesus' mission. John may have expected something different from the Messiah. So, he sent a chosen delegation to meet with Jesus and tell him that they had been sent by John, and he wanted to know if Jesus was "the one who is to come," or should they look for another?

> At that very time, Jesus was healing many people of their afflictions and evil spirits and restoring to many their sight. So Jesus told the delegates, "Go, tell John what you have seen with your own eyes and heard with your own ears: the blind see, the crippled walk, the lepers are cleansed, and the deaf hear, the dead rise, the poor have the Gospel preached to them. And blessed are they who are not scandalized in me." Jesus knew that when the delegates returned to John and told him what they had seen and heard, John would immediately recognize it as the fulfillment of the prophecy of Isaiah concerning the Messiah. (Lk. 7:18–23)

While in Jesus' presence, the envoys would have recognized many of their own former followers of John, who had gone over to Jesus. The envoys were among those still loyal to John, although John had told his followers originally that Jesus was the one they should follow, and that he should increase while John would decrease, and it was John's mission to prepare the way for his coming. It seems many did obey John and became Jesus' disciples, and the envoys spotted them in the adoring crowd with Jesus. They would naturally have difficult feelings about these former followers of John, since these envoys had remained staunchly loyal to John.

As the envoys were leaving, Jesus broke into a beautiful and emotional eulogy to John:

> What did you go out to the desert to see? A reed shaken by the wind? But, what did you go out to see? A man clothed in fine garments? I tell

you, those who are luxuriously dressed live in the palace of kings. But, what did you go out to see? A prophet? Yes, I tell you, and much more than a prophet. You went out to see him of whom it is written, "Behold, I send my messenger on ahead, and he will prepare the way before you." And I tell you, among those born of woman, there is no prophet greater than John; and yet the least important in the kingdom of heaven is greater than John. (Lk. 7:24–28)

Why is John greater than all the other prophets? Because, if you can believe it, Jesus tells the people, John is Elijah, who is to return, and John's work was not just to prophesy but to introduce the Messiah himself and the inauguration of the kingdom of heaven on earth. And with John's ministry, Jesus said, "The kingdom of heaven has been under assault, and the violent will bear it away." Not a bad thing, but a sign of the success of John's ministry. The people believed John and went to follow Jesus in great numbers, like an army storming a fortress, and the violent were bearing it away. Not a bad thing, indeed, though it is hard to understand Jesus' colorful language. What he seems to be saying is, the rush of those to enter the kingdom is so great, it is hard to restrain the vehemence of the pressure. Some of these ideas the Dominican Scripture scholar Father Pierre Bernard describes in detail in his beautiful two-volume series, *The Mystery of Jesus,* which I would strongly recommend if you can find a copy. It is available on the Internet.

Jesus' life was now becoming more complicated. Herod's agents were appearing more and more in the crowd that followed Jesus. In the beginning they rubbed elbows with the Pharisees, and eventually joined forces with them. Even the Sadducees had become part of the coalition, since none of them were capable of outwitting Jesus on their own. Even their combined efforts would prove to be no match for his vastly superior intelligence.

19

JESUS' JOURNEY TO JUDEA

Jesus' most successful engagements with the people were in Galilee. Life, while busy, still provided the freedom for the people to gather at times during the day to listen to Jesus talk about God, and the things of God, and of the things that mattered to people.

Judea was different. The people there were sophisticated. The Pharisees and the scribes were experts in the Scriptures and the Law. The Sadducees were steeped in Greek culture and philosophy and for the most part believed in a diluted form of Judaism. Strangely, from their ranks came the high priestly families, which were deeply resented by the Pharisees, who followed the strictest interpretation of their religious laws, and the religious traditions, and believed that the high priests should come from priestly stock, not just political appointees. The political and religious elite lived in Jerusalem, and there always seemed to be electricity in the air. Relations between the Sanhedrin, the seventy-one Judean rulers of Jerusalem, and the Roman governor were always tense. The governor tolerated the Sanhedrin as long as they could keep the peace and prevent the people from causing disturbances. Among the members of the Sanhedrin were Pharisees and Sadducees, as well as other Judean elders. The governor, Pontius Pilate, was a severe administrator who had little patience with his Israelite subjects and held a tight rein even over the Sanhedrin.

Whenever Jesus journeyed to Judea and especially to Jerusalem, the capital, tense incidents seemed inevitable. Strong feelings of animosity and jealousy against Jesus were so intense, even visitors coming to the feasts from foreign countries could sense the tension. Whereas Herod let Jesus be and allowed him to wander unimpeded in his territory, the religious elite in Jerusalem were so jealous of Jesus and his popularity, they were constantly driven to create issues and public confrontations with him. One would think they should have been more discreet, as every time they created a situation with Jesus, they ended up being totally vanquished by the force not only of Jesus' logic, but of his vastly superior knowledge of the Scriptures and the Law. Every time they confronted him with a new issue, they ended up being shamed or humbled by the brilliance of his response.

Since the feast of Passover was approaching, and the tour through Galilean towns was behind him, Jesus, together with his apostles and other disciples, decided to travel south and work their way up the high hills to Judea and Jerusalem. By now Jesus' mother and her sister and a handful of close friends and loyal relatives formed an entourage that accompanied Jesus wherever he went. The women particularly were concerned about Jesus not taking good care of himself in his enthusiasm to do his Father's work. And besides, they wanted Jesus and these rough emissaries he chose to represent him to look presentable when they went to meet with the public. Among this select group was the wife of Chuza, the majordomo in Herod's court.

Luke mentions that Jesus and the little caravan took the road down through Samaria, where Jesus had previously been warmly received and where his reputation as a friend of the Samaritan people, as well as one sent by God, had spread throughout the country. When Jesus' advance group entered a Samaritan town, telling of Jesus' coming, the Samaritans' first reaction was joy, probably thinking Jesus would be celebrating the Feast of Passover with them. However, when they were told that Jesus was on his way to Jerusalem, they were offended and told the group that they were not welcome, since they were on their way to celebrate the feast with the Jews. They then shunned him and treated him and his group roughly, refusing them lodging and other ordinary gestures of hospitality.

James and John were furious, and they asked Jesus if they should not call down flaming sulphur upon the Samaritans. Jesus was horrified that they should even think like that. "You do not know what you are saying. The spirit that prompts you is not my spirit. I have come to save people's lives, not destroy them." (Lk. 9:52–56) For this outburst, Jesus labels the two brothers the "sons of thunder," as Mark relates in his Gospel.

When they finally arrived in Jerusalem, John mentions a visit to the Temple as the first place Jesus went on entering the city. That makes good spiritual sense. It was his Father's home, and to pay his respects to his Father was an example he wanted to show the people. When he arrived there, however, he was horrified at the scene before him. John describes in detail his anger at seeing the Temple desecrated by the authorities having turned it into a stockyard for the selling of animals, big and small, for the Passover sacrifices. In righteous fury, he picked up some lengths of rope and made a whip that he flailed about, spooking the animals—bulls and heifers, and sheep and goats—causing chaos. Picture the money changers, with their vast piles of coins from all the neighboring countries from which worshipers came for the feast, including gold and silver coins in neat piles for the rapid currency exchange required for the thousands of people rushing around. "Get this stuff out of here!" Jesus yelled out above the bellowing of the bulls and bleating of the sheep. "My Father's house is a house of prayer. You have turned it into a den of thieves." Walking over to the money changers, he overturned their tables, as they made a mad dash to make sure their coins would not roll away and get lost among the money of their competitors. Then, walking over to those selling doves, or pigeons, the sacrifices for the poor, Jesus merely told them to take the cages out of there. In no time at all, total chaos reigned, as Jesus calmly walked away, looking up toward the altar of sacrifice where the priests were slaughtering the animals and sacrificing them, with the smoke and smell of burning animal flesh hovering over the altar like a cloud. What a detestable insult to God! In the midst of such bedlam, how could people pray or even collect their thoughts in prayerful meditation as they stood before God in His holy sanctuary on the most sacred day of the year? How could they walk away feeling they had offered pleasing sacrifices to God admist this foul desecration of His home?

It is possible, that, in the confusion, none of the officials or the Temple police confronted Jesus over what he had done, but in his repeat of the same action toward the end of his life, the Temple officials were lying in wait for his appearance in the Temple, and a vigorous confrontation occurred.

Although what Jesus did could not but infuriate the chief priests and the members of the Sanhedrin, it seemed to have pleased the people. We can be sure there were many decent people who shared Jesus' disgust at the ongoing sacrilege against the sacred presence of Yahweh in their midst. They surely, though quietly among themselves, applauded his bold courage in doing what he did. So, Saint John writes that "during his stay in Jerusalem for the Passover, many believed in his name when they saw the signs that he performed." However, John adds a strange qualifying comment: "But he did not open himself up to them, because he knew what they were like, not that he needed anyone to warn him, but because he knew what was in people's hearts."

Although there is nothing recorded by the evangelists about the many healings and other remarkable signs like he performed in Galilee, word soon spread among the populace and also reached the ears of the officials that this new teacher, whoever he was, was reputed to be working miracles, and not just simple things, but giving sight to people born blind, and healing cripples whose limbs were deformed. These were awesome signs that impressed the officials. He also had a hypnotic effect on the people because, unlike the scribes and Pharisees, who dabbled in opinions, he taught on his own authority. Who was he? Where had he come from? Some of the official scholars of the Law and the Torah most likely witnessed Jesus' doings, since it was his practice to gather in the Temple precincts early in the day and teach the people in the various Temple porticoes.

This would explain why some of the well-disposed among the Sanhedrin were not only curious about Jesus, but secretly admired him, and had a strong desire to learn more about him. How to do that, however, was a problem, as it would not be politically wise to be seen conversing with this popular nobody openly. Their attitude was, "After all, he is a Galilean, and all we ever hear coming out of that place is trouble." One of them, however, did get a message to Jesus that he would like to meet with him secretly, some night after dark, so he could learn more about his teachings. The man's name was Nicodemus, not necessarily a man of unconventional thinking, but an old man of aristocratic stock, and a Pharisee; a man who was unwilling to make rash judgments about a man even if he was from Galilee; a man who seemed to radiate an aura of genuine holiness reminiscent of John, but more refined and without John's abrasive manner. Another side of Jesus that impressed not only Nicodemus, but other scholarly scribes and expert lawyers, was Jesus' uncanny knowledge of Scripture, that same depth of understanding that had impressed the scholars in the Temple when Jesus was only twelve years old. It is possible that some of those same scholars were still around, and might have been wondering if this was the same boy from Nazareth who impressed them so much when he was only a child. The signs that Jesus now performed could have brought back memories of that young boy in the Temple twenty years before. This would have only increased their curiosity. He could very well be an instrument of Yahweh. Nicodemus needed to meet with this young teacher, whoever he was. His teaching and his knowledge of the Law and the Scriptures was too authentic to come from a mere amateur.

The meeting was arranged. And they met. But where? John does not mention the place, though one translation mentions Jesus' "home." But Jesus had no home in Jerusalem. Who did Jesus know in Jerusalem who would have let him stay at his house and entertain guests, in the late of night until early morning? Mark's father had a home in Jerusalem, apparently the place where later on the Last Supper would be celebrated. Perhaps it was there that Nicodemus and Jesus met. Or did they meet out where Jesus usually stayed when in Jerusalem, in a grove of olive trees? Wherever they met is not critical. That they met is significant. Also, it is not clear when this visit took place, after John the Baptizer's death or before it. The chronology in the Gospels is very confusing.

It was late one night, after the crowds had left the streets, that Nicodemus found his way to wherever Jesus was staying. Nicodemus spent much of the evening speaking with Jesus. "Rabbi, we know that you are a teacher come from God, for no one could perform the signs that you perform unless God was with him." It is interesting that Nicodemus says "we." It would seem that there were other Pharisees and high officials who shared his willingness to accept Jesus, or they may have been there with him. Nicodemus' concern then was, "Now that I am willing to accept you and your teaching, what is expected of me if I am to please Yahweh?" But Nicodemus did not get a chance to put it into words. Jesus knew what was on his mind, so he gave the answer before Nicodemus had a chance to frame the question.

"I tell you with great emphasis, unless a man is born again from above, he cannot see the kingdom of God."

"How can a grown man be born again?" Nicodemus asked him. "Can he go back into his mother's womb and be born again?"

"Again I emphasize, unless a man is born through water and the Spirit he cannot enter the kingdom of God." It is important to remember here that Jesus is talking to a Jew who knows the importance of the ritual of circumcision as a necessity for Jewish people's acceptance by God, and already knows of Jesus' teachings and wants to learn more. Some Christians mistakenly apply these words of Jesus to people who have never had the teaching of Jesus preached to them or who have been turned away from Jesus by the behavior of so many Christians, and gratuitously make the judgment that these people without faith cannot be saved. Jesus continues, "You must be born from above. The wind blows where it will, and although you hear its sound, you cannot tell where it is coming from or where it goes. This is how it is with those born of the Spirit." The Spirit gives his gift of faith to whomever He will.

The thought now comes to mind, was John present during this conversation? Or was he eavesdropping? That's possible. He had done it on other occasions, though I cannot imagine him staying up all night just listening. Later we will see him and James and Peter falling asleep in Gethsemane, when Jesus needed their prayers and support. He does record a few pieces of the conversation between this learned Pharisee and Jesus, but it is also clear that most of the dialogue is missing, and what is recorded does not do justice to Jesus. Jesus seems to be almost insulting Nicodemus for not understanding and refusing to see the truth. It is hard to imagine Jesus treating so harshly this old man who is reaching out to him for understanding. It is possible, as some think, that colleagues of Nicodemus knew of the man's intention to visit Jesus and wanted him to let Jesus know he was representing them, as well. If that is true, then Jesus' words do not seem so harsh, if he is referring to things Nicodemus told him about his fellow members of the Sanhedrin. Maybe also Nicodemus was not alone. Possibly others close to him, and who shared his curiosity, were also present. These words of Jesus then make sense: "I tell you in truth, we speak what we know, and witness to what we have seen, and yet you people reject our evidence. If you do not believe me when I speak about things in this world, how are you going to believe me when I speak to you about heavenly things?" It is too bad John did not record more of what was exchanged between the two, or even if there were other friends of Nicodemus present, so we could have a better picture of just what did take place and what was said. What *is* recorded would have taken at most two minutes, and yet it seems that the conversation went on the whole evening till daybreak, as Jesus makes mention of "the light that has come into the world, yet there are some who prefer the darkness," perhaps alluding to the coming of the dawn; he also mentions that the man who has come into the truth now comes out into the light. Was that a reference to the two men having finished their all-night discussion and now that the light was coming up, Nicodemus, having found the truth, was walking out into the light? Jesus' mind was always so playful and so beautifully subtle.

What is significant about the meeting of the two men is Jesus' explanation of baptism by water and the Spirit being essential for entrance into the kingdom of heaven, the kingdom of God. It is this spiritual rebirth that is essential as an expression of acceptance and commitment to the Son of Man, who has come down from heaven and who will be lifted up, and will be the source of eternal life to all who accept him. Jesus is saying in a subtle yet very real way that he is the one whom Yahweh has sent down from heaven. Jesus also gives Nicodemus something to think about for the future, saying to him, "The Son of Man must be lifted up as Moses lifted up the serpent in the desert, so that everyone who believes may have eternal life in him. All who are willing to see the hand of God in the signs that the Son of Man performs and accept him as sent by God will possess eternal life in the kingdom of heaven." By the end of the night, Nicodemus had found what he had come for, and we will see him in the future, speaking out boldly for Jesus, though for some strange reason nothing is recorded about him having said anything in Jesus' defense during the illegal trial before the high priest on the night before his crucifixion. Perhaps he was not invited.

The meeting of Jesus with Nicodemus seems to have been one of the reasons why Jesus made his presence in the Temple area so open—so Nicodemus, who as a ruler in Jerusalem would be aware of his presence, would come to see him. It reminds me of the time Jesus went way out of his way to meet another person whose life he wanted to touch, the woman at the well in Samaria. He went far off the beaten track to meet this foreign woman at Jacob's Well in Sychar. But that is another story that reveals so much of Jesus' mind, and the depths of his understanding of human spirituality. The two longest conversations of Jesus that have been recorded in the Gospels are the one with Nicodemus and the one with the Samaritan woman. They are both critical dialogues packed full with theological ideas that still have not been fully developed.

After the episode with Nicodemus, Jesus takes his apostles and wanders around the Judean countryside, meeting people, announcing to them the good news of the kingdom, and baptizing those willing to commit their lives to God by accepting Jesus as the One sent by Yahweh for their salvation. This is the only activity Jesus performed while in Judea. It is a very different kind of activity and shows how Jesus is beginning to involve the apostles in an active way in his ministry.

At the same time, John was baptizing at Aenon, near Salim, where there was plenty of water, and people were going there to be baptized. This was before John had been put in prison.

Now some of John's disciples had opened a discussion with a Judean about purification, so they went to John and said, "Rabbi, the man who was with you on the far side of the Jordan, the man to whom you bore witness, is baptizing now, and everyone in going to him." John replied, "A man can lay claim only to what is given him from heaven. You yourselves can bear me out; I said: I myself am not the Christ; I am the one who has been sent in front of him.

"The bride is only for the bridegroom; and yet the bridegroom's friend who stands there and listens, is glad when he hears the bridegroom's voice. This same joy I feel and now it is complete. He must grow greater and I must grow smaller. He who comes from above is above all others; he who is born of the earth is earthly himself and speaks in an earthly way. He who comes from heaven bears witness to the things he has seen and heard, even if his testimony is not accepted, though all who do accept his testimony are attesting the faithfulness of God, since he whom God has sent speaks God's own words. God gives him the Spirit without reserve. The Father loves the Son and has entrusted everything to him. Anyone who believes in him has eternal life, but anyone who refuses to believe in the Son will never see life; the anger of God stays on him." (Jn. 3:22–36)

John still had his loyal following. It is easy to see the jealousy of John's disciples. One could understand how they would have a difficult time abandoning their master, since many of their spiritual lives had been saved by John and his strong spiritual teaching. They needed the strength that came from their friendship with him. And although he encouraged them to go with Jesus, he could understand their loyalty. They were not totally convinced who this newcomer really was. John they knew. They knew they could trust John. He was strong and would stand by them. They were like family to him. It took a long time for them to feel comfortable with Jesus, and even after John's beheading, they went with sad and humbled hearts to find Jesus.

Word came back to Jesus that some Pharisees had found out that Jesus was not only preaching now, but baptizing, as well. That, however, was not totally true. Jesus had his apostles do the baptizing and was allowing them to play a greater role in his ministry. Rumor was also spreading among the Pharisees that Jesus was baptizing even more disciples than John. Why that would bother the Pharisees is difficult to understand. Were these Pharisees friends of John, at least secretly? Or were they concerned because they calculated that Jesus could be even more of a threat than John in his ability to raise vast numbers of loyal followers in Judea, just like he had been doing in Galilee? They had to wonder what would happen if all Jesus' followers from Galilee to Judea were gathered together in one show of strength.

Whatever their reason, Jesus saw them as threatening the progress of his work, so he left the countryside of Judea and decided to go back to Galilee, but by way of Samaria, which was unthinkable for religious Judeans and Galileans.

From Jerusalem along the road to Gibeon to Bethel to Ephraim to Sychar was not far at all, hardly thirty miles. It was pretty much a direct route, but through dry, rocky, robber-infested country. It was probably a three-day journey, or four if the weather was hot and humid. Then they might have rested more often. Sykar was Jesus' destination. The Gospels do not mention Jesus ever having been in this area previously, but he was on a definite mission this time. As the group approached Jacob's Well, just outside Sykar, they realized they were running out of provisions and needed to find a place to shop. Who was with Jesus at this point? His close disciples were definitely part of the group. It is possible that the others who had accompanied Jesus on the way down from Galilee for the Passover were no longer with him, having returned home to their families when the festivities were over. A few close friends, possibly including his mother, may have still been with him, though it is more probable that they had gone back to Galilee with the others as soon as the festivities were over, leaving Jesus to do whatever ministry he needed to do with the apostles.

As the group arrived at the well, Jesus sent the others on their way to take care of whatever business they needed to transact. Jesus, tired from the long journey, sat down on the well. Centuries before, the patriarch Jacob had dug this well, which was near the land he had given to his son Joseph. It was about noon when Jesus arrived. His timing was perfect. He had known that a woman would be coming to the well at that time. This is uncanny, and gives us another rare insight into the workings of Jesus' mind, and his ability to know beforehand what will be taking place in people's lives. It helps us to realize how he could be so understanding of people; it is because he could see deeply into everyone's heart and knew the intimate details of their lives, which we are about to witness in his conversation with this woman.

When the woman, a Samaritan from the town, came to the well, Jesus asked her if she would give him a drink. She got quite huffy. "Huh! You, a Jew, are asking me, a Samaritan and a woman, for a drink of water?"

Jesus replied to her, "If you only knew what God is offering, and who it is who is asking you for a drink, you would ask him to give you a drink, and he would have given you living water."

"You do not even have a bucket, sir, and the well is deep. How are you going to get this living water? Are you greater than our father Jacob, who gave us this well, and who drank from it himself, and also his sons and their cattle?"

Jesus was very patient with the woman. He had gone there for a reason and was moving very patiently, in spite of her cynical attitude. "Whoever drinks this water will become thirsty again. But, the one who drinks the water that I will give will never grow thirsty again. The water that I give will become a wellspring within him, flowing into eternal life."

"Sir, give me this water so that I don't have to keep coming out here." Was she serious or was she just being sarcastic? She knew he had nothing to draw water with. How could he give her anything? She probably said it with her tongue in her cheek, testing him, in case he should be serious.

Jesus decided to end the conversation and get down to business.

"Woman, I would like to talk to your husband. Get him and bring him here."

"I don't have a husband," she replies.

"I know. You have been married five times, and the one you are living with now is not your husband. You have spoken truthfully."

"Sir, I can see you are a prophet. Our fathers worshipped on this mountain, while you people say that it is in Jerusalem where we ought to worship."

Her tone suddenly changed. Putting aside her attitude, she nervously thought of something serious to say to this stranger, whom she now realized she had treated rudely. Her voice offered a note of apology as she respectfully asked Jesus a question that had been on her people's conscience ever since they broke with the religion Yahweh had established.

"Believe me, woman, the time is coming when you will worship the Father neither on this mountain, nor in Jerusalem. You worship what you do not know. We worship what we do know, for salvation comes from the Jews. But, the time will come, and in fact it has already come, when true worshipers will worship the Father in spirit and in truth, in your hearts and in the way you live your lives. That is the kind of worship the Father wants. God is spirit and those who worship must worship in spirit and in truth."

"I know that when the Messiah comes, and he is coming, he will tell us everything."

Jesus then responded to her, "I who am speaking to you am he."

The woman immediately left her bucket on the well and ran back to the village. (Jn. 4:4–28)

At that point the disciples came back and were surprised at seeing Jesus talking to a woman, and the two of them alone. It was considered very improper for Jewish men to speak to a strange woman, especially in public. But, they did not dare to ask him about it. It is interesting that John hints that they were thinking about asking him, but thought better of it and kept quiet. They apparently had picked up lunch while they were away, and offered some to Jesus, and were again surprised when he turned them down. They had been traveling a long distance and thought

Jesus would be hungry like themselves. The long response of Jesus shows a very childlike enthusiasm over a very challenging and successful mission to the ordinarily hostile Samaritan people, since Jews and Samaritans had had bad feelings for centuries. While they were talking in this vein a large crowd of Samaritan townsfolk were coming along the road toward the well. When Jesus saw them, his heart filled with joy that these heretofore hostile people were coming out to meet him and welcome him. They were not coming for healings, but to hear his message. He was so happy that his little mission there was turning out so well. He compared the large crowd to a field of ripe grain waiting to be harvested. He had planted the seed. Some day, others would have to come and reap the harvest. But who? He told his disciples to pray to the Father to send workers to continue the work of harvesting these souls. Again, Jesus seems to have been referring to the wheat in the fields waiting to be harvested. All it needs is the workers.

The apostles were mystified. They were in hostile territory. They had long ago learned, perhaps from personal experience, to expect nothing good from these people. Possibly fearful of this crowd closing in on them, they did not have the slightest idea what Jesus was talking about. None of what he was saying made any sense to them. It was one of those occasions when even those closest to Jesus had a hard time understanding him, and wondered if something had happened to him. They certainly could not fathom his intense enthusiasm at this particular time for the mission his heavenly Father had entrusted to him. They had no idea what had transpired between him and the woman who left the well in a hurry and ran back to the town, forgetting even to take her bucket. Nor did they dare to question him about what had happened.

However, when the townsfolk arrived at the well and were friendly to Jesus, the apostles could only conclude that the woman must have had a profound experience of some kind that had prompted all her neighbors to come out to meet this Jewish holy man and see for themselves what he was like.

What was interesting in Jesus' conversation with the woman was his revelation of his identity to her. That is unique. In going through the Gospels, that is the only time Jesus revealed so precisely to anyone that he was the Messiah. He seconded what Simon said when he blurted out under divine prompting, "You are the Christ, the Son of the Living God." And Jesus remarked that Simon's revelation came from the Father in heaven. Why would he single out this woman for such a stunning revelation? Who was *she*? There is something very mysterious about this meeting and why Jesus went out of his way to meet this woman. She certainly was not the epitome of sanctity or a model of virtue, that he should single her out for something special. He had such an uncompromising attitude toward the sanctity of the marriage bond, and now went out of his way to meet a person who had violated that sacred ideal not once, but five times. What was the lesson or the message he was trying to teach? Could it be that even though she had fallen from the ideal that Jesus preached, he understood her real-life situation and saw not just her failure to observe what was expected, but also an inner goodness that prompted him to see in her what he saw in the publican in the Temple: a humble, repentant attitude toward God that justified her in his eyes, and inspired him to pick her to be the missionary to that Samaritan village. Perhaps we could adopt that same Good Shepherd attitude toward people whose marriage situation we do not approve of. Jesus could preach the highest of ideals and when he came across a person who fell far short of those ideals, he showed an exquisite compassion. If we showed that kind of understanding we might not have forty percent of our people being refused the Eucharist.

Jesus once made the remark, "You judge by what you see on the surface of people's lives. I judge by what I see in their hearts." That is the key to understanding how Jesus saw people—not the surface of their lives, but what they were like inside. Even though this woman broke the sacred law of the indissolubility of marriage, he did not judge her just on that. He obviously saw something good about the person deep down inside. Maybe it was not her fault that she'd had five husbands. Maybe it was her fault. Jesus may not have approved of her five marriages, but he did *recognize* that she had been married five times, and commented that the person she was living with presently was not her husband.

It seems Jesus picked this woman to announce the coming of the Messiah into her village to teach us a lesson. Imagine asking a person like that to be a Eucharistic minister, or a greeter, or a reader in church. People would be horrified. Then you think, "What would Jesus do?" That is what Jesus meant when he called himself the Good Shepherd. The legalistic

Pharisees ostracized people when they broke the laws. They looked upon them as sinners. We only too easily fall into the same trap and consider as sinners people who do not measure up and treat them accordingly. Jesus looked beneath the surface of this woman's life and saw a life full of goodness and caring for others; that was always the key. So, he chose her, a nice person in his eyes, to be the missionary announcing the good news to that village. And she was thrilled.

What did she do next? Without even thinking, she left her bucket on the well, left immediately, ran down through the village announcing to everyone she met just what had happened. Could this possibly be the Messiah? She did not tell them, "Come, meet the Messiah." She knew they would not believe the likes of her. They would probably have laughed at her. Word soon spread through the whole town. They went out to meet Jesus, were impressed, and invited him to stay in their town. He stayed there for two days, then had to continue on his journey back home. While he was there, many of the Samaritans came to believe in him and were converted. The woman, however, was given no credit. Although they accepted what she had told them, they had the nerve to tell her, "We believe because we have seen with our own eyes, not because the likes of you told us." (Jn. 4:4–42)

There are a lot of lessons in this story, lessons that Jesus clearly wanted to teach. This woman with her irregular and unacceptable lifestyle was clearly an outcast, and was not accepted by the women who went out in the cool early morning to draw water. She had to go out at the worst time of the day, high noon, when the sun was the hottest, to avoid the mean and contemptuous comments from her neighbors. Jesus knew how she was being treated and the shame she endured, but still he could see her as a good person, so he chose her. People in ministry often feel unworthy of the call they received. Did God make a mistake? Why did He pick me? Doesn't He know what I am really like? I don't even like myself. No, God does not judge us according to the mistakes we make, or by our failings. Even our sense of unworthiness is a plus, because it will be important when we serve others. He knows we limp badly, even the best of us. But if He sees in our hearts sensitivity to the loneliness and the pain in other people's lives, which is what *is* important to Him, He then overlooks the rest, like He did every day with the apostles, who were so frightfully dense and had so many failings. He still picked them to be apostles. We see it in the story of the prostitute who comes barging into the dining room of Simon, the chief Pharisee in Capernaum. We see it in the way He treats Peter after Peter commits the horrible sin of denying even knowing Jesus, right after he made his First Communion at the Last Supper.

I think we have missed so much of what Jesus is really like by just skimming across the surface of his life and not carefully contemplating what he meant when he referred to himself as the Good Shepherd. When we understand what he meant by that, we have the key to understanding how he felt and how he judged sinful people, and how he wants us to judge people. The beautiful message here is the compassion of the Good Shepherd, so different from the righteousness of the religious officials, so prone to punishing violators of the Law rather than drawing them by love into a more observant attitude toward the Law. Jesus could preach the highest of ideals, and then when he found someone who fell far short of those ideals, he could still treat that person with compassion. That was what made him so different from the Pharisees. They rejected sinners. Jesus went out to embrace those whom the Pharises excommunicated as sinners. We ourselves have to be careful not to fall into that same practice and tell people whom we judge to be sinners that they are not worthy of Jesus' embrace. We have no right to forbid them to welcome Jesus into their hearts, often at times when they need his love in Communion more than ever. How can we judge the state of their souls? If the Good Shepherd decided to go out and embrace sinners and lost souls, who are we to say they are unworthy? I would never want that on my conscience.

20

JESUS' QUICK RETURN TO GALILEE

All during these times while Jesus was traveling with the apostles, he had been instructing them and teaching them many things he did not share with the general public. It had been almost a year now that they had been traveling with him from village to village throughout Galilee, and again on his way to Jerusalem, stopping off in villages along the way, preaching repentance for their sins and announcing the arrival of the kingdom of God. Having celebrated with the apostles the recent Passover in Jerusalem and evangelized in Judea, and in Samaria, and now returned home to Galilee, they took some time to rest before the crowds realized they were back in the neighborhood.

While it is hard to follow Jesus' itinerary in its original order, there are certain events that seemed to have been part of a particular chain of activities and connected in some way. We try our best to order these events in a way that makes some sense. After the long strenuous trip to Jerusalem and then back home to Galilee, we have to assume Jesus did not start on the very next day preaching all over the neighborhood again, though John does say that after their two-day stay in the village near Jacob's Well, he returned to Galilee, where the Galileans received him well, because they had seen all that he had done in Jerusalem, during the festival which they also had attended. It makes good sense that he and the apostles had to rest up for a few days. Did they come quietly into the town at night so as not to be noticed, so they could hide? Maybe they camped in a quiet place along the coast of the Sea of Galilee, or in a secluded place on the banks of the Jordan. Or maybe they did go back to Capernaum and slip into town in the dark of night and quietly return to their homes to rest, with Jesus staying at Simon's house.

We do see them after a short time taking up their busy schedule again. John mentions that Jesus went to Cana again. A court official, hearing of Jesus' whereabouts, went out to meet him and ask him to come and cure his son, who was gravely ill, indeed, at the point of death, at Capernaum. The man apparently did not believe in Jesus but knew he had the power to heal. Jesus then commented, "You people do not believe what I have to teach unless I work miracles for you."

"Sir, come down before my son dies."

"Go home. Your son will live."

The man believed what Jesus had said and went on his way. While he was still on his journey, his servants met him with the news that the boy was alive. He asked them when it was that the boy began to recover.

"The fever left him yesterday at the seventh hour."

The father realized it was at that exact time that Jesus had said, "Your son will live," and he and his household believed. (Jn. 4:43–54)

It is not easy to tell just when the following activities took place, whether at this point or when they were home previously. They seem to fit logically into the present context, so we will place them in the order that follows.

Assuming that Jesus and the apostles rested up after their long trek, during which Jesus had been training the apostles on how to conduct themselves when preaching the good news of the kingdom, it would seem that this was a good time to start them out on their own. So, after giving them authority and power over demons, and to cure diseases, he sent them out on their first missionary journey to preach the good news and heal the sick. All Saint Luke writes about that journey was that they went about from village to village preaching the Gospel and working cures everywhere. He does not say where they went, nor does he give any details as to what happened along the way. (Mt. 9:35–38; 10:1, 10:5–16)

Word apparently did get back to Herod Antipas, however, that these things were going on and that Jesus' work was expanding, and it made him concerned and curious. But he did not want to make a second mistake and do something precipitously, like he'd done with John the Baptizer, which still troubled him deeply. So, he allowed Jesus and his disciples to move freely throughout his tetrarchy.

While the Gospels do not say how long the apostles were away on their missionary journey, Luke writes that they returned and reported to Jesus all that they had done. They must have been quite excited about their experiences, because Jesus decided to take them with him to a quiet out-of-the-way place so they could have some peace and quiet to share with him all that had happened. The out-of-the-way place was on the quiet outskirts of Bethsaida, which was around the northern tip of the Sea of Galilee and across the river from Galilee. This was in the land of Herod Philip, Herod Antipas' brother. Jesus thought it would be a nice place to rest and have some quiet time with the apostles. It was, indeed, for a short time, as the people soon got word that he had escaped and withdrawn to that area. In no time the crowd began to gather. It must have been frustrating for Jesus as well as for the apostles. Was there no place they could go to have some peace and quiet? Hopefully, the apostles did have enough time to share with Jesus what had taken place on their first solo mission. Even though the Gospel writers did not spell out the details of what happened on the journey, they do say that the apostles preached the Gospel and healed many people.

I wonder how careful the apostles were in following Jesus' detailed instructions, especially about taking nothing with them, not even money. They did have a hard time believing things Jesus told them, and I think this mission was for them a real test of their obedience to Jesus' instructions as well as to their faith in him.

I always had a difficult time accepting Jesus' instructions to the apostles as sensible until my life changed after I had to retire for health reasons. I had written *Joshua* and published it myself. I knew I had to write a book about Jesus before I died, and I was haunted by my conscience until I finally did, though when I was reaching the end of the manuscript, I began to get nervous and subconsciously found myself writing more and more slowly, thinking that when I finished I was finishing my life's work and I would then die. But that was not to be. The published book became my mission, my life's work.

One of the first calls for me to speak came from Belgium, from a man by the name of Michael Devlin, an international tax lawyer for Levi-Strauss, the jeans company. Michael was living in Belgium and had had a dream in which he saw a dark red book with Hebrew-looking lettering that he could not make out. A voice told him to read that book. The next morning the dream was still vivid, but it was only a dream, so he forgot all about it. Shortly afterward, he was sent to Florida on business. One day he visited a bookstore to look for something to read. His eyes immediately alighted on a reddish-colored book standing by itself. It was the same book he had seen in the dream, with the same kind of lettering for the title. It was *Joshua.* An inner voice told him, "That's the book. Read it!"

He bought the book and read it that night, then ordered a whole case and had them shipped back to Belgium for the parish community he belonged to. The whole parish read it. The man then tracked me down and asked if I would come to Belgium to speak to their parish. It was my first missionary journey, though I did not look at it in that light at the time.

Their priest called me and was concerned about what I would charge.

I told him I don't charge to talk about Jesus; he then invited me to come to Belgium and speak to his people. It was a time in my life when I had nothing. I didn't realize it then, but I went to Belgium with nothing. I had no money, no worthwhile clothes, as I had no money to buy nice clothes. What I wore didn't match.

When I arrived in Belgium, the priest told me that it was a bad time, as people in his parish were very busy at that time of the year. Ambassadors and important people from NATO were part of the parish, and members of the European Parliament, as well as people from various international corporations. I felt out of place, as I had always associated with people like the people in *Joshua,* with whom I always felt more comfortable. The priest told me not to feel bad if only fifteen or twenty people showed up. I wished he had told me that before he invited me to come, as I was scheduled to speak for five consecutive nights, each night going deeper into Jesus' personality and teachings.

The first night was rather discouraging, as there were only 19 people there five minutes before the talk was to begin. By the time I was ready to start, there were 250, and the same number each of the following nights. They had canceled or postponed whatever duties they had scheduled for that week. One person who came every night was the military officer in charge of the computers for the NATO maneuvers that were to take place that week. I never found out what happened to the scheduled maneuvers.

That was my first introduction to a real mission of preaching the Gospel. Without intending to, or even realizing it at the time, I was following the detailed instructions of Jesus to the apostles when he sent them out on their first mission. I took nothing. I had nothing. I was treated graciously by the parishioners, who showed me various sites in Waterloo, and in nearby monasteries and convents, which were all but empty. I had the sad feeling that people did not walk away from the Church because they'd lost faith in Jesus. I had the feeling that Jesus was never preached to them, and they were walking away from a Church that to them was an institution that was not feeding the people, while the people hungered for intimacy with God. They hungered for someone to come and make Jesus real for them so the Holy Spirit could rekindle in their hearts the fire of their faith.

Shortly after that I met Admiral Hamm, who was head of the United States liaison to NATO. He told me he had put *Joshua* on the list of recommended books for the U.S. Navy. It was a great learning experience for me to see Jesus' message spreading in such a remarkable way with hardly any help from me.

I came back home with my own faith reinforced, a realization that Jesus' instructions to the apostles were realistic and sensible, but realistic and workable only within the spiritual environment of Jesus' thinking, his kind of reality. Within that environment his instructions worked. I needed no money nor a lot of baggage to go four thousand miles away and preach the good news of Jesus' kingdom and make Jesus real to people who hungered for him. I came back no richer materially, and I had the comfort of knowing that I did not charge people to drink of the life-giving waters of Jesus' wellspring.

But, as time went on, God took care of me in ways I could never have imagined. My faith was also rekindled in the mystery of Jesus' presence in the world wherever his Word is preached. He becomes in some mystical way present to the people listening. I could see hearts on fire when the beauty and mystery of his life was preached. It made no difference who the people were. I was to see it later when I spoke to well-educated Hindus. They hungered to hear more about Jesus. It is different from the effect preachers have when they preach Scripture by quoting and analyzing Scripture texts. There is something very mysterious about how Jesus seems to become almost physically present when someone talks about him in a way that makes him real. Preaching Jesus as a living person is like a sacrament, which accomplishes and makes happen what it signifies. I was beginning to learn that this is what is needed in the Church: for clergy to speak about Jesus and make Jesus real for the people. I think if this was done in Europe it would rekindle the fire of Christianity that spread throughout those countries when Jesus was first preached there eighteen hundred years ago. Preaching doctrines leaves people cold. The apostles did not teach doctrines; they brought Jesus to life in the people's hearts. Jesus, the Word of God, was the message. The doctrines were absorbed as people learned about Jesus in depth, and in the messages that Jesus shared in his own preaching. As necessary as it is for us to understand the doctrines about Jesus and what he taught, doctrines are ineffective as an evangelizing tool. People crave intimacy with God and a deeper spirituality. They crave to meet a real Jesus. When we bring them Jesus, they respond. And as their attachment to Jesus grows, we share with them all the things that Jesus taught, because then they hunger to learn more about him.

21

THE DEATH OF JOHN THE BAPTIZER

John was an uncompromising prophet with a passion for God's truth and for his mission to prepare the people for the coming of God's Anointed. He delivered that message loudly and clearly. "Confess your sins and repent! Prepare your hearts for the coming of the Lord's Anointed." There was no mincing of words. No one who listened to him could fail to understand his message. His integrity and innocence and simplicity and lack of self-righteous hypocrisy appealed even to the jaded, diseased soul of a pathetic king, who had been caught in the web of the scheming wife of his half-brother, Herod Philip. Defining the location of these minor kingdoms will be helpful in understanding the significance of the various events as they occur in the Gospels. Galilee was a section of Palestine just south of present-day Lebanon, in ancient days Phoenicia, where Tyre and Sidon were located. To the east of Galilee, across the Sea of Galilee, was the tetrarchy of Philip, which included Gaulanitis, Trachonitis, and Batanea. To the south of Galilee was Samaria, forbidden territory for Israelites loyal to the Temple worship in Jerusalem. Across the Jordan River from Samaria was Perea, which was part of Herod Antipas' tetrarchy. Samaria also separated Galilee from Judea, which lay south of Samaria.

Judea was governed by a Roman official, who at this time was a tough and cold-blooded administrator named Pontius Pilate. Galilee and Perea were ruled by one of Herod the Great's sons, Antipas, called by the people Herod Antipas. Herod the Great had another son who was still alive, the others having been killed by their father. This son's name was Herod, whom the people called Philip, Antipas' half-brother. Philip, although himself a tetrarch, had little standing in the people's eyes and even less political influence. He had married a woman named Herodias, a granddaughter of Herod the Great by one of his wives named Miriamne. On the occasion of a visit to his half-brother, Philip's wife Herodias became infatuated with her much younger brother-in-law, Antipas, and traveled with him back to his palace. In time they married, causing outrage among the populace by this brazen adultery. It was an open insult to the religious population, and put John the Baptizer in the predicament of having to speak out against such a flagrant violation of morality. Had Herod's offense been of lesser magnitude, John could have spoken to Herod privately, since Herod had a certain respect for John and liked to listen to him speak. But the situation was so flagrant, and John had so become the moral spokesman for Yahweh, he had to speak out publicly against this crime, as did the prophets of old. And speak out he did, loudly and without mincing words. What he said cut Herodias to the heart. She vowed never to forgive him for the insult and plotted for the time and the day when she could demand his imprisonment and finally his execution.

Caving in to Herodias' continuous nagging, Herod Antipas had John arrested and confined for almost a year in the prison at Machaerus, one of Herod's heavily fortified mountaintop palaces, on the eastern shore of the Jordan River. This place was at the northeastern point of the Dead Sea, and a great distance from his kingdom of Galilee. Machaerus was on the same side of the Jordan as Perea, the other part of Herod's kingdom, which was north of the Nabatean kingdom, which lay spread out beneath Herod's mountaintop perch. The two kings were at odds over an old and considerably large debt Herod owed to the king of Nabatea. It was to Herod's advantage that his scouts could keep an eye on any possible troop movements from the south.

Having put John in prison to satisfy Herodias, Herod felt secure that he had settled the issue with her. While spending part of the year at the mountaintop fortress, he enjoyed holding long conversations with John, whom he secretly revered, which made Herodias all the more uneasy, fearful that John would talk the king into dismissing her and sending her back to her husband. This stressed her out to the point where she would feel comfortable only if the prophet was eliminated completely.

That chance came on the occasion of Herod's birthday banquet, to which all the officials and important people in the region were invited. It must have been a real wild party, with wine flowing freely and any moral restraints long abandoned soon after the party was in full swing. Herodias now saw her chance, knowing that Herod was drunk and devoid of any sense of reason. She sent her voluptuous adolescent daughter into the banquet hall to perform one of her more salacious dances. The dance turned out to be a stunning success. Proud of this successful show, Herod called the girl over and told her to ask for whatever she wished and vowed he would give it to her, even though it be half his kingdom. She immediately went to talk to her mother, who told her to ask for the head of John the Baptizer on a platter. When the girl went back and told Herod, he was deeply grieved, but not wanting to insult his guests, who had heard his vow to the girl, he sent an executioner down to the prison. A short time later, the man came back with the head of the prophet on a platter, which the daughter dutifully brought to her mother. It is hard to imagine that Herod's guests were pleased that he kept his oath when it meant serving a severed bloody head on the king's table while everyone was eating supper. (Mk. 6:17–29)

As difficult as it may be to give Herod credit for any kind of moral decency, he did grieve over the death of his unlikely friend for a long time afterward. This explains why he was so tolerant of Jesus' great success in his ministry of fulfilling John's prophecies, and preaching the kingdom of God the length and breadth of his kingdom, even allowing important people in his court to become devoted followers of Jesus.

Herod did allow John's disciples to come and carry away the body of their beloved prophet and provide a decent burial for the holy man who had had such a profound effect on the lives of so many. According to Saint Jerome, John's followers buried him in Sebastiyeh, ancient Samaria. Many years later, a church was built on the site, and what is left of the building survived into modern times.

When Jesus was informed of John's death, it affected him deeply. They were more than just cousins. John's whole life had been spent in total dedication to Jesus and his sacred ministry. They were partners of the best and most intimate kind, bonded by no less than Holy Spirit himself, who coordinated each of their ministries as the Father was establishing his kingdom on earth.

At the time of John's death, Jesus was in Galilee. Herod had been staying at Machaerus, his fortified mountaintop castle, over a hundred miles away, where he'd had John beheaded. Jesus still felt comfortable in Galilee, though shortly after John's death, he quietly moved over to the neighboring territory of Gaulanitis, which was outside Herod Antipas' jurisdiction and in the territory of Herod Philip. It gave him the time and the privacy to grieve the death of his devoted friend, and the last of the prophets. The quiet time also provided the rare chance for Jesus to teach the apostles, which was impossible in busier places.

Jesus had been working in the area of Capernaum, which was important for him. It gave him the opportunity to speak to a wide variety of people, not all of whom were Israelites. In this way Jesus was preparing these Gentile peoples for the mission of the apostles later on. This explains why so many of the Gentiles from the area were so easily converted after Jesus' Ascension. They were already familiar with Jesus' teachings and the harvest was ripe for the apostles to reap what the Master had sown.

Capernaum had become too busy. It was time for Jesus to find a place where he could meet new people and have time to teach the apostles, a place where they could relax and bond with one another, a place quiet enough where Jesus could explain in more depth what he was teaching the people, the underlying reasons for his teachings. The area around the northern edge of the Sea of Galilee was ideal. It was not far from Capernaum, and in the tetrarchy of Philip, Herod's brother. A village nearby had been built up into a city and beautified by Philip and given the name Bethsaida Julias, undoubtedly in honor of the emperor. It was one of the most beautiful areas in all of Palestine.

No sooner had Jesus and his little band arrived by boat at their quiet retreat, than people were already arriving by boat to join them, having seen where Jesus was headed. Others were coming along the land route around the tip of the Sea of Galilee. The hoped-for retreat was no more. As tired and frustrated as Jesus must have been, his thoughts were not on himself, but on the emptiness and insecurity of the people who followed him everywhere like infants clinging to their mothers. It was as if they could not bear for him to leave them even for the peace and quiet he needed. His heart went out to them, and the apostles heard him thinking out loud, "I feel so sorry for the people. They are like sheep without a shepherd."

It is so revealing of the tenderness of the heart of God, a phenomenon difficult to understand, that God could be so concerned for simple creatures He had made out of nothing, *nothing*. We have no real value, yet He feels our pain. He feels our insecurity and inadequacy. So, forgetting his own needs for the rest of the day, Jesus rose to the occasion and, as the crowds gathered around him on the hillside, he began to teach them all over again.

22

JESUS' MISSION BEYOND THE JORDAN

"Come apart into a quiet, deserted place and rest a little" is the way Jesus expressed his concern for the apostles' condition after their stressful mission. They needed a rest and a chance to unwind. How thoughtful! Jesus had been teaching and healing all day, and had to be tired himself, yet he was concerned about his helpers, these tough, earthy fishermen, and hardened laborers. They were used to their ordinary jobs. They enjoyed the daily contact with their customers, even the incessant haggling over the price of fish on a particular day. That was fun to them. But preaching: That was totally out of their line. Talking about the kingdom of God, and about things of the spirit, this was new to them and was not easy. Preaching, even for a seasoned preacher, can be stressful. Jesus knew his apostles must be tired and also must have many things to share with him. When it came to himself, Jesus never seemed to care. This beautiful God! Whoever heard of a God like this, so thoughtful of people's needs and feelings?

But no sooner had they arrived than people began to inundate the hillside. Some had spotted Jesus when he left and had a good idea where he was heading, so they alerted the others. As word spread so did the crowd that wanted to follow him. Soon there were over five thousand people milling around the incline, waiting for Jesus to signal them to be seated so he could begin speaking to them. When it came to preaching his message or healing someone, Jesus never said no, and this occasion was no different.

Today, however, the mentality is different. "You have an obligation to yourself, and to your health," we are told. "You cannot let others' demands control your life." I have never found that workable, and Jesus could not, either. How many times he tried to escape, but the people would not let him go! They craved what he had to give them. They could not get enough of him. For Jesus their needs came first. His own needs were rarely considered.

The little hill where Jesus stationed himself was not far from Bethsaida Julias, a beautiful city that Herod Philip had built to honor the emperor. It was also the area where Jesus' disciple Philip came from. As the people began to settle down, Jesus climbed to a spot above his audience, an area flat enough for him to speak out to the crowd. The crowd was spreading out on a relatively level area around him, where they could be close enough to hear him speak, and where he could walk comfortably through their midst and talk to small groups about their individual personal concerns. Jesus always made his gatherings intimate, so individuals could receive personal attention, especially if they needed physical, spiritual, or emotional healing. Each individual felt bonded with Jesus because they sensed he knew them; this was something that only a person like Jesus could handle, since he could see into each one's heart, and could feel their pain.

Jesus spoke to the people for quite a while, then wandered through the crowd talking to small groups and individuals, conversing with them, blessing the children, comforting the desolate and troubled, healing the sick, and calming those with emotional and mental problems. Time passed quickly, and the apostles reminded Jesus that it was getting late, and the sun would soon be setting, and all the people would be stuck there in the dark, with nothing to eat and no place to sleep.

Jesus told them to feed the people. They were mystified. "Where are we going to get food away out here in the desert? And besides, we don't have enough money to buy food to feed them all." Jesus said this to test them, because he already knew what he was going to do. So he told them to direct the people to break into groups of fifty and a hundred and spread out on the grass. How picturesque that must have been with everyone wearing brightly colored robes! The scene reminded the Gospel writers of a vast flower garden. Then Jesus asked if anyone had any food, and they found a boy with a few loaves and some fish. They brought the little basket to Jesus. He blessed it, gave thanks to his Father, and told the apostles to distribute it among the thousands of people. The apostles looked at him with disbelief. Distribute it? What—a few loaves and a few fish? But, keeping their thoughts to themselves, they did as they were told and, to their shock, found that the basket did not empty. They kept putting what they had into a number of other baskets that the people had with them, and in a short time fed the whole multitude, to everyone's shock. They kept eating, and as much as they wanted. Even then there were full baskets left over, which Jesus instructed the apostles to gather together so it would not be wasted.

Jesus certainly did not do this to awe people with his power. In fact, he was shocked when he saw their reaction. Saint John writes very bluntly that he "fled" from the crowd up into the hills to escape, for they wanted to take him by force and make him king. In the chaos, he quickly ordered the apostles to get in the boats and leave immediately, which they eventually, and reluctantly, did. The whole scene is something Jesus certainly did not want to happen. He had tried so hard to avoid situations like this, knowing it would be looked upon as a move against the king. In situations like this you can see that Jesus' concern for the people overrode his realization that things could get out of hand and cause trouble with the authorities. He did it even though it seemed to be against his better judgment. The people had not eaten in hours and had come a long distance. There were elderly and children in the huge crowd. Where would they sleep? Where would they take care of their necessities in this out-of-the-way place? People were always afraid of snakes in those rocky hill areas. The huge crowd had to return to their homes, and they had to have something to eat before they left for the long journey. Jesus solved the problem in the shrewdest way he could. He fed them, and, as at Nazareth when the mob wanted to toss him down the hillside, he escaped from their midst. So now, in the confusion, he fled. The crowd could not find him to make him king. He had adroitly avoided a potentially tragic situation. (Mk. 6:30–34; Mt. 14:13–21; Lk. 9:10–17; Jn. 6:1–13)

This was not the only time a situation like this came up. It seems there may have been another similar situation where it was necessary for Jesus to feed a large crowd who had wandered far from home to listen to his wisdom and to be healed of their ills. That seems to have taken place much later on. On this occasion, however, the story did not end there. The apostles had already spent considerable time sailing across the sea and had made little headway because of adverse wind currents, that slowed down their progress. So, after escaping the crowd, and spending private time with his Father, Jesus decided to catch up with the apostles and leave the area. What follows is fascinating. The Gospel says that the apostles had traveled a mere fraction of the distance toward Capernaum, because of the adverse current and the strong wind. Jesus could have just appeared on the opposite shore and waited for them to arrive, then gone home with them. But he decided not to do that. What follows seems to indicate Jesus' sense of humor. It was close to Passover, which is early spring, the time of almost a full moon. It was bright on the surface of the water. So, Jesus decided to place himself a few yards from the boat, walking on the water toward the boat. The apostles were naturally scared beyond belief, thinking they were seeing a ghost. Jesus called out to them, "Be glad. It is I. Don't be so frightened."

"If it is you, Lord, tell me to come out to you!"

"Come on!" the figure answered. And Peter stepped out of the boat and began to walk toward Jesus. When he realized he was walking on the water, he lost his nerve and immediately began to sink. "Lord, save me! I am drowning."

"Simon, you of little faith! Why did you doubt?" Jesus responded, as if to say, "As long as you believed, you were doing what you thought was impossible. When your faith faltered, you began to sink."

Then Jesus reached out and held Peter's hand, helping him back into the boat. Then he climbed in and straightaway they found themselves at shore, at a place called Gennesaret. That in itself was striking, as just a few minutes before they were hardly a third of the way, and still had almost five miles to go to reach the opposite side. (Mk. 6:48–52; Jn. 6:14–21)

We had not seen Jesus in this area of Galilee before. It is called the Plain of Gennesaret, and was one of the most beautiful sites in all of Palestine. It was in Jesus' day an unusually fertile piece of land, with fruit trees of every imaginable variety, producing fruit practically the whole year round. The weather was perfect for growing not just fruit but a wide variety of unusual nuts, as well as dates and figs.

As soon as Jesus and the apostles disembarked, a crowd was already gathering. Some were among those who had been with Jesus the night before. Others from the neighborhood were familiar with Jesus, though he had not been in their area before. The crowd kept growing larger, and Jesus recognized that most of them had been with him just a few hours before. They were here again, out of increased curiosity. What was he going to do now?

Jesus had always been willing to give the people the benefit of the doubt, hoping their curiosity would mature into a deeper understanding of his message and his mission, and hopefully a commitment. But he seems to have finally come to the realization that the people were more concerned about his providing distractions from the boredom of daily living than they were about their spiritual life. It bothered him that they could be so shallow. The apostles were probably right. They had known these people all their lives, and had little confidence in the depth of their commitment to anything but themselves. On this occasion Jesus decided to raise the level of their understanding of what he had to offer them, namely, an authentic escape from this monotonous and painful life through a life hereafter filled with unending happiness, and the promise of a more beautiful life here on earth, based, not on material things, but upon a more intimate relationship with God. This was much more awesome than what their forefather, Moses, had offered to their ancestors.

23

"IF YOU EAT THIS FOOD YOU WILL LIVE FOREVER"

I don't know how Jesus could do it. He had gone to the other side of the lake to have some peace and quiet time with the apostles. The crowd had followed him there. He felt sorry for them and fed them miraculously, then had to slip away because they wanted to take him by force and acclaim him king. He spent the night quietly in the hills after sending the apostles back to the opposite shore by themselves. Then after meeting the apostles in the middle of the lake, he mysteriously arrived at the Capernaum side with the apostles, and was immediately confronted with the same crowd he had just escaped from.

What is so impressive is that Jesus never showed the slightest trace of irritation with the people. And the apostles were always watching Jesus' change of mood. They noticed when he had tears in his eyes. They noticed when he seemed to feel sad. They noticed when he was angry. They noticed when he was tired. So, when they do not mention him becoming impatient or annoyed with the people tagging along with him wherever he went, it strongly suggests that he took it in stride. It shows how Jesus could rise above our humanness and manifest that part of himself that transcended our pettiness and manifested a divine compassion for the poor creatures who craved the love and warmth that radiated from him. These grown human beings, hardened by the meanness and injustice they'd suffered all their lives, were so desperate for the attention and healing love of this stranger. And that was what he was to them, just a stranger, a stranger who loved them without condition and cared for them when they were hurting and even when they were just hungry. It was as if he was, in some way, a part of their life, as if he belonged to them.

The people were surprised to see Jesus with the apostles. They'd noticed that the apostles had left in their boat without him. "Rabbi, when did you come here?"

In response he said to them, "I tell you in truth you are here today because yesterday I fed you. But, you should learn to hunger for the bread that lasts forever, which I will give you."

They then demanded a sign as his credentials from God that they should follow him and obey him. How strange, how superficial, how forgetful! Just a few hours before they had been so impressed that they'd wanted to declare him their Messiah King. Now they demand a sign that they should believe what he was telling them.

"Moses fed our ancestors the manna in the desert, as it is written, 'Bread from heaven he gave them to eat.' "

"The food that Moses gave you did not come down from heaven. The bread that comes down from heaven gives life to the world."

"Lord, give us this bread always."

It is important to remember that Jesus, in talking like this, knows that the people are aware of the approaching Festival of the Passover, the time for the celebration of the Feast of the Unleavened Bread, which was the official sacrificial meal of the Jewish Passover, when the Passover lamb was slaughtered and eaten, and also the unleavened bread.

"I am the bread of life, the true bread that has come down from heaven and gives life to the world. He who comes to me will never hunger, and he who believes in me will never thirst."

This they could not digest. "We know this man. We know his family. How can he say, 'I came down from heaven'?"

Jesus continued:

"Do not murmur among yourselves. Only those who listen to the Father can come to me. My Father will draw them to me, and I will raise them up on the last day. And it is written, 'And they shall all be taught by God.'

"I am the bread of life. Your fathers ate the manna in the desert and they died. This is the bread that comes down from heaven, so that if anyone eats of this bread he will not die. I am the living bread that has come down from heaven. If anyone eats this bread he will live forever; and the bread that I will give is my flesh for the life of the world."

"How can this man give us his flesh to eat?"

"Unless you eat the flesh of the Son of Man and drink his blood you cannot have life in you. He who eats my flesh and drinks my blood has life everlasting, and I will raise him up on the last day, for my flesh is real food and my blood is real drink. He who eats my flesh and drinks my blood lives in me and I in him. As the living Father has sent me, and as I live because of the Father, so he who eats me, he also shall live because of me."

This took place in the synagogue in Capernaum. The response was negative. "This is a hard saying. Who can accept it?" From that time on, many of his disciples left and never again followed him.

With sadness in his heart Jesus turned to the apostles and, worried even about their response, asked them, "Will you also leave me?" And

Peter immediately answered, "Lord, to whom will we go? You have the words of eternal life, and we have come to believe and to know that you are the Christ, the Son of God." It is Jesus they love, not what he can do for them. The crowds did not have that same attachment to Jesus. When he disappointed them, they thought nothing of abandoning him

It is so easy to see why Jesus loved Peter so much. As weak and impulsive as Peter was, Jesus could count on him. Peter would never abandon him, even though he could at times lose heart and say ridiculous things that he repented of.

Jesus, still concerned, answered, "Haven't I chosen you twelve, yet one of you has a devil?" He was obviously referring to Judas, whose faith had grown cold. The loyalty of Jesus is a strange phenomenon. Jesus saw great potential in Judas. He even put him in charge of what little money Jesus and the apostles had received as gifts from thoughtful followers. But there was a flaw in Judas' personality that turned out to be fatal. His loyalty seems to have been based on his faith in Jesus as the powerful Messiah who would be the one to free Israel from the oppressive Roman yoke. One of the Fathers of the Church commented that on the night before, when the people wanted to take Jesus by force and proclaim him king, Judas had been ready to furnish the crown. It seemed that when Jesus turned that down and then offered his flesh and blood as the pledge of eternal life, Judas finally realized that his kingdom was only in his mind, like some ancient Don Quixote fighting windmills. But Peter spoke not only for himself but for the rest of the group, that no matter what Jesus taught, and as difficult as it might be for them to understand, they believed in *him* and would be loyal to him. (Jn. 6:48–71)

When Jesus promised his flesh and blood as the food that gives eternal life, he was offering to the people a gift that in his thinking was the greatest gift he could offer them. They had followed him like lost sheep. He had given them more than adequate reason to believe not only in him as a person, but in whatever he should teach them. They had faith in the sensational things he did, and in his healing power. But faith in his message and his mission, and in the mystery behind the divine signs that were the Father's endorsement of his teachings, was lacking. He tried on this occasion not just to spark that faith, but to show them that if they were impressed with the manna that they *thought* came down from heaven, he would give them the real bread that *did* come down from heaven, and then in plain language they could not misunderstand, he told them that he was the real bread that came down from heaven, and that he would give them this bread as food for their souls. In their eating this bread they would be assured of eternal life, and in the eating of this bread they would become one with him in a most intimate way. In the way the Father had given life to him, so in eating this bread he would share his life with them. How beautiful, how intimate! They could not accept it. It sounded like cannibalism. After all his stunning miracles, they were too dense to realize the living presence of Yahweh in Jesus, and never saw past his humanity. In that void of supernatural light, all they understood was an irrational human, who had now gone too far. "This is a hard saying. Who can accept it?" was their response. And they walked with him no more.

It has always surprised me that Christians who believe in the literal interpretation of Scripture have a problem with that episode and those words of Jesus. Even though Jesus reiterated over and over, and in stronger language each time, that it really was his flesh and blood that he was offering, they cannot believe that that is what he meant, so they make it a symbol with no relevance to life. Yet Jesus said it was necessary for eternal life and for intimacy with himself. What Jesus did not say to the crowd was *how* he would give them his flesh and blood as the food of their souls. For this he demanded faith in him. The Eucharist will always be the mystery of faith, and the test of faith. It was the test that Judas failed.

It was at the Last Supper that Jesus finally showed what he meant. At the official sacrificial meal of the Old Testament, the Passover meal, in which Jesus and his family shared the Passover Lamb, Jesus inaugurated the official sacrificial meal of the New Testament in his blood, when he gave them the bread and wine and told them, "Take and eat; this is my body. Take and drink; this is the cup of my blood, the blood of the new and eternal covenant which will be shed for you for the forgiveness of sins." He was the true Lamb, the Lamb of God, who had come to wash away our sins in his blood, not the blood of an animal lamb, but in the blood of the Lamb of God. In giving his body in the form of bread and his blood in the form of wine, he gave them the new Passover Lamb, the Lamb of

God, as John the Baptizer called Jesus, to share for the forgiveness of sins. The whole early Christian Church taught by the apostles was unanimous in its acceptance of the Eucharist as the real and living presence of Jesus, the true Lamb of God. And that belief persisted until the fifteen century, and is still held by Catholics, Lutherans, Eastern Orthodox, and a few other Christian groups. In fact, for almost a hundred years in early Christianity, when the Christians came together they came together not for Bible reading, but for the Eucharist. And Christians risked their lives to bring the Eucharist to Christians in the Roman prisons waiting for their execution as martyrs.

In some mysterious way, Jesus created a whole new kind of presence in the Eucharist, different from his divine presence throughout the universe, different from physical presence, different from presence over the telephone or radio or television. It was a presence so intimate that it is impossible to define, a presence in which Jesus and our souls become bonded in a love that is beyond human comprehension, but a presence that makes Jesus available to us in an intimate way, as our strength in difficult times, our comfort in painful times, our light when all is dark, and our joy and peace at all times. It is a presence in which he fulfilled his promise not to leave us orphans. "Those who eat my flesh and drink my blood live in me and I in them" is the way Jesus described this presence.

24

JESUS WANDERS INTO PAGAN COUNTRY

The chronology of Jesus' whereabouts after the painful rejection of his gift of living bread from heaven is not clear. John's Gospel jumps from Passover to the Feast of Tents. That is more than a five-month gap. Mark's account has Jesus doing ministry for a while after his rejection by the people and his unhappy encounter with the scholars from Jerusalem, but then has him abruptly leaving Galilee and wandering up into the pa-

gan territory of Phoenicia. This as the next item on his itinerary seems to
make sense. What is clear is that Jesus was deeply discouraged from the
people's rejection of the gift of living bread. Reading the account, you can
feel his grief, which seems to have led to a serious depression. He had
spent so much time cultivating the faith of the Galileans, the people of
Capernaum, the people of Bethsaida, the people of Corazain, and other
peoples in the region. And they coldly rejected him. We will see him later
on lashing out against them in stern warning: "Woe to you, Capernaum!
Woe to you, Bethsaida! Woe to you, Corozain! If the miracles worked
in you had been worked in Sodom and Gomorrah, they would have long
since repented. And you, Capernaum, you think you will be lifted up to
the heavens. You will be cast into the depth of hell."

These were not vindictive threats. Jesus was not like that. They were
dire warnings from a heart that had given so much to those people, and
when he was offering them the most beautiful gift he could, the living
bread come down from heaven, the gift of himself as an intimate companion of their life, they coldly and cynically walked away from him forever. Jesus used strong language to make the people realize the chance
they had and thrown away. He had invested a major part of his ministry
preaching to those people, and not just preaching, but healing their sick,
and blind and deaf, and their lepers, even raising their dead back to life.
He had become a member of each of their families. He had been more
than a friend. He had been like a brother to them. To Jesus none of them
was a stranger. He had given of himself to the point where his relatives
thought he had gone beyond reason, even verbalizing that he was beside
himself, which was their way of saying he was losing his mind. He really
had given his all. I think it was at that point that Jesus was so depressed
that all these people who had meant so much to him could in just one moment so easily turn their backs on him. It was a frightful blow to his confidence that he could bring his people back into his Father's love. That they
could just coldly walk away from him was devastating because it showed
how shallow was their loyalty and their faith in him. What was so beautiful about Peter was that his loyalty and the loyalty of his comrades was
to *Jesus*, and not to what he could give them or do for them. Even though
they could not always understand what he was saying, they would believe
whatever he said because he had said it, and if he said it, it must be true.

That was real love. And that was why Jesus loved Peter so much. He could always *trust* his love, in spite of Peter's frightful weaknesses.

I am convinced it was right after this incident that Jesus with his loyal apostles left Israel and, after saying so often that his mission was to the children of Israel, he wandered off into pagan lands up north. It is strange and difficult to understand what the rationale was for this unusual departure from a lifestyle that until this point seemed so predictable. Perhaps he just needed to get away from it all and take a retreat with his friends. He did need a good stretch of quiet time to train them, which he knew was not an easy job.

The small group slowly worked its way north, stopping here and there to rest and take their meals. Judging from the narrative in the Gospels, Jesus went a considerable distance into Phoenicia, as far as Tyre and maybe even as far as Sidon, which would have been almost a hundred miles north and deep into pagan territory. There is nothing mentioned in the Gospels about Jesus preaching there or performing any ministry. Mark mentions that he went to a certain house intending to visit people there. That is interesting, as there are ancient stories among the Maronite Catholics living in Lebanon today that Mary and Jesus had visited there and spent time in that country, probably before Jesus began his ministry, probably at this particular time. Perhaps Mary had relatives there. Mark does not mention whose house it was, or who lived there, so it is left to our imagination. To this day there are still shrines in Lebanon dedicated to Mary and Jesus and commemorating their visit to that country. Mass offered in the Maronite rite is still celebrated in the language that Jesus spoke, Aramaic. The only other item Mark recounts is the unsettling scene with the Syro-Phoenician woman who pestered him to heal her daughter who was possessed by an evil spirit. The woman somehow recognized Jesus. We know his reputation had spread far and wide into the neighboring countries, and even pagans would make the journey to Galilee to meet this famous healer. When these foreigners returned home they had many stories to share about Jesus, so his reputation grew throughout those far-away places. So, somehow this woman recognized Jesus and knew that he could heal her daughter if he so chose. Jesus apparently just ignored her, but she was persistent, so persistent that she was getting on the apostles' nerves. But nothing could dissuade this woman who was so concerned about her daughter, and knew that this Jewish healer was the only one who could save her. So, she continued to nag him, which was annoying the apostles to the point where they could not take it any longer. Finally one of them remarked, "Lord, can't you give her what she wants so she will leave us alone?"

"My mission is to the lost sheep of the house of Israel," Jesus replied, looking at the woman.

The woman sensed Jesus might be softening, so she approached him and fell down at his feet. "Lord, help me," she pleaded.

"It is not right to take the food from the children's table and give it to the house dogs," Jesus told her.

But she was not offended. She knew that Jesus was not calling her a dog, but was referring to the attitude the Israelites had toward their pagan neighbors. "But, sir, even the house dogs eat the scraps that fall from the children's table."

Jesus was impressed, and you can easily picture him breaking into a friendly laugh. "Woman, you have great faith. Go on home! Your prayer is answered. Your daughter is already healed." The woman left and went home, and found the child in bed, and at peace. (Mk. 7:24–30)

Mark then has Jesus wandering around the territory of Tyre. He mentions nothing more about the house that Jesus intended to visit or perhaps spend an extended period of time. Traveling to Tyre from Gennesaret, a distance of approximately thirty miles, would have taken two or three days. The Gospels make no mention of how long Jesus rested in Tyre. It seems he was not in any particular hurry to do anything except rest and spend time discussing important matters with the apostles. After wandering in the area of Tyre, for an unspecified time, according to Mark, Jesus came back to Galilee by way of Sidon. This is interesting, as Sidon was not on the way back; it was roughly another thirty miles farther north, so it was a roundabout route home. There is no mention of how much time he spent in that area. Jesus certainly did not seem to be in a hurry. From Sidon the small band wandered east toward Lake Huleh, and spent time in the refreshing foothills of Mount Hermon, and in Trachonitis, and later, down in the area of the Decapolis, the Ten Cities, where again there were few Israelites.

These were centers of heavy Greek and Roman influence. Why

Jesus would spend time there is not easy to understand. In fact, during this whole journey, which seems more like an extended retreat, a time of prayer and serious reassessment, none of the Gospels mention Jesus doing any missionary work: no preaching, no healing, no visiting, nothing, but just wandering in areas where he was either unknown, or little known, in a region filled with pagan people. This is difficult to understand considering Jesus' constant focus on the mission given to him by his heavenly Father to bring the good news of salvation to the Israelites. The whole journey into Phoenicia and the foothills of the snowcapped Mount Hermon, and Gaulanitis, and Caesarea Philippi, had to take at least a month, probably longer. It haunts the imagination of anyone trying to comprehend Jesus, and his reasons for doing things, most of which are predictable. His whole public ministry had been so consistent, and much the same each day. He went from village to village preaching and healing all who were suffering in any way. When all of a sudden he leaves it all and just wanders up into this foreign land, it presents a mystery to the student of his life, especially as the Gospel writers are mysteriously silent as to what happened during that time. They say absolutely nothing. They seem almost secretive.

Maybe it was just a simple vacation. God knows, he needed one, especially after his recent crisis. Spending time in the area of Tyre and Sidon, along the beautiful seacoast, at remarkable architectural sites, and then days at the beautiful snowcapped mountains of eastern Phoenicia, near breathtaking Lake Huleh, suggests that it was a time for rest and restoration of spirit. The most logical explanation is that, away from the pressing crowds, it was the only time when he could teach the apostles and thoroughly train them for their difficult ministry ahead. Jesus could see on occasion from their unguarded comments that they were still seriously lacking in understanding of what he was trying to teach, and of the attitudes that were critical to their ministry. This extended retreat was the perfect time to fill them with his spirit and a thorough understanding of what he meant by salvation, and repentance and forgiveness of sin, and God's forgiving love, and the kingdom of God, and how it was to function when once they were sent out to bring that kingdom to the whole world.

But the vacation soon came to an abrupt end as he approached the eastern area of the Sea of Galilee. They were now in the area of the Decapolis. A crowd spotted Jesus and immediately brought to him a deaf and dumb man for him to heal. They asked Jesus to lay his hand on him. It seemed everyone knew that Jesus healed by touching a person, so, even in this out-of-the-way place, the person asked Jesus to lay his hand on the afflicted man. Jesus took him aside in private, at a distance from the crowd, and put his fingers into the man's ears, and touching his tongue with spittle, looked up to heaven, and sighed, and said, "Ephphratha," which means, "Be opened." And immediately the man's ears were opened, and his tongue was loosened and he began to speak clearly. Jesus then told them all to tell no one about what had taken place. But the people were so amazed at the stunning miracle that they could not help but tell everyone they met. It seems that this took place in an area where people had not previously witnessed Jesus' miracles, but just knew of his reputation, and some of them recognized him as he was passing through their town. It seems he still did not want the news to spread that the miracle worker, the Galilean healer, was in town. While willing to heal the poor fellow, he tried to make the event as private as possible, as he took the man away from the others and healed him quietly. It is hard to remember Jesus acting this way on any other occasions. They were still deep in pagan territory, though the presence of Israelites was considerably more noticeable as he was approaching the Sea of Galilee. (Mk. 7:31–37)

Leaving there, he continued on toward the Sea of Galilee, where he was met by a large crowd, including, no doubt, some of those who had walked away from him previously. Mark does not say where this crowd came from or in what place they met Jesus, but he says that as they gathered around him, he led them to a deserted place apart, and spent three days with them. As the new day began at sunset, the crowd was probably with him in the afternoon, which would have been considered one day, then the day which had begun at sunset, and late the following afternoon would have been the second day, and close to the beginning of the third day. So, it may have been to our way of thinking only a day and a half, like the three days of Jesus in the tomb before his resurrection, from late Friday afternoon to Sunday morning.

Jesus felt sorry for them because they had been with him all that time and had nothing to eat. So, he repeated what he had done with the last crowd that followed him to an out-of-the-way place. He multiplied a few loaves and fishes and had the apostles distribute them to the crowd of four thousand this time, then soon afterward dismissed the crowd and he and the apostles climbed into the boat and sailed over to the area of Dalmanutha, a town near Magdala, on the western side of the Sea of Galilee. (Mk. 8:1–10; Mt. 15:32–39)

No sooner had Jesus arrived on the shore, than a group of Pharisees heard of his coming and immediately went out to confront him. From their insistence it seems they were the same ones who had previously come up from Jerusalem and confronted him about his disciples not performing the prescribed ritual washings. Probably still smarting from his devastating indictment of their hypocrisy on that occasion, they were laying in wait for his return. They seemed more sure of themselves this time, and more arrogant. They probably had more support, maybe real Temple scholars, as well as some Sadducees. This confrontation seems to have been a quasi-official hearing, with the Sadducees present, which certainly did not intimidate Jesus. They immediately began their questioning by demanding a miracle or some other sign from heaven as proof that he had been authorized by Yahweh to do what he was doing. Mark records Jesus' reaction: "With a sigh that came right from his heart, he said, 'Why does this generation demand a sign? I tell you once and for all, a sign will not be given to this generation. It is an evil and faithless generation that demands a sign. I tell you, a sign will not be given other than the sign of Jonah.' " Then, just like in his previous confrontation with them, he immediately turned his back on them and got back into Peter's boat, as if to say, "Let's get out of here. I can't take any more of these people." So, they rowed away and left the team of bewildered clerics standing there with open mouths. They were not used to people turning their backs on them and treating them with such contempt.

One might ask, could Jesus not have been more diplomatic, since these people were in a position to destroy him? He knew they hated him. And after this confrontation, they surely would stop at nothing to kill him. Jesus' abruptness is understandable once you realize that these people hounded him, and had spies taking notes every time he spoke or healed. They had effectively ruined his ministry, poisoning people's minds against

him. It wasn't as if Jesus had not been gracious toward them on other occasions, hoping to penetrate their hard hearts. By now he knew they were
determined to obstruct his mission, so he was ruthless in his condemnation of their hypocrisy. Jesus knew full well that they were not sincerely
looking for light from on high in an honest attempt to understand him,
and possibly embrace his message. They were simply trying to start a
fight. Jesus knew it and was going to have no part of it.

As they were sailing along, the apostles remembered that they had
forgotten to bring more bread with them; they had only one loaf in the
boat. Seeing their annoyance and their concern over it, Jesus said to no
one in particular, "Keep your eyes open, and beware of the yeast of the
Pharisees and the yeast of Herod." He was still upset over the Pharisees'
pigheaded resistance to God's grace, but also, for some reason, he began
to show concern about Herod, who as yet had not shown any opposition
to his ministry. The apostles thought it was because they had no bread
that Jesus said what he said. Knowing what they were thinking, Jesus said
with obvious annoyance in his voice:

> "Why are you talking about having no bread? Do you still not under-
> stand? Are you so dense? Have you eyes that do not see, and ears that
> do not hear? Why are you concerned about bread? It was only yester-
> day that I multiplied the loaves and fed four thousand. And how many
> baskets did you have left over?"
>
> And the apostles sheepishly answered, "Seven."
>
> "And it was only a short time ago that we fed the five thousand. And
> how many baskets were left over?"
>
> Again they sheepishly answered, "Twelve."
>
> "And you're still worrying about bread?" he responded. (Mk.
> 8:14–21; Mt. 16:5–12)

This kind of treatment was unusual for Jesus. It is easy to see that
something was weighing heavily on his heart for him to be so agitated,
and talk so brusquely to these men who had given up everything for him
and loved him dearly. But, underneath his irritable remarks, the apostles
knew he was hinting that if they needed bread it would be readily available, no matter where they were. Did he favor them with another little

miracle, just for them? It seems so. What he said was clearly a hint that when they needed the bread it would be there. No doubt when they were having lunch later, they were pleasantly surprised to find they were not short of bread.

What was it that was troubling Jesus so grievously? It was not just the mean spirit of the Pharisees; it was also the inability of the people to understand him, and realize the crucial importance of his message, and what it meant for the salvation of their souls. This concern was also very personal. He had spent so much of himself on these people, only to be coldly rejected by them, because they failed to understand, and now he was expressing doubt even about the apostles themselves. He was wondering if they too were unable to understand what he was and who he was. He was beginning to wonder, "Are they also so dense that even they cannot understand what I am all about? And they are the ones to whom I am entrusting my mission when I leave."

You can feel the pain and the sadness and the doubt that were torturing Jesus. He was, more than at any other time, feeling a terrible aloneness. He had come to take upon himself the sins of us all, the burdens weighing down upon us. "Is this what it meant?" must have crossed his mind. All alone on this planet, far from the joy and security of his real home, with no one who had the capacity to understand what he was trying to say, to teach, and what he was offering to them, the divine gifts of a healing reconciliation with the Creator. They were not even aware they needed reconciliation or salvation. He loved these simple creatures with all his heart, a heart that beat with a divine fervor, a heart that could find no emotional equal who could return the love that he offered to all, especially his closest friends, a heart that was destined never to receive in return a love equal to his, a love now so badly needed. He was beginning to realize with a fearful anxiety that he was alone. The breadth and depth of his mind was so far beyond the reaches of human intelligence. Looking at the apostles, he could see their feelings of inadequacy. They had the look of an understanding puppy dog that could feel the master's pain, but was helpless to reach out to offer any meaningful comfort. They knew he was hurting, but what could they do? How do you comfort a God, or at least one who is so close to the Almighty that you dare not even try to reach out with a comforting gesture? Jesus could see all that in their timid, pathetic looks. His heart broke for them, too, because they were trying so hard to understand, but had no ability to see into his soul, which they would need to do if they were to be of any solace to him.

It was not long before they arrived at Bethsaida. Immediately the little band was spotted and some people were leading a blind man down to Jesus, begging him just to touch the man. Jesus took the blind man by the hand and led him outside the village. Putting spittle on his eyes and laying his hands on him, he asked if the man could see anything.

"I can see people, but they look like trees walking around."

Jesus then laid his hands on the man's eyes, and he could see clearly and everything was sharp and distinct. Jesus then told him not even to go into the village. (Mk. 8:22–26)

Jesus left the village immediately and went up to Caesarea Philippi. Again, this strange behavior! Jesus is escaping people again. Why this need to distance himself from the people? I am sure the apostles have no idea what is happening. Caesarea Philippi is a way up north, twenty miles distant from Bethsaida, again deep in pagan territory. Whatever is it that is troubling him? He clearly is having a very difficult time processing whatever it is, and needs a place where he can be alone. The presence of his friends, these simple fishermen, is his only earthly comfort, even though they can do nothing for him but just be there. Where is Jesus' Heavenly Father? Why has He withdrawn the comfort of His constant presence? What is He doing to His beloved Son? How can He be so far away when His Son is suffering so intensely? I am sure these are thoughts that haunted him. He was to be like us in all things. It is so much a part of our lives as humans to wonder where God is when we need Him. Seeing Jesus so disconsolate strongly indicates that his Father has distanced Himself from him for some reason and the pain is difficult for him to endure.

Part of our burden of being human is that we experience alienation from God, especially when we are trying to reach out to Him when we are deeply troubled. This feeling of alienation is particularly painful when we are advancing in contemplative prayer, and to strengthen our faith, God withdraws the comfort of His presence and we are left, seemingly, alone. We then go through the terrible dark night of the senses and later the even more terrifying dark night of the soul. That is part of being human. If Jesus came, as Isaiah prophesied, to carry our burdens, then what Jesus was suffering at that time was the dreadful feeling of alienation from his Father, something he had never known before, and the pain was unbearable, especially because his Father was really all he had to give him strength, and comfort. As he had said, "I receive life from my Father." Everything else was more like an illusion. His Father *was* reality.

The question might arise that Jesus *is* God, and how could he be confused and have doubts. That question we cannot answer, but other occasions show clearly that he could undergo these kinds of human crises. He shows it in the Garden of Olives when he cries out, "My soul is sad even unto death," and "Father, let this chalice pass from me, but not my will, but your will," and "If this is what I must do, then your will be done." On the cross he experienced the same frightful loneliness: "Father, why have you abandoned me?" Jesus certainly could feel our pain, our doubts about our mission in life, our sense of failure, and our desperate loneliness, our broken dreams and broken hearts. It had a purpose. He wanted to understand what our life is like, and our pain and anguish and also our joy and happiness. He could do that only by being one of us. In letting us see his own pain, he is telling us he understands our pain, our loneliness, our broken dreams and broken hearts.

25

BACK AGAIN IN PAGAN COUNTRY

Mark records that on their way to the villages around Caesarea Philippi, Jesus raised the question, "Who do people say I am?" A strange question, but it seems to give the key to what has been troubling him ever since the crowd rejected him when he promised to give himself as the living bread from heaven. It seems to be part of the reason he became irritable with the apostles when they realized they were short of bread, as if Jesus' multiplying the loaves and fishes had made no lasting impression on them, and they were still having problems not just under-standing him but understanding who he was. Jesus was so humble, I am sure his extraordinary humility veiled the majesty of not only his divinity, but also the towering brilliance of his human person.

Even though Peter confessed his loyalty to Jesus after the crowd turned their backs on him, and in that confession expressed the feelings of the other apostles, as well, Jesus still had doubts about the stability of Peter's faith, and what he and the others really thought of him. So, on this oc-casion when they were near Caesarea Philippi, Jesus raised the question, "Who do people say that I am?" In raising that issue, he was finally ex-pressing what was really troubling him.

"Some say, 'John the Baptizer'; others say, 'Elijah'; still others say, 'Jer-emiah or one of the prophets.' "

"But, who do you say I am?" he asked, perhaps looking straight into Simon's eyes.

"You are the Christ, the Son of the living God," Simon spoke out boldly.

Jesus responded, "Blessed are you, Simon, son of John, for flesh and blood has not revealed this to you, but my Father in heaven. So, now I say to you, you are Rock, and upon this Rock I will build my Church, and the powers of hell will never triumph over you. I will give you the keys of the kingdom of heaven. Whatever you shall bind on earth, I will bind in heaven. Whatever you loose on earth, I will loose in heaven." Then he gave them strict orders to tell no one that he was the Christ. (Mt. 16:13–20; Mk. 8:27–30; Lk. 9:18–21)

Jesus finally heard from the apostles what he needed to hear. They did know who he was, even though Simon needed the prompting of the Heavenly Father to help him understand it. Simon's response broke the mood of sadness troubling Jesus. He was all of a sudden back to his ordi-nary self, and went on talking about the kingdom, and the future of his ministry. The kingdom of which Jesus spoke is a kingdom built on heav-enly truths. And in these words Jesus gave his guarantee that his teach-ings of these heavenly truths would be transmitted in their wholeness through the apostles until the end of time. This was the first time Jesus used the word *Church* in referring to the community of his followers. That term would be used continually and consistently from then on throughout history. Paul would continually talk about the Church as the body of Christ, and also the bride of Christ without blemish. John in Revelations would talk about the Church as the kingdom of God and as the bride of the Lamb, come down from heaven and founded on the layers of rock with the names of the apostles on them.

The Church was then beginning to be understood by the apostles as the embodiment of the mystery of Jesus' continual redemption of the human race throughout all future generations. The Church in its metaphysical entity was revealed as the bride of the Lamb, the perfect spotless creation of the Christ, like glittering crystal, but in its human condition, filled with human members reflecting both brilliant holiness and humiliating shame. What will always be difficult to understand and even more difficult to live with is that the two are totally distinct. The metaphysical entity is the sacred creation of Jesus as his mystical body enshrining the Holy Spirit as the living source of divine life and grace to the human members of Jesus' body. The members of the body of Christ on earth will always be in the process of redemption, so the Church will always be filled with sinners if it is fulfilling Jesus' mission of saving sinners. It is critical to keep the two concepts separate. Though we may become disillusioned with people, we can never logically become disillusioned with the Church. It *is* Jesus present in our midst. And to it we owe our loyalty in spite of the weakness of its members.

This expression of Simon did not come from himself. Jesus said it was the result of a direct revelation from God, prefiguring how the Holy Spirit would guide and direct the apostles and those who would succeed them in guiding the Church throughout future generations, thus assuring the integrity of Jesus' teachings until the end of time. What took place had to be a comfort to Jesus. It showed his Father had not left him, and was giving Jesus a clear sign assuring him that, although the present might seem dark, the future "will be well taken care of, my beloved Son, so be at peace."

It was also around this time that Jesus seemed to become more keenly aware of the future problems he would face; not that he had been unaware of them previously, but like us, he could not help but concentrate on pressing issues. In the past, his future sufferings had not been a top priority for his concern, but now as he knew difficult times were coming he focused on what he knew would be taking place in his life, but it was with a renewed optimism. He shared these concerns with the apostles. "The time is coming when I will journey to Jerusalem, and I will suffer greatly at the hands of the elders, the chief priests and the scribes, and be put to death, and then will be raised up on the third day." (Mt. 16:21–23)

Peter would listen to none of this kind of talk. He took Jesus aside, and began to scold him for such talk: "Don't even think of such things. God forbid anything like that would ever happen."

In spite of Peter's obvious concern for the Master's welfare, Jesus could still become upset with him, and he looked upon what Peter had said as a temptation to doubt the Father's expressed will. So, Jesus sharply put Peter in his place: "Get behind me, Satan. You are putting a stumbling stone in my path. You think as humans think, not as God wills."

Then Jesus explains, apparently not just to the apostles, what is necessary for a person who wants to follow him as a disciple. This would seem to indicate that there were small pockets of disciples in the area whom Jesus was visiting to strengthen their commitment to him. They could have been Jewish people living in the area or pagans who had become disciples of Jesus after hearing him speak and witnessing his miracles in Galilee in the months past.

"If anyone wants to be my disciple, he must deny himself, take up his cross, and follow me. For anyone who wants to save his life will lose it, but anyone who loses his life for my sake will find it. What then will a man gain, if he wins the whole world and loses his soul, or what can a man offer in exchange for his life?

"I tell you all this, for one day the Son of Man will come clothed in his Father's majesty, and when he comes he will reward each one according to the goodness of his life. And when will this be? I tell you, there are some here who will not taste death until this all takes place and the Son establishes his kingdom with great power and majesty." (Mt. 16:21–28)

Wherever this dialogue took place, it seems Jesus was either just leaving the area of Caesarea Philippi, or was already on this way back to Galilee. Matthew, Mark, and Luke all talk about six days later, though Luke mentions about eight days later, and the three Gospel versions tell of Jesus taking Peter, James, and John up a very high mountain. If Jesus had been coming back down from Caesarea Philippi at that time, a six-day walk south would have brought the little group back down well into Galilee, and not far from the mountains in central Galilee near Mount Tabor.

Mount Tabor has been traditionally considered as the place where Jesus took Peter, James, and John to pray with him and where the Transfiguration occurred. It is a likely site, as the view from there is magnificent. At 3,100 feet high, it is not the tallest mountain in the area, but it has a panoramic view of the valleys in every direction. However, as there were military fortifications on Mount Tabor in Jesus' day, it is not likely that that was the site Jesus chose for such an important event, especially since crowds would have followed him there. Besides, it was a day's journey south of Capernaum, and we see Jesus in Capernaum after the Transfiguration. It does not seem that he would have taken his apostles that far south just for the site, and then go right back up to Capernaum, when he was passing through much more spectacular sites in mountains not far from Caesarea Philippi before he turned south to go back to Galilee. One mountain in that area was Mount Merin, almost 4,000 feet high, also with a spectacular view. As not many people in that area knew Jesus, he would have had the privacy he needed for the sacred event that was to take place. This would have been a perfect place for Jesus to take the disciples. At the top of that mountain they could rest and pray, far from everything earthly, and in a sacred silence. Moses and Elijah could visit with Jesus in a magnificent epiphany that the apostles needed to reinforce their understanding of Jesus in the destiny of God's people, and the importance of Jesus in their own lives. It certainly was a good preparation for the tragic events that would take place in Jerusalem in the not-too-distant future. This was a perfect setting for the kind of experience Jesus was planning for his apostles. Jesus seemed full of enthusiasm over his renewed ministry and all that the future held out to him.

Jesus picked Peter, James, and John to ascend the mountain with him, and left the others behind. Why did he take only those three? It seems that since the beginning these had been the charter members of the group, and they were already familiar with Jesus when he came to Capernaum, and they most likely were the ones who introduced the others to him.

Running their family businesses conditioned them to be take-charge persons, which the others could clearly see. They came to recognize them for their leadership roles. The others seemed to have understood that Jesus counted on these three when something had to be done. The others also looked to them when decisions had to be made. In every group certain people stand out for their leadership qualities; the others recognize it and in time learn to accept it, even though on occasions it may arouse certain envy. Among the apostles Peter, James, and John were there from the beginning of Jesus' ministry; most of the others came later, and the pecking order had already begun to fall into place.

So, when Jesus told Peter, James, and John to come with him up the mountain, while the others were left either at the foot of the mountain, or somewhere on the mountainside, they probably did not feel left out, but knew that Jesus had something important to discuss with them. These three also took the blame for things—things they did or should have done—and were sternly corrected and put in their place; you hardly ever see the other apostles being criticized for anything. Peter, James, and John always stood out, while the others were content staying in the background, and just enjoyed being with Jesus.

The hike up the mountain was not an easy climb, especially for Peter. The doctor who analyzed his bone structure from remains found in the Vatican estimated that Peter was not very tall, and that he was quite wide, as well. That also explains John's description of Peter on Easter Sunday morning, when the two ran out to the tomb. John arrived first and had to wait for Peter to catch up, no doubt huffing and puffing and out of breath. That was most certainly his condition when the small group reached the top of the mountain. One can almost imagine Peter complaining how exhausted he was, and Jesus making fun of him. "That was good for you, Peter. We should do this more often." Jesus' happy spirit had fully returned.

After resting for a while from the strenuous climb, Jesus went off by himself to pray. While he was praying, two figures appeared and began conversing with him. They were the two most important people in Israel's history—Moses, the Law-giver, and Elijah, the great prophet. The apostles were awestruck by this epiphany. They recognized the figures from their conversation with Jesus; Moses was talking with Jesus about the Law, and Jesus' fulfillment of the Law, and Elijah was conversing

with their Master over the prophecies, and how carefully he was fulfilling everything that had been said about him in times past through the
prophets.

The apostles, simple as they were, even with their assumed air of
sophistication, were stunned at what they were witnessing. Seeing the
greatest figures in all of Israelite history meeting with their Master and
conversing with him about the future of Israel, Jesus' approaching death,
and other weighty matters impressed them mightily. Who really is our
Master that even Moses and Elijah come to him, and discuss with him so
very humbly such weighty matters as the destiny of Israel itself? In discussing his approaching death, the persons in the vision shared with him
their dismay that the leaders of Yahweh's people could so coldly reject
their Messiah and turn him over to the pagans for execution. They tried
humbly to offer him some small measure of comfort.

The evangelists tell the story best. While Jesus was praying,

> His garments became dazzlingly white, even like snow in the sun. And
> Moses and Elijah appeared, and were talking with him about his death,
> which he was to fulfill in Jerusalem.
>
> Now, Peter and his companions were half-asleep, and when they
> woke up, they saw the glory and the two men standing with Jesus. And
> as the figures were parting from him, Peter said to Jesus, "Master, it
> is good for us to be here. Let us set up three tents, one for you, one for
> Moses, and one for Elijah," not knowing what he said. But, as he was
> speaking, a cloud came and overshadowed them, and they were afraid
> as they entered the cloud. And there came a voice out of the cloud, say-
> ing, "This is my beloved Son; listen to him." When the disciples heard
> this they fell on their faces, and were filled with awe. But, Jesus came
> and touched them, saying, "Rise, and don't be afraid." And when they
> lifted up their eyes, they saw no one, but Jesus alone.
>
> As they came down from the mountain, he warned them to tell
> no one what they had seen until after the Son of Man had risen from
> the dead. They faithfully observed what he had told them, although
> they discussed among themselves what "rising from the dead" meant.
> And they asked Jesus why the scribes said that Elijah had to come first.
> "That is true. Elijah is to come first, to see that everything is as it should
> be. However, I tell you that Elijah had already come, and they treated

him as they pleased, just as the Scriptures say about him. And the Son of Man will be treated in the same way."

When they reached the bottom of the mountain and rejoined the rest of the disciples, they saw a large crowd around them and some scribes arguing with them. The moment they saw him, the whole crowd was struck with awe at his appearance and ran over to greet him. "What are you arguing about with them?" he asked. A man in the crowd spoke out, "Master, I have brought my son to you. He is afflicted with a spirit of dumbness, and when it bothers him, it throws him to the ground and he foams at the mouth, and grinds his teeth, and grows rigid. I asked your disciples to cast it out, but they were unable to." "You faithless generation," he said to them in reply. "How much longer must I be with you? Bring the boy to me!"

They brought the boy to him, and as soon as the spirit saw Jesus, it threw the boy into convulsions, and he fell to the ground and lay writhing there, foaming at the mouth. Jesus then asked the father, "How long has this been happening to him?"

"From childhood," he said, "and it has often thrown him into the fire and into the water, trying to destroy him. But, if you can do anything, have pity on us and help us"

Jesus retorted, "If you can; everything is possible to anyone who has faith."

Immediately the father of the boy cried out, "I do have faith; help me to have greater faith."

And when Jesus saw how great the crowd was that was pressing around him, he rebuked the unclean spirit, "Deaf and dumb spirit, I command you, come out of him and never enter him again." Then throwing the boy into violent convulsions, it came out of him, shouting, and the boy lay there like a corpse, so that the people said, "He is dead," but Jesus took him by the hand and helped him up, and he was able to stand. When he had gone indoors, his disciples asked him privately, "Why could we not cast it out?" And he answered, "This kind can be driven out only by prayer." (Mk. 9:14–29; Mt. 17:14–21; Lk. 9:37–43)

Mark mentions Jesus going into a house. Where are they? Perhaps the healing took place near the victim's house, and the father invited Jesus and his disciples in to show his gratitude. There is no explanation. The

Gospel writers say nothing about any of Jesus' family or friends having a house in that faraway location. The house could be the home of the family whose boy Jesus healed.

> After that, the little group continued on their way through Galilee, and again, he did not want anyone to know his whereabouts, because he was instructing his disciples, trying to impress on them that he would be put in the hands of evil men who would put him to death, but that after three days he would arise again. Even though this was the second time Jesus had told the apostles about his impending death, they still could not grasp what he was talking about, but they were afraid to ask him any questions. (Mk. 9:30–32)

They finally arrived at Capernaum and went to Peter's house, where they at last had a chance to relax. Apparently, the apostles were having a discussion among themselves on the way to Capernaum. They were arguing about who was the most important among them. It is hard to imagine what was going through their minds. Jesus had just told them, for the second time, that he was going to die, and they started arguing among themselves about who was the most important among them, who Jesus would appoint to run the organization after he died. Jesus must have been walking faster than the others, and they thought they were out of earshot when they carried on this discussion. But although he said nothing at the time, he knew full well what they were talking about. Once they all sat down and started to relax and enjoy some refreshments, Jesus casually raised the question, "What were you fellows arguing about back there on the road?" You can picture them all of a sudden becoming tongue-tied, because they had been talking about who was the greatest among them. It is easy to imagine the way it went, each of the apostles giving reasons why he should be considered the greatest: Nathaniel saying, "Look what he said about me, 'A true Israelite in whom there is no deceit.' " And then James and John jumping in with their argument: "We're blood relatives, and blood is thicker than water. We've got it made; our mother will make sure of that," and one day we will see her trying. And then Peter: "But look at what he said to me the other day: 'Blessed are you, Simon, son of John, because flesh and blood has not revealed this to you, but my Father in heaven. And I tell you, you are Rock, and upon this Rock I will build my Church, and the gates of hell will not prevail against it. And I give to you the keys of the kingdom of heaven.' Top that if you can!"

Imagine these saintly men, whose images we have been accustomed to seeing in stained glass, whom we've honored in our churches as extraordinary saints, arguing about something so petty.

Jesus obviously did not say anything to them at the time, but just let them talk on, perhaps quietly chuckling at their childishness, but realizing that they could not be allowed to foster that kind of thinking about themselves. So, he talked to them quietly, out of earshot of others in the house, and taking a little child, possibly one of Simon's grandchildren, he placed the child in their midst, and putting his arms around the child, said to them, "Whoever wants to be first among you has to be like this little child. He must be willing to make himself the least of all, and be willing to be at the service of all the rest. And whoever welcomes one of these little children welcomes me, and in welcoming me, welcomes Him who sent me." That is clearly what Jesus was expecting of his apostles when they took over the guidance of the kingdom after his departure. This is what he expects of his bishops and priests today. As time went on, Peter seems to have finally become that simple childlike servant. We see it in the Acts of the Apostles. Although he was conscious of his role as the leader, he was most gracious in his relationship with the rest of the apostles, even allowing Paul to insult him to his face, without responding, when Paul called him a coward for not taking a strong stand against the observance of the dietary laws by Jews who had become Christians. We see it when, at the first Council of the Church in Jerusalem, Peter convenes the group and delivers the opening speech setting forth the agenda, but allows James to be spokesman, since he was the head of the Church in Jerusalem. Then at the end, as Peter and the apostles approved of James's ruling, it became the official teaching of the Church. (Mk. 9:33–37) What a striking change in Peter's personality, and the humble way he guides the young Church, allowing another apostle to be spokesman, while he feels comfortable just expressing his approval together with the rest.

26

Jesus Tours Other Galilean Towns; a Secret Trip to Jerusalem

After his wanderings through Phoenicia and the area of Gaulanitis and parts of the Decapolis, there is little record of Jesus doing much more preaching in and around his base in Capernaum.

Jesus decided to tour other Galilean villages, bringing his message to those he had not yet visited, intending in a few months' time to make his trip to Jerusalem for the Festival of Tents, Succoth, the harvest festival. The people in the outlying area of Galilee were of a simpler mentality and gentler disposition. Jesus was beginning to feel more comfortable with these people. They lacked the sophistication and the cunning of the businesspeople, who looked at religious things with a more cynical attitude. These farming people worked hard, spent more time with their families, and were not as anxious and harried as the stressed-out city people. They were more open to Jesus, and that helped to heal the hurt that Jesus had been feeling for the past few months. But, as far away as Galilee was from Jerusalem, the scribes and Pharisees still received daily reports of Jesus' whereabouts and his escapades. So, even here in these quiet villages, Jesus was not free from their harassment, and it did not take long before they found out his whereabouts, and showed up, immediately creating a public confrontation. It had to be very close to the Festival of Tents, as people were preparing to take up the wheat harvest.

Wherever it was, someplace in Galilee, Jesus and the apostles were walking along a road that passed through a field of standing grain. The apostles were hungry and they started to pluck heads off the stalks; rubbing them in their hands, they were eating them the way we would eat peanuts. Some scribes and Pharisees, who were watching, immediately began accusing them of violating the Sabbath. Jesus turned around and angrily confronted them. "What are they doing now that is so evil?" he demanded.

"Well, can't you tell? They are harvesting grain; they are doing what is forbidden on the Sabbath."

Jesus looked at them and, clearly irritated, said, "Have you not read what David did when he and his companions were hungry, how he entered the holy place and took the sacred showbread, which only the priests were allowed to eat [because it symbolized the presence of God], and gave it to his companions because they were hungry. When are you going to learn that the Sabbath was made for man and not man for the Sabbath?" He was also saying implicitly, "And the Law was made for man and not man for the Law." (Mk. 2:23–28; Mt. 12:1–8; Lk. 6:1–5) It is his children that God cares about. The purpose of the Law is to protect his children. God's laws are not arbitrary. They are protective and productive. So, if a law no longer has meaning or is damaging to God's children, it should be changed or abrogated.

And the showbread that Jesus was talking about was kept in special gold containers in the holy place, and symbolized God's presence among the people, like our reserving the Eucharist in the tabernacles in our churches, though the Eucharist is not merely symbolic, but the real divine Presence. The showbread, however, was still sacred to all Israelites, so when Jesus justified David taking the showbread and giving it to his troops for lunch because they were hungry, the Pharisees must have been horrified. They dared not say a thing because David was their all-time national hero, and held up by Yahweh himself as "A man after my own heart." This made them all the more furious with Jesus, because he had bested them again using their own weapons, passages from Scripture.

And Jesus drew out this issue on Sabbath work even further. "And have you not read in the Law where Temple priests are free to work on the Sabbath without committing sin? I tell you there is something here greater than the Sabbath. Had you understood the words, 'It is mercy I desire, not sacrifice,' you would not have been so quick to condemn the innocent. The Sabbath was made for God's people, and not God's people for the Sabbath. And I tell you further, the Son of Man is Lord even of the Sabbath."

That last statement is a stunning commentary. What Jesus is saying it that the Law was made for man and not man for the Law. Who would have ever thought that God had created the Sabbath for people's benefit? Everyone always believed the purpose of the Sabbath was to focus people's attention on God, and his worship. It was always called the Lord's Day. Jesus said it was intended as people's day. Confused about that myself, I asked a rabbi friend, a saintly scholar by the name of Rabbi Michael Szenes, if Jesus was right. He told me that Jesus *was* right. God originally established the Sabbath rest as a way of protecting slaves, so their masters could not work them to death. They had to have a day off, and to make sure, he mandated the Sabbath as a day off from work for everyone, from the king down to the lowliest slave. Nobody could work on the Sabbath. It was a day to rest, a family day when the family could get together and enjoy one another's companionship, and refresh themselves for the upcoming week. As time went on religious leaders felt uncomfortable with everyone having such a good time, so they created all kinds of rules forbidding physical exertion of any kind, and turned the beautiful gift of God into a veritable nightmare. Jesus tried to restore the Sabbath to God's original purpose, and made it quite clear that he was doing this on his own authority, for "the Son of Man is Lord even of the Sabbath."

It seems there was not a day when Jesus was not harassed by scribes and Pharisees. There was no escape. Shortly afterward Jesus entered a synagogue in the neighborhood. Present were some Pharisees who went right up and took the prominent seats in the room. They were watching Jesus intently, and also watching a man there who had a withered limb, his right hand, as Saint Luke points out. Seeing the Pharisees and the man with the withered hand, Jesus sized up the situation immediately, and knew full well that the Pharisees were maliciously hoping that Jesus would do something. He did not disappoint them. He called over the man with the withered hand, set him in the midst of the assembly, and looking right at the Pharisees, asked them, "Is it lawful, on the Sabbath, to do good, or to do evil, to save life or to destroy it?" They said nothing, but just watched, with evil in their eyes. Then Jesus followed up with another question. "Which of you, if his donkey or his sheep fell into a pit on the Sabbath, would not feel justified in doing what he had to do to pull it out of the pit?" Such a practice was approved by the Pharisees' own experts in the Law. Jesus knew that and ended with the comment, "Since a human being is of more importance than a donkey or a sheep, it is therefore legal to help a human being on the Sabbath." Then,

Jesus healed the man and let him go. Nobody said a word. The Phari-sees feigned anger, but with hypocritical glee immediately teamed up with the Herodians (Jews loyal to Herod's party, and whom the Phari-sees despised), and plotted a way to kill Jesus. (Mk. 3:1–6; Mt. 12:9–14; Lk. 6:6–11)

Jesus then left there and continued on his journey to the vicinity of the Sea of Tiberias, where a crowd began to form over the next few days with people from throughout Galilee and from farther away. He still drew crowds from far and wide in the area there, even after losing that huge crowd who had walked away from him weeks before. This does not mean that some of their number did not drift back to him when they'd had a chance to think things over and reevaluate this kind man who did so much for them. Saint Luke, as well as the other Synoptics, men-tions the areas from which people were now flocking to Jesus. They were coming from other parts of Galilee, from Judea, from the regions around Tyre and Sidon, and the Decapolis; from Perea on the eastern side of the Jordan, and from Idumea, south of Judea. These groups apparently were different from the ones he had been speaking to previously and who had walked away from him, though no doubt some of them came back and mingled with this new crowd, which contained many people from pagan territories. This was a very mixed group, not just Jews, but many pagans, as well. Jesus was made to feel much more comfortable with this crowd. They seemed to be a simpler type of people, and more open to his mes-sage.

His manner of speaking to these people is different in tone from his former talks. He now is much more matter of fact, and lays right on the line what following him really means and what is involved:

"If anyone comes to me and does not hate his own father and mother and wife and children and brothers and sisters, yes, and even his own life, he cannot be my disciple. Whoever does not bear his own cross and come after me, cannot be my disciple. For which of you, desiring to build a tower, does not first sit down and examine the cost, whether he has enough to complete it? Otherwise, when he lays the founda-tion, and is not able to finish it, others who see it will begin to mock him, saying, 'This man began to build, but was not able to finish.' Or what king, going out to engage another king in war, will not sit down first and take counsel whether he is able with ten thousand men to go against him who is coming toward him with twenty thousand. And if not, while the other is still a great way off, he sends an ambassador and asks his terms of peace. So, therefore, whoever of you does not renounce all that he has cannot be my disciple."

It is as if Jesus is saying, "If any of you are serious about following me, that is one thing, but if you cannot make up your mind and are only willing to commit yourself halfheartedly, you might as well not bother." He had learned a bitter lesson from his experience with the former crowd. He had been too trusting and too easy on them. It reminds Jesus of salt that has lost its taste: "It is no longer of any use and it might as well be thrown away. It is the same for those who halfheartedly commit themselves to the kingdom, then lose the fire of their enthusiasm. Pay attention to what I am trying to tell you." Jesus' mission needs followers who are wholeheartedly committed to furthering the reign of God on earth. They must be willing even to die in their efforts to bring his love and message to the world. Anything less is of no help to him. Their lack of enthusiasm will be a drag on the other disciples, who are fired with enthusiasm to spread God's message of salvation throughout the world, and are willing to die for it if necessary.

When Jesus was talking earlier about hating father or mother more than the kingdom, we have to understand the way people expressed themselves in those days. How we would express it today would be different. "If you cannot detach yourself enough from your family and loved ones, so they will not be a total distraction in your ministry with me, then you are not really fit for this kind of work." I have seen marriages destroyed by either the husband or wife being so attached to a parent that they were not able to totally commit to their spouse, but had to get approval from the parent for everything, even decisions in minor matters. The parent was involved in almost everything of any importance. So, the words, "A man and a woman leave father and mother and cling to their spouse, and the two become one flesh," is made meaningless.

When my book *Joshua* became popular and began to spread around the world, and requests for talks came from all over, I knew that eventually I would have to have someone to work with me to continue the ministry when I died, or when I could no longer keep up the pace. I tried so hard to find someone whom I thought would be good. One person I asked said he would have to be guaranteed a salary of fifty thousand dollars a year before he could consider it. Another person said that he admired me for having a ministry of making Jesus real around the world, but he was very much aware that being faithful to what Jesus taught, and preaching that kind of message, would generate all kinds of controversy and opposition. "My life as a clergyman is difficult enough," he said, "without putting up with persecution for preaching a real Jesus. Being faithful to Jesus will always get you into trouble, especially when you make it your full-time ministry. Jesus promised as much. People don't really want to know the real Jesus; it disturbs their carefully protected comfort zones. So, you either preach the undiluted Jesus and upset people, or compromise what he taught to keep your fans." Jesus' comments about the singleness of purpose required of those who would follow him showed how well he understood the human heart.

It was now time to think of another trip to Judea. Jesus' work in Galilee was winding down as the Festival of Tabernacles, or the Festival of Tents, was approaching. This was a happy time of the year, and Jewish families looked forward to it. It was a festival that the whole family could take part in, and was the most popular festival of the year. During the time of this festival, the countryside around Jerusalem was covered with booths, or tents, where the families lived during the week of celebration.

John's Gospel has a very curious introduction to this event. The caravan of Jesus' family and friends is being organized to take off on the journey to Jerusalem.

Now the Jews' feast of Tabernacles was at hand. So, his family said to him, "Leave here and go to Judea, that your disciples may see the works you are doing. For no man works in secret if he seeks to be known openly. If you do these things, show yourself to the whole world." For even his family did not believe in him.

Jesus said to them, "My time has not yet come, but your time is always here. The world cannot hate you, but it hates me because I testify of it that its works are evil. Go to the feast yourselves. I am not going up to this feast, for my time has not yet fully come." Having said this he stayed in Galilee.

This is interesting, watching Jesus telling his family that he was not going up to Jerusalem, and that they should go on by themselves. Then shortly after they left, he started out on his own. Why? It seems rather mysterious. Why did he not want to go with his family? Did he need to be alone? Were there a lot of things on his mind that he had to process, which he could not do if he was traveling with a crowd? Perhaps he realized that the Pharisees' spies would be expecting him to be with a crowd, and would be laying in wait for him, so he decided to go down by himself and mingle with strangers when he arrived in the vicinity of Jerusalem. This way he could relax and not be the center of attention, and talk to strangers and listen to all their gossip, and the comments they would have picked up about himself. It would be a good sounding board for what he could expect when his presence became known. He did hear what people were saying about him, some that he was a good man, while others thought he was a troublemaker. Others were wondering if the authorities had come to accept him.

But, after his family had gone up to the feast, then he went up, not publicly, but privately. The Jews were looking for him at the feast, and saying, "Where is he?" And there was very much discussion about him among the people. While some said, "He is a good man," others said, "He is leading the people astray." Yet for fear of the Jews, no one said anything openly about him.

About the middle of the feast, Jesus went up into the Temple and taught there. The Jews were in awe at his teaching, and commented, "How is it that this man has such knowledge when he has never studied?" Overhearing what they said, Jesus answered them, "My teaching is not mine, but His who sent me. If any man's will is to do His will, he will know whether the teaching is from God, or whether I am speaking on my own authority. He who speaks on his own authority, seeks his own glory, but he who seeks the glory of Him who sent him is true, and in him there is no falsehood. Did not Moses give you the Law? Yet none of you keeps the Law. Why do you seek to kill me?"

The people answered, "You have a devil! Who seeks to kill you?"

Jesus answered, "I did one deed, and you all marvel at that. Moses gave you circumcision, not that it came from Moses, because it really came from the fathers, and you circumcise a man on the Sabbath. If on the Sabbath, a man receives circumcision, so that the Law of Moses may not be broken, are you angry with me because on the Sabbath I made a man's whole body well? Do not judge by appearances, but judge with integrity." (Jn. 7:2–24)

Still, Jesus' ministry in Jerusalem was effective. There were many who listened to him and followed him. No doubt many were from foreign countries, from which many of the pilgrims came to celebrate the festival. These most likely were the ones who formed the nucleus of the communities that were to accept the apostles later on, after Pentecost. They had already heard Jesus speak, were convinced that he had to be the Messiah, and later on were ready to receive the apostles into their communities when they went out to bring Jesus and his message to the world.

Seeing that people were gathering around Jesus, and the numbers were increasing, the authorities were feeling even more threatened, not just by his rising power, but for fear the Romans would be concerned that another Galilean was gathering followers. They were really more concerned for themselves and angry that Jesus had exposed in front of huge crowds that they were phonies, and even worse, doing the work of Satan by not accepting him. They just wanted to get rid of him, so they sent out the Temple police "to arrest him, but no one laid hands on him because his hour had not yet come. Yet many of the people believed in him, and said, 'When the Christ comes, will he do any more signs than this man has done?' " (Jn. 7:30–36)

The Pharisees heard the crowd talking about these things, and Jesus, seeing them and the priests standing around in the crowd, said, "I shall be with you a little longer, and then I go to Him who sent me, and you will look for me, but will not find me. Where I am you cannot come."

They asked themselves, "What does he mean, 'to go where we cannot find him?' Does he intend to go to the Diaspora, and be with the Jews abroad, and teach the Greeks? What does he mean by saying, 'You will look for me, but you will not find me, and where I am you cannot come?' " (Jn. 7:30–36)

This response the authorities could not understand. They were totally bewildered. What was he saying? Would he leave the country and preach to the Jews of the Diaspora in foreign countries? And Jesus did not intend to settle their minds. It was his intention to give them no peace of mind. They did not deserve more. They still wanted to arrest him, but the security police could not get themselves to do it. They were too impressed with the honesty and sublimity of his teaching, and sensed the injustice in demanding his arrest. It was a happy festival for most of the people and the people loved Jesus, so why spoil the celebration by causing a riot among the whole populace of Jerusalem? That is what would have happened if the police had tried to arrest Jesus.

One of the ritual ceremonies decreed for this festival was the water gifts brought to the Temple amidst singing and dancing and prayers for rain, especially during times of drought, which were very common in the area. Sometimes a drought would go on for months; occasionally it would continue for years, as happened in the time of Elijah the prophet, when no rain fell for six years. This time of the year was the dry season. The earth was parched, and heavy dust filled the air from the movement of people and animals. Parched throats expressed painfully the desperate need for water, and symbolized the thirst, an even more painful thirst, in their souls. This was an annual phenomenon, and on the last day of the feast the whole nation prayed desperately for their dry and parched lives.

As Jesus watched the crowds pouring into the Temple with their libations, and saw their physical and spiritual craving for relief from the heat and oppressively dry air, picture him standing above them, motioning to them for silence. Then in the dramatic silence of that hot afternoon, looking down across the crowd from where he was teaching, not far from where the Temple scholars were teaching, and watching, Jesus cried out in a strong, loud voice, "All you who are thirsty, come to me, and I will give you drink. Believe in me, and rivers of living water will flow from within you." (Jn. 7:37–38) Jesus was talking about the Holy Spirit, whom those who believed would one day receive, after Jesus had accomplished his mission.

Those who knew Jesus knew full well that he was not just saying empty words. He was comparing himself to the rock in the desert, from which water had gushed forth in such abundance as to slake the thirst of the vast hordes of Israelites wandering with Moses through the hot, parched desert, so many centuries before. Those present that day in the Temple knew what Jesus was talking about. They knew he was using their thirst to make them aware of the more gnawing thirst in their souls that demanded relief. They had heard him speak. They felt the wonderful, comforting sensation of experiencing the closeness of God and the satisfying joy that poured through their souls as this man Jesus spoke to them of his Father. His words that day gave real meaning to the feast they were celebrating. Never before had they looked on this festival in the same way, nor would they again. Everything he said gave greater depth and meaning to their lives, and an experience they would never forget, and would pass on to their children.

Jesus' words went like an electric shock among the people. If anyone else had said what Jesus said, the people would have thought him odd, or crazy. But, coming from Jesus, whom the common people had learned to respect for his earthiness and sublime spirituality, it all made sense, and gave them much to think about. They had already had a taste of the spiritual waters Jesus poured into their souls, and they craved more. As they continued on their way into the Temple, they talked among themselves: " 'This man is truly the Prophet!' But, others were saying, 'This man is the Christ,' while still others commented, 'How can the Christ come from Galilee? Do not the Scriptures say it is from the family of David, and that it is from Bethlehem, David's town, that the Christ should come?' And there was confusion among them." (Jn. 7:40–43)

The authorities tried on any number of occasions to have Jesus arrested, but each time, the security police came back empty-handed. This particular time was one of those occasions. The chief priests had sent the Temple police to apprehend Jesus, but they returned without him. The Pharisees asked, "Why have you not brought him?" Their response came from their conscience: "Never has anyone spoken the way this man does." To which the Pharisees replied, "You are also allowing yourselves to be seduced by this man? Have any of the leaders or even a single Pharisee put faith in him? As for the people, they are ignorant of the Law, and they are cursed anyway." (Jn. 7:44–49)

It was on this occasion that Nicodemus showed his true colors, although not with the greatest courage. While the chief priests and Pharisees were trying to arrest Jesus, Nicodemus spoke up and protested, "Since when does our Law condemn a man before he even has a hearing, and the facts made known what he has done wrong?" The others did not answer, but merely ridiculed Nicodemus for defending Jesus. (Jn. 7:50–52)

When that day ended, the people left for their own homes, since the festival was over. Jesus retired to the Mount of Olives, apparently alone. Nothing is mentioned about the apostles being with Jesus. Perhaps Jesus really did get lost in the crowd, like he seemingly intended to, and not even his family knew of his whereabouts. On the following morning, however, he appeared again in the Temple area. As soon as word spread among the people concerning his whereabouts, and that he was speaking, the crowds began to gather around him in the cloistered area, where the scholars of the Law usually taught groups of their own followers. Jesus was still attracting great crowds. Whether they were coming because they were convinced his message was from God and were willing to commit their lives to him, or because his comforting way of speaking provided pleasing entertainment and a nice spiritual uplift, was something that was difficult to understand. Possibly, they were sincere and would have liked to commit their lives to him, but nothing in the Gospels indicates that they were willing to make that difficult commitment. Considering what was involved personally for persons who committed their lives to Jesus, whose fate seemed ever more precarious as each day passed, it was indeed a most difficult decision to make. Jesus could see that reflected not only in their eyes, but in their hearts, as well. To make a commitment to Jesus meant jeopardizing one's standing in the local synagogue and in the Temple worship, too. As time went on, especially after Jesus' arrest and execution, there were even more threatening penalties.

Late that afternoon, Jesus left the Temple and probably walked through the Lion's Gate, and down the valley, across the road to the Garden of Gethsemane, where he spent the night. It was his favorite haunt when he was not visiting Mary and Martha and Lazarus in Bethany. It seemed he still needed quiet time alone. John makes no mention of the apostles and his family meeting up with him so far. It seems Jesus' need for privacy on this trip worked out the way he had planned. Alone in the Garden of Gethsemane, he was thrown back totally on his thoughts. There were heavy things weighing down upon him. He knew the atmosphere in the city was like weather before a violent storm. He could feel the tension. The authorities were ready to attack him at the slightest provocation, and arrest him, if they could find someone willing to carry out their orders. He had evaded arrest already because "his time had not yet come." One can only imagine his prayer and his communication with his Father that night. He would not be human if he was not worried or anxious. His Father was his refuge, his only comfort. He could not help but feel a sense of failure. He knew he had come to redeem the world by his death, but there were so many other things he wanted to accomplish. It meant so much to him to bring his people back into his Father's love. But free will made that impossible. "How often I would have gathered you together as a hen gathers her chicks under her wings, but you would not allow me." And there was the relentless hounding by the authorities. There was, in his Father's plans, no rest from the daily confrontations and hostile attacks from the authorities, his Father's own religious authorities, which had to be particularly painful. They were the very ones Yahweh had nurtured through the centuries with prophetic guidance and warnings when they strayed from their loyalty to God. Indeed, the whole purpose of Judaism was to be the vehicle for the recognition and enthusiastic reception of the Son of God when the Father sent him as their Savior. For Jesus to find he was not only unwelcome, but hated by his Father's chosen instruments created a cosmic disruption of God's plan for the thousand years of peace and prosperity. These religious authorities had now become, perhaps unknowingly, the vehicle of Satan for the destruction of their long-awaited Messiah. Jesus knew this and tried so many times to tell them they were doing the work of Satan, and that they were locking the door for others to enter God's kingdom. But their hatred of him rendered them deaf to his warnings. As futile as his mission was becoming, there were still important messages that had to be delivered, and as usual, the messages were delivered through his response to events that took place almost daily. The lessons learned from these events and his response to them would be passed on until the end of time, and would affect the lives of millions for centuries to come. Some of these events took place the following day.

27

Dramatic Happenings in Jerusalem

The next morning Jesus left early for the Temple, and soon upon his arrival people gathered around him. He taught in a section along the same long cloistered area where the Temple scholars were accustomed to seating themselves to conduct discussions with their own disciples. It must have grieved them sorely to see this unschooled rabbi gathering huge crowds around him, and hanging on to his every word, when he had no official standing in the elite community of Temple scholars. But who had more right to teach in the Temple? It was his home. Isaiah had prophesied that when the Messiah came, the people would be taught by God. Here it was all happening, and no one had the slightest idea that the culmination of their destiny as God's people was already taking place, and no one had the slightest idea of its meaning.

Jesus had just begun to teach when a disturbance broke out at the fringe of the audience. It was early morning. Some Pharisees or their spies had been out during the night playing amateur sleuths or only-too-willing voyeurs, hoping to catch a couple in the act of adultery. How do you catch people in the act of adultery? These fellows obviously were quite adept at it. Strangely, however, they caught only the woman. Maybe the partner was a friend of theirs. They dragged this woman out of bed and down through the city streets right into the Temple courtyard itself, and flung her at the feet of Jesus.

Jesus' first reaction was to turn his back on them, more to save the woman further humiliation.

"We caught this woman in the act of adultery. Moses said in the Law we should stone such women. We now ask you, what do you say?"

This obviously was an attempt to trap Jesus into saying something that would put him in contradiction to the Law, and then accuse him of a crime. Disgusted with their hypocrisy, Jesus bent down and began to write something in the soil with his finger. However, since they persisted in demanding a response, he stood up and said to them, "Let him who is without sin among you cast the first stone." And stooping down again, he wrote in the soil. When they realized what was happening, they slipped away, one by one, beginning with the eldest, so that Jesus was left alone with the woman cowering at his feet. Then, standing there, he said to her, "Has no one condemned you, Woman?" "No one, Lord." "Then neither will I condemn you. Go, and do not ever again commit this sin." (Jn. 8:3–11)

Sin is an offense against God. In this episode it is the humans who demand the ultimate punishment for this woman's act of adultery. Something is wrong here, terribly wrong. Humans are demanding the punishment for a sin against God; humans who are themselves sinners against God. God is embarrassed, not for himself, but for the sinner. Why does Jesus turn his back on the scribes and Pharisees? It is an expression of disgust, disgust at the self-righteous who cannot smell the odor of their own sins, which is only too real to Jesus. They may boast of their ability to observe the Law. But the Law is not God's greatest concern. The first commandment and the most important of them all is to love God, to honor God by reflecting God's love back to Him and to others. The sin of these scribes and Pharisees is the worst kind of sin. It consists in that their lives are a living denial of all that God is. God is love. Love is the one most important element missing in their spirituality. Without love, *spirituality* is an empty word. It is the symptom of the death of a soul.

Although the Gospel writer did not mention what Jesus wrote on the ground, one of the Fathers of the Church said that what Jesus started to write in the soil was the secret sins of the scribes and Pharisees. In their shame they slunk away without another word, and in the deathly silence, the woman found herself there at Jesus' feet, surrounded by the large crowd, all choked with tearful emotions. One can almost hear the loud clapping applause for the wretched woman, and at seeing the despised Pharisees totally routed. Were there still people there who were disciples of the Pharisees? Did everyone approve of what Jesus did? He showed the difference between the compassionate justice of God and humans' malicious thirst for punishment of sinners other than themselves. It is Jesus' subtle warning of how the divine Judge will judge those who have been merciless in their own conviction and judgment of sinners. God will judge us with the same compassion with which we judge others. This does not mean that judges and prosecutors should not convict and punish criminals. It is whether they punish out of vengeance and destroy sinners, or treat them in a way that the image of Christ within them is not desecrated but can still have hope of a new life of genuine godliness. Only an authentic Christian society is capable of reforming the bruised and damaged spirit of a person trapped in evil.

In the diocese where I live there is a priest who has dedicated his whole life to the healing of broken souls. He has been a dear friend over the years. He had a parish in a seriously blighted area of Albany, New York. His very presence drew the bruised and damaged and broken people from all over. There were the homeless and the alcoholics and the drug addicts, and every type of people no one wanted. Father Peter Young became their good shepherd. They were his friends. They were his family.

When he started his ministry in that neighborhood, public intoxication was a crime, punishable by jail time. The state legislature was not far away from the parish, so Father Young would go up to the legislature day after day after day, and haunt each of the legislators in the Senate and the Assembly until after years of unrelenting persistence, he wore them down. They finally changed the law and decriminalized public intoxication.

But that was only the first step. Most of the people in his neighborhood were homeless. He invited as many as he could to sleep in the church buildings, and he fed them. There was a detective lieutenant stationed in the local precinct who was a friend of Father Young. His name was Ted Flint. Ted and I had been altar boys together. I was their family's paper boy. At one time Ted went into the seminary to become a priest, but eventually he left and joined the Albany police force. There are some police officers who have a reputation for being brutal to people not of their kind. Ted was an anomaly. With a Jesus-like compassion he befriended these outcasts. When he picked up his paycheck, he would immediately cash it and go to the supermarket and fill his car with food for the homeless and the addicts in Father Young's parish. It was all done under the cover of darkness, known only to Father Young.

But even that was not enough. Many of Father Young's parishioners were arrested for various things, mostly drug-related, and were sent to prison. So, the priest started another program, similar to halfway houses, and talked the judges and other officials into sending the offenders to his houses. Some of these houses were schools and former seminary buildings that were no longer in use. Counselors and people with experience were needed to administer these kinds of programs; the priest managed to round up such professionals from all over. Gradually, these programs became so successful that after many years and many more similar programs that the priest set up in other places and other states, the State University of New York decided to do a study of how successful these programs were. To date, preliminary data indicate that the success rate is well over 90 percent. One of those helped had at one time been an assistant attorney general of New York State, and he praises the program for what it has accomplished for so many battered souls.

That is what Jesus meant when he tried to teach us to be compassionate and to heal rather than destroy. There are a lot of lessons in the story of the woman caught in adultery. Unfortunately, there are still so many Pharisees who would rather destroy than be a living, compassionate Jesus to broken souls. Persons like Father Young who do this kind of work are rarely appreciated, except by those they live for, because their work holds up a mirror to a society that is bent on punishment. He once offered the expertise of his counselors to help priests having problems, but his offer was rejected because his superiors did not consider his counselors professional, though they were. He knew it was just a way of disparaging his work. Working with the homeless and the broken often generates envy and other unpleasant reactions, so these people rarely receive the honor they should receive from those who should be proud of them. We were sitting on the porch of Joshua in Altamont not too long ago, talking about our lives as priests through the years. Now we are both old and a lot more fragile, and do our best to make a difference. After his visits, I always have tears in my heart for all that he has gone through, and the way he has been treated in his long life so dedicated to others. I hope some day the Vatican will honor him for the remarkably Jesus-like work this real "street priest" has done all his life. And what a joy it is to see how the lives of so many of his salvaged souls have been beautifully transformed into strong and productive people in society, so different from the millions of lives that are being reduced to subhuman level and destroyed in our vindictive criminal justice system. Applying Jesus' love and compassion to solve the problems of our broken society can make a difference. "It is not the death of a sinner that I desire, but his conversion leading to a new and fruitful life."

28

"I AM THE LIGHT OF THE WORLD"

During the Festival of Tabernacles, or the Festival of Tents, there was another celebration, the Feast of Lights. One author, a Scripture authority whom I had read many years ago when I was in my last year of theology, mentioned that during this time, at night, the whole Temple was brilliantly illuminated. At some point, probably when there was an eerie lull in the noise and a silence fell over the massive crowd in the Temple courtyard, Jesus raised his voice and, in a powerful, dramatic tone cried out to the vast multitude, "I am the Light of the world. He who follows me will not walk in darkness; he will have the light of life." (Jn. 8:12)

Picture the area filled with religious officials, scribes, Pharisees, priests of various ranks, as well as thousands of people from every country where Israelites lived. The authorities must have been beside themselves with bewilderment. "What is this man going to do next? Now he is making himself the light of the world. Is he mad? Does he really think he is the light of the world? He is either mad, or he should have credentials justifying his claim." So, they decided to confront Jesus and demand justification for his preposterous claim to be the light of the world. They accused him of claiming for himself a divine attribute, "[B]ut you are rendering testimony to yourself. That is not valid."

> Jesus responded, "Even if it were I who testify to myself, my testimony is truthful, because I know from where I come, and where I go. You judge according to the flesh [limited human knowledge]. I judge no one.

Still, if I do judge, the judgment that I make is true, for I am not alone. I and He who sent me are together. In the Law, your Law, it is written that the testimony of two men is valid. I am the witness for myself, and there is also the witness of the Father who has sent me."

Of course, they asked him, "Where is your Father?"

"You know neither me nor my Father," Jesus retorted. "If you knew me you would also know my Father." (Jn. 8:13–19)

What Jesus was saying was clear. It was as if he had said to them, "You should know my Father. He has been teaching you through the prophets for hundreds of years, preparing you for my coming. And if you listened to the prophets you would know me because they were preparing you for my coming. But of course your fathers killed the prophets and you buried them, so how could you know? If you listened to the prophets, you would know me, and know that I am truthful, and my testimony about myself would be valid, and the signs that I work would be evidence of my Father's testimony on my behalf. That is all the evidence you need. But, because you are blind, you cannot see."

Then, for some reason, Jesus told them that he was leaving. "I go and you will seek me, and in your sin you will die. Where I go you cannot come." (What he was saying was that in the future, when the time of destruction came upon them, they would look for their Messiah, but they would not be able to find him because he had already come and gone, and it would be too late to go and look for him. But they could not understand that.) They kept asking, "Will he kill himself, since he says, 'Where I go you cannot come?' "

Jesus then said to them, "You are from below; I am from above. You are of this world; I am not of this world. That is why I said to you that you will die in your sins. It is because you do not believe that 'I am' that you will die in your sins."

The key to understanding Jesus' assertion that they "do not believe" is that it is not from ignorance that they did not believe in Jesus, but because they chose not to believe. Jesus seemed to reveal their real evil when he told the parable about the tenants hired to care for the vineyard. In the parable the owner sends servants to collect what is due him, and the tenants beat and kill the servants. He finally sends his son, and the tenants remark, "Let us kill him. He is the heir. If we get rid of him, the vineyard will be ours." Whatever it was that the chief priests and scribes and Pharisees clung to so ferociously, their clinging made even God's Son an unwelcome intruder in their business, and the only and final solution to this threat was his elimination. They had come to that conclusion very early after Jesus' appearance. In short, their long-awaited Messiah was a threat to their business, and to their power over the people. Their greed for material wealth and power was such an obsession that they let it blind their consciences to the overwhelming evidence of Jesus' identity as God's Anointed.

This blindness of which Jesus accused the religious authorities may seem hard for us to believe when the divine identity of Jesus is so obvious to us, but the blindness of the scribes and Pharisees is a very common phenomenon in human nature. In all the years I have been a priest and have heard confessions, I have never had a penitent come to confession and confess that he or she had ever committed a sin of injustice toward another human being, especially in business practices, or that they had destroyed another person. Only rarely did anyone admit they had been unable to forgive someone who had injured them or someone they loved. I know good people, heads of multinational corporations, who, just before financial reports were due, would lay off thousands of workers at an age where it would be almost impossible for them to find other employment. The devastation to these loyal workers and their families often drove many of them into the ranks of the homeless, and some to suicide. This was all done to enhance the executive's genius as a shrewd businessman, or to pad his severance compensation when he was plotting his retirement. And these were upstanding Christians. The human ability to justify personal evil is pervasive throughout our race. Every evil act performed is done because we convince ourselves that what we are doing is good. Only later on, when we look back on our lives with more objectivity, can we see what we have done and feel disbelief that we could have so deceived ourselves.

At this point the Jewish authorities were thoroughly confused as to what Jesus was claiming.

They said to him, "Who are you?"

"Why do I even speak to you?" Jesus replied. "I have many things to say and to lay bare about you, but know this, that He who sent me is true, and the things that I heard from Him, these I speak to the world." They did not understand that he was speaking to them about the Father.

Then Jesus said, "When you have lifted up the Son of Man, then you will know that 'I am' and that of myself I do nothing. What I say I say just as the Father has taught me. He it is who sent me, and He is with me. He has not left me alone, because I do always the things that are pleasing to Him." While he was saying these things many believed in him. (Jn. 8:21–30)

These new believers are *really* new. They have just been touched by what Jesus is saying, but their understanding of him is new. Their belief is shallow and can be fickle. Jesus said to them, "If you live on in my word, you shall be my disciples indeed, and you shall know the truth, and the truth shall make you free." Some in the crowd—whether it was some of those standing by who were beginning to believe in Jesus or those who did not believe in him is not clear—took exception to what Jesus had just said:

"We are the children of Abraham, and we have never been slaves to anyone. How can you say, 'You shall be free?' "

" 'I tell you in truth, everyone who commits sin is a slave of sin. But the slave does not live in the house forever. The son lives there forever. If therefore the Son makes you free, you will indeed be free. I realize that you are the children of Abraham, but you still seek to kill me because my word has not taken hold of you. I speak what I have seen with the Father; and you do what you have seen with your father.' "

"Abraham is our father," some protested.

Jesus then said, "If you are the children of Abraham, then do the works of Abraham. But as it is, you are plotting to kill me, one who has spoken the truth to you, what I have learned from God. This Abraham did not do. But, you are doing the work of your father."

"We have not been born of fornication; we have one Father, God."

"If God were your father, you would surely love me, for I came forth from God and have come down here. I have not come of myself; He it is who sent me. Why do you not understand what I am saying? It is because you cannot bear to listen to what I have to say. The father from whom you are is the devil, and you do the will of your father. He was a murderer from the beginning, and he has not stood for truth, for there is no truth in him. When he tells a lie, he speaks from his very nature, for he is a liar and the father of lies. But, because I speak the truth you do not believe me. Which of you can convict me of sin? If I speak the truth why do you not believe me? He who is of God believes the words of God. The reason you do not hear is that you are not of God."

From that point, the Pharisees accused Jesus of being a Samaritan, and of being possessed by a devil. Jesus told them they accused him of having a devil because he honored God, and then went on to tell them that whoever kept his word would never see death, which really infuriated them.

"Now we know you have a devil. Abraham is dead, and the prophets are dead, and you say, 'If anyone keeps my word he will never taste death.' Are you greater than our father Abraham, who is dead? And the prophets are dead. Who do you make yourself out to be?"

"If I glorify myself, my glory is nothing. It is my Father who glorifies me, and holds me before you as a witness of Himself, of whom you say that He is your God. And you do not know Him, but I know Him. And if I say I do not know Him, I would be like you, a liar. But, I know Him and I keep His word. Abraham your father rejoiced that he was to see my day. He saw it and was glad."

They then laughed at him. "You are not yet fifty years old, and you have seen Abraham?"

To which Jesus responded, "Before Abraham came to be, 'I am.' " At that point they picked up stones to throw at him, but Jesus slipped away from them and left the temple. (Jn. 8:30–59)

What Jesus was claiming here was said so bluntly, it should have stunned them into at least taking him seriously enough to consider what he had said. Jesus used the same words that God had used on Mount Horeb when Moses asked Him for his name. He responded, "Tell the people 'I am' ('Yahweh') sent you."

The following incident must have been shortly after this confrontation with the religious authorities; it ties in logically with where that discussion left off. Jesus had come across a man who had been born blind. The apostles were now with Jesus again. Did they just come across him by accident in the Temple environs, or had they met up with him earlier? No matter, they were with him when he encountered this blind man. They asked Jesus, "Rabbi, who has sinned, this man or his parents, that he should be born blind?"

> Jesus answered, "Neither this man nor his parents have sinned, but that the works of God might be made manifest in him. I must do the works of Him who sent me while it is day; night is coming, when no one can work. As long as I am in the world, I am the Light of the world."
>
> When he had said these things, he spat on the ground and made a paste with his spittle, and spread the paste over the man's eyes, and said to him, "Go, wash in the pool of Siloam" (which means One Sent). So he went and washed and returned seeing.

People who had known him were shocked, and he told them what had happened. Eventually, he encountered the Pharisees, who questioned him. He told them the same story, about this man who'd told him to go and wash in the pool of Siloam, which he had done, and immediately he could see. What the Pharisees naturally picked up was the message Jesus knew they would eventually get, that the man had gone to the One-Who-Was-Sent and was healed immediately. The Pharisees could not but be stunned by the cleverness and the force of Jesus' stratagem. He had been telling them consistently that he was the One Sent by the Father to teach God's word. He had told them so many times that if they listened to the One Sent they too would see. But, because they refused to accept the One Sent, they remained blind. A powerful lesson, but their hatred of Jesus was so deep it hardened their hearts against him and they remained adamant in their refusal to acknowledge him. (Jn. 9:1–21)

The story ends with Jesus looking for the man in the Temple precincts. He found him, approached, and asked him if he believed in the Son of God. The man's answer was so simple and so open: "Who is he, Lord, that I may believe in him?" "You have both seen him and he it is who speaks with you." And the man said, "I believe, Lord." And he fell down and worshipped him. And as might be expected, there were Pharisees present who witnessed this. Jesus tried once more to reach out to them: "For judgment I have come into this world, that they who do not see may see, and those who do see, may become blind." Some of the Pharisees asked him, "Are we also blind?" Jesus' response was unequivocal: "If you were blind, you would not have sin, but because you insist 'We see,' your sin remains." (Jn. 9:35–41)

Jesus knew that in their obsession to hold on to the power and material benefits of the vineyard entrusted to them by his Father, they had willingly blinded themselves to the truth of his identity and the divine source of his message. So, he was making an observation as to the state of their souls, warning them that in the eyes of their God, they were living in the worst sin, the sin of usurping the Kingdom of God for themselves from God's own Son.

In John's Gospel the narrative moves on to another parable that Jesus shared, which does not seem aimed at the religious authorities. He talks about the sheep and the sheepfold and the shepherd. It does not seem to follow immediately after this last confrontation in the Temple. Jesus was probably outside of Jerusalem, in an area where there were sheep grazing, and possibly a large sheepfold where several shepherds would lead their sheep at the end of the day so they would be protected at night from foxes or wild animals or even human thieves.

Jesus started out by talking about the gate of the sheepfold:

> "I say to you in all truth, he who does not enter by the gate into the sheepfold, but climbs in another way, he is a robber or a thief. He who enters by the gate is the keeper of the sheep. The gateman opens to him, and the sheep listen to his voice. Then he calls his flock by its name and they recognize him as he leads them out. When he has brought out all his own he walks before them and they follow him because they recognize his voice. A stranger they will not follow. They will flee the stranger because they do not know the voice of strangers." (Jn. 10:1–5)

When Jesus told parables they dealt with something that was on his mind, and were prompted most often by his surroundings. On this occasion, it is possible he was considerably removed from the city. The parable is a long and extended one and there seems to be a large number of flocks in the area. Also, something seems to be troubling him since his recent encounter with the Temple officials. It is still on his mind, and seems to raise concerns about the future. So, he describes a very complicated scenario about sheep and shepherd and other handlers of the sheep. It is difficult to decipher what are all the meanings in this complicated parable puzzle. What is the sheepfold with not just one flock but several flocks? Is Israel the sheepfold, from which only a small number of the sheep recognize the Messiah's voice? Who is the gatekeeper? Could it refer to the guardians of the Temple, the chief priests, who ran the sacred place like their private business, and allowed foreign nonbelievers illegal entrance into important Temple affairs? Strange they were not able to prevent Yahweh's Shepherd access to the sheepfold. None of the things mentioned in the parable seems to apply to the scribes and Pharisees unless we include them as gatekeepers. He does refer to himself as the gate, through which the sheep pass as they enter and leave the sheepfold. He is the gate, we know, to the kingdom, and the gate to understanding the Father, and the gate to the kingdom of heaven after death. Jesus hints there are other flocks of sheep in the fold. Who are they and what are they doing in the sheepfold with Jesus' flock? Are they in any way related? Are they the Jewish people who do not recognize the shepherd's voice, the voice of the Good Shepherd? They have their own shepherds, the scribes and the Pharisees. Who are the robbers and thieves who break into the sheepfold to ravage the sheep? All these questions seemed to have no current answers.

Jesus had made a remark to the Pharisees earlier, saying they would one day look for him, realizing too late his true identity, but would not be able to find him, because he had already left. Where he had gone they could not go. He had hinted there would be bad times, possibly years later when they would be fatally locked in the besieged city of Jerusalem, and they would finally realize that he was truly their Messiah, but it would be too late. They would have already killed him. Maybe now Jesus was defining those times when people would enter the sheepfold and stir up trouble that would bring Roman disaster upon the flock. Could he have been referring to the false prophets, who sprang up every so often? Could he be thinking of Barabbas and other revolutionaries who would bring disaster upon the people?

Could this unusually complex parable refer to the future, when false prophets, as in the early Church, would enter the sheepfold and tear apart the flock? They would come to steal the sheep, and breed their own sheep living side by side with the flock of the Good Shepherd. Is this parable intentionally confusing because Jesus' vision into the future saw the confusion that would occur as the flock was tampered with?

The constant harassment of the scribes and Pharisees must have had a discouraging effect on Jesus. Their endless accusations and the verbal traps they laid for him, interrupting every speech he gave, creating confusion among the people, had to cause him to wonder about the future, when his simple apostles would be the target of relentless persecution.

Then, immediately after John lays down this parable, he shows Jesus telling the parable of the Good Shepherd, the only one who really cares for the flock.

> "I am the Good Shepherd. The Good Shepherd lays down his life for his sheep. The one who works for pay is not the shepherd. The sheep do not belong to him. When he sees the wolf coming, he abandons the sheep and flees. The wolf then attacks the sheep and carries them away and scatters them. The hired hand does this because he works for pay and has no concern for the sheep. I am the Good Shepherd. I know mine and mine know me, as the Father knows me and as I know the Father. And I offer my life for the sheep.
>
> "I have other sheep who are not of this fold. These also I must bring under my care, and they will hear my voice. Then there will be one flock and one shepherd. The Father loves me for the reason that I lay down my life so I can take it up again. No one takes my life from me; I offer it, of my own free will. I have the power to lay down my life and I have the power to take it up again. Such is the command I have received from my Father." (Jn. 10:11–18)

When Jesus referred to himself as the Good Shepherd, he was not just talking about times past when he was walking among the flock, although it was those circumstances that prompted him to tell that parable. He had witnessed the pain and the damage done to the sheep by the hired hands, the scribes and Pharisees. By their lack of understanding of the difficult situations in the people's lives, which often made it difficult if not impossible for them to live up to all the ideals of the Law, the Pharisees drove them away and excommunicated them from Temple worship. They did this because they had no real love for the sheep, and could without any qualms abandon them to the wolves. But the Good Shepherd who loves the sheep went out to look for the bruised and troubled and hurting sheep, and when he found them, he picked them up, placed them on his shoulders, and carried them back home. He did this because he loved the sheep. And he still does this today.

So, Jesus was projecting the meaning of this complicated combination of parables into the future, when this parable will make sense. There will be those who enter the sheepfold surreptitiously and cause mayhem among the flock. This began early in the Christian communities and will continue forever. But the loyal sheep will still recognize the voice of their shepherd, and will follow him when he leads them out of the sheepfold.

Only Jesus understands the pain of the sheep, who too often have been hurt and bruised and damaged, sometimes critically damaged, and driven away by some of their own unfeeling shepherds. In his compassion, the Good Shepherd knows their pain, and will always go out in search of them. And he is referring to sinners, people hurt and bruised by sin. He knows they are hurting, and because he loves them he never gives up his search, and when he finds them he tenderly carries them back home. It is so beautiful to see the Savior going out in search of sinners, whom, interestingly, he does not call sinners, but hurting sheep. If the Savior chooses to embrace sinners, we might ask ourselves if it is right for us to say that these people are not worthy of his embrace. Is not their coming home painful enough, and humbling enough, without demanding even more of them before we will accept them fully, and allow Jesus to embrace them?

This seems to be a good time to end this phase of Jesus' ministry, because it is a natural conclusion to Jesus' mission in Galilee. He does not seem to have ever gone back to Galilee, his place of so many memories beginning from his childhood and ending with this phase of his ministry. There were good memories for him, as well as most painful memories as he was winding down his preaching there with great disappointment and the cold rejection by those people for whom he'd spared nothing of himself to heal them of sickness, blindness, and diseases of every description, only to see them turn away from him with cold indifference, as if he really meant nothing to them other than their daily entertainment.

After warning them of the danger of their rejection, and comparing them unfavorably with Sodom and Gomorrah and Ninevah, he left them forever, and seems to have never looked back.

So now we end that chapter of Jesus' life and see him burdened with ominous premonitions as he travels alone to Judea, where he knows he will preach to the people from there and to Jews from the Diaspora, who will come there regularly from many countries to celebrate the great feasts of their religion.

29

A WHOLE NEW CHAPTER IN JESUS' MISSION

In preparing the apostles for their work in the future, he told them they were to go out and teach all nations. "Some will accept you, some will reject you. If a town rejects you, leave that town and shake the dust of that town off your sandals as a testimony against them." That counsel Jesus seems to have put into practice when he left Galilee for the last time and went to Judea. After he gave so much of himself to those people for well over a year, they coldly turned their backs on him and walked with him no more. After leaving this time, he never returned to Galilee. There was still his ministry in Judea ahead of him, and much for him to accomplish before his work was finished.

Did he write off the people of Galilee who rejected him? That is a frightening thought, that God would treat anyone that way. He gave them strict warning about what their fate would be if they did not change, and if they continued in their resistance to God's grace, but it is not in the nature of God to write off any of His children, who were created with such love. We may write off sinners and condemn them to death as unredeemable, or to a life of inhuman degradation for the rest of their natural lives. Redemption of a sinner is not a popular value in the political life of many people. Punishment and retribution is the accepted response of so much of today's society.

Fortunately, God is more humane. He never abandons His children but goads us constantly with His redeeming grace right to the end, determined to win our repentance and change our hearts, until we accept His love. We humans do not have that kind of persistent love. We cannot tolerate sinners the way God does. When people do evil we demand the ultimate in punishment and rarely see any reason for compassion or redemption. That crowd in Galilee turned their backs on Jesus. They made their decision. He still made himself available to them for the next few weeks, in the unlikely chance they might have a change of heart, until the time came for him to continue his ministry in Judea and Jerusalem and its surrounding area.

The last time he was in Jerusalem they'd tried to kill him. This time he knew what to expect. His return after past unpleasant experiences reflects his determination to reach out even to those whose hearts were already turned against him, many of whom were still only too willing to find an excuse to kill him. It could not but be a sad journey. He had already warned the apostles on various occasions that he would be betrayed by the chief priests, and be tortured and put to death. His willingness to put himself in these circumstances was impossible for the apostles to understand, especially if he foresaw that it was about to happen. They had seen the Master slip away and mysteriously disappear in the past from precarious situations. Maybe that was what he was planning this time, as well.

We saw Jesus working as the Festival of Tents was winding down. Toward the end was celebrated the Festival of Lights, when he dramatically declared himself as the Light of the world. He had tried to open the hearts of the Pharisees to the light that he brought into their world. But no matter how hard he tried, they *chose* to remain blind to even the most convincing evidence, as when he gave sight to a blind man after he sent the fellow to wash in the pool named Sent, cleverly hinting that the blind man received his sight from the One Sent. And that was what the fellow told the Pharisees when they questioned him. "I went to Siloam, the One Sent, and now I see."

At some time while Jesus was in Judea, he traveled to Transjordan, on the eastern side of the river, in Herod's other territory, where very large crowds followed him to hear him speak and to be cured. It was a wise move on Jesus' part to preach in that area, especially with the large crowds gathering around him. If he had gone closer to Jerusalem, especially with a large crowd gathered around him, he would have aroused suspicion and created a distraction from his preaching. It was a wise move for still another reason. The spot in Transjordan where he stayed and preached was the place where he'd first met John while he was baptizing. Many of John's loyal followers lived in the surrounding area. Seeing Jesus not only preaching and his apostles baptizing, but also curing people of diseases of every kind, made very real John's testimony about Jesus as the Lamb of God, and the anointed one whose way John was sent to prepare. Many of John's followers who remained loyal to John's memory now could understand why John had insisted that they follow Jesus.

Being there on the spot sacred to the memory of John's loyal disciples, it was clear Jesus could not tarry there for long, because of its proximity to Herod's palace. As it happened, Herod happened to be residing there at this particular time. That was where his mountaintop fortified palace of Machaerus was located, and where John had been imprisoned and beheaded. Hearing that Jesus had relocated from Galilee down to where John used to meet and baptize brought back nightmares to Herod. Whereas he had tolerated Jesus and his ministry in Galilee, he was now suspicious of why Jesus would come down here so close to Herod, and at the same place where John had preached, unless it was to haunt him. Jesus' stunning miraculous cures of people with all kinds of diseases unglued Herod's sense of security. What was the source of this man's powers? Jesus' ability to hold the crowds spellbound unsettled him. What did he plan to do with all his talk about a kingdom?

Word of Herod's fears spread among the local aristocratic elite, including influential Pharisees. Apparently there were many Pharisees who admired and respected Jesus, and were present among the crowds Jesus preached to at the Jordan. They may not have been followers, but they were touched by his intimacy with God, and sensed he was a good man. They had heard of Herod's attitude toward Jesus and were concerned for Jesus' welfare. One day a small group approached him to warn him, "Leave this place! Herod is plotting to kill you." Jesus' reply was sharp. "Go, tell that fox: Know that today and tomorrow I cast out devils and on the third day accomplish my mission. But, for today and tomorrow and the next day I will go on, for it would not be right for a prophet to die outside Jerusalem."

These were bold words. It is obvious what Jesus thought of Herod, and he was telling him in language that was unmistakable, "No matter what you intend to do to me, you will fail. There is nothing that you do that could harm me. My time has not yet come. And when that time comes, it will not be here in your jurisdiction. I am in control of my own life. When I die, it will be in Jerusalem."

The Gospels do not say how long Jesus stayed in that area. It was probably long enough to give John's disciples a chance to come and enjoy the experience that John had prophesied and was willing to die for. Whatever fading feelings of envy they may have held previously about Jesus' popularity were now replaced by a joy that John's prophecies about this man were powerfully fulfilled, and they had no scruples in becoming wholehearted disciples of Jesus. "Many people who came to him there said, 'John gave no signs, but everything he said about this man is true.' And many of them believed in him." (Jn. 11:41–42) The delegation of leading disciples whom John had previously sent to evaluate Jesus paid off. John knew they would be impressed when they saw the stunning evidence of his divine mission. When they came back and told John and his disciples about Jesus, that was all that was needed. John could finally die in peace, knowing that his mission was accomplished. John's mission was well launched, and the crowds gathering around his Master were vast, greater than he could have ever imagined. And John knew his work was done.

When Jesus came down from Galilee to Judea this time, even though he came in his own good time and not with his family, he eventually met up with not just the apostles, but also the seventy-two disciples whom he had previously in Galilee sent out two by two to prepare the people in the towns and villages he intended to visit. This does not mean that they were with him every place he went, but they were scattered throughout the area in Judea to announce Jesus' coming to various places, probably telling the people the approximate day of his arrival, and how long a time he would be able to spend there. While there these men, and there could have been women as well, would have met with various people in these villages and discussed with them the message that Jesus would be bringing to them, and that he most probably would be willing to heal whoever was sick in the village. They would have also discussed the details of whatever hospitality the people might be willing to offer to Jesus and his apostles during the time they would spend with them. They couldn't just sleep in the streets. The eastern people were always noted for their hospitality.

Luke records the instructions Jesus gave to this advance contingent:

"The harvest is great but the laborers are few, so ask the Lord of the harvest to send laborers into his harvest. Start off now, but remember, I am sending you out like lambs among wolves. Carry no purse, no backpack, no sandals. Don't dally talking to people on the way. Whatever house you go into, let your greeting be, 'Peace to this house,' and if peaceable people live there your peace will rest on them. If not it will come back to you. Stay in the same house, accepting whatever food and drink they offer you, for the laborer is worth his keep. Do not move from house to house. In whatever town you enter, eat what is set before you. Cure the sick and say, 'The kingdom of God is very near to you.' And whenever you go into a town and they do not welcome you, go out into its streets and say, 'We wipe the very dust of your town from our feet and give it back to you, but know this, the kingdom of God is very near.' And I tell you when the time comes, it will not go as hard on Sodom as on that town." (Lk. 10:2–12)

They were practical instructions. It was all about focus on their mission, and they must realize they were not asking favors from people. They were offering them a priceless gift, the greatest gift of their lives. The people should know the purpose of their coming. They were already aware of Jesus and his work, and they should be glad to offer his disciples hospitality. But he also warned his representatives to be respectful of what the people offered them, and whether they were rich or poor, they should be gracious to all.

30

Jesus Tours the Judean Villages

In the meantime, Jesus went on with his apostles to other villages, preaching his message of the kingdom and healing the sick and troubled, and enjoying the fellowship of the friendly villagers, most of whom had heard of him since his previous visit to the area during the festivals. These people seemed for the most part to be very accepting of him, and had a much healthier appreciation of his teachings. They also seemed to be sufficiently knowledgeable of the Scriptures to do their own thinking and not be afraid to disagree with the Pharisees' and priests' opinions about Jesus. We see many of them later on defending him when he is being attacked by emissaries of the chief priests and other rulers.

Trying to place the happenings described in the Gospels from this time on is difficult. Some events seem to have taken place earlier. Some of the stories and parables may have been at other occasions previous to Jesus' present visit to Judea. But the exact order of events is not critical, and certainly the Gospel writers never considered it critical. What were critical were the teachings of Jesus, and we will content ourselves to listening to Jesus as well as watching him in our attempt to understand him and what he was experiencing.

We do know it was after the Festival of Tents and the Festival of Light. That was at the time of the wheat harvest, and the harvesting of other crops and certain fruits, as well. September was winding down, and October was approaching. Luke writes that "Jesus traveled through the towns and villages, teaching and setting a pathway for himself on his way to Jerusalem." (Lk. 13:22) Then Luke relates incidents that do not necessarily seem to have taken place at that time. They seem to reflect things that had happened on other occasions, but that is of little importance. John, however, totally ignores the time from the ending of the Festival of Tents, which was late September, until the Festival of the Dedication of the Temple, which was celebrated in December, well into winter, and the winter cold.

So, we will take a little freedom and walk with Jesus through the various towns and villages, and listen to what he has to say, and learn something of his experiences. Remember: It is early October and the harvest has been taken in and the grapes have all been picked and pressed. This is always a fun time for the people in whatever country—the local inhabitants partake of the wine-making event. It is a fun time, with music and dancing and singing, as everyone takes part in the joyful occasion. The grapes were crushed and the wine poured into large containers, or into wineskins, which were then stored in cool places, often in caves dug out of the soft sandstone rock. These caves might be the common storage places where a number of families' wine was stored.

This brings back so many fond memories of my time in Italian parishes. In October every year I used to get invitation after invitation to visit the parishioners' homes when they were making wine. Walking down each street, you could almost become intoxicated from the fumes pouring out of all the open cellar windows. It was all new wine, but they wanted the priest to taste it, and then when it was fully fermented months later, they would call up and ask me to come down and taste their finished product. After fifteen or twenty visits it was a task to work my way back to the rectory, carrying at least six or seven bottles of their best wine. Some of the wine was delicious and could have been marketed. It was much better than some of the costly wines sold today.

Some of the best wine in the neighborhood was made by an eighty-year-old man who lived next to the rectory. We had become dear friends. His name was Peter Della Ratta. One day he called up his son, Richard, who has since been my lawyer for years, and told him that he was shocked when he saw me doing heavy work like a common ditchdigger, and that I was strong like a bull, and that he was going to ask me to help him turn his wine press. He was too weak to turn it anymore. So, I helped him, and unfortunately, after he told me to turn it once more, the cast-iron shaft broke. He couldn't wait to tell his son. But his wine was delicious. He made a white muscatel and a zinfandel, which tasted nothing like what they sell in stores. His wines were alive and delightful. On Sunday mornings, Pete would go to the bakery and get two loaves of freshly baked Italian bread, and on his way back home, he would call me as I was coming from the church, and we would sit on the bumper of a car and tear apart one of the loaves and enjoy our own personal breaking of bread. Pete is now long dead, and all his wine-making equipment is in my cellar.

Another winemaker was Dominic Leone, who is still alive, and after my being out of that parish for almost forty years, we are still dear friends, and he and his wife Antoinette still come to visit and bring jugs of their red and white wine. His wine is the same excellent quality it was forty years ago; there is still nothing comparable to it even in the stores.

Now let us take a trip with Jesus around these towns and villages. The common people loved Jesus, and I am sure that as he strolled down the streets of these little towns, he could smell the fragrance of those fermenting grapes floating through the air. And men of these cultures being as they are, so proud of their wine—I am sure they had to have invited Jesus into their caves to sit and chat with them as they did their work. Everybody made wine in those countries, and Jesus as a young man most probably helped his own relatives as they pressed the grapes and stored away their family's wine each year.

And even though Jesus was not a heavy drinker, the Pharisees made a thing of Jesus drinking wine all the same. So, I am sure when he met with the people in these little villages, the local men were only too happy to have this famous preacher taste their wine while they waited excitedly for his approval.

The time when Jesus made the comment about the wineskins, it was something he probably learned from relatives he was helping as they made wine for the family. "They do not put new wine into old wineskins, because the new wine when it ferments will burst the skins. They put new wine into new wineskins, so they will work together." (Mt. 9:16–17)

The wine-making season was, and still is today, a happy time for the villagers. They have street dances and music and fun. If Jesus worked his way through these villages, he must have had a lot of fun, something he needed at the time to distract him from what he knew only too keenly awaited him in Jerusalem. These townsfolk must have had beautiful memories of Jesus' time spent in their midst, preaching to them about the kingdom and sharing in their simple parties and in their daily lives for the few days he spent in each of those places.

When you see how these simple villagers took to Jesus, and saw how playfully human he was, it makes sense to see them later on taking Jesus' side when he is criticized by the religious leaders. These leaders were frightened by the people's reaction when they tried to hurt Jesus. On at least one occasion they were afraid the people were going to stone them. This was all a new and encouraging experience for Jesus. After all the time and caring Jesus had spent with the vast crowds in Galilee, he'd never had this warm bonding with those people. Here it was entirely different. These people appreciated him and enjoyed him, and developed warm feelings for him.

One day as Jesus was touring the villages, the seventy-two returned all excited, bursting with the wonderful experiences they'd had expelling demons from people possessed. They could not get over the thrill of the experience. These seventy-two seem to be more childlike than the apostles, who were all too easily prone to feelings of self-importance. Then, Jesus said to them, as if to reassure them that Satan is real, "I watched Satan fall like lightening from heaven. Yes, I have given you power to tread on serpents and scorpions, and all the wiles of the enemy, so nothing will ever hurt you. But, do not rejoice that spirits are subject to you, but that your names are written in heaven."

> Then, Jesus, filled with the joy of the Holy Spirit, prayed, "I bless you, Father, Lord of heaven and earth, for having kept these things hidden from the learned and the clever, and revealed them to these childlike souls. Yes, Father, it has so pleased you that it be this way. Everything has been entrusted to me by my Father, and no one knows who the Son really is except the Father, and no one knows the Father except the Son, and whoever the Son chooses to reveal Him." Then, turning to them privately, "Happy are the eyes that see what you see, for I tell you, many prophets and kings desired to see what you see and never saw it, and to hear what you hear and never heard it." (Lk. 10:17–24)

As Jesus and his companions continued their tour of the villages, they gradually worked their way to a village higher up in the Judean hillside called Bethany. It was there that Mary, Martha, and Lazarus lived. Reading carefully the Gospel texts, you get the impression that Jesus' manner of teaching was different here than in Galilee. In Galilee, there were wide open hillsides with grass and places for the crowds to sit and relax while listening to Jesus preach. There were no such accommodations in the dusty rocks of the Judean hills. His style here had to be different, and commentators think that he met with people in small groups at their houses, or perhaps in a village gathering place.

In Bethany, he had an ideal spot at Mary, Martha, and Lazarus' place. Hopefully he did not still have the seventy-two advance messengers with him when he arrived there. Even the twelve apostles were enough of a crowd to spring on any host, however gracious they might be. No doubt the seventy-two were already on other assignments, though Jesus might have sent somebody up to alert Martha that he was on his way. Luke does not say whether the seventy-two were still with them, or just the apostles. Judging by the size of the present remains of the compound or villa where this family lived, this must have been a place that could accommodate a good number of visitors. Other parts of the Gospels give the impression that this family did quite a bit of entertaining, always including high officials of the government and the Temple at their social gatherings.

Jesus and the apostles finally arrived at the house and were no doubt welcomed with great excitement. You can imagine that Martha gave them a chance to refresh themselves and offered them a local beverage and some snacks. But, knowing how gruff the apostles were, they probably did not consider sitting around talking to women their idea of relaxation, and besides, they were Jesus' friends and not theirs, so they could easily feel out of place. So they probably excused themselves, giving the family some private time with Jesus and promising to be back in time for supper, then walked down through the village to chat with the local villagers about things men in those days talked about, or perhaps played a popular game with the old men in the village gathering place.

It is interesting that Bethany is not far from the Jordan River crossing where Jesus had been preaching just a short while before. It was the same place where John used to baptize, on the eastern bank of the river in Perea, which was about seventeen miles from Bethany. Bethany was on the way up the hillside road on the way to Jerusalem. I had always wondered how Mary, Martha, and Lazarus had originally met Jesus and became such dear friends. It could easily have been when they were visiting John at the

Jordan, since they were a religious family. They always seemed to be a cut above most other people in the Gospel stories, and although they were quite wealthy, they were also deeply religious. It is very possible that they had been John's disciples before they met Jesus, and it may have been at one of John's gatherings that they first met. Again, Luke said previously that after Jesus finished preaching at the Jordan, he worked his way through the villages with his eye on Jerusalem, and sure enough, while on his tour of the villages and towns, as he approached Jerusalem, he was already in the vicinity of Bethany.

It is also a possibility that when Jesus left John after John had baptized him almost two years earlier, and went on his forty-day retreat, that retreat was on the rocky cliffs overlooking Jericho and not far from Bethany. After that retreat he must have been in a weakened condition and would have had to recuperate before making his hundred-mile trek back up to Galilee. What better place to stop and recuperate than at the home of these new friends, Lazarus and his two sisters at Bethany? The road out of his retreat was only a short walk to Bethany. This seems a very credible possibility, as we do not see him having any other close friends in the vicinity where he could stay to rest and recuperate. Bethany was a logical place for him to visit, and these very friendly folks probably would have invited him to stay and rest before starting out for that long trip northward. As strong as Jesus may have been, there is no way he could have walked a hundred miles back to Galilee in such a weakened condition.

So, again we find him and his apostles visiting this gracious family. It is very convenient, only two miles from Jerusalem and the Temple, where we will find Jesus after his short visit at Bethany.

When writing about this trip, it is hard not to wonder what Jesus did with the small army of seventy-two scouts that had been with him. Surely he did not descend on Martha with eighty-five guests dropping in for supper. As gracious as Martha was, I am sure Jesus would not have done that to her. He had brought the seventy-two down to Judea for a reason. They had their own work to do. They were assured of hospitality in the villages where they went to prepare for Jesus' visit in the near future. While the messengers were there, the villagers, who already knew of Jesus, would have had a thousand questions about him and his teachings, questions the messengers would have been only too happy to answer. So, those seventy-two messengers of Jesus would not have felt left out when Jesus went to Bethany. They had important work to do, which they were clearly excited about, and enjoyed immensely, and for the most part were treated with the customary eastern hospitality.

The setting in the house at Bethany, in the meantime, was relaxed, except for Martha. She ended up out in the kitchen by herself, busy getting everything organized for dinner for seventeen people, while Mary, seemingly oblivious to all the work that had to be done, was sitting at Jesus' feet listening to him. The apostles obviously had already taken their leave.

It did not take long before Martha not only felt she was being taken advantage of, but felt left out of a chance to sit and talk with Jesus, too. So, in a bit of a huff, she walked in where the two were chatting and chided Jesus for letting her sister just sit there and relax with him while she had to do all the preparations for dinner. "Lord, doesn't it bother you that she just sits there listening to you while I have to do all the work myself?" And who could say she was not right, though Jesus does not give her much satisfaction. The ease with which she could be so candid with Jesus shows that this family was more accustomed to Jesus' visits than the Gospels seem to indicate. It seems they were longtime friends.

"Martha, Martha, you are anxious and concerned about so many things, when only one thing is necessary. Mary has chosen the better part and it will not be taken from her."

Martha is gracious enough not to say more, but she could have just as easily said, "All right, Jesus, I'll stay here and sit with you, too, if you and your crew don't mind going without dinner." However, I cannot imagine Jesus letting Martha continue doing all the work herself. And where was Lazarus, their brother with the name meaning "leper"? Was he once a leper whom Jesus had cured of the horrible disease? Was he out working at his place of business, whatever that may have been? The family does seem to have lived comfortably, and later we will see important people visiting their home for social gatherings. Lazarus does seem to have had considerable social standing in the community for his sisters to enjoy their comfortable living, and for them all to be able to entertain lavishly on occasion. (Lk. 10:38–42)

There is nothing more said by Luke about this beautiful visit. He merely whets our appetite to imagine the most enjoyable conversations and special things Jesus shared with these dear friends, and speaking to them in a way he would not ordinarily speak to strangers or even the apostles. He did talk about life after death and the resurrection, and about his followers' resurrection after death, which we do not see him speaking about in the same way to others. It seems he had talked quite pointedly about the resurrection of the body at the last day, which we don't see him discussing anyplace else. Martha mentions this later, on the occasion of Lazarus' death, when she says to Jesus, "I know that he will rise again at the resurrection on the last day." It would have been more satisfying, though, if Luke had told us more about intimate details of what really took place on the occasion of that pleasant respite in Jesus' grueling schedule.

Luke does not indicate that Jesus stayed at his friends' house for any extended period of time; however, since neighbors of Mary and Martha certainly knew of Jesus from the sisters sharing with them, it is hard not to imagine that the family did not invite the neighbors to come to visit Jesus. This certainly had to happen. It would not have been very gracious of them not to have invited friends and neighbors to visit this famous teacher whom Mary and Martha and Lazarus had talked about so often.

When I used to travel, giving talks about Jesus, a great part of the time was spent at local family gatherings. If I did not stay at a hotel, I often stayed at someone's house, and for days after my talk, the hosts would ask if I minded visiting with their friends and neighbors. It is hard not to imagine the same thing happening to Jesus when he visited Bethany and other places as he traveled around Judea. The next time we see him will be at Mary and Martha's for Lazarus' shiva (period of mourning); it is clear that the mourners already knew Jesus when he finally showed up, indicating that they must have met him on other occasions in their neighborhood.

But now, while he was with Lazarus' family, and friends and neighbors they may have invited over, what did he talk about? He was not in the habit of just indulging in small talk. He had messages to deliver, and the time was growing short. Some of the things that Luke relates may have been the substance of what Jesus shared with those people, even though he does not explain the details of the precise situation.

Jesus' favorite subject was his Father. Though Jesus told his apostles to pray as if they were talking to their Father, he then went on to tell them about the prayer we call "The Our Father." It is very possible that when Luke placed this teaching within the context of Jesus' visit to Bethany, he was explaining to them the intimacy they should feel when they were praying to God. He told them to call God "Father." That was unheard of among Jews. He was the Awesome One, the Lord of the Universe. To call him "God," or in the endearing term that Jesus used, "Dear Father," or "Dad," was totally incomprehensible to the Israelite mentality, and not only the Israelite community then, but even in our own time, though I have heard that some Jews recently have felt more comfortable using the term "Father," after hearing Christians say it so often. In teaching them to pray this way, Jesus broke down the thick veil that distanced people from God, who loved them and wanted them to feel close to Him.

Call him "Dear Father," or whatever term you use when talking to your father. "Who are in heaven": Where is that? Heaven is where God is, and God is everywhere, so heaven is everywhere, all around us, just in another dimension. Our Father is so very close always. We live and breathe in Him, as He holds us in His protecting embrace. "Hallowed be your name!" May your name and the glory that reveals you to us be held in profound reverence. "Your kingdom come." The kingdom is already in your midst. When you open your hearts to the Father, you then enter the kingdom and become one with the kingdom. "Your will be done." As the kingdom spreads, the Father's plans for his children's welfare begin to take deeper root in the world until in time the world reflects the peace of heaven. "Give us today our daily bread." We really do not need much; we ask you, Father, for what we need for today. Tomorrow is in your hands. We know you always care for us. "Forgive us our sins, as we forgive those who sin against us." That is hard, Father. Teach us to forgive those who have hurt us so we can earn your forgiveness for all the wounds we have caused you. And "Lead us not into temptation, but deliver us from evil." Father, you guide our every step. Guide us away from those things that are dangerous for us, so you can protect us from evil and the evil one.

It seems in teaching the small group of listeners the way to pray, it was still too new for them. People are used to asking God for things and are always concerned about what to do when God does not answer. Someone seems to have asked Jesus what to do then. Jesus was very blunt. "Keep pestering Him!" He tells them a homey little story. "Imagine one of you has a friend who lives nearby, and you go to him in the middle of the night and wake him up, 'My friend, lend me some food. A friend just stopped off at my house on his travels and I have nothing to offer him.' And without even opening the door, the friend yells out, 'Don't bother me! The door is bolted and we are all in bed. I cannot get up and give you anything now.' I tell you, if your friend does not get up and give you what you want out of friendship, if you persist, he will give you what you want just to get rid of you."

It is enjoyable to see Jesus being so earthy. It is not that he is saying that God does not want to be bothered, like the man in the parable. But what he is saying is that the Father knows what is good for you, and for some reason may be reluctant to give you what you want, but if you keep persisting, He will answer your prayers in some way just to stop your pestering.

Then Jesus continued to develop on people's persistence when they want something from God. "So, I tell you, ask and it will be given to you; search and you will find; knock and the door will be opened to you. For the one who asks, will always receive; and the one who searches, will always find; and the one who knocks will always have the door opened to him. For what father among you would give his son a stone when he asks for bread? Or hand him a snake when he asks for a fish? Or hand him a scorpion when he asks for an egg? If you, then, who are evil, know how to give your children what is good, how much more will the heavenly Father give the Holy Spirit to those who ask Him?"

Jesus carefully encouraged that little group, possibly at Mary, Martha, and Lazarus' place, to continue praying, even if the heavenly Father does not grant what people ask for, because what they ask for, and sometimes almost demand, may not be for their good. But persistence in prayer often strengthens people's need for God's help, and often, if God does not grant their requests right away, it gives them a chance to realize that maybe what they are asking for is not good. Often people, after waiting, change their mind and begin to realize that maybe God was right in not granting what had seemed so important.

Jesus gives the real key to understanding the Father. He will always give the Holy Spirit to those who ask Him. If what they ask for is really needed for the good of their souls, that they will always receive. When it is material things, persistence will always prompt the Father to answer in a way that is for His children's good. Jesus showed sensitivity to the merely human way we approach God with our requests and was careful not to ridicule the childish way we pray, but encouraged us to continue praying. The Father will always answer, but not like the genie in fables. He is not our servant. We are the servants; He is God, a God who cares, and always gives us what is good for us.

Jesus eventually moved on and continued his tour of the villages. He was warmly received by almost everyone. It was a wonderful experience seeing Jesus so widely accepted by the people in the little villages he visited. This time it was different. There was more comradeship between the people and Jesus. They liked him personally, so different from the Galileans, who enjoyed what he could do for them. These people genuinely liked Jesus and were willing to fight for him when the authorities tried to arrest him.

Remember Jesus was now in Judea, and not far from the City of Jerusalem. Officials and their spies wandered through these little villages to listen to Jesus, not because they wanted to learn, but because they needed information to bring back to their superiors, who were preparing a case against him. So, many of the things Jesus talks about or makes reference to in his talks to the villagers were for the benefit of the scribes and Pharisees present. There were still messages he wanted to get back to the Temple, things he must preach for their benefit, even though he knew beforehand they would still insist on being blind and deaf to whatever he had to say.

On one occasion the subject of the kingdom of heaven came up. One of the apostles raised the question. "Who is the greatest in the kingdom of heaven?" What was he asking? About the kingdom of heaven on earth? Whatever the apostle had in mind, Jesus seems to have answered in terms of the kingdom of heaven after death. He called over a little child and, putting his arm around the child, told the crowd, "Unless you are willing to become like this little child, you will not even enter the kingdom of heaven. So, whoever is willing to be like this little child, that one is the greatest in the kingdom of heaven." (Lk. 18:1–4) But maybe Jesus is still talking about the kingdom of heaven on earth. Without a humble spirit a person will not possibly have the proper attitude for the kingdom of heaven to even appeal to him. The more childlike a person is, the deeper the person's humble spirit before God—that determines the person's standing in the kingdom of heaven. John the Baptizer gave up everything on earth, and denied himself of all that he might have treasured, living only to serve the Master. Jesus remarked that he was the greatest of all.

That was sure to baffle them. What was he talking about? What value has a little child? Who wants to become like a little child? We struggle our whole lives to grow up, and Jesus says we should be like little children. I am sure Jesus explained what he meant, but the Gospel writers never went into detail when Jesus said something that was confusing. We are left trying to search our own minds and search Jesus' mind in an attempt to understand why a child was so important to Jesus.

Searching like this always brings me back to experiences in the parishes where I served. In one parish there was a senior high school student who took a liking to me and was always available to help when I needed him. There was a beautiful simplicity about him, bright but childlike. His family were dear friends, and they were so glad that their son was close to me, and willing to help me work with the younger kids in the parish.

After graduation he went to college and I did not see him for the longest time. Years later, after I had been sent to another parish, he called up one day and asked to see me. I was delighted. He came over and said he was planning to get married and wanted to know if I would do the wedding. I was only too happy. But then he said, "There is one thing I feel I should tell you, Father. I do not believe in God." I was totally shocked, and asked him why he'd come to me to get married. And he told me it was because it was important to his grandmother that he be married in the Church.

I told him that that was not honest, and I could not be part of that, but that I would be willing to talk to his grandmother and help her to understand. He agreed to that, and eventually we had the wedding outside of church. When he told me that all he wanted me to do was just receive their exchange of vows and that he and his friends would do the rest of the ceremony, I told him that I was not going to go through all this trouble unless I could put my two cents in at the ceremony. So, I gave the sermon. After the ceremony, the best man came up to me and said, "Father, I have to admit your sermon was the most beautiful part of the ceremony. Thank you for what you have done for us."

When people become too sophisticated they lose that beautiful child-like innocence that was so precious to Jesus, and often their pride makes it difficult if not impossible to see the beauty and authenticity of that reality based on faith. I have often admired with tears in my eyes the simple women and also some men who would with such childlike simplicity and love kneel in church and say their rosary, repeating the same Hail Mary over and over and over, with such tender love in their childlike hearts. I would get so upset when I heard some priests ridicule those simple loving souls for the way they prayed. Yet, those simple souls are the ones who will have no trouble entering the kingdom when their time comes, while the rest of us, so well educated and so sophisticated, can only hope that God will have mercy on us. We know only too well the ones He favors, the faithful souls who believe so simply and love so sincerely.

"See that you never despise one of these little ones, for I tell you that their angels in heaven stand continually in the presence of my Father in heaven." (Lk. 18:10)

And suddenly the subject drifts off into talk about a lost sheep. What caused that? Did a villager come running down the street with a lost lamb he had just found? Whatever, Jesus used the occasion to talk about his favorite subject, a lost lamb, which he always saw as a lost or wandering soul. "Tell me, imagine a man has a flock of a hundred sheep and one of them wanders off. What do you think, will he not leave the ninety-nine and go out in search for the one that is wandering? I assure you, if he finds it, that gives him more joy than the ninety-nine that did not wander. Likewise, it is never the will of your Father in heaven that one of these little ones should ever be lost."

Then the subject changes again, this time to a family problem. It is possible someone asked Jesus how to resolve a family issue when someone has done something wrong. Simon may have been the one who brought up the subject. Jesus' answer is quite blunt:

> "If someone has done something wrong, discuss it with him between
> the two of you. If he listens, you have won him back. If he does not
> listen, go and talk to others in the family and have an intervention. It

takes two of you to uphold a charge. If he still refuses to listen, report it to the whole family, and if he still refuses to listen, then treat him like an outcast, a pagan or a tax collector.

"I assure you, whatever you bind on earth will be bound in heaven, and whatever you loose on earth will be loosed in heaven."

Was he saying this a second time to Simon the Rock?

Then the subject of prayer came up. This is interesting. Jesus had not talked like this before. "I will repeat what I said once before, if two of you on earth agree to ask anything at all, it will be granted you by my Father in heaven, for where two or three are gathered in my name, I will be there with them."

Then Peter brought up another subject that was troubling him. This may have been done when they were off by themselves. "Lord, how often must I forgive my brother, seven times?" Now seven times is quite generous, or so Peter thought. You get the impression he had been struggling with this after Jesus had talked about forgiveness on another occasion, and had managed to talk himself into seeing how he could forgive up to seven times, but that was it. Jesus' reply was unsettling, "Not seven times, but seventy times seven times." And the conversation came to an abrupt end. And you picture the Rock walking away, shaking his head in disbelief. "Impossible, impossible!"

But Jesus does not end it there. He continues with a parable. This time he elevates the whole issue of forgiveness to a global dimension that extends right up to the judgment day.

There was a king who decided to settle accounts with his servants. When the reckoning began, a servant was brought in who owed ten thousand talents of silver, an incredible amount of debt. As he had no way to pay, the master ordered that he and his family be sold, together with all he owned, in payment of the debt. The servant broke down and pleaded with the master, who forgave him the whole debt. But, then that servant went out and encountered a fellow servant who owed him a hundred denarii, by comparison a very small amount. He grabbed the servant by the throat and shook him, demanding, "Pay me what you owe me." The man pleaded with him to give him time and he would pay him in full, but the other servant refused, and had him thrown into prison until he paid his debt. His fellow servants were upset and reported what had happened to the master, who then sent for him. "You wicked servant, I forgave you your whole debt when you pleaded with me. Should you not then have had pity on your fellow servant as I had pity on you?" In his indignation, the master turned him over to the torturers till he paid all his debt. And that is how my Father in heaven will treat you unless you forgive your brothers and sisters from your heart. (Lk. 18:12–35)

This is the lost and too easily forgotten teaching of Jesus. Every year when election time comes round, and the politicians are parading their wares, I cringe when lawyers and judges are campaigning. Candidates for district attorney almost to a man compete with one another as to who will be the most perfect Pontius Pilate and satisfy the demands of the rabble for blood. Losing all sense of personal pride and dignity, they grovel to please the public. And the worst of it is that when elected they carry out their vows by over-indicting individuals for crimes they know they did not commit, with the hope they will plead to a lesser crime, but still serious enough to put them in prison for years. Then at the next election, when they may be campaigning for a judgeship, they can boast of all the lives they destroyed by trick convictions. And these officials parade themselves as good Christians. One cannot help but hear Jesus saying, "It is not the death of a sinner I desire, but his conversion to a new and holy life." Our system makes that impossible. If Jesus meant what he said about his heavenly Father at the Judgment Day, then it is going to be one sorry day for those who have so lightly destroyed the lives of so many by their cold-blooded meanness in condemning them to a personal hell on earth.

When Jesus said that the one servant owed his master ten thousand talents, he was telling us that even though we may consider our offenses against God insignificant, in his eyes they are monstrous compared to any offense humans can commit against one another, and we had better forgive one another, or he will act in strict justice toward us and demand the ultimate of what we owe Him, even though we look upon ourselves as righteous.

31

Jesus Is Again Confronted by the Pharisees

It is very possible that the story about Jesus meeting the Samaritan woman at Jacob's Well two years earlier had reached the ears of the religious leaders in Jerusalem. That woman had been married five times and had not legalized her present relationship. Yet, Jesus saw fit to use her in his ministry to the people in that village. What a chance for the legalists to catch him on a legal issue and trap him into admitting he did not accept the marriage laws!

A group of Pharisees approached Jesus and asked him, "Is it against the Law for a man to divorce his wife for any reason whatever?" Jesus answered, "Have you not read that the Creator from the beginning made them male and female and that he said, 'This is why a man must leave his father and mother and cling to his wife, and the two will become one.' They are no longer two, but one. Therefore, what God has joined together, let no man break apart."

Well said. He answered that question, but now the trap. They put to him the question, "Why, then, did Moses legislate that a writ of dismissal must be given in the case of divorce?"

"It was because you were so mentally dense that Moses allowed you to divorce your wives, but it was not so from the beginning. Now, listen to what I tell you, the man who divorces his wife and marries commits adultery; though notorious lewdness is a serious issue that must be considered."

The case was settled. The Pharisees were again reduced to silence. But now Jesus' disciples had a problem, which they expressed. "If this is the way things are between a husband and wife, why bother getting married?" Jesus replied, "It is not everyone who can accept this teaching, but only those to whom it is granted. There are eunuchs born that way from their mother's womb; there are eunuchs made that way by men, and there are some who choose to be celibate for the sake of the kingdom of heaven. If anyone can accept this let him be free to choose." (Mt. 19:1–12)

This last comment of Jesus is interesting. "There are some who choose to be celibate for the sake of the kingdom of heaven. If anyone can accept this let him be free to choose." If Jesus said that it should be freely chosen, is it not better for the long-term benefit of the kingdom that Jesus' warning should be taken seriously? Why do we pick and choose which of Jesus' admonitions we will take seriously?

Jesus was still on the outskirts of Jerusalem, visiting the villages, but there seem to have been people from all around who had heard of his visit to the area, so outsiders found him and joined the crowds where he was speaking. In one particular village parents were bringing their children for him to lay his hands on them and bless them. This is a first, showing how accepting and respectful these people were in comparison to the brusqueness of the Galileans. Seeing this feeling of intimacy with Jesus as an intrusion, the apostles were indignant, and came up and tried to shoo the children away. But Jesus scolded them. "Let the children be, do not stop them. It is to such as these that the kingdom of heaven belongs." He then laid his hands on them and went on to the next town. (Mt. 19:3–15)

In this place also, a crowd gathered and welcomed him. They had already been prepared for his coming. It could very well have been an upscale village with residents belonging to important families, and people with considerable wealth. A young, well-dressed, refined young man came up to Jesus and asked him with deference, "Good master, what is it that I must do to possess eternal life?" This is an interesting question because eternal life was not an idea that was common in the thinking of the day. The question itself indicates that the man had either heard Jesus speak on another occasion, or had been talking to people who had heard Jesus talking about life after death or eternal life.

Jesus was struck by the man calling him "good," and picked up on it.

"Why do you call me good? There is only One who is good. But if you wish to enter into life, keep the commandments."

And he said, "Which ones?"

"These are the ones: 'You shall not kill, you shall not commit adultery, you shall not steal, you shall not bring false witness, honor your father and your mother, and love your neighbor as you love yourself.'"

The young man said to him, "These I have kept all my life. What more must I do?"

And Jesus said, "If you wish to be perfect, go sell what you possess and give to the poor, and you will have treasure in heaven, then come follow me."

Hearing these words, the young man went away sad, for he was a man of great wealth. And to the rest of those standing around, Jesus looked at them, and seeing that many of them were people of means, many of them his disciples, he remarked, "I assure you, it will be hard for a rich man to enter the kingdom of heaven. In fact, it is easier for a camel to pass through the eye of a needle than for a rich man to enter the kingdom of heaven."

When the disciples heard this they were astonished. "Who then can be saved, Lord?"

Jesus looked at them for a moment and then said, "For men it is impossible, but for God all things are possible."

Then Peter, who was giving up not a little to follow Jesus, was concerned. "What about us, Lord? We have given up everything to follow you. What will we have?"

Jesus knew they had sacrificed a lot to follow him, and he knew to this point they had nothing to show for it but his love and friendship, so he told him, "I assure you, when all is made new and the Son of Man sits on his throne of glory, you yourselves will sit on twelve thrones to judge the twelve tribes of Israel." Then Jesus went on, as he thought of the future, and promised, "And everyone who has left houses, brothers, sisters, father, mother, children, or land for the sake of my name will be repaid a hundredfold, and also inherit eternal life." (Lk. 18:18–30)

The response of Jesus to the rich man is very interesting. He did not immediately suggest giving up everything. He answered precisely the question the man had asked him, about what he must do to attain eternal life. When the man expressed surprise that that was all that was required, and commented that he had done what Jesus said, and kept the commandments since his youth, Jesus then did not tell him he had to sell all his possessions, but said, "If you *wish* to be perfect, go and sell all your possessions, and give to the poor and come, follow me." It important to realize that Jesus did not say it was mandatory, or necessary, or that there were not other options. Since the man seemed to be aspiring to a nobler way of living, Jesus set before him the ideal: Give up everything, and come, be one of my disciples. He does not usually invite individuals to become his disciples, but when he does, it is usually an invitation to be not just a disciple, but a coworker or an apostle.

It is also important to notice that Jesus did not say that in order to attain eternal life he had to give up his possessions. That was an option, leaving open the other options for the proper use of material wealth on the part of Jesus' disciples. To Jesus' way of thinking, wealth is like any talent God gives us. He does not expect us to use it all on Him, but to share the richness of those talents to help others, by being the instruments of God's love for those less blessed than ourselves, and share those talents for the betterment of the community or to help those who need what our talents can provide.

Jesus seemed at that point to be in the vicinity of a large agricultural area. The most prominent agricultural region in that part of Judea would have been Jericho, with its sprawling farms, rich soil, and moist climate.

It had not been long since the Festival of Lights. The thought of light was still on Jesus' mind, and he spontaneously spun a parable about the importance of light. And this seems to be a pattern of Jesus. Although nothing around him might prompt him to develop a message, at times he seemed merely to be thinking about something, and decided to draw a lesson from it, and express it to his little group. On this occasion he burst out with the thought,

"No one lights a lamp, and then hides it, or puts it under a large container, hiding it from view, but puts it on a lampstand so people in the room may see the light. The lamp of your body is your eye. When your eye is healthy, your whole body is filled with light; but, when the eye is damaged, your body too will be in darkness. See to it then that the light inside you is not darkness. If your whole body shines with light, with no dark corners, then you will surely live in its radiance."

When he had finished speaking a Pharisee invited him to dinner at his house. He went in and sat down at the table. The Pharisee watched him and noticed with surprise that he did not perform the complex ritual of hand washing before the meal. Though the Pharisee said nothing, Jesus knew his thoughts and responded to them immediately, so the Pharisee could wonder how he knew what he was thinking about.

"You Pharisees, I know, clean the outside of the cup and dish, but inside your own selves you are filled with all kinds of evil and greed. You foolish people, did not He who made the outside make the inside also? Give alms generously of what you possess and you will then become clean. It is hard to understand that you can pay a tithe of mint and rue and all varieties of herbs, but overlook justice and love of God. These you should have *indeed* practiced while not leaving the others undone. It is so pathetic when you Pharisees rush to take the seats of honor in the synagogues, and crave being greeted with such ostentation in the marketplace. You remind me of unmarked tombs that men walk on, not knowing they are treading on the graves of men already dead. Thus, in passing you closely on the street they contract legal uncleanness as if they were passing a corpse." (Lk. 11:37–44)

Jesus' sarcasm here was cutting. He accused them of being so beautifully clothed, people did not realize they were encountering walking dead men. As searing as his criticism was, it was not made from meanness, but it was like a doctor trying one last painful measure to save a diseased patient. Jesus had patiently tried rational explanations and realistic interpretations of the Law and the Scriptures, and reached out to them by going to their houses for dinner, and directed the people to respect them because their authority came from God, even though they should not imitate their behavior.

And now he was speaking to them as God, furious at what they had done to His people and to the religion He had entrusted to them. By their endless and merciless laws, they continually drove people away from their religion, driving a wedge between themselves and God. The scribes, the legalists standing there with them, were also offended. "Rabbi, in talking like this, do you refer to us as well?"

"Woe to you as well, for you bind up heavy burdens for people to bear and do not lift one finger to lighten those burdens. Woe to you also, for you are the ones who have built the tombs of the prophets whom your fathers murdered. It is true, your fathers murdered them, but you sealed their tombs. That is why divine Wisdom has said, 'I will send them prophets and apostles; some they will kill, others they will persecute, so that the blood of all the prophets which has been shed from the beginning of time, this generation will have to answer for, from the blood of Abel, to the blood of Zacharias who was cut down between the Altar and the Holy Place itself. I tell you, all the blood of the past will be demanded of this generation. Woe to you lawyers, for you have hidden the key to knowledge; you yourselves have never entered, and those who wished to enter, you kept out.' " (Lk. 11:45–52)

It is painful to hear Jesus speaking like this to these men. They were the very ones who could and did eventually decide his fate. It is so different from the way he treated the people. He treated them with tenderness and affection. He identified with them, and felt their pain and the frustration and hopelessness they felt from the way the religious leaders treated them and the damage it had done to them spiritually. Jesus, in a way, was making the officials pay for what they had done. He was giving them a small taste of the judgment they would be in for when they appeared before God, who had entrusted them with the care of the Father's hurting sheep.

Rather than stirring up their consciences, it drove them to fury. Immediately after Jesus left the house, the scribes, who were the lawyers, and the Pharisees gathered together and decided to ambush Jesus every chance they got, and bombard him with one question after another, rapid-fire, to catch him off guard, in an attempt to trip him up and say something on which they could indict him. From that day on they tried to make his life miserable, and arranged for groups of their colleagues to be at each of his gatherings and confront him with a barrage of questions.

This drama frightened the apostles. This was not what they wanted to experience. They'd had the hope deep down that this time in Judea would be the climax of Jesus' mission. Hopefully, he would be accepted not only by the whole Judean populace but by the ruling elite, as well. This confrontation blew away whatever dreams they'd had about their Master being accepted and acclaimed as the Messiah. Now they were fearful that a dangerous storm was brewing. Jesus knew their fears and addressed what they were feeling. "Let me tell you, it is not those who can kill the body, and can do nothing more, you should be afraid of. Fear the One who after He puts you to death, also has the power to send you into hell. Are not five little sparrows sold for just a few cents? Yet not one of them is ever lost sight of by the eyes of God. And you are worth more than a whole flock of sparrows, and your heavenly Father knows you so well, not a hair of your head falls to the ground without your heavenly Father knowing it. So, do not be afraid." (Lk. 12:4–7) You are never alone.

The villagers and other visitors witnessed this angry dispute, and were delighted when Jesus indicted the leaders for the way they treated the people. They were all on his side. They expected more drama to come. Perhaps he would declare himself the Messiah. Each day the crowds grew, numbering in the thousands. This time they were cheering crowds of not just simple villagers but people with influence and wealth, very different from what he had faced in Galilee.

Jesus' talks from then on were powerful—not political, as the people would have liked, but powerful in the depth and strength of their spiritual messages. He knew full well that it was not easy or even safe for people to commit themselves to accept and follow him. He reached out to them and told them in so many words, "Do not be afraid, my friends. If you are willing to declare yourself as my disciple, I will acknowledge you before the angels in heaven. But I will also not recognize those who disown me before others. If people say bad things against me, I will forgive them, but if they insult the Holy Spirit who inspires me, that sin will not be forgiven, because they are blaspheming and rejecting the very Source of life and forgiveness."

These gatherings seem to have been casual, even though the numbers were great. On one particular occasion, a man broke in with the request, "Master, tell my brother to give me a share of the inheritance!"

"My friend, what authority do I have to act as judge over a dispute between you and your brother, or to act as arbiter of your claims?" and then, looking around the crowd, he sent a bit of strong advice to all.

"Watch and be on our guard against excessive love of money and material things, for material things do not really give you security, even if your possessions are more than you think you need. I will tell you a story. There was a very wealthy man who had one year an abundant harvest. He thought about it, and what he should do. 'I know what I will do. I will demolish my barns and build bigger ones and store my grain and other goods in them. Then I will say to myself, "Self, you now have good things to last you for many years; relax, eat, drink, and enjoy your life." ' But, God said to him, 'You foolish man, this very night you will be called out of this world. To whom will all this stored up wealth go? What treasure will you take with you to present to God?' " (Lk. 12:13–21)

When my many brothers and sisters and I were young, my father used to say to us, "It is not how much money you make in this life that matters to God, but how much you give away." It is one of the things that I could never forget. And one day, a friend came to me and asked me if I could lend him fifteen hundred dollars. It was very important to him. All I had in the bank at the time was not much over fifteen hundred. I remembered what my father had said, and what Jesus said about always giving when someone in need asks you. Sister Dorothy Ederer, a Grand Rapids Dominican sister, was working with me at the time. So, I excused myself and went to talk to Sister, and told her, since she was my co-director. She knew we needed the money to pay bills, and was concerned, but finally said, "God seems always to take care of us, so do what you feel you have to do." Still worrying about how I would pay my bills, I gave him the money and forgot about it. The next morning, when Sister Dorothy and I walked down to the mailbox, she took out the mail, noticed a letter from my agent, and handed it to me. I opened it, looked at it, and gave it to Sister. When she looked at the contents, she almost fainted. It was a check for a hundred thousand dollars, with a note saying the check was from my publisher, who'd decided to make a series of calendars using quotations from my Joshua books. We both had tears in our eyes at realizing how generous God is in repaying all of us for the little token kindnesses we do for others. We can never outdo God in generosity. And now that I am older and I struggle again, I realize what a blessing it is to be free of material things.

Jesus knew he had blown any possible chance for reconciliation with the officials. They were too filled with hate for him to even entertain that possibility any longer. Now his concern was for the apostles, who, in spite of their love of Jesus, were still weak and fearful. He was also concerned for the brave people who'd managed to summon up enough courage to commit their lives to follow him and his way of life. They were not strong people, certainly not strong enough to withstand the recriminations of the officials, who would forbid anyone to follow him under the threat of severe penalties. He continued to allay their fears, instilling in them a bravery to withstand the Pharisees' meanness.

"That is why I tell you not to worry about your life, or even about what you are to eat and what you are to drink, and how you will find the means to obtain the necessities of life like the clothes you wear." Yes, after the things he'd said to the scribes and Pharisees, the disciples were now greatly concerned about all those things. The Temple authorities were mean enough to confiscate and strip them of everything, even a livelihood. And Jesus was very honest with them. His description of the reality of the situation was stark. It was not going to be easy to follow him. The price would be high. But they would not be alone. The Father Himself would take care of them and also their needs.

"Life means more than food, and the body more than clothing. Look at the ravens over there in the field. They do not store or reap or gather into barns. God feeds them. You never see them going hungry. How much more you are worth than birds! Can any of you add a brief span to your life by worrying about it? If small things you cannot control, why worry about big things?

"Look at the flowers over there in the field. Are they striking, spread out like a vast carpet, swaying in the breeze? They don't have to do anything, and even Solomon in all his majesty was never clothed with such splendor."

A few years ago, I had a small package of California poppy seeds. I threw them on a patch of ground no bigger than a few square feet. The first year they came up and looked pretty. The next year I could not believe what I saw. Those few seeds had multiplied after the first season, and after being spread by the wind there were poppies all over. My rose garden also was a thick carpet of golden poppies. It was so spectacular that

I took out the rosebushes and let the poppies multiply. That is what Jesus was talking about. And it was probably the same kind of flowers growing in the field that he told the people to observe.

> "Now if God so clothes the grass in the field, which is here today and burned up tomorrow, how much more he will look after you, you of little faith. So, do not worry about what you are to eat and what you are to drink and what you are to wear. It is the pagans who spend their lives concerned about these things. This life here is their only concern. Your Father knows you need these things. Set your hearts on the kingdom and all these things will be provided for you. So, do not be afraid, little flock, for it has pleased your Father to give you the kingdom." (Lk. 12:23–32)

It is clear that Jesus was very much concerned about his disciples' fear for the future. It is easy to sense his pain over their anxiety. They knew, now more than ever, how much the authorities hated Jesus and were determined to kill him, and punish those who followed him. He did not try to diminish or deny that things looked bleak. These people were too intelligent for that. He knew he had the strength to endure what had to happen. They did not have his kind of strength. He knew that, and all he could do was share some of the strong convictions that drove him, and offer them hope and reasons to rise above their fears. In the end, he told them, they would come through the ordeal, as difficult as it might be. And quietly, to the apostles, he said, "If they haul you before synagogues and magistrates and authorities, do not worry how to defend yourselves or what you are to say, because when that time comes, the Holy Spirit will teach you what you are to say." (Lk. 12:11–12)

32

I Have Come to Set Fire upon the Earth

R ealize that the closer his tour led him to the City, the more the tension mounted. People were nervous. The crowds were still supportive of him. They took his side against their own religious leaders, whom they knew were phonies, and whom Jesus had bravely exposed for their hypocrisy and secret crimes. It had cost him, and caused some of his more timid followers to waver in their loyalty to him. Jesus was aware of what loyalty to him cost his disciples. He knew what happened in each family when one of the members decided to follow him. The whole family was torn apart. Siblings might not agree, but they supported their brother or sister. Parents fought, in-laws got involved and entered the fray. The whole family ended up taking sides. This was far from what Jesus had intended, but he was always realistic, always faced real life, just as it was.

He said he had come to set fire upon the earth. When he spoke these words his meaning was far different from a literal interpretation. He did come to set fire on the earth, but it was the fire of divine love, which he hoped would spread throughout the whole world, gathering the whole family of God back into His love. "I have come to set fire upon the earth and what more could I desire but that it be enkindled. There is a baptism I must still receive, and how distressed I am until it is accomplished." Jesus related this fire to his passion and death and resurrection. He could not wait, for then, after the resurrection, that fire would be ignited and would spread far and wide. He could not wait. But would this spreading of his message bring peace? He knew it would, but it would also be the cause of much anguish and conflict, as people reacted to it in many different ways.

"Do you think I have come to bring peace on earth? No, I bring division. From now on a household of five will be divided against itself, three against two and two against three; the father against the son, and son against father; mother against daughter, and daughter against mother; mother-in-law against daughter-in-law, daughter-in-law against mother-in-law." It is a striking image and description of his whole ministry, and to see it turning into family turmoil and alienation between members of so many families when someone becomes his disciple is indeed painful. He expressed in his own words how his mission of spreading love and peace had taken a disturbing, undesired turn. He had said so many times that he'd come to bring peace, but sadly he saw that his coming also brought about conflict between those who loved him and those who refused to accept him and his message of love. It certainly was not what he wanted, but sadly it would eventually have to happen. People just could not be neutral when the subject was Jesus. Either people loved him, or they wished he had never come to disturb their comfortable lives.

It seems the enemies had regrouped and were back on the attack. A contingent of them showed up at one of the village gatherings. Jesus had been talking about many things—about learning to share and to care for one another, and to be sensitive to those in need. A question was brought up by some people who had just arrived. Some people! Luke does not say that they were Pharisees or scribes. They may have been students of the Pharisees. They reminded Jesus of the time when Pilate had crucified certain Galilean rebels, and mixed their blood with the blood of the sacrifices. This does not sound like Pharisees or scribes. They would have been more direct. It sounds like students, perhaps students of the Pharisees, sent to challenge Jesus. They do so by asking a question, like students at a lecture, timidly hinting for the speaker to reply. Jesus responded with a rhetorical question. "Do you think those Galileans who suffered such shame were greater sinners than other Galileans? No, I tell you, and unless you repent of your sins, you will all perish the way they did. And do you think those eighteen on whom the tower of Siloam collapsed and killed were more guilty than the rest of the people in Jerusalem? No, I tell you, and unless you repent you will all perish the way they did."

Strong words to people who'd merely asked a simple question. But, though those recent arrivals might have looked innocent enough, Jesus knew who they were and why they were there, and he was not going to let them break up the group, so he immediately let them know he was wise to them. They seem to have been amateurs in raising issues. Jesus knew that their first question was just the prelude, so he took control of the conversation right at the beginning, and asked the questions and answered them himself, then threw warnings back at the group. They said nothing more. When Jesus warned them about their need to repent, he made them realize he had read their souls and forced them to wonder just who was this man who knew their private lives.

Then he talked about the signs of the times. The group of new arrivals was present for this issue. Not only they, but many people were anxious about the signs in the world predicting bad times coming, maybe even the end of the world. This seems to have been a perennial concern. They could also be wondering if signs in their local world seemed to indicate the arrival of God's Anointed. "When you see a cloud coming in from the west, you say a storm is coming, and so it does, and when the wind comes from the south, you say it is going to be hot, and so it is. Hypocrites, you know how to interpret the signs of the weather by reading the heavens. How come you do not know how to interpret the times?"

Jesus then seems to tie in a parable about a fig tree as a way of bringing home the same point. A man had a fig tree planted in his vineyard, and he came looking for fruit on it and he found none. He said to the man looking after the vineyard, "Look, I have been coming here now for three years looking for fruit on this fig tree and have found none. Cut it down! Why should we waste the space?"

"Sir, leave it one more year, and I will dig around it, and manure it. It may bear fruit next year. And if it does not, you can cut it down."

Three years was the time Jesus had spent cultivating the Jewish people. So far they had not produced any fruit. Again, he was directing this parable to the visitors who had just posed the question about Pilate and the Galilean rebels, who he knew would bring it back to their superiors.

After this incident, as Jesus moved on to the next village, he was invited to speak in their synagogue. He noticed there were Pharisees present, as well, another contingent sent to harass him. It was the Sabbath, and a woman was there who had been possessed by a devil for eighteen years. The torment left her feeble and bent over and unable to stand up straight. When Jesus saw her, he called her over and said to her, "Woman, you are healed of your infirmity," as he laid his hands on her. She immediately stood up straight and burst out in praise of God.

The head of the synagogue was upset that Jesus had done this on the Sabbath, and immediately arose and said to the people present, "There are six days when work can be done. Come and do your healing on one of those days, but not on the Sabbath."

Jesus retorted, "Hypocrites! Is there one of you who does not untie his ox or his donkey from the feed trough and lead it out to water on the Sabbath? And this woman, this daughter of Abraham, whom Satan has held bound for eighteen years, was it not right to untie her bonds on the Sabbath?" Seeing how Jesus had shamed and embarrassed his enemies sitting there, the people were filled with glee and astonishment at the wonders he worked.

Jesus seems to have been moving closer to the City, as the concentration of Pharisees and lawyers is more noticeable. In this particular village, which was populated by prominent persons and persons of wealth, one of the leading Pharisees invited Jesus to dinner. Jesus always accepted their invitations, as he never passed up a chance to try to reach these people's hearts. Early in the meal, or before it even started, Jesus had healed a man with a very bad case of fluid buildup in his body. Whether he was a Pharisee or a lawyer, or an invited guest, Luke does not say, but Jesus did not make a big issue of the situation. He just cured the man and said he was doing nothing more than all the guests there did every Sabbath for their animals that needed watering. They said nothing, probably because the man cured was one of their own.

Into the meal, however, Jesus noticed how the guests vied with one another for the seats near the hosts and prominent guests, which is human enough. Luke writes that Jesus told those reclining at the table a parable about guests at a wedding banquet. As the guests arrived, they made sure they found the most prominent places to recline. When the host arrived, he went to those sitting in the prominent places and asked them to move down lower, because there were some very important people who must occupy those places. Then, embarrassed in front of all the guests, they shamefacedly went and took the lower places. And they all realized it would have been wiser for them to seek the lowest places; then they would have been in a position for the host to say to them, "No, you must go up higher," and then they would have felt honored in front of everyone. (Lk. 14:1–11)

I always wondered where the evangelists acquired all the details about Jesus' presence at private situations like this. Did Jesus tell them about it afterward, or were they also invited and did they observe it for themselves? It makes no difference. Wherever the details come from, they often make Jesus look boorish in the way he insults people, people who seem to be well-intentioned and even favorable toward him, as on this occasion. And it is so unlike Jesus to be boorish. He was a most gracious person and possessed a warm love for everyone. I cannot imagine him going from place to place insulting people. It does not make sense. Another example also happened at this meal. All the people invited were prominent people. Jesus noticed this. During the meal, and it seems everyone became quiet whenever Jesus started speaking, Jesus made a suggestion. Since the host seemed well-disposed to Jesus, I would like to think that Jesus made a suggestion to the man rather than a criticism, like the Gospel implies. I would like to think Jesus would have expressed his thoughts perhaps in this manner: "The dinner is enjoyable and the learned host has been most gracious, and has many important friends. But, it might be nice sometime to have a dinner that would be most pleasing to your Father in heaven, inviting the poor, the crippled, the lame and the blind, those who could in no way repay you, except your heavenly Father, who will certainly reward you richly when the time comes." (Lk. 14:12–14)

Immediately, one of the guests said, "Happy the man who will be at the feast in the kingdom of God." This indicates the atmosphere was friendly, one of the few times it is made to seem obvious in the Gospels. Jesus would certainly not have been invited to dinner as often as he was if he had a reputation for being rude or boorish. The comment this guest makes seems to follow directly from Jesus' suggestion about having a party that would be pleasing to God. People in those days did not think that way, so this comment shows that Jesus' teaching about happy times in the kingdom of heaven had made an impression on at least this one man.

Then, Jesus picked up on what the man had said, which shows there were lively conversations going on, and he continued, explaining what might happen if God had a party.

> "There was a man who threw a great banquet, and he invited a large
> number of people. When the time came for the banquet, he sent his

servants out to say to those invited, 'Come, everything is ready.' But they all began making excuses. The first said, 'I have bought a piece of land, and I must see it. Please hold me excused.' Another said, 'I have bought five yoke of oxen, and I am on my way to try them out. Please hold me excused.' And still another said, 'I just married, and I certainly cannot come. Please hold me excused.'

"The servant returned and reported this to his master. Then the man in charge of the banquet, in a rage, said to the servant, 'Go out quickly into the streets and alleys of the town, and bring in the poor, the crippled, the blind and the lame.' 'Sir,' the servant reported, 'your orders have been carried out and there is still room.' Then the master said to the servant, 'Go out to the open roads and the hovels, and tell them they must come to the banquet so that my house will be full; for I tell you, not one of those invited will partake of my banquet.' " (Lk. 14:15–24)

This is Jesus at his best. He had all the dinner guests thoroughly enjoying the exciting conversation. One of the guests could not wait until the great feast in the kingdom of heaven. Jesus then told a parable about what that great party would be like. First of all, it will be full of surprises. The problem Jesus always faced was the false opinion people had of themselves. It was as if these good people felt that they were all that God expected of them. They did not realize it, but they felt very comfortable with themselves and felt that God had to be pleased with them. It is surprising how many people feel that way, mostly men. Women so often are not pleased with the way they are and pressure themselves to be better. Jesus, knowing what these guests were really like, realized that a lot of changes were needed in their lives if they were to be pleasing to God. This parable is carefully crafted so as not to hurt, but also to make sure the lesson was clear. Jesus ended the parable by telling all the guests that there would be a stunning surprise at who would end up being the guests at the great feast in heaven. All said so delicately, but so incisively and leaving so many unanswered questions that they would be thinking about the meaning of that parable long after the dinner ended. When each of them went to bed that night, the last conscious thought would have to be, "That Galilean fellow has one sharp mind. He was talking about all of us there at the dinner and we did not even realize it then. Now, after thinking about it all day long, it finally dawns on me what it was all about, and it was so true."

So, Jesus' times spent at parties were not always fraught with confrontations. In fact, I am beginning to wonder if the atmosphere on those occasions was not a lot more fun than the Gospels seem to intimate. Otherwise, Jesus would not have been invited to so many parties—especially by the Pharisees, if they expected to be insulted in front of their guests every time he came. I am sure he was a most charming and entertaining guest, and from his lips flowed pleasantly phrased gems that the guests could take home with them and ponder long after the party.

As Jesus moved closer toward Jerusalem, the crowds grew larger. People had been coming in from the Diaspora, preparing for upcoming celebrations. By this time, there were not many who had not heard of this famous Galilean holy man, who spoke to people's hearts, and talked about life with Yahweh and all our loved ones in heaven after death. Their curiosity to see and hear Jesus in the flesh was one of their greatest desires in going to Jerusalem that year.

Now the crowds were traveling with him. That had to alarm the authorities. Great crowds were always threatening. No one could predict their intentions or what might occur purely by chance. Jesus, seeing how attached this group was to him, wanted to make sure that if they were intending to become his true disciples, they knew what they were in for. It was not going to be easy. "If anyone comes to me and does not hate his father and mother, wife and children, and even his own life, he cannot be my disciple. Whoever does not carry his own cross and come after me cannot be my disciple." So, he tells them to think it over thoroughly before they make their decision, for it will not be easy to walk with him. He tells them they must plan, as they would for any serious undertaking. "Which of you wishing to build a tower does not first sit down and calculate the cost to see if there is enough money to complete the project? Otherwise, after laying the foundation and finding himself with insufficient funds to bring the undertaking to completion, all those standing around will laugh at him and tell everybody, 'This fellow started to build this great project, but ran out of money and was unable to finish.' "

And Jesus did not stop there; he went on and told the crowd another parable, hoping, if not to cool their enthusiasm about following him, then at least to strongly urge them to be prudent in understanding what their lives would be like if they accepted the challenge in earnest to follow him. And as was explained before, when Jesus talked about hating father and mother, he did not mean *hate* in the real sense of the word, but not being so attached to them that they could not give themselves wholeheartedly to their new life. Their dedication would be at best halfhearted, and they would often be distracted by anxiety about home, and family concerns. Perhaps a way of wording Jesus' remark that we can understand would be this: "Unless you are willing to love your loved ones less than God, you are not worthy of God's kingdom. God and his kingdom must come before all else."

Luke then follows with the simile about salt. Jesus had said this on another occasion, but Jesus, like all preachers, will use a catchy simile on many occasions. So, here, Jesus is talking about disciples who may not have totally renounced their love of the world, and who are enticed back into family affairs or material attractions. He compares their enthusiasm for the kingdom to salt. If salt ever loses its tang, how can it be restored? It is the same with love of the kingdom. Love of material things and excessive anxiety over family affairs can cause people to lose their taste for the work of the kingdom. How can you restore that taste for things of the spirit? (Lk. 14:25–35)

33

JESUS RETURNS TO THE REGION OF PEREA

They wanted to arrest him right then, but he eluded them. This is all that John says about this trip of Jesus to Jerusalem. He then has Jesus and his disciples leaving Jerusalem and going down again to where John used to preach and baptize. It was too early for Jesus to be there. He had entered the city for a purpose. According to John, he went into the Temple and just wandered back and forth along the portico, met a group of officials who questioned him as to his identity. He told them in words that shocked them, and when they tried to stone him he slipped away and left the city. He had tested out the city and the atmosphere. They were lying in wait for him. He had other things to do before the final showdown. Leaving the officials with something to ponder, he left and went back down into Herod's territory of Perea with his apostles. There does not seem to have been a crowd with him, so he had time to further instruct the apostles. (Jn. 10:22–42)

It is difficult to follow precisely Jesus' tour of the villages. He was very much aware that he'd had an unpleasant confrontation with a group of Pharisees and their interns. He knew they were planning more unpleasant confrontations, so he seems to have wandered off to a place where Pharisees would be most unwelcome and would not be inclined to create a scene. The most likely place was just across the Jordan in Perea, the southern part of Herod's tetrarchy. Since it was the crossing between two separate territories, the area was well covered by officials collecting all kinds of taxes and tolls. The place was filled with publicans, the official tax collectors for the Romans. But there were also Herod's spies, ever on the alert for anything suspicious.

This also explains why on this part of Jesus' tour he was swamped by publicans and others having business in the area who were not in good standing with the Pharisees. These, Luke seems to indicate, came to him in great numbers. Strangely enough, some Pharisees and scribes were bold enough to track Jesus down and complain that there were many sinners gathered around Jesus, and not only gathered around him, but sharing their food with him. This bothered them immensely. Either Jesus knew what they were thinking, and answered their nasty thoughts, or they were bold enough to express their criticism out loud, which would have been dangerous, since they would have been calling sinners many of those standing around. Whichever it was, Jesus answered with a parable.

"What man among you, having a hundred sheep and losing one of them, would not leave the ninety-nine in a safe place and go out in search for the lost sheep until he finds it? And when he does find it, he picks it up and places it on his shoulders with great joy. Upon his arrival home, he calls in all his friends and neighbors, and says to them, 'Come, celebrate with me, because I have found my lost sheep.' I tell you, in the very same way, there will be more joy in heaven over one sinner who repents than over ninety-nine righteous people who have no need of repentance." (Lk. 15:1–7)

We may find it hard to understand how a man could make such an issue out of finding a wandering sheep, that he would have to invite the whole neighborhood in to celebrate, but a short time ago, an elderly man where I live had no family. All he had was a dog that had been his faithful companion for years. One day, the dog got out of the house and accidentally wandered off and could not find its way home. The man was beside himself, as if he had lost a child. The fellow called his neighbors and asked if they had seen his faithful friend. No one had. He called the police but was told they do not go looking for lost animals. The old man went out looking, and wandered through the neighborhood, calling the dog's name. No response. For hours he kept wandering farther and farther from home, frantically calling the dog's name. As he wandered into a different neighborhood, calling out the dog's name, some thought he was demented. Finally, as he was growing weak, he decided to start back home, still calling the dog's name as he went along. As he approached his house, he saw the dog pawing at the front door, whining and barking. The old man called the pet, and it came running excitedly. Both were beside themselves with the thrill of finding each other. As soon as the old man went into the house, he called his neighbors and invited them over for a simple celebration, and like a child, all he could say was, "Thank God, thank God!" Jesus knew people so well.

After experiencing this man's reaction, I could not but think that Jesus must have witnessed the same thing, and in telling the parable, it was not just made up. He knew what finding a lost sheep meant to a man, and why he would call in his friends and neighbors to celebrate with him.

This little trilogy of parables about something or someone being lost is a good example of how Jesus tried so hard to help the Pharisees and scribes understand him, and his scandalous (to their way of thinking) association with sinners. The next parable is about a woman who had ten coins and lost one. She lit a lamp and looked high and low for the lost coin. She swept the whole house, carefully looking for the coin. Finally she found it. It was always difficult for me to understand why anyone would make a big fuss over finding a coin, especially if it was not a gold coin, or a silver coin, but a coin of little value. This could have been a coin that had value; Jesus does not say. One commentary states that it was a drachma, a silver coin. Another commentary mentions the headband women wore at their wedding, a band of ten coins, and identifies this lost coin as one of that set of ten, so to her it was valuable. After finally finding the coin she calls in her friends, and neighbors too, saying to them, "Rejoice with me; I have found the coin that was lost." Jesus ended the parable with, "In just the same way there will be rejoicing among the angels of God over one sinner who repents." (Lk. 15:8–10)

That was particularly hard for me to appreciate until one day I remembered when I was a little boy, perhaps five or six years old. It was late, and as I never like to go to bed early, I managed to avoid the unpleasant experience. My father retired early, and my mother always did the ironing or sewed socks at night. I think she let me stay up just so she would have some company. One night while she was ironing, she reached into her housedress pocket and got all upset. "What's the matter, Mother?" "I had a quarter in my pocket and it must have fallen out, Joseph. Would you help me find it? It has to be here somewhere." We looked all over and finally found the quarter. My mother was so happy. She said, "Joseph, do me a favor. Go down to Henny Murphy's before he closes, and get a small loaf of two-day-old bread, so I can have bread for tomorrow morning, and get one popcorn square and a maple bell, so we can celebrate for finding the quarter. The bread will cost only six cents and the popcorn square and the maple bell a penny each. And make sure you don't forget the change. That's all I have."

I did as she told me, and when I came home, she took the popcorn square (about a two-inch square), and the maple bell (a maple flavored crème coated with chocolate, and shaped like a half a golf ball), put the maple bell on the popcorn square, pressed down the maple bell, broke the square in half, and gave me half. That was our celebration, the celebration of the poor over finding a lost quarter. So, we can see how realistic Jesus is in his understanding of us simple humans.

This next parable is a masterpiece of what we might today call pastoral theology and pastoral counseling. Jesus was still weaving tender, thought-provoking stories in an unrelenting effort to touch the hearts of the legalists. This parable has always been labeled the Parable of the Prodigal Son. It could be even more fittingly called the Parable of the Prodigal Father.

"A man had two sons. The younger son said to his father, 'Father, give me my share of your estate that will one day be mine anyway.' So, the father divided the property between them. A few days later, the younger son collected all his belongings and went off to a foreign country and wasted all his inheritance on a dissolute life. After he had spent everything, a severe famine struck that country, and he found himself in dire need. He hired himself out to one of the local citizens, who sent him to his farm to feed the pigs. There he craved to eat the pods he was giving to the pigs, but no one offered him any. Coming to his senses, he began to think, 'How many of my father's hired hands have more than enough to eat, and here I am dying of hunger. I will get ready and go back to my father and tell him, "Father, I have sinned against heaven and against you. I no longer deserve to be called your son. Treat me as one of your hired hands." ' So, he got ready and went back to his father. While he was still far off, his father caught sight of him and was filled with compassion. He ran to his son, embraced him and kissed him. His son said to him, 'Father, I have sinned against heaven and against you. I no longer deserve to be called your son.' But, his father ordered his servants, 'Hurry, bring the finest robe and put it on him. Put a ring on his finger and sandals on his feet. Then take the fatted calf and slaughter it. Then let us all celebrate with a feast because my son who was dead is now come back to life again. He was lost and now he is found.' Then the celebration began.

"Now the older son had been out in the field, and on his way back, as he came closer to the house, he heard the sound of music and dancing. He called one of the servants and asked what it all about. The servant told him, 'Your brother has returned and your father has slaughtered the fatted calf because he has him back alive and well.' The brother was angry, and when he refused to enter the house, his father came out and pleaded with him. He said to his father in reply, 'Look, for all these years I served you, and never once have I disobeyed your orders, yet you never gave me as much as a kid goat to celebrate with my friends. But when this son of yours returns after wasting all your money on prosti-tutes, you slaughter the fatted calf for him.' The father said to him, 'My son, you are here with me all the time; all I have is yours. But, now we must celebrate and rejoice, because your brother was dead, and has come back to life; he was lost and has been found.' " (Lk. 11–32)

The pathos with which Jesus recited this story is filled with such force, it reflects the psychological genius Jesus used in trying to touch the hard hearts of the Pharisees and the scribes. It shows the love that Jesus had for these stubborn men who resisted every impulse of God's grace in their hateful resistance to him. He never gave up on them.

There is such a profound insight, in this parable, into the mind and heart of God that a person could develop many theological principles from the way Jesus describes the father and the two sons. The parable is mostly about the father, as Jesus compared the reaction of the scribes and Pharisees, who delighted in condemning sinners, with the reaction of God Himself, who does not condemn sinners but desires only their conversion that they may have life.

The reaction of the religious authorities was brutal. They had no love for the unwashed rabble. The religion would be better off without them. Get rid of them and, though we might have smaller numbers, we would have better quality. Some religious leaders today, even at the highest level, have expressed that same attitude. Our politicians and criminal justice officials often have that same mentality. "Get rid of the scum. Execute them. Let them rot in prison."

It is well worth our while to examine this parable more thoroughly. The story is not about the son. This father *is* the story; look at him! He gives half of his possessions to this spoiled kid because he cannot wait for his father's death to get his inheritance. He wants it now. The father na-ively gives it to him. What father in his right mind would do such a thing? But this father does. Then the fellow goes off and lives a totally immoral life, and finally runs out of money.

Hard times come upon him and the only way he can survive is on the charity of a stranger who gives him a job of feeding pigs. Such an insult to a Jew! The fellow finally comes to his senses and dreams up a line to soften up his father, perhaps sincere, more likely not, but shrewd. "I know what I will do. I will go back and tell my father how wicked I have been, and how sorry I am. I know he will forgive me." And that is what he does.

Jesus then so delicately laid bare the father's heart in the way he painted the homecoming scene. "The father saw his son in the distance." How many mornings and evenings had that poor father scoured the distant horizon, hoping he would one day spot his son walking over the hill? And finally he does. What does he do then? Most fathers would wait until he came in the house crawling, and then the first thing out of their mouths would be, "Well, kid, did you learn your lesson?" Then after a pathetic confession and proof of contrition, the father might relent and give him a conditional welcome, as long as he would be on his good behavior. Of course, that is only common sense.

Jesus showed that this father, his Father in heaven, is devoid of what we call common sense, the way humans think. This father runs out to greet his son. And when he does, he seems to pay little attention to the son's carefully prepared speech. He is just so thrilled to have him back home, and in one piece. After throwing his arms around him and choking on the odor, he tells the servants to bring the son inside, wash him up, dress him with the finest robe, put rings on his finger, and sandals on his feet, and then, kill the fatted calf that he has been saving, and have a great celebration. "My son is back home! My son is back home!" It breaks one's heart to see God, who designed, created, and controls this whole vast universe, being so frightfully vulnerable, and so devastated by his love for a sinner who seemingly does not deserve His love. What a strange God, who pours His love so generously into our lives, and receives so little in return. And to think that our society, which so self-righteously boasts that it is Christian, can have such hatred for those whom God loves with such infinite love, and eagerly snatches them out of God's hands to execute them before God can finish His work of redeeming them. We have a long way to go in understanding the mind of God. "As you judge others, so will you be judged."

Then, there is the other son. What do we say about him? He is all of us. He is the scribes and Pharisees who do not share the Father's love for his children, and have no pity when people break the law. The son refuses to celebrate and berates the father as he boasts of his own integrity and righteousness. If this parable did not touch the hearts of the Pharisees and scribes to whom it was directed, then they would have to be beyond even God's powerful grace.

34

JESUS TALKS TO HIS DISCIPLES

As Jesus continued his trek through the villages, he seemed to take short breaks to spend time alone with his disciples. They could not spend all their time with him, as they still had bills to pay and other responsibilities to their families and to their work. That did not mean that they were not fully committed to Jesus. They were there whenever he needed them. Even Jesus took time away from them. He needed his private time, especially when he wanted to spend time with his Father. The apostles had to go looking for him. So, Jesus wasn't that rigid in his demands on them. There was a beautiful freedom of spirit they all enjoyed. Rarely do we see all the apostles with Jesus at any particular time. But, even when they were all with him, they would spend so much time with Jesus, travel a few miles into different villages, then go back to their homes and to their work. While alone on their walks Jesus taught them.

On a particular occasion as Jesus was walking through a village, it seems there were large estates in the area where the owners had a considerable number of workers. He was a keen observer of people, and at some time or other came across a situation where a wealthy landowner had a problem with the manager of his workers. Whether it was while on this tour or on another occasion when he witnessed an incident, or when someone brought the problem to Jesus, he made it into a parable, and though he was apparently addressing his disciples, others were listening.

"There was a wealthy man who had a servant who was reported to him as having squandered his property. He called in the servant and said to him, 'What is all this talk I hear about you? I want a full accounting of your stewardship, for you can be steward no longer.' The steward thought, 'What shall I do now that my master is taking my steward-ship away from me? I am unable to dig. I am too proud to beg. I know what I will do, so that when I am removed from my position, they may welcome me into their homes.' He called his master's debtors one by one. To the first he said, 'How much do you owe my master?' 'One hundred measures of olive oil,' he told him. 'Here is your promissory note. Sit down and write one for fifty.' Then to another he said, 'How much do you owe my master?' 'One hundred kors of wheat,' he replied. He said to him, 'Here is your promissory note. Sit down and write one for eighty.' And the master commended the dishonest steward for his craftiness. And Jesus continued commenting, "The children of this world are more astute in dealing with their own kind than are the chil-dren of light. So, I tell you, make friends for yourselves with ill-gotten wealth, so that when it fails they may welcome you into their eternal resting places. Whoever is trustworthy in small matters can be trusted with greater ones. Whoever cannot be trusted with small matters can-not be trusted with important things. So, if you cannot be trusted with dishonest wealth, who will trust you with wealth that you have coming to you? No servant can serve two masters. He will either hate one and love the other, or be devoted to one and despise the other. You cannot serve God and this world." (Lk. 16:1–13)

Why was Jesus talking like this? Who was he talking about? Was it a reference to one of the apostles about whom he had reason to be con-cerned, or was he telling people that love of money and material posses-sions can be an obstacle to real, dedicated loyalty to God? If you are so in love with money and material possessions that you think about them day and night, that is where your heart is, and that is where your loyalty lies. That is the god you worship. There is no room left for God. "You cannot serve God and money," as Jesus expressed it.

Luke mentions Pharisees hearing this, though he mentioned at the beginning that Jesus was specifically addressing his disciples, and not the local villagers. The Pharisees may have just wandered on to this gathering of Jesus' close disciples and stayed at the edge of the group, eavesdropping. They were offended by what Jesus was saying because he was talking about dishonest people who could not be trusted. Luke said, "The Pharisees, who loved money, heard all these things and sneered at him." Jesus, noticing them present, said to them, "You excuse yourselves in the sight of others, but God knows your hearts; for what humans consider acceptable is often abominable in God's eyes." (Lk. 16:14–15)

To go back to the parable Jesus was telling about the dishonest manager, Jesus was showing how shrewd people could be when it came to money and material things. It bothered him that people were nowhere near as shrewd when it came to spiritual matters and important things that pertained to their eternal salvation. He was hinting strongly that people should have the same shrewdness in their handling of spiritual riches as they did when they were managing material possessions.

Then Jesus made an astounding remark that must have totally bewildered the Pharisees: "The Law and the prophets lasted until John, but from then on the kingdom of God is proclaimed, and everyone who enters does so with violence. It is easier for heaven and earth to pass away than for the smallest particle of the Law to be considered invalid." (Lk. 16:16–17) It was a criticism of the Pharisees' attachment to the Law, so it would seem that what Jesus was saying was, "It is easier for heaven and earth to cease to exist, than for you people to abandon your obsession with the Law."

In those few phrases Jesus explained the whole problem he was having in proclaiming the kingdom for people to embrace. The problem was their attachment to the old ways, the ancient Law and the prophecies, which were only a preparation for the Messiah's coming. They were so obsessed with the things of the past that they could not accept their fulfillment, which was taking place before their very eyes. The Messiah had already come, and they were still dreaming about his coming. They would rather cherish the prophecies' dream than accept the Messiah himself, who was preaching in their streets. This was a phenomenon that mystified Jesus, and he finally saw its absurdity. Departing from the old ways was done only with violence to one's attachments to childhood ways of thinking. That was the violence needed to storm the kingdom of heaven.

Jesus told another parable. What prompted this parable, and who was present, and where it was spoken, are difficult to know. It probably was spoken to a different audience, an audience in a neighborhood where there were very wealthy people; again, one of those trendy enclaves where the recently wealthy moved, near the villas of the old rich. Wherever this location was, there were always, of course, the ubiquitous destitute, begging for food and pricking the consciences of the rich, which Jesus himself also did so well.

"There was a rich man who dressed in purple garments and fine linen, and feasted sumptuously every day. Lying outside the gate of the rich man's mansion was a poor man named Lazarus, covered with sores, who would have been overjoyed to eat the scraps that fell from the rich man's table. But no one offered them. Dogs even used to come and lick his sores. When the poor man died, he was carried away by angels to the lap of Abraham. The rich man also died and was buried, and from the regions below where he was in torment, he raised his eyes and saw Abraham far off and Lazarus at his side. And he cried out, 'Father Abraham, have pity on me. Send Lazarus to dip the tip of his finger in water and cool my tongue, for I am suffering torment in these flames.' Abraham replied, 'My child, remember that you received good things during your lifetime, while Lazarus received only bad things; but now he is comforted here, while you are in torment. Besides, there is a great chasm between you and us to prevent anyone from crossing over from our side to your side, or from your side to our side.' He said, 'Then, I beg you, Father, send him to my father's house, for I have five brothers, so that he may warn them, lest they too end up in this place of torment.' But, Abraham told him, 'They have Moses and the prophets. Let them listen to them.' He said, 'No, Father Abraham, but, if someone comes back to them from the dead, they will surely repent.' Then, Abraham said, 'If they will not listen to Moses and the prophets, neither will they be convinced even if someone should rise from the dead.' " (Lk. 16:14–31)

This parable may have been taking place in real life right there at that moment. Perhaps it was near a very wealthy man's villa. Could that man have also been standing around out of curiosity, listening to what this preacher had to say? Was there a poor beggar over near the gate of the rich man's estate? The name Jesus used for the beggar was Lazarus, which means "leper." Could the poor man have been a leper driven by desperation to dare to approach a neighborhood where wealthy humans lived? Most probably this parable was not taking place, but is just true to life, with a powerful message Jesus wanted spread throughout that particular neighborhood.

So often when people become rich, they no longer see poor people. It is as if they suddenly become invisible. We often make unpleasant things disappear from our consciousness so we do not have to deal with them, though they will haunt us in different ways, usually in our dreams or at vulnerable times. Just tonight a congressman was being interviewed on television, and I could not believe what he said, that "There are no poor people in our country, just people too lazy to work. Anyone who really wants to work can always find a job."

What Jesus was talking about in the parable was not people who happen to be wealthy, but people blinded by greed to the existence of poor people to the point where they no longer see them when they walk past them on the street. It is an attitude they have to develop to deaden their consciences. I will never forget one bitterly cold day in the early 1980s. It was snowing. I had just exited the Thruway in South Albany, New York, and was entering Route 9W, when I saw a respectably dressed old man walking south on the road. When I turned left I was about to pass him, but decided to stop and ask him if he would like a ride. "I would really appreciate that," he said. He got in the car, and I asked him where he was going. "To Coatesville, Pennsylvania," he replied. "Coatesville, Pennsylvania?" I asked, bewildered. "What are you doing walking, and way up here?" "I just left a shelter, my tenth one since I left Coatesville."

It struck me that this neatly dressed man, close to eighty years old, was living in shelters. I asked him what was in Coatesville. He told me he had a post office box there where he picked up his pension check and social security check at the beginning of each month. Then he went on to tell me he had worked for the railroad all his life, and when he retired he got a pension, but it was not worth very much anymore, so he had to make a decision as to whether he would live in an apartment or eat. He could not afford to do both. Since he had no family, there was no one for him to live with. So, he started out at the beginning of each month going to a shelter to live. He was allowed to stay for only two or three days in each shelter, and then he moved on to the next one. And between Coatesville and Schenectady, New York, he ended up staying at nine or ten shelters before it was time to go back to Coatesville. Then he went on to tell me that many of his old railroad friends were in the same situation. In fact, he had met one not too long before sitting on a park bench. They sat and talked for a long time, and then he had to say good-bye to his friend. It was the last time he saw him. He died a short time later.

I felt so sorry for the man, and after him telling me that his old railroad friends were in the same predicament, I decided to write to the president of the United States. I did get a letter a few weeks later from the Secretary of Health and Human Services or whatever the official name of the cabinet-level department was. She told me that I must be misinformed, as there were no people in our country in such dire situations as I described. I guess there are some people whose lives have been so insulated from ever encountering destitute people that it is almost impossible for them to believe that such people exist.

In Jesus' day, however, the poor and the orphaned wandered through every neighborhood. You could not avoid them. Jesus had seen so many situations where the poor were treated like scum, and referred to as the unwashed rabble. In this parable you can feel his anger, almost rage, at the cold, callous indifference to human suffering by this rich man in the parable, even at his very door, pleading for something to eat, anything. He paints the picture in frighteningly stark contrasts, both in describing the two situations in this life and the two situations in the life to come. And he does not in the slightest soften the edges of the parable. The whole situation is black and white.

This problem so troubled Jesus that in another parable he described the Last Judgment, and decreed that the basis for the Last Judgment will be not perfect observance of the commandments as people in Jesus' day were taught, and as we also were all taught since childhood, but how we treated the poor during our lifetime.

Whether on this same occasion or on another occasion, Jesus talked about scandalizing the innocent and causing them to sin. This subject had come up at another time, when Jesus was surrounded by little children. The same may have occurred at this time, as well, since children were always drawn to Jesus. He used the situation to stress the lesson, a lesson very much an issue in Jesus' day, just as it is today, as so many children learn to sin from the bad example of their parents or other family members, and the scandal caused by family friends. The innocence of so many children is destroyed by scandalous experiences at home, and from association with relatives, so by the time they are emerging from childhood they have already lost their innocence, not just in matters of sexual behavior, but in good moral living. "Things that cause sin will inevitably occur, but woe to the person through whom they occur. It would be better if a millstone was tied around his neck and he was tossed into the depth of the sea than that he scandalize one of these little ones." (Lk. 17:1–2)

Then, on to another subject essential to Jesus' way of living, and a subject he talked about frequently, and something that he practiced consistently in his own life. "Be alert! If your brother offends you, and he repents, forgive him. And if he offends you as much as seven times in one day, and comes back seven times to ask forgiveness, telling you he is sorry, forgive him." (Lk. 17:3–4)

One day, the apostles, troubled because they felt they did not have enough faith, said to Jesus, "Lord, increase our faith." Jesus said to them, "If you have faith the size of a mustard seed, you could say to this tree, 'Be uprooted and plant yourself in the sea,' and it would obey you." (Lk. 17:5–6) Think about that. It is not easy to understand. Faith, where does it come from? Is it born in us? It is something parents teach us? Is it something that can be taught? Or is it a gift from God?

I have thought about this question for many years, and am still trying to understand how Jesus looked upon people's faith. It sometimes appears that Jesus *expected* us to believe, and that he thought we could do something about whether we believe or not. Here we see that the apostles were also concerned about their own lack of faith, and apparently had tried to deepen their faith, but had not succeeded at it. So, they asked Jesus to increase their faith. Is our faith something we can increase or deepen? If we do not have faith, can we determine on our own that we are going to have faith, as if it is under our control?

I know of a Jewish man who went to church every day, and before the Blessed Sacrament prayed that God would give him the gift of faith. No matter how hard he tried, he could not believe. For years he continued, never giving up, pleading with God to give him faith. I do not know whether he was ever given the gift, though I am sure he was pleasing to God, perhaps more pleasing than many people who have faith. Other people shared with me the same concern. My physics professor at Columbia University told me a similar story about himself. He wanted so much to believe and join the Church, but he could not get himself to. believe and asked me humbly, "How do you get faith? I try so hard." I told him that I thought it must be a gift from God, and he said, "I think you're right." Clearly, their willingness to believe did not make it happen. Perhaps faith-filled parents can instill faith in their children, though some children seem to resist and grow up with very little faith. It is rare to see a child who has faith when the parents had no faith, so parents do have an influence over a child's ability to believe.

For adults who have grown up without faith, and would like to believe, that is a separate issue. No matter how hard they try, just willing it does not bring about an attitude of belief. It must be a gift from God. It is the same with deepening our faith, though it seems that life's experiences can affect people's faith either positively or negatively. When good things happen unexpectedly and for no apparent reason, and at a time when the good was something we needed, that often lights a spark of faith, which can grow into a flame. And when other good things follow that seem to have no natural explanation, it can prompt a person to consider that maybe it is the hand of God. Also, when we read the Bible or spiritual books, that can deepen our awareness of spiritual realities and, in the process, bring about a deepening of faith and trust in God. Also, faith, like love, can grow cold and die if we do not practice it regularly. Being involved in good works or in things involving God can stimulate faith, and deepen it.

The artist who did the beautiful thought-provoking paintings for one of my books called me one day after the book came out. She shared with me that at the time she had been experiencing a very difficult problem, but when she started working on the painting, the problem seemed to lessen. When she finished the painting, the problem that had seemed so overwhelming and unsolvable just evaporated as if it had never existed. She was convinced it was the work of God.

So, it seems that faith is fundamentally a gift of God's grace. If God uses parents as the vehicle of that grace, it still comes from God. We may nurture that gift and help our faith to deepen, but when it comes to an extraordinary kind of faith, that is not the fruit of our human efforts, but an extraordinary gift of God, which He gives to whomever He chooses. I would love to have the kind of faith my mother and father possessed. My mother had been told by her doctor that she should never marry, because it was medically impossible for her to have a child and survive. She had had scarlet fever as an infant and it had seriously damaged her internal organs. When she was pregnant with me, the doctor pressured her to have an abortion, which both she and my father refused to agree to. Reluctantly she started to go to another doctor. In time she ended having twelve children, which was my parents' dream. The previous doctor, whom she had known from her childhood, was so impressed, he told her one day, that he'd learned to believe in God from the powerful witnessing of her life. A divine purpose was so clear.

As the apostles asked Jesus to increase their faith, another issue arose in Jesus' mind about the apostles, and how difficult it was for them to practice the kind of humility that he himself lived. The apostles were only too ready to take great pride in the work they were doing, which is not wrong. But it is not the way Jesus thought. He'd come to serve. That is a concept the apostles had a difficult time applying to themselves. Jesus' ministry, in which they were very involved, and were playing an ever more important role, made them feel justifiably proud. But that could be a problem as Jesus saw it. So, he raised another issue for them to consider. It was his way of teaching them another important lesson.

"Who among you would say to his servant who had just come in from plowing or tending sheep in the field, 'Come here immediately and recline at your place at the table?' Would he not rather say, 'Prepare for me something to eat. Put on your apron, and serve me while I eat and drink. You may eat and drink when I am finished?' Is he grateful to that servant for doing what he was commanded to do? So should it be with you. When you have done all that you have been commanded to do, say, 'We are unprofitable servants, we have done no more than was our duty.' " (Lk. 17:7–10)

One day a scientist, one of my father's customers, came into the shop to pick up his meat order. He was talking to my father, who had only a sixth-grade education—formal education, that is. He learned his most valuable knowledge from life's experiences. The scientist was elated over some stunning findings that he and a colleague had discovered. "Yes, Peter, there is no limit as to what scientists will produce in the future," he boasted. The man and his friend did not believe in God. My father replied, "That is a wonderful thing you and your friend accomplished. But, you are a scientist who spends his life analyzing. Tell me, did you create what you found, or did you find what God created and blessed you and your friend with intelligence to discover what was hidden there all the time? None of us can take credit for our great accomplishments. I thank God for the privilege and the responsibility of raising His children, whom He entrusted to me and my wife. And after we have finished, we will have done nothing more than was our obligation to God."

"What a unique way of looking at life, Peter. I will have to think about that. I know my wife will appreciate it. She likes to thank God for everything," the man replied.

35
_____

ON THE WAY TO JERUSALEM

When the evangelists remarked that Jesus was working his way to Jerusalem after leaving the Transjordan area, they gave no itinerary, which leads a reader to assume that the direction Jesus took was on a continuous straight line toward Jerusalem. But we now find him, to our great surprise, in an area much farther north, probably up along the Jordan valley near Scythopolis at the edge of both Samaria and the southern tip of Galilee, far out of the way, and certainly not, to our way of thinking, on the way to Jerusalem. Scythopolis is over sixty miles north along the Jordan valley from where Jesus began his tour of the villages. So, rather than going westward through the villages and towns, he zigzagged, veering in a northerly direction, possibly to visit some of the villages along the border of Samaria near the Jordan.

Jesus is now in an area quite far from Jerusalem. We never know what is going on in Jesus' mind. Perhaps there was some work he felt was unfinished among the Samaritans, since he had once created a favorable attitude among them toward his message, and now, knowing his mission was in its final months, he could plant some lasting memories of his time spent there and his message of the kingdom.

Another possible reason why Jesus went to this area was because he, in his far-seeing vision, saw a situation occurring in that area that he wanted to respond to, specifically to meet somebody as he did when he wanted to meet the Samaritan woman at Jacob's Well. When he finally arrived there and was about to enter a village, he was met by ten lepers, who stood at a distance from him. The wording here is different from the evangelists' description of other encounters with people needing healing. Luke does not say, "as Jesus entered a village," but, "as Jesus was entering"—he had not as yet entered. This is significant. These lepers were observing of the laws forbidding them to enter a village. Luke also writes that they stayed at a distance from Jesus and spoke loudly so Jesus could hear them: "Jesus, Master, have pity on us!" In hardly any of the previous places where Jesus went was he treated with such reverence and respect by diseased persons. Jesus usually touched people, especially lepers, when he healed them. These lepers kept their distance from Jesus, so he merely said to them, "Go, show yourselves to the priests."

As they were going on their way they were cleansed. A short time later, one of them, realizing he had been cured, came back and glorified God in a loud voice and, falling at Jesus' feet, thanked him. And he was a Samaritan. Jesus said to him, "Were not ten cured? Where are the other nine? Has no one come back to give thanks to God except this foreigner?" Then he said to the man, "Stand up and go; your faith has saved you." Jesus never looked for thanks, but it must have hurt him that his own never appreciated him enough to thank him. This is the only time in the Gospels where anyone ever thanked Jesus. You cannot but feel his hurt that it was only a Samaritan, and not one of his own.

Luke does not say the nationality of the other nine. They could have all been Samaritans, but they most probably were mixed, with some being Galileans or even Judeans. The significant thing is that it was the Samaritan, noticing he had been cured, who returned to thank God. To which Jesus responded, "Stand up and go on your way. Your faith has saved you." (Lk. 17:11–19)

It is impossible to know why Jesus was in that part of Palestine. Could he have decided to travel out of his way to that place, knowing that there was a gathering of lepers there, like the time he made the trip to Samaria on that other occasion, intentionally, knowing that a woman would be at Jacob's Well at noontime? This is another example of Jesus' ability to see things far away. He'd had a mission to accomplish there in that Samaritan village. Was there a similar purpose in his taking this out-of-the-way detour to meet these unfortunate lepers? It was a mission, a mission that brought hope and a whole new life to those ten tortured outcasts from the society of nice people. It would have been a worthwhile undertaking for any doctor, even if he had to travel far out of his way, to be able to instantaneously cure ten people afflicted with that hideous disease. Whatever Jesus' motive was for him to make that detour, the evangelists recount no other happenings, no preaching, no other healings, only a brief encounter with a band of Pharisees, and then Jesus started back on his way to Jerusalem.

As far away from Galilee and Judea as Jesus was, the Pharisees were still hounding him. They could have been local Galilean Pharisees, wandering clergy of a lower class. Most probably they were Pharisees from Jerusalem sent out specifically to harass Jesus, though these Pharisees seem to have been a decent group who wanted to learn. They ask a fair enough question: "When is the kingdom of God coming?" Jesus' answer provides important information for all of us: "The coming of the kingdom of God cannot be observed, and no one will announce its coming, saying, 'Look, here it is,' or 'There it is.' For I tell you, the kingdom of God is among you."

There is a profound message in Jesus' response for all of us, especially for people searching for God. When we reach out to him and express our openness to receive Jesus' message and his love, he and his Father come and live within us. By our embracing the divine Presence within us the kingdom has already come to us, and we become citizens of the kingdom. There may still be more expected of those who have newly decided to embrace the kingdom, but the first step has been made, namely, welcoming the Lord. Grace upon grace will follow.

Jesus went further in explaining this to his disciples and, in doing this, made a complete break from his response to the Pharisees. He shifted from talking about the kingdom of God within the reach of people who accepted him into their hearts, to the final unfolding of the Last Days, the end of time, when the Son of Man will come in all his glory. He did not take much time saying what he had to say:

> "The days are coming when you will long to see one of the days of the Son of Man, but you will not see it. There will be those who will say to you, 'Look, there he is,' or 'Look, here he is.' But, do not go there, or go looking. As lighting strikes and lights up the sky from one end to the other, so will the coming of the Son of Man be just as striking. But, first he must suffer greatly and be rejected by this generation. As it was in the days of Noah, so it will be in the days of the Son of Man. People were eating and drinking, and marrying and giving in marriage right up to the day that Noah entered the ark, and the flood came and destroyed them all. So it was in the days of Lot. People were eating and drinking, buying and selling, planting and building. On the day when Lot left Sodom, fire and brimstone rained from the sky and devoured them all. So it will be on the day the Son of Man will be revealed. On that day, a person who is on the housetop, and whose belongings are in the house, must not go down to get them, and also a person in the field must not go back to what he left behind. Remember the wife of Lot. Whoever seeks to preserve his life will lose it. But, whoever loses it will save it. I tell you, on that night there will be two people in one bed. One will be taken and the other left. And there will be two women grinding meal together. One will be taken and one will be left."
>
> They asked Jesus, "Where, Lord?" "Where the vultures gather, there you will find the body." (Lk. 17:22–37)

Though he did not give a very clear answer to the question, as if that was not important, what he did consider important he made very clear. "You do not need to know when that time comes. When it does come just make sure you are ready. When the Son of Man comes, you will not have to wonder where he is or if it is really he. The coming of the Son of Man will be as stunning as lightning flashes across a darkened sky." It is as if Jesus was telling us not to make a big issue out of his final coming. We should just make sure we are all ready, when we are called home. That will be the end of the world for us. That is what is important.

What follows seems to be a break, as Jesus moved into a totally different subject, the subject of our need to pray often and with persistence. Did this follow from what we have just discussed or did Jesus say this at a different time? There is no way to know, though there could be a connection. If we are to be ready when God calls us to judgment at the end of our life, we had better start taking our lives seriously, and evaluate ourselves in the light of that day. That will not be easy if we work at it full-time. And what is going to be critical in determining whether we are going to be successful or not is our prayer. We need God's help more than we realize, and Jesus was saying that we should pray constantly and persistently, really pestering God for what we need, and not give up even if God does not answer our prayer after a long time. Just keep pestering Him. He will eventually give us what we need. There is really good humor in the parable Jesus used to tell us how we should persist in hounding God when something is important for us.

> "There was a judge in a certain town, who feared neither God nor man. There was also a widow who lived in the same town, who kept coming to him, demanding, 'I want justice from you against my enemy.' For a long time he refused, but eventually, he finally decided, 'Maybe it is true. I fear neither God nor man, but this woman is so demanding, I had better give her justice before she does me violence.'
>
> "Now see what the unjust judge concludes. Will not God also give you what you need, especially when it is something that you have a right to expect of Him?"

But, he then adds, with all this talk about being ready when the time comes, "Do you really think the Son of Man will find faith on the earth when he comes?" (Lk. 18:1–8) Is Jesus telling us that with all the grace God may give us, and no matter how many prayers He may answer, there will still be some who will not be ready when the time comes? They will be like the Galileans, to whom Jesus gave all he had and they still turned their backs on him.

What follows in Luke's Gospel could be a continuation of the same theme, except the message in this next parable is a hint of what will be important to God when the time comes for us to stand before Him.

"He told this parable to those who boasted of their holiness, and loathed others as sinners. 'Two men went to the Temple to pray; one was a Pharisee, the other a tax collector. The Pharisee stood there before the Holy Place and prayed, "I thank you, God, that I am not like the rest of men, adulterers, thieves, corrupt, or like that tax collector back there. I fast twice a week; I pay tithes on all I take in." The tax collector stood off at a distance from the Holy Place, so conscious of what he was, he could hardly raise his eyes to heaven, but he beat his breast and pleaded, "God, be merciful to me. I am a sinner." This man, I tell you, went home justified in the eyes of God, and the other went home rejected by God. Everyone who exalts himself will be humbled and those who humble themselves will be exalted.' " (Lk. 18:9–14)

Thus Jesus tells us the attitude we must have when the Son of Man comes and we are called to stand before him.

Surprisingly, the next incident describes another attitude that God desires to see in us, and that will be important when we appear before Him. People were bringing their children to Jesus for him to bless them, but the disciples were driving them away. Jesus called the children back to him and said, "Let the little children come to me, and do not stop them, for it is to such as these that the kingdom of heaven belongs. And let me assure you, anyone who does not approach the kingdom of God like a little child will never enter into it." (Lk. 18:15–17)

Jesus had just left Scythopolis up between Samaria and Galilee, and was now on his way back down to where he'd started well over two months before. We see him not far from Jericho, which is on the approach to Jerusalem. A crowd seems to be with him the whole time, as he has been talking all along the way, healing those afflicted and telling parables with messages that all tie in together, all clearly spelling out what attitudes and virtues are necessary if one wants to be ready when God calls us home. Prayer is one thing that is necessary, and persistence in prayer. The simplicity of a child is also necessary for entrance into the kingdom. Humility and sincere recognition of our sinfulness and sorrow for our sins are what God wants when we approach our judgment.

And now we see a rich man, a very wealthy man, a member of one of the aristocratic families in the area, approaching Jesus. This was after

Jesus said that unless you have the simplicity of a child you cannot enter heaven. Did this wealthy young man have the simplicity of a child? He asked Jesus, "Good Master, what must I do to possess eternal life?" An interesting question! Jesus often talked about the kingdom of heaven, but rarely did he talk about eternal life. He talked about eternal life with Nicodemus. He talked about eternal life when he promised the Eucharist as the heavenly food that assured eternal life. Where did this young fellow hear about eternal life? Was he a friend of Nicodemus, who had shared with him the conversation he'd had with Jesus? Jews did not know about eternal life, so where would he have picked up this idea? Had he been with Jesus on another occasion when he talked about life after death, and living on in heaven for eternity?

The man addressed Jesus with utmost refinement and respect. "Good Master," he addressed him. Jesus answered his question precisely. The man had asked him what he *must* do to possess eternal life. Jesus told him exactly what he *must* do.

> "Keep the commandments. You must not commit adultery; you must not kill; you must not steal; you must not bear false witness against your neighbor; honor your father and your mother."
>
> The man replied, "I have done these things since I was a child."
>
> Then Jesus told him, "One important thing is lacking. Go, sell all that you have, and give the money to the poor. You will then have treasure in heaven. Then come follow me." When the man heard this he became deeply sad, for he was very wealthy. (Lk. 18:18–23)

There is more than meets the eye in this conversation. Jesus told the young man just what was necessary for his salvation. That was all the man had asked for. But, when he was not content with Jesus' answer, as if he was expecting more, then Jesus told him what he might do, though it was not necessary, and that was strip himself of his wealth, give the proceeds to the poor, and become one of his disciples. Jesus was inviting him into his group of close friends, his disciples. You do not see Jesus doing that very often. This man clearly was someone very special in Jesus' mind. He was a good man, with great potential.

Luke says that Jesus looked upon the man, insinuating that it was a look of love and sadness, because here was a man who was good, and Jesus could see the struggles the fellow would have all his life with his great wealth and the complicated situations that would compromise and maybe jeopardize his basic goodness. The Gospel does not say whether the man stayed there or walked off. But, Jesus went on to expound on what a danger riches are, and how love of material things can make it so difficult to enter into the kingdom of God. "It is easier for a camel to walk through the eye of a needle than for a rich man to enter the kingdom of God." "Then who can be saved?" someone shouted out. "With men it is impossible," Jesus replied. "With God all things are possible." (Lk. 18:18–23)

It was still winemaking season. As Jesus and his apostles were walking through villages he spotted a wealthy man walking out to the village square, where men were hanging around, looking for someone to hire them. The man needed a good-sized crew, and there were only a handful there at that early hour. Seeing this scene made Jesus think. "You know," he said,

> "the kingdom of heaven is like that man looking for workers in his vineyard. The owner of the vineyard went out early in the morning looking for workers. He made an agreement with them for a denarius a day and sent them into his vineyard. Going out again at the third hour, he saw more men standing around. He told them to go into his vineyard and he would pay them a fair wage. He went out again at the sixth and again at the ninth hour, and the eleventh hour, which was five o'clock, and did the same."

This parable of the workers in the marketplace is very carefully constructed. Only a keen observer of hiring practices in those days could have described so well the psychology of day laborers.

It brings back memories of my days as a seminarian, when I was on summer vacation. I was seventeen at the time and needed summer work. My cousin suggested I go down to the port of Albany and stand around with the crew waiting to be hired to unload the ships.

There were about a hundred men standing there, waiting for the foreman to come out and pick whom he needed for that shift. This particular night it was a grain ship being loaded for Russia. Those of us who were hired climbed on board and jumped down into the hold, on top of the grain, and with large four-gallon scoops we started shoveling grain so it would spread along the floor of the hold, as the elevator chute kept discharging a never-ending torrent of grain on top of the pile already there.

We worked nonstop for four hours, with no time to rest or a break. If one of us slowed down, the foreman made sure we kept up the pace. As time passed it became hard to breathe, as the cloth masks that protected us from the thick dust became clogged with perspiration and moisture from exhaling. The whole time we hoped no one would forget and light a cigarette anywhere near us, as it would cause an explosion.

At the end of the four hours, exhausted, we climbed out of the hold and crossed the gangplank to the dock. When the men went to their cars I was too tired to walk anywhere. I sat down at the edge of the dock and tried to hold down the terrible feeling of nausea. My six-mile walk home that night at least helped clear my lungs, and prepared me for the best sleep of my life. But the next morning, when my mother put cereal out for my breakfast, I must have looked at her real funny, because we both broke out laughing. I could not eat cereal for at least three months after I stopped working there that summer.

When you are hired as a day laborer, a supervisor watches over the workers and allows no slack. You work hard. It was the same in Jesus' day. Those day laborers worked hard, nonstop, until the end of the day. For us at the dock, one day it was the grain ships; another day it was unloading pulp shipments from Sweden for the paper mills.

So, it is easy to feel sympathy for those who were hired at dawn to work in the vineyard until nightfall. For as we are about to see, they would be paid the same wage as the latecomers. It is easy to understand why those who bore the heat of the sun all day were angry when those who came in the last hour received the same pay as they did.

"When evening came, he [the owner] went out to the vineyard and paid the workers, giving them all a denarius, beginning with the first and right to the last. When those who worked from six o'clock in the morning until the end came, they received their denarius. And when those who came at three o'clock in the afternoon came, they received the same as the others. Those who worked all day right from the start complained that they got the same as those who came at the end of the day, thinking they would receive more, since they endured the heat of the whole day.

"The owner said to them, 'Did we not agree for a denarius a day? Are you upset because I am generous, choosing to give to those who worked only an hour the same as you who worked the whole day? Can I not do what I want with what is mine? Why should you be envious because I am so generous?' "

Jesus summed up with the lesson, "The last shall be first, and the first last." (Mt. 20:1–16) That is God's justice. Is it fair? What is the missing factor?

This is a parable that troubles many people, yet it is so real. In Maryland there is a landscaper whose crew of immigrant workers cut my lawn and care for the grounds. He is a good employer. The workers are dependable and very professional, and always do an excellent job. Usually there are four in the crew. When they finish, I give them a little something extra. Occasionally when they come, there may be one or two extra workers, older men. Even though they do not come regularly I give them the same as I give the others. I know the work is not as easy for them, as they are considerably older. They are most grateful. Fortunately, the younger men smile when I give the bonus to the old men.

I can understand Jesus' thinking when he told that parable. It seems so natural to show appreciation for a job well done. And the owner was generous in showing kindness to those who were hired later in the day. Was Jesus teaching in this parable that God is like the owner of that vineyard? Or is he telling a parable about a wealthy farmer who has no feelings for those who worked hard all day? It is a parable that makes the reader feel uncomfortable.

What Jesus was thinking about seems to transcend human conditions, and is describing a much more spiritual aspect of life. It seems to concern the world at large and how people spend their time in the vineyard of life. The denarius becomes a symbol not of recompense for a job done, but a symbol of the eternal reward that God will give at the end of life. There are some who spend their whole life working hard in the kingdom, and others who finally come back to God when their lives are almost ended. God rewards them all with the same reward, entrance into heaven. Is God unjust? No. But His kindness toward those who come late is hard for humans to understand, because it is impossible for us to understand the love that God has for all of us, and His joy and happiness when sinners come back to Him.

All that Jesus had been talking about was closely connected, and was intended as preparation for the apostles' work later on. It was the closest thing to a retreat that Jesus gave to a group of his followers, who were walking along with him on his way to Jericho. At this point, knowing they were not far from Jerusalem, he took aside his twelve apostles and shared with them what was going to happen. "Now we are going up to Jerusalem, and everything that is written by the prophets about the Son of Man will take place. He will be handed over to the pagans and will be made sport of, and will be badly treated, spat upon, and when they have scourged him, they will put him to death, and on the third day he will rise again." But they could not understand what he was talking about. It was all very mysterious and made no sense to them.

36

JESUS ENTERS JERICHO

Jesus finally reached Jericho. It is one of the lowest spots on the face of the earth. If the Dead Sea is hundreds of feet below sea level, Jericho is not much higher. It is warm and damp and a perfect place for agriculture. This is probably why it is one of the oldest cities in the ancient world.

As Jesus entered the city with his apostles and disciples from the village who had recently accepted Jesus, they passed a blind man lying on the side of the road. He'd heard people saying that Jesus, the teacher from Galilee, was coming into the town. The man had heard of Jesus, and knew he now had a chance to be healed, so he called out, "Jesus, Son of David, have pity on me." The people standing near him tried to shut him up, and told him to keep quiet, but he shouted all the louder, "Jesus, Son of David, have pity on me."

Jesus stopped and ordered those standing nearby to bring the man to him. When he came up, Jesus asked him, "What is it you would like me to do for you?" "Sir, let me see again." Jesus said to him, "Receive your sight. It is your faith that has healed you." And he immediately received his sight. And he joined the disciples and followed Jesus, praising God. And all the people who witnessed gave praise to God for what had happened. (Lk. 18:35–43)

As Jesus walked through the town, there was a man there, a tax collector named Zacchaeus, who had heard about Jesus, but had never seen him. When he heard that Jesus was coming down the street he immediately climbed up a sycamore tree growing along the road and crawled out on a limb so he could see Jesus as he passed. The man was very short and was afraid he would not see Jesus otherwise. Luke makes a point of mentioning that this man was not just an ordinary tax collector, but a chief tax collector overseeing the unjust extortion of people's taxes, and a man despicable in the people's eyes. To the patriots he was nothing more than a traitor to his own neighbors. I am sure our own super-patriots who cannot tolerate anyone who disagrees with their brand of patriotism would never have tolerated this fellow and his ilk. Even at that time he would have been assassinated, but for his protection by the Roman authorities. And there he was, like an excited little boy anxious to see a famous man who talked about God, and who cared for people and had a reputation for healing people of terrible diseases.

An old priest friend, who works in a parish where there are many Mafia families, told me stories of how these hardened criminals have a simplicity that is hard to square with their reputations. Knowing so many of them, he told me stories of how helpful they are when he needs help for poor people and how generous they are to families who are destitute and in desperate need of help. And they want no one to know where the help came from. He could write a book on the number of people they have helped. Of course, the priest never justified their criminal activities, but the contrast between their reputation and what he had seen so often when he asked them to help someone was bewildering. He attributes that to their mothers, who like Saint Augustine's mother never gave up her storming heaven that one day her son would find God.

As Jesus walked closer to the sycamore tree, he knew the publican would be up there on the limb, so he stopped under the tree and, looking up and seeing the fellow, he called up to him by name, "Zacchaeus, come on down. I am to stay at your house today." The fellow shimmied down the tree and, all excited, welcomed Jesus, with joy. The crowd was not only shocked but hurt. "How could this holy man visit a family like that when he must know how that man has stripped us of our hard-earned money, and made some of us almost beggars?"

The publican knew what the people were thinking, and how Jesus had put himself in such a compromising position by favoring him, so he loudly announced for all to hear that, "If I defrauded anyone I will pay him back four times more than what I owe, and besides that," he then said to Jesus, "to show my appreciation, sir, for your kindness, I will give half my property to the poor."

In one place where I worked, a stranger asked if he could meet with me. I made an appointment and we talked. He told me stories about his life, and how difficult it was, and delicately hinted he was part of the Mafia, and not just a lowly soldier. After he had read *Joshua*, he said it touched his heart and made him see things he had never understood before. Then he told me about plans he had to better people's lives. I listened half cynically, and half hopefully, as he went on. By the time he finished and asked if I would hear his confession, I was convinced that Joshua, the real Joshua, had touched his heart. How long it would last was another story. I felt guilty for being so cynical, but I had heard too many stories all my life to take people's promises too seriously. It was only years later that I heard from other people that what he had told me that day and what he had promised to do really happened. It was unbelievably beautiful. It made the Gospel story about Zacchaeus suddenly become real life. It also made me understand why some priest friends who work in "Mafia" parishes live in such hope that they can make a difference by working there. It is because they see so much and know there is, deep down, a goodness of heart that in time, with prayer and God's grace, can be touched and changed, a change that no one will ever know or learn of, other than God and the priest.

While the people were complaining that Jesus was visiting a sinner's house, he stood up to them, telling them, "Today, salvation has come to this house, because this man, too, is a son of Abraham. The Son of Man has come to seek out and save those who were lost." (Lk. 19:1–10)

While people were listening to what he was saying, he continued, telling them a parable, because he was near Jerusalem, and they were thinking the kingdom of God was going to be established very soon. "A man of noble birth went to a distant country to be made king, and then return. He summoned ten of his servants and gave them ten pounds and told them, 'Trade with them until I get back.' But, his fellow countrymen hated the nobleman and sent a delegation before him with the message, 'We do not want this man over us as our king.'

"Now when he returned, having been made king, he sent for those servants to whom he had given the money, to find out what profit each had earned. The first came in and said, 'Sir, your one pound has earned ten.' The king replied, 'Well done, good servant. Because you have shown yourself trustworthy in a small matter, you shall be put in charge of ten cities.' Then the second servant came. 'Sir,' he said, 'your pound has earned you another five.' To this one he also said, 'You shall be in charge of five cities.' Then the other servant came in. 'Sir,' he said, 'here is your pound. I put it safely away in a cloth, for I was afraid, knowing that you are a hard man, demanding what you have not advanced, and reaping what you have not sown.' He said to that servant, 'You evil servant! Out of your own mouth I condemn you. You knew that I was a demanding man, demanding what I have not advanced, and reaping what I have not sown? Then why did you not bank my money, so I could at least have interest on my return?' Then he turned to the others standing there, saying, 'Take the one pound and give it to the one who has ten pounds.' And they said to him, 'He already has ten pounds!' 'I tell you, everyone who has will be given more. But, anyone who has not will be deprived even of what he has. As for my enemies who did not want me to be their king, bring them here and execute them in my presence.' " (Lk. 19:11–27)

Those are razor-sharp words coming from the gentle Jesus. What prompted such a blunt retort to this crowd who had been following him for days? It is seemingly connected to the situation that had just taken place. The people were obviously angry because Jesus had hurt them all by choosing to dine with someone they hated. We can suppose that some people in the crowd used much more colorful language than Luke quotes in his Gospel. Did their language lay bare the hypocrisy in some persons there who were so critical of Jesus? It sounds very much like there were Pharisees present in the group. Even Luke's toned-down quote reflects wording the Pharisees regularly used in criticizing Jesus. And typical of Jesus, he was not going to let them insult this man who was humbling himself, publicly admitting he was a crook and promising to make amends. In the process he changed his heart.

Who, then, was the nobleman going to the foreign country? Clearly it was Jesus himself. Who were the servants? Just as clearly, they were the Pharisees and whatever other religious authorities were present in that crowd. They were all specially gifted by God to bear a profit for Him. Some of them were indeed profitable servants and would be rewarded. This is the first time Jesus shows a distinction among the Pharisees and other religious authorities. Some were sincere. Others were hateful. There were many who hated the nobleman who was to become their king, and did everything they could to prevent his being made king. It is interesting that these Pharisees seemed to have stalked Jesus all along that long and circuitous route that took Jesus to all those villages and towns. One would think his enemies would have learned something from Jesus' sermons after all that time. It is strong evidence how much they hated him.

Something that struck me years ago, and it is so true in the case of the Pharisees: If you like someone they can't do anything wrong. If you don't like them they can't do anything right. And in Jesus' case, they hated him so much that he could never do anything good in their eyes. Imagine someone finding fault with God! In this last parable Jesus ends with a thinly veiled, dire warning to the authorities that in refusing the accept the king sent to them from on high, they are running the risk of facing their worst nightmare when they appear before the king on Judgment Day. This was the only time Jesus threatened his enemies, not with hell, not with eternal punishment, but with death at the hand of God. Eternal death is a concept Jesus never talked about before. Eternal punishment, yes; but, eternal death? Does that mean that his enemies will be eliminated from existence? Whatever he meant by having his enemies executed before his eyes, it shows his exasperation with these men whose hearts were so full of hate and evil that even God was tempted to abandon them to eternal destruction. It is well worth studying further.

There seems to have been no response whatever from the Pharisees after that shocking and humiliating denunciation in front of the crowd following Jesus. Then Jesus told another parable, one that gives us a graphic insight into how God will judge us at the great Judgment. Actually it will be Jesus who will be the judge.

"When the Son of Man comes in majesty, and all the angels with him, he will take his seat upon his glorious throne, and all the nations of the earth will be spread out before him. He will separate them one from another, like a shepherd separates sheep from goats. The sheep he will place on his right, and the goats on his left. Then the king will say to those on his right, 'Come, you who are blessed by my Father. Inherit the kingdom prepared for you from the beginning of time, for when I was hungry you gave me food; when I was thirsty you gave me drink. When I was a stranger, you welcomed me, I was naked and you clothed me; ill and you cared for me; in prison and you visited me.' Then the righteous will say to him, 'Lord, when did we ever see you hungry and feed you, or thirsty and give you drink, or a stranger and welcome you, or naked and clothe you, or ill or in prison and visit?' And the king will say to them in reply, 'In truth I say to you, As long as you did it for the least of my brothers and sisters, you did it for me.'

"Then he will say to those on his left, 'Depart from me, you accursed ones, for when I was hungry you gave me no food; when I was thirsty, you gave me no drink; when I was a stranger you never welcomed me; naked and you never clothed me; ill or in prison and you did not care for me.' Then they will answer him, 'Lord, when did we see you hungry and not feed you, or thirsty and not give you to drink, or a stranger or ill or in prison, and not attend to your needs?' And he will answer them, 'As long as you refused to do it for the least of my brothers and sisters, you refused to do it to me.' And these will go off to eternal punishment, but the righteous to eternal life." (Mt. 25:31–40)

After that scene Jesus made his move to Jerusalem. Saint John says it was the time of the yearly celebration of the Dedication of the Temple. He also specifies that it was winter. No sooner did he arrive with his apostles and some disciples, and begin walking up and down in the Temple area, the Portico of Solomon to be specific, than officials gathered around him and badgered him into answering the question once and for all: "Are you the Christ? Tell us clearly and without equivocating." Jesus replied, "I have told you but you do not believe me. The works I do in my Father's name are my witness, but you do not believe me, because you are not of my sheep. The sheep that belong to me listen to my voice. I know them and they follow me. I give them eternal life, and they will never be lost, nor will anyone steal them from my hand. The Father, because of what He has given me, is greater than I, and no one snatches anything out of the Father's hand. The Father and I are one."

The officials immediately picked up rocks to stone him. Jesus stood there and coldly looked at them and demanded for which of the good works he had done were they stoning him. "We are not stoning you for any good works but for blasphemy, for claiming to be God, when you are only a man."

Jesus then said to them, "Is it not written in your Law: I said, you are gods? So it uses the word 'gods' concerning those to whom the word of God was addressed and Scripture cannot lose its force. And yet to someone the Father has consecrated and sent into the world you say, 'I am blaspheming,' because I said 'I am the Son of God.' If I am not doing my Father's work, there is no need to believe me, but if I am doing it, then even if you refuse to believe in me, at least believe in the work I do; then you will know for certain that the Father is in me, and I am in the Father."

37

THE DEATH AND RAISING OF LAZARUS

While casually spending time with the apostles the first time they had a chance to be alone and away from crowds, Jesus received news by way of a messenger sent by Mary and Martha. It is interesting that they knew where Jesus was staying. He obviously had been in contact with them very recently. Again it shows the intimacy of the relationship Jesus had with this little family. The last time he had left them, either before his ascent to Jerusalem or after the atttempted stoning, he returned to the Jordan River area. They must have been concerned about something, whether it was their brother's health, or the possibility of something happening to Jesus. They could not just let him go away from them without letting them know how to contact him in an emergency. It is human for friends to be concerned and say to one another, "Now, where are you going to be in case something happens, or in case we need you. Don't you dare leave without letting us know where we can find you." That would have been natural.

I am sure we have all been treated this way by those who love us and are concerned about us; they may want to know in case something happens to those close to us and they need us to be with them. Or the persons asking for information may just be possessive and need to cling to us. People are often like that in my own life, and I do not particularly like it. It gives people too much control. If they are dear friends, that is one thing, but if they just want to draw me into their close circle, when I do not want to be there, I resist it.

Jesus was very protective of his freedom and independence, and on no other occasion do we see him letting others into the privacy of his personal life. However, he clearly felt differently about this family, and so he told them where he would be, and precisely where. "We will be down at that exact spot where John used to baptize, across the Jordan in Herod's territory, where we will be safe. You know where that is; where we met you and your brother the first time." How beautiful is the tenderness of this God who came to live like us, and among us. He had never shown this kind of familiarity with any other people during his whole ministry. This gives us another tiny glimpse into Jesus' private life with close friends. Had Lazarus been sick when Jesus last visited the family? It would have been only right for these dear friends to stay in touch with one another when a family member was not well. Jesus apparently told them his whereabouts in case they needed to contact him, so the messenger arrived at the precise spot with the message, "Lord, the one you love is ill."

After the messenger left, Jesus told the apostles, "This sickness is not unto death. It is for God's glory so that through it the Son of God may be glorified." Now let John tell the story.

Jesus loved Martha and her sister and Lazarus, yet when he heard that he was ill he stayed there two more days before saying to the disciples, "Let us go back to Judea." The disciples said, "Rabbi, it is not long since the Jews tried to stone you. Are you going back there again?"

Jesus replied, "Are there not twelve hours in the day? No one who walks in the daytime stumbles; he has the light of the day so he can see. Anyone who walks around at night stumbles, as he has no light to guide him." He then added, "Our friend Lazarus is at rest. I am going to wake him." The disciples said to him, "If he is resting, he will get better." But, they misunderstood Jesus. He was speaking of the death of Lazarus, but they thought that by "rest" he meant "sleep." So, Jesus said plainly, "Lazarus is dead. And for your sake I am glad I was not there, because now you will believe." Then Thomas, known as the Twin, said to the other disciples, "Let us also go to die with him."

That remark of Thomas is a clear indication that the apostles had finally taken seriously Jesus' warning about his approaching death, though they still could not grasp what he was talking about when he also told them about his rising again after three days. This remark of Thomas also shows the complete dedication and loyalty of the apostles to Jesus. Being ready to "die with him" meant that they were prepared to leave every other human attachment behind—wife, children, loved ones, businesses, and, totally unprepared to die, they were willing to die if Jesus was going to die. That shows the difference between the apostles and the previous disciples in Galilee. The apostles were totally dedicated to Jesus, even if it meant dying with him.

On arriving at Bethany, Jesus found that Lazarus had been in the tomb for four days already. As Bethany is only two miles from Jerusalem, many Jews had come to Martha and Mary to comfort them about their brother. When Martha heard that Jesus was coming she ran out to meet him. Mary remained sitting in the house. Martha said to Jesus, "Lord, if you had been here my brother would not have died, but even now I know that God will grant whatever you ask of him." Jesus said to her, "Your brother will rise again." "I know he will rise again at the resurrection on the last day." Jesus said, "I am the resurrection. Anyone who believes in me, even though he may die, he will live, and whoever lives and believes in me will never die. Do you believe this?" "Yes, Lord, I believe that you are the Christ, the Son of God, the one who was to come into this world."

When she had said this, she went and called her sister, telling her in a low voice, "The Master is here and wants to see you." Hearing this, Mary got up quickly and went to him. Jesus had not yet come into the house. He was still at the place where Martha had met him. When the Jews who were in the house to comfort Mary saw her get up so quickly and go out, they followed her, thinking that she was going to the tomb to weep there.

Mary went to Jesus and as soon as she saw him, she threw herself at his feet, saying, "Lord, if you had been here my brother would not have died." At the sight of her tears, and those of the Jews who had come with her, Jesus was greatly distressed, and with a heartfelt sigh, he said, "Where have you put him?" They said, "Lord, come and see." Jesus wept. And the Jews remarked, "See how much he loved him." But there were some who commented, "He opened the eyes of the blind man. Could he not have prevented this man's death?" Sighing again, Jesus reached the tomb. It was a cave with a stone to close the opening. Jesus said, "Take the stone away." Martha, the dead man's sister, said, "Lord, by now there will be a stench. This is the fourth day since he died." Jesus said, "Did I not tell you that if you believe you will see the glory of God?" So, they took away the stone. Then Jesus lifted up his eyes and said, "Father, I thank you for hearing my prayer. I know that you always hear me, but I speak for the sake of all these who are standing around me, so that they may believe that you have sent me."

When he had said this, he cried out in a loud voice, "Lazarus, come out." The dead man came out, his feet and hands bound with strips of cloth, and a cloth over his face. Jesus said to them, "Unbind him and let him go." (Jn. 11:1–43)

This event is so revealing of Jesus' inner life and his capacity for human friendships. In closely analyzing the Gospels, and the way ordinary people responded to Jesus, you cannot help but conclude that Jesus' whole life was relationships. When he walked into a village or a town, people immediately gathered around him. No one seemed to be afraid of him or to feel that he was aloof from them. What is surprising is that people knew he was a saintly man, and intimate with God, as they could see from his healing powers. But even the worst sinners were not afraid to approach him, knowing that he would never turn them away or be in any way critical of them, as were their religious authorities. I will never forget many years ago when a very difficult young man came up to me and said, "You really like me, don't you?" "Why do you think that?" I asked him. "Because I can tell by the way you look at me, even though I am not a nice person." "Yes, I do, because I see a lot of good in you, and when you realize that yourself, your whole life will change."

Every individual who ever met Jesus had to have the feeling when Jesus looked into their eyes that this man loved them. "I can tell by the look in his eyes, and I know he sees right through me and knows everything about me." Being God, Jesus had a deep personal relationship with each human being he met. As a human he may not have felt the same about everyone he met, but that is just the way we are made. Some people we are drawn to, some we find it difficult to be close to. The whole Gospel story is about relationships, all different kinds of relationships in Jesus' life. Here in the story of this little family in Bethany, we see a very rare facet of the warmth of Jesus' love for three people that is tender, and so absorbing of his attention. These three, Mary, Martha, and Lazarus, were clearly the most intimate friends of his life. They were really family to him, closer to him in his feelings than Mary Magdalen, whose relationship so many authors make so much of. Who else in the Gospels did Jesus have to tell where he was going off to, so they could contact him if he was needed? They knew just where to find him when Lazarus was ill, asking him to come home because they needed him.

In his telling of this story, John reveals very interesting emotional reactions on the part of Mary and Martha and also Jesus. When it was reported that Jesus was approaching the compound where they lived, Martha immediately jumped up and ran out to meet him, at some distance still from the house. Mary stayed in the house. Interesting! Martha's first words were not, "Thank you so much for coming," but, "If you had been here he would not have died." Jesus knew that she was upset with him for not coming right away when they sent the messenger, and when he could have done something to save their brother, and so she scolded him. Who else in the Gospels would ever have talked with such familiarity to Jesus?

And Mary—she also knew Jesus was approaching the house. She did not even get up and go out to meet him. She also was upset with him, and Jesus knew it, so after telling Martha that her brother was going to rise again and seeing her belief in the final resurrection, Jesus told her, "I am the resurrection and the life, and whoever believes this, even if they die, they will live." Martha did not understand what he was telling her.

Rather than walk back into the house with Jesus, Martha went back into the house and went immediately over to her sister and whispered to her, "Mary, the Master wants to see you." John does not have Jesus telling Martha that he wanted to see Mary. But Martha knew her moody sister and how attached she was to Jesus, and that she was upset because he had not come right away when they sent the messenger to him. Martha also realized that she did not know how her sister would react to him if Jesus came right into the house, and it could be embarrassing. And Jesus knew Mary was upset with him, and, understanding what Martha was doing, he stayed right where he was and waited outside the gate where Martha had met him, for Mary to come out, which she did. It is interesting. Jesus did not budge. She was going to come out to him. How human! Isn't that the way someone acts who has been hurt by the one he loves?

Mary came out running, and her friends from Jerusalem followed her. And although John says that when she met him, she fell down at his feet and cried, it would be hard not to imagine that when Mary reached Jesus, she threw her arms around him and cried, "Why did you come so late? If you'd gotten here on time, my brother would not have died." Possibly whoever of John's scribes wrote the Gospel for John, maybe even after John's death, they had a clear idea of the divinity of Jesus and may have considered it more proper for her to fall at his feet, though it does seem a bit unrealistic. Clearly Jesus and Mary both had deep feelings for each other. More than anything else in the Gospels, this incident shows a very tender, affectionate side in Jesus' personality, especially in the scene that follows.

Jesus' reaction tells a lot, and shows how deeply he loved Mary. When he saw her crying, and her friends with her also crying, he was overcome and tried to hold back his own tears, which ended in a deep, heartfelt groan or sigh. He then broke down and cried, as he asked Mary where they had buried their brother. They answered, "Lord, come and see."

If the present-day site believed to be Mary and Martha's house is authentic, the tomb was around the outside wall of the compound. A doorway leads down a circular stone stairway to the grave site and the slab on which Lazarus was buried, at least ten or twelve feet below the road. Now, who was there watching this drama unfold? This is significant, and a reader can very easily miss the subtle dramas aside from a dead man rising from the dead. John points out very carefully who was there that day, and you can picture John, who was so shrewd and had a touch of cynicism, scanning all the faces and recognizing people present whom he had seen previously at Mary and Martha's place for one or another of their social gatherings. As he watched the reactions of each one of the mourners, John could easily identify the phonies and the sincere friends.

The men moved away the stone covering the entrance to the tomb, and stepped back. No one knew what to expect. They were all thinking, "Is he going to go down into that tomb with the horrible stench?" Then, all of a sudden, amidst the dead silence of the crowd, Jesus cried out in a loud voice, "Lazarus, come out from there!"

Everyone waited. It would take a while for the corpse to revive, and for Lazarus to wonder where he was and what was happening, then to stand up and stumble toward the steps, and slowly walk up each step. Finally he would have reached the entrance to the tomb and appeared in the doorway. The crowd of onlookers was stunned, terrified, and thrilled and was feeling whatever any of us would feel at such an extraordinary experience. We can only imagine the thrill and concern of the two sisters at seeing their brother alive. What would he be like? Like he had been dead for four days? Then Jesus told them to free him from the shroud and bring him inside so he could dress.

This was a most unique miracle because of the scientific ramifications. Lazarus had been dead for at least four days. His body and all his organs would have started decomposing. What made this miracle so unique was the power Jesus had over nature. Although he was roughly fifteen miles away from Bethany when Lazarus died, either he from that distance prevented the body from decomposing until he went there, or if the body did decompose, as Martha had already hinted, then he showed even greater power over nature by recomposing all those complex molecular chains to bring the body to a state where it could function perfectly and immediately. He did this just by the power of his will, without even touching the body.

Even Jesus' enemies did not dare to deny what had taken place. Those spies who were there later went and told the authorities what had happened, and in their hatred, all they could think of doing was to kill Lazarus so they could destroy the evidence that Jesus had the power to raise the dead, even those dead for four days. They could not tolerate the fact that this person they hated so much could raise the dead. Much less could they tolerate the effect of such a miracle on the people who were already beginning to see Jesus as more than human. And while all the friends of Martha, Mary, and Lazarus were celebrating this wonderful gift of God, Jesus' *religious* enemies were already plotting ways to kill not just Jesus, but Lazarus too.

What happens at funerals is always interesting. John again notices the reactions of everyone. I have done the same thing at funerals in parishes where I was stationed. People's interests and attitudes at funerals are eye-openers. I will never forget one funeral. After Mass at the church, the burial took place at the Gate of Heaven cemetery in Yonkers, quite a long trip. I sat in the frontseat of the limousine with the driver. The widowed husband sat in the backseat with his sisters-in-law. I knew the man quite well. He was a quiet man, kept a lot to himself. I knew he was grieving deeply over the death of his wife, but could not express his pain.

I listened to the conversation in the backseat for the whole trip to the cemetery and back to the Bronx. The man's in-laws were berating him for not grieving over their sister's death. Then they started discussing things in the house that belonged to their sister and commented about each item. I could tell they had an eye on just what they wanted from his house. That is what was uppermost in their minds while the husband just sat there, quietly grieving. They then started listing the things they wanted and said they would be over to pick them up the first chance they got.

At the gravesite during breaks in the prayers, I watched the expressions on the faces of everyone standing around. Over the years faces reveal so much. When we arrived back at the church, I got out of the limousine, and opened the back door and shook the man's hand, and said to him, "John, I know you well, and know how deeply you are grieving, though it means little to others. You are a very sincere man, John, and your feelings are deep, too deep to show. But, don't be too trusting of anyone. They will strip you of all that is dear to you, and leave you with nothing, and all alone, and you will never see them again. Jesus warned us to be 'simple as a dove, but as sly as a fox.' Good advice, John. You will be in my prayers. If you need me, you know how to get in touch with me."

That was the mentality John had at Lazarus' gravesite. He knew the drama that was beginning to unfold. The family at Bethany was very well known in Jerusalem. Pharisees and other political and religious notables were regular guests at their house, and they were there that day. Mary apparently was the popular one in the family. Let John tell us:

Many of the Jews who had come to visit Mary, and had seen what he [Jesus] did, believed in him, but some of them went to the Pharisees to tell them what Jesus had done. Then the chief priests and Pharisees called a meeting. "Here is this man working all these signs," they said, "and what are we doing about it? If we let him go on like this, everybody will believe in him, and the Romans will come and take over both our Holy Place and our authority." One of them, Caiaphas, the high priest that year, said, " 'You know nothing at all of what is going on. Can you not see that it is necessary that one man be sacrificed to save the nation?' "

Then John adds, "He did not say this from his own mind, but being the high priest that year, he prophesied that Jesus should die for the nation, and not just for the nation, but to gather into one the children of God who are scattered throughout the world. So, from that day on, they looked for a chance to kill Jesus." (Jn. 11:45–54)

John knew what was going on behind the obvious, as he knew personally confidants of the high priest's family, and you can be sure he told Jesus what he'd noticed about the different kinds of people who were among the mourners, so after spending time with Mary, Martha, and Lazarus, Jesus left there and went north across the hilltops past Jerusalem on the east, to Ephraim, today a Palestinian Christian village (Taybeh), at the edge of the wilderness, and stayed there with his disciples. He knew it was no longer safe for him to walk among the Judean religious people. There were too many spies and allies. We can assume that during this time, Jesus was not with the apostles only, but also with those loyal disciples who always traveled by his side, and would be with him to the bitter end. That would be Mary, his mother; Mary Magdalen; probably Mark, at whose father's house, apparently, they would celebrate the Last Supper; Cleopas, the husband of Mary's sister; Mary, Jesus' aunt; then Joanna; Mary, the mother of James and John; and other relatives of Mary and Jesus, members of their extended family who would be there to celebrate the Passover with Jesus. About these events John is very knowledgeable. For some reason he had friends among relatives of the high priest's family and had access to information about which the other Gospel writers knew nothing. That is why John speaks so authoritatively about these details.

John says that they stayed in that village. The question keeps coming to mind, where did they stay in that village? If there was a large group accompanying Jesus, where could they find accommodations? It would be unthinkable for all of them, with women among them, to just live out in groves of trees, of which there were few in the area, or in caves, since they were in the Judean wilderness. From our following Jesus on his recent tours it is easily seen how many people took to him and committed themselves to his teaching. Presumably, a number of these people were people of means and may have had villas, or large houses surrounded by a protective wall. Jesus chose that village for a reason, most likely because he was offered accommodations there, most likely by wealthy disciples. This would have given Jesus more quiet time with his family, particularly with his mother, as he knew the end of his life was not far off. Also, he needed more time with the apostles in his continuous effort to help them understand and believe what they found impossible to accept, that he was going to die, and die a violent death in just a short time. It seems he did little more than that at this time, as the evangelists mention no other activities that Jesus performed during that short period before he left there to go back to Bethany.

38

JESUS' LAST MINISTRY IN JERUSALEM

The Passover was not far off. People were coming from all over the known world, and also from those villages where Jesus had been preaching and healing during the past few months. These local villagers showed an unusual liking for Jesus, and were looking around for him as they approached the city, and later on when they were wandering around in the Temple. Those who had come from other countries and had heard Jesus preach on previous visits were asking among themselves, "Do you think he will be here for the Feast? Do you think he will finally be accepted by the authorities?" Those who lived closer to the Temple and in Jerusalem itself knew better. They had been informed that the order had been issued by the chief priest that anyone who had knowledge of Jesus' whereabouts should report it to the authorities so they could arrest him. The city was tense. Everyone was on edge.

Then Saint Mark has something to insert at this time, and it is interesting that he is the only evangelist who records this story.

When they were approaching Jerusalem, at Bethphage and Bethany, close to the Mount of Olives, he sent two of his disciples, and said to them, "Go, to the village facing you, and as you enter it you will immediately find a colt tied, that no one has yet ridden. Untie it and bring it here. If anyone says to you, 'What are you doing?' You will answer them, 'The Master needs it and will send it back here at once.'" They went off and found a colt tied near a door in an open space. As they untied it, some people said to them, "What are you doing untying that colt?" They told them what Jesus told them to say, and the men let them go. They then took the colt to Jesus, and spread their cloaks on its back, and he mounted it. Many people spread their cloaks on the road, and others olive branches, and branches from trees which they had cut along the road. And those who went in front, and those who followed, were all shouting, "Hosanna, blessed is he who comes in the name of the Lord. Blessed is the coming of the kingdom of David our father. Hosanna in the highest heavens." (Mk. 11:1–10)

Luke adds that there were Pharisees in the crowd who took offense at the people proclaiming Jesus as the son of David and as the Messiah. "Tell your disciples to stop chanting that." And Jesus replied, "I tell you, if these keep silent, the very stones will cry out," as if to say, "The truth is so obvious to everyone but you people." Then, as they were descending the Mount of Olives, and Jesus looked across the Kedron Valley, at the Holy City and the Temple, his Father's house, he was overcome, and broke down and cried.

"Jerusalem, Jerusalem! How often I would have gathered you together as a hen gathers her chicks under her wings, but you would have no part of me. If you only knew on this day the way to peace, but now it will be hidden from your eyes! The time will come when your enemies will build siege works around you and hem you in on every side and they will dash you and your children inside your walls to the ground, and there will not be left standing one stone upon another within you, for you did not recognize the day of your visitation." (Lk. 19:41–44)

He went into Jerusalem and entered the Temple area, and after looking around, in deep thought, as it was already late, he went out to Bethany with the twelve. (Mk. 11:11)

At this point Luke relates that Jesus entered the Temple and drove out those trading there, but it seems Mark tells what really happened, that Jesus walked around in the Temple precincts and, after spending time deep in thought, left. This makes sense, because we see Jesus, even according to Luke, teaching in the Temple daily during the days that followed and spending much time there, which he would have never been allowed to do if he had created such havoc just the day before; they would have had a good pretext to arrest him. As it turned out, the time Jesus spent in the Temple precincts on those days was extremely tense, but there was nothing with which they could legally charge him, and the local people who had become so fond of Jesus as he worked his way through their villages

and towns were strongly on his side, which was threatening to the officials. All they could do was challenge his teachings, and every time they
did that, he held a mirror up to them and showed them the true image of
how spiritually corrupt they were, and how God saw them, which shamed
and infuriated them. On one of the days that followed, Jesus would tell
them a parable which would reveal to the chief priests just how evil they
were, and the real motives they had for wanting so badly to kill him.

It is interesting that Mark says nothing about Jesus' stay in Bethany or
what happened there. Perhaps he was not there. He knew about the colt
on Palm Sunday, but it does not seem that he went back to Bethany with
Jesus and the apostles, and you wonder why. Then you realize that he was
not one of the apostles. The thought then comes to mind that perhaps the
owner of the colt was a relative or friend of Mark's family who lived in the
neighborhood across the valley from the Mount of Olives, at the house
where some Scripture scholars think Jesus held the Passover meal, his
Last Supper. Again, we will see Mark, not at the Last Supper, but in the
garden afterward, when Jesus was arrested, so, even though he was not
an apostle, he must have also been at the Last Supper, which leads one to
believe it was his family's residence.

For the story about what took place at Bethany, we depend on John.

Six days before Passover, Jesus went to Bethany where Lazarus was,
whom he had raised from the dead. They gave a dinner for him there.
Martha waited on them and Lazarus was among those at table. Mary
brought in a jar of very costly ointment, pure nard, and with it anointed
the feet of Jesus, wiping them with her hair. The house was filled with
the fragrance of the ointment. Then Judas Iscariot, one of his disciples—the man who was to betray him—said, "Why was this not sold,
and the money given to the poor?" He said this not because he was
interested in the poor, but because he was a thief; he had been given
charge of the purse, and he used to take money out of the purse for
himself. So, Jesus said, "Leave her alone. She has done this for the day
of my burial. You have the poor with you always. You will not always
have me."

Meanwhile a great number of important Jews from the neighborhood had heard that Jesus was there and came out as if to see Jesus
but also to see Lazarus, whom they had heard Jesus raised from the

dead. Then the chief priests decided to kill Lazarus too, since he was the cause of so many of the influential families walking away from the priests and following Jesus. (Jn. 12:1–11)

It was at this time that Judas Iscariot, who by now was disillusioned with Jesus, having given up hope that he would proclaim himself the Messiah, went to the chief priests, offering to hand Jesus over to them. They were delighted and offered him thirty pieces of silver in payment. From that time on, Judas was looking for an opportunity to betray Jesus.

It is painful to continue meditating on what is happening, as you feel the intensity of the pain Jesus must have been suffering, spending each day in the thick hate-filled atmosphere created by the religious authorities, who had begun threatening the people if they showed Jesus any recognition. They had also sent out strict instructions forbidding people to join his disciples. The chief priests and their cronies tried in every way they could to arrest Jesus, but he was always surrounded by caring people who had recently become his disciples from the local countryside. They guarded him zealously and protected him from the authorities, who were afraid of these people. On occasion they threatened to stone the chief priest himself and those with him if they tried to harm Jesus. This was a totally new experience for Jesus, who had been so disappointed by the attitude of the people in Galilee.

One day while Jesus was teaching in the Temple, and proclaiming the good news and the kingdom, the chief priest and the scribes, together with some of the elders, confronted Jesus with the question, "On whose authority do you do and teach the things you do? Who gives you this authority? We certainly did not."

"I will ask you a question and if you answer that question I will tell you on whose authority I do and teach the things I do. What was the origin of John's baptism: from heaven, or was it human?"

They knew they were checkmated again, and struggled to find a way out of the dilemma. Debating among themselves, they decided that if they said, " 'From heaven,' then he will say to us, 'Why did you not accept him and follow him?' If we say it was human, then the people will stone us because they believe John was a prophet." So they ended up saying, "We don't know." "Then neither will I tell you where my authority comes from." (Lk. 20:1–8)

But then Jesus went on to tell where his authority came from by means of a very cutting parable, which he appeared to be delivering to the crowd standing around, though it was aimed right at the chief priest's heart, as well as the hearts of all his cronies standing there listening. They would not have walked away, because they were trying desperately to catch him in a slipup in something he might say, so they could indict him.

"A man planted a vineyard and leased it out to tenants, and went abroad for a long time. At harvest time he sent a servant to the tenants to get his share of the produce of the vineyard. But the tenants brutalized him and sent him away empty-handed. The owner sent a second servant, and they beat him and treated him viciously, and sent him away empty-handed. The owner sent still another servant, whom they also wounded and drove out. Then the owner of the vineyard said, 'What am I to do? I will send my beloved son. Him they certainly will respect.' But when the tenants saw him, the plotted among themselves. 'This is the heir. Let us kill him; then the vineyard will be ours.' So they dragged him outside the vineyard and killed him.

"What will the owner do to those tenants? He will come himself and make an end of those tenants and give the vineyard to others." Then they said, "God forbid!" Then he looked right at them and said, "Then what does this text of Scripture mean, 'The stone which the builders rejected has become the cornerstone?' Anyone who falls on this stone will be dashed to pieces, and anyone it falls on will be crushed."

The chief priests and the scribes wanted more than anything to kill him on the spot because they knew he had directed the parable at them, but they were afraid of the people. He had bluntly accused them of being willing to kill their Messiah to protect their business.

We saw Jesus delivering this parable on another occasion to Pharisees. This time it is to the chief priests and scribes assigned to the Temple. In this parable Jesus goes right to the heart of the issue of why these men wanted to kill him. It was not to protect the people because Jesus was a threat to the state. The prophets always spoke of Jerusalem and the Jewish people as God's vineyard. The chief priests knew that that was what Jesus was referring to. The tenants were the chief priests and the religious authorities, to whom God had entrusted his precious vineyard.

The servants sent by the owner were the prophets, whom their ancestors had treated brutally. Then the owner decided to send his beloved son;
certainly they would respect him. Then Jesus revealed the real reason
why the chief priests wanted to eliminate him. It was because they had
turned their religion into their own personal business operation. They
knew in their hearts that Jesus was the Messiah, and that their own days
were numbered if he took over. They knew he would never tolerate what
they were doing, so they decided, "We'd better get rid of him before it's
too late; otherwise we will lose everything. You can see how the people
already love him."

Jesus finally exposed their true motives, which they had hidden even
from themselves, because they could not let themselves think that they
were killing their Messiah just so they could keep their lucrative Temple
business operation.

Again they lost another match of wits with Jesus, so they regrouped,
and after consulting with their strategists, they picked men loyal to them,
with reputations for honesty, and sent them to Jesus to pose to him a
conscience problem. This was a clever trap that seemingly had no escape.
If he fell for it, they could turn him over to the Roman authorities for
treason. With feigned respect for Jesus' reputation for honesty, they posed
the question, "Master, we know that you say and teach what is right. You
show favor to no one but teach the way of God in all honesty. Is it permissible for us to pay taxes to Caesar or not?" But Jesus could see their hypocrisy and said, "Show me a coin used to pay the tax. Whose image and
title are on it?" "Caesar's," they said. "Well, then, since you recognize
him already, pay what you owe him, but make sure you are as faithful in
fulfilling your obligation to God." (Lk. 20:20–26)

They had sent their shrewdest men, and they were reduced to silence.
Being unable to catch him in anything he said, they could not help but be
amazed at his answers.

Shortly after, another contingent tried to take him on. By this time,
Pharisees, scribes, and Sadducees, who had always been implacable enemies, decided to work together in an attempt to trap Jesus, since none of
the groups on their own had keen enough minds to outwit his brilliance.
This time the Sadducees tried their hand. These people, the aristocrats in
Jewish society, were highly educated and very wealthy, most of them having been trained in Greek schools. They rejected many of the teachings of

Judaism and were devotees of Greek philosophy. They were hated by the Pharisees, who were fanatically loyal to all the teachings and traditional practices of Judaism. But their mutual hatred of Jesus was so intense that they became allies in their attempt to destroy him. On this occasion the Sadducees posed to Jesus this dilemma, in an attempt to hold him up to ridicule.

"Master, Moses prescribed for us, if a man's married brother dies child-less, the man must marry the widow to raise up children for his brother. In this case there were seven brothers. The first brother, having married a wife, died childless. The second, and the third married the widow; and the same with all seven. They died leaving no children. Finally, the woman died. Now at the resurrection, whose wife will she be, since she had been married to all seven?"

Remember, the Sadducees did not believe in the resurrection, so they thought they could make Jesus look ridiculous no matter how he answered. But, Jesus' answer was calm, and precise.

"On earth people take wives and husbands, but those worthy of the resurrection and a place in the other world do not marry, for they can no longer die, but they are as the angels in heaven, and being children of the resurrection they are children of God. It was Moses himself who implied that the dead rise when, in the passage about the bush, he calls the Lord, the God of Abraham, the God of Isaac, and the God of Jacob. He is God, not of the dead, but of the living. To him they are all alive."

Some scribes who were part of the crowd and who believed in the resurrection were delighted that Jesus had bested their enemies, and they spoke out, "Well said, Master." And his enemies did not dare ask him any more questions. (Lk. 20:27–39)

On another occasion, Jesus brought up an issue that could only con-fuse those who were listening. He said to the people, "How can people claim that the Christ is the son of David, for David himself says in the Book of Psalms: The Lord said to my Lord, 'Sit at my right hand till I have made your enemies your footstool.' David here calls him 'Lord.' How then can he be his son?" (Lk. 20:41–44)

This is a most remarkable riddle that Jesus threw at those scholars, questioning the human origin of the Messiah, and using God's own inspired word, calling the heir to David's throne, David's Lord, not his son, pointedly declaring the Messiah is the Lord Himself, even though in some mysterious way he is also descended from David. He is also telling them that they were looking at their Messiah and were too blind to recognize him. They were looking at their Lord Himself, and in their blindness, *refused* to see. That was a verbal time bomb that would torture them with guilt for the rest of their evil lives.

When the people were in rapt attention with what Jesus was saying, and the officials were still smarting from his cutting accusations, he turned to his disciples and said to them, "Beware of the scribes who love to walk around in long robes, and love to be greeted with ostentatious deference in the market place, to take the front seats in the synagogues, and the places of honor at banquets, while they devour the property of widows, and for show offer long prayers in public. The more severe will be the sentence they receive." (Lk. 20:45–47)

On one of those days, when Jesus was speaking in the Temple, he was positioned near the treasury, where he could see people putting their offerings into the coffers. Jesus noticed an elderly lady who had come into the treasury. Watching her, he noticed she put two small coins into the treasury, and he commented to his disciples how the well-to-do people put in small tokens of their wealth as offerings that were no hardship for them, but this poor widow put in all she had to live on, which was worth more than all the money of the rich people. (Lk. 21:1–4)

Then, as Jesus and his friends were casually walking around the courtyard of the Temple, it was always a wonder to just look around and admire the vast dimensions of the building, and the excellent stonework, and artistic carving, and the gold façade glittering in the sun. One of Jesus' disciples remarked that it was breathtaking. Jesus looked around and felt a sense of pride that this was his Father's house, and his, as well. But then sadly he said to his disciples, "All these things you are admiring, the time will come when there will not be left one stone upon another. It will all be destroyed." Shocked at what he had just said, one of them asked, "Master, when will this happen, and what signs will there be telling us when it is going to happen?"

He told them, "Be careful not to be deceived; many will come using my name and telling people, 'I am the one' and 'The time is near.' Do not believe them and do not join them. When you hear of wars and revolutions, do not be terrified, for this is something that must happen first, but the end will not come immediately. Nation will fight against nation, kingdom against kingdom. There will be great earthquakes and plagues and famines in various places. There will be other terrifying events and great signs in the sky. But before this happens you will be arrested and persecuted; you will be handed over to the synagogues and be imprisoned, and brought before kings and governors for the sake of my name. That will be your opportunity to bear witness. Remember, do not prepare what you are to say in your defense, for I will give you a clarity and wisdom that none of your opponents will be able to resist or challenge. You will be betrayed even by parents and brothers, relatives and friends. Some of you will be put to death. You will be hated wherever you go on account of my name, but not a hair of your head will be lost. Your perseverance will guarantee your lives.

"When you see Jerusalem besieged by armies, then you must know that it will soon be laid waste. Then those in Judea must escape to the mountains, those inside the city must leave it, those in the country must not take refuge in the city, for this is the time of retribution when all that Scripture says will be fulfilled. It will be sad for those with child or with babies at the breast, when these days come. There will be signs in the sun and the moon and the stars; on earth nations in chaos, bewildered by the turbulence of the sea and its tsunamis; people collapsing from terror and fear at what is threatening the world, for the powers of universe will be shaken. Then they will see the Son of Man coming in a cloud with power and magnificence. When these things begin to take place, stand up straight, hold your heads high, because your liberation is already at hand."

Then Jesus shared a parable.

"Look at the fig tree, and in reality every tree. As soon as you see the buds appear, you can see for yourselves that summer is already upon us. So it will be when you see these things taking place; know that the kingdom of God is near. In fact, I tell you before this generation has passed away, all will have taken place, but what will never pass away is what I have taught you. My teachings will never pass away.

"Be aware, that your hearts may not be dulled by sinful living and drunkenness and life's worries, for that day will come upon you unexpectedly, like a trap. It will come down hard on all those living on the face of the earth. So, stay awake, praying at all times for the strength to survive all that is going to happen, and to hold your ground before the Son of Man." (Lk. 21:5–38)

This extended and complex series of warnings Jesus delivered while in the Temple precincts teaching. At night, however, he would leave and spend the night in the grove of olive trees in the open air of the Mount of Olives across the valley.

In the morning he would walk across the Kedron Valley and up the opposite hill to the Temple, where the people were waiting for him in great numbers to hear him speak. A large number of scribes and Pharisees mingled in with the crowd. When Jesus arrived he began to speak to the people, immediately indicting them for all the crimes they had committed against God's people, whom they were charged by God to protect and teach.

"The scribes and Pharisees occupy the chair of Moses. You must do therefore what they tell you. But do not imitate them, for they are hypocrites who do not practice what they preach. They build up heavy burdens and lay them on people's shoulders and do not so much as lift a finger to lighten those burdens. Everything they do they do to attract attention. They wear broad headbands and longer tassels. They love to take the place of honor at banquets and the front seats in synagogues, and to be greeted ostentatiously in the market place, and have people call them 'Rabbi.'

"You, however, must not allow yourselves to be called Rabbi, since you have only one Master, and you are all brothers. You must call no one on earth your father, since you have only one Father, and He is in heaven. Nor must you allow yourselves to be called teachers, for you have only one Teacher, the Christ. The greatest among you must be your servant. Anyone who promotes himself will be humbled, and anyone who humbles himself will be honored.

"As for you scribes and Pharisees, you hypocrites! You shut up the kingdom of heaven in people's face; neither going in yourselves, nor allowing others to enter who want to enter.

"As for you scribes and Pharisees, you hypocrites! You travel over sea and land to make one convert, and when he converts you turn him into more a son of hell even than you yourselves.

"Alas, have you no shame, you blind guides. You say, 'Anyone who swears by the Temple is under no obligation, but if he swears by the gold on the Temple, he is obligated.' Blind fools, which is greater, the gold, or the Temple which consecrates the gold? Again, you say, 'If anyone swears by the altar it has no force, but if anyone swears by the offering on the altar, he is bound.' You blind men, do you not understand? By your swearing by the altar you are swearing not only by the altar but by everything on it. And anyone who swears by the Temple, swears not only by the Temple, but by all that is in the Temple and by the One who lives there. And anyone who swears by heaven is swearing by the Throne of God, and by the One Who sits there.

"Be ashamed, you scribes and Pharisees, you hypocrites! You pay tithes on mint and dill and cumin, and neglect the weightier matters of the Law: justice, mercy, and integrity. These you should have done first, while not leaving the others undone. You blind guides, you strain out the gnat and swallow the camel.

"Be ashamed, you hypocrites, you clean the outside of the cup and the dish, and leave the inside full of extortion, and avarice. Blind Pharisee! Clean the inside of the cup and dish first, so that the inside and the outside will both be clean.

"Be ashamed, you scribes and Pharisees, you hypocrites! You are like whitewashed sepulchers, looking so pure and clean on the outside, but inside full of filth and dead men's bones. In the exact same way, from the outside you look like men of integrity, but inside you are full of treachery and licentiousness.

"Be ashamed, you scribes and Pharisees, you hypocrites! You build the sepulchers of the prophets and decorate the tombs of the upright, saying, 'We would never have joined in the shedding of the blood of the prophets, had we lived in our ancestors' day.' So, your own evidence indicts you. You are the children of those who murdered the prophets. Very well, finish the work your ancestors began.

"You serpents, brood of vipers, you think you can escape being condemned to hell? Let me show you why. I am sending you prophets and wise men and scribes. Some you will murder and crucify; some you will scourge in your synagogues and hunt them down from town to town; and thus you will draw down upon yourselves the blood of every righteous person that has been shed from the blood of Abel the holy to the blood of Zechariah, the son of Barachiah, whom you murdered between the altar and the Holy Place. In all truthfulness, I tell you, it will all come back to haunt this generation.

"Jerusalem, Jerusalem, you who kill the prophets and stone those sent to you! How often I wanted to gather you together as a hen gathers her chicks under her wings, but you would have nothing to do with me! Now, I tell you, your house will be deserted, for I tell you, you will not see me anymore until you say, 'Blessed is he who comes in the name of the Lord!' " (Mt. 23:1–39)

As Jesus was walking around the Temple precincts, Andrew and Philip approached him to tell him there were some Greeks nearby who had come up to the festival, and asked if they might see him. Jesus did not answer directly, but told the apostles that the timing was not good, as he had a critical message to share with those close to him, and that was that

[T]he hour is come for the Son of Man to be glorified. And I tell you emphatically that unless the grain of wheat falls into the earth and dies, it remains just a grain of wheat, but if it dies it yields a rich harvest. Anyone who loves his life will lose it. Anyone who hates his life in this world will preserve it for eternal life. Whoever serves me will follow me, and my servant will be with me wherever I am. If anyone serves me my Father will honor him. Now my soul is troubled, and what shall I say, "Father, save me from this hour?" No, for that is why I have come to this hour. So, I say, "Father, glorify your name."

At that point a voice came out of heaven, "I have glorified it and

I will continue to glorify it." The crowd standing by thought it was a thunderclap; others said it was an angel speaking to him. Jesus told them the voice was not for him but for their benefit. "Now sentence is being pronounced on this world. The prince of this world is being cast out. When I am lifted up I will draw everyone to myself." This indicated the kind of death he would suffer.

The crowd then remarked that "the Law has taught that the Christ will remain forever. So, how can you say, 'The Son of Man must be lifted up'? Who is this Son of Man?" Jesus answered, "The light will be with you only a little while longer. Go on your way while you have the light, or darkness will overtake you, and no one who walks in darkness knows where he is going. While you still have the light, believe in the light, so that you may become children of the light."

Once Jesus said this, he left and was hidden from their sight. There is no mention whether the Greeks heard all that Jesus had to say, or whether they stood back from the crowd while Jesus was speaking. Presumably, all they had to do, since this scene took place in an open space, was just walk closer to the edge of the crowd and be part of what was happening. That would seem likely, because Jesus never turned anyone away who asked to see him. It would seem they heard the message Jesus wanted them to hear. (Jn. 12:20–36)

The week was passing by fast. Early in the week, probably Tuesday, Jesus had walked up to the Temple and entered the Court of the Gentiles, and was confronted by a stockyard, with herds of sheep and goats and pigeons and money changers handling currencies from all the countries of the known world at that time. The odor and sight of fresh manure must have stunk to high heaven, and this was God's house. The religious authorities had made it a place of lucrative business for themselves by licensing wealthy businessmen to bring their animals there to be sold for the sacrifices. Jesus had never been so angry as he was at this time, seeing how they had desecrated his Father's house.

Taking a length of rope lying on the ground, he knotted it, and making a whip, he drove out the animals and overturned the tables of the currency dealers, creating pandemonium as animals began running in all directions and currency dealers started crawling all over the floor of the courtyard trying desperately to keep their coins from rolling away into other bankers' piles of money. Interestingly, when he approached the cages of those selling doves, he merely told them to "take these things out of here." They were the poor, selling doves for a pittance to other poor who could not afford to buy the more costly animals for sacrifice. In the midst of all this turmoil and in the height of his anger, Jesus still pitied the poor and showed a delicate consideration for them. Then, in a loud voice, he shouted out for all to hear, "My house is a house of prayer and you have made it a den of thieves." Interesting that he did not quote the Scripture passage saying the Temple was the House of God. He said, "*My* house is a house of prayer," stating very clearly his true identity. Then blind and lame people who were wandering around the Court heard Jesus was nearby, and when Jesus noticed them, he went over to them, all crowded together for mutual support and protection, and as upset as Jesus was over the desecration of God's house, he healed them, manifesting remarkable emotional control. When Jesus left and was confronted by the chief priests and other elders, who demanded on what authority he did what he did, he told them he would not tell them from where his authority came. "The only sign I will give you is, 'Destroy this temple, and in three days I will rebuild it.' " They did not know then that he was talking about the temple of his body. But Caiaphas will remember the incident, and also Jesus' remark, which will prove he knew what Jesus meant. One wonders how evil a person can be.

John, before beginning his account of Jesus' Passion and all that follows, provides a summary of the important things that Jesus taught about his identity and the importance of people accepting him as their salvation and as their light showing them the way to the Father, as all that he has been teaching has come from the Father. He does nothing except what the Father tells him. And those who accept him honor the Father, and the Father will also honor them.

39

The Beginning of the End

The feast of Unleavened Bread, or the Passover, was only hours away. The atmosphere in Jerusalem was tenser than ever. Word had spread among the people that the officials were determined to arrest Jesus and kill him. Everywhere Jesus went the people gathered around him, not only to listen to him, but to protect him. They made Jesus' enemies nervous. The chief priests and the Pharisees knew they could do nothing to him as long as the people were guarding him. Even Luke says as much: "The chief priests and the scribes were looking for some way of doing away with him, but they were afraid of the people."

The only way they could arrest Jesus would be if one of his own betrayed him by alerting the authorities of Jesus' whereabouts when he left the Temple at the end of the day and was without the people's protection. "Then Satan entered into Judas the Iscariot, who was one of the Twelve. He approached the chief priests and the officers of the guard to discuss some way of handing him over to them. They were delighted and agreed to give him money (thirty pieces of silver, the contemptuous value of an incompetent shepherd). He accepted and began to look for the right time to turn him over to them without the people knowing it." (Lk. 22:3–6)

The feast day was about to begin. Preparations had to be made. They had to have a sacrificed lamb. They had to purchase the bitter herbs, and prepare all the other ingredients for the solemn ritual meal, which by Law was a family affair. So Jesus sent Peter and John to do what had to be done to get everything ready to eat the Passover. They had to go and purchase the lamb, and the other items needed. But before that they had to have a place to bring all these things, since they had no living quarters themselves. So, Jesus told them before sending them out to go into the city,

"Where you will meet a man carrying a pitcher of water. Follow him into the house he enters, and tell the owner of the house, 'The Master said to ask you, "Where is the room for me to eat the Passover with my disciples?" ' The man will show you a large upper room furnished with table and couches. There make preparations for the supper." The two apostles left and found everything just as Jesus said, and they made all the preparations for the Passover, including the roasting of the lamb.

Now, an interesting question comes to mind. Who was invited? The reason this occurs to me is that the Passover was, by Law, for the family. Jesus redefined family by including all those who accepted him and became his disciples, opening up the possibility that some of his closest disciples may have been invited. And what happened to the seventy-two who were with Jesus during his trek through the villages in Judea? Were they still there, waiting for their families to come down and celebrate the Passover with them? It does not seem likely Jesus would have needed to invite them since they had their own families who would be coming to the feast.

All of which leads us to the strong conclusion that there were more than Jesus and the apostles celebrating that Passover meal. Most probably, those persons who were at Calvary the next day would have been in the upper room the night before. Who would they have been? Jesus' mother, Mary; her sister Mary and her husband Cleopas; James and John's mother; and Mary Magdalen and Salome and Joanna, as well as the apostles and Mark. It is difficult to imagine them not being there. I cannot see Jesus, who had been near his mother during his whole public ministry, celebrating his last meal on earth and excluding her. It would not make sense. It would have broken her heart, which was already broken over what she had been witnessing of late in the hatred of the religious leaders whom she had respected all her life as God's appointed teachers and shepherds. And Jesus was always so sensitive to the pain in people's hearts. And this was the woman who made it possible for him to come to redeem the world and reconcile the children of this world to his Father. She had suffered from the very first day he came into her life. This would be their last meal together. The words that Jesus would speak at the Passover meal will be much richer as we read them, knowing that his mother was there listening to each word, and understanding them in a way no stranger possibly could, not even the apostles. She would in the future be the one to interpret and make sense out of those words and out of his life that he had given for all of them, and it would be her role to strengthen and inspire them in difficult times. She had his strong spirit and readiness to sacrifice that he often talked about when trying to teach them about dedication to take up their crosses and follow him.

When the Passover meal began, Jesus opened the ceremony, "I have eagerly longed to eat this Passover with you before I suffer, because I tell you, I shall not eat it again until I eat it with you in a whole new setting in the kingdom of God." If the Passover, or Seder, ritual was followed, there would have been a prescribed ceremony, which was quite flexible depending on the family.

First the festive candles or lamps would be lighted, accompanied by a blessing. This would be done at sunset or just before. Then the wine would be blessed, four cups for each of the people partaking, and a cup for Elijah in case he might come. At this point in the ceremony the first cup of wine is consumed. Then there is a washing of hands in preparation for the eating of the green vegetable, most often parsley, which is dipped in salt water. The green vegetable symbolizes the new life and hope that comes in the springtime. The salt water symbolizes the tears the children of Israel shed during their time of slavery in Egypt.

There should have been placed on the table three matzos. The middle one is taken and broken in half. One half is put back with the other two, and the other half is hidden for children to look for afterward, and consumed at the end of the meal. Next the story of the Exodus is told, or read, and following that the second cup of wine consumed. The hands are washed again while a blessing is said, and each person takes a piece of blessed matzo and eats it. Then another piece is eaten. Then a blessing is said over some bitter vegetable, usually horseradish, which is spread between two pieces of matzo and eaten. This symbolizes the bitterness of the times spent in Egypt. Then follows the Passover meal, usually a roasted lamb, and the third cup of wine is consumed. Then after the meal is finished, the piece of matzo that had been hidden is consumed, as a prayer of thanks is said. Then someone opens the door to the room for Elijah to enter, announcing the coming of the Messiah. If this full ritual was performed at the Last Supper, Jesus would have said, Elijah had already come in the person of John the Baptizer. Then psalms are sung and the fourth cup of wine is consumed.

How the Passover was performed that night no one knows. Being the last official one, it probably was performed in the traditional way because of its significance in bringing together the two covenants. It provides for us a good picture of what the table looked like, during that meal, everyone with four cups of wine, and the bowls of a green vegetable, and the bowl of salt water, and the matzos, the flat pieces of unleavened bread, probably made of barley flour (the bread of the poor), since it was the time of the barley harvest. Then there would be the huge platter with the roasted lamb, which the guests would cut a piece off of with a knife, or tear a piece off with their fingers, and dip it in a gravy of some kind and eat it with pieces of matzo. During the festive meal the vegetables could be anything the family preferred. It was the great feast of the year, the yearly celebration of their freedom.

That night the greater part of the evening was taken up by Jesus' masterpiece of divine eloquence as he delivered his divinely inspired message to his family and to the world. He told how much God loved us, so much he had had to show us by giving his life for us, and proving it by submitting to a most shameful and humiliating death by torture and crucifixion. As Jesus delivered this testament of love, it is hard not to imagine his eyes filling up with tears more than once, as he reminisced over all the experiences he and his family and his apostles had lived through over the years. And now that he was leaving, as you listen to his words, you can feel his broken heart, as he laid bare his soul to these children, as he called them; to a person who was eternal, they were mere children.

Then, as they were finishing the Passover lamb, Jesus took a matzo, blessed it, broke it, and gave it to his disciples, saying, "Take, eat, this is my body." Then he took a cup of wine and after blessing it, gave it to them saying, "Take and drink this, all of you; this is the cup of my blood, the blood of the new and eternal covenant which will be shed for you for the forgiveness of sins." And then, as they are passing the cup from one to the other, Jesus continued, "I will no longer drink this fruit of the vine until I drink it new with you in the kingdom of my Father." Then, after singing a hymn, they went out to the Mount of Olives. (Mt. 26:26–30)

Much of the profound significance of what had just taken place was probably lost on the apostles. They did, however, understand that what he had promised months before at the synagogue in Capernaum, he was now fulfilling. He had promised to give his flesh and blood as the food of their souls. The crowd thought that what he was saying was ridiculous. How can this man give us his flesh and blood to eat and drink? The apostles probably thought the same thing, but did not dare to utter it. They had learned to accept whatever he would tell them, even though they could not understand him. Now they saw what he meant. So, this is how he will give us his flesh and blood. Now it all makes sense. If he is going to give us his flesh and blood, he can do it, by creating a whole new type of presence, present to each of us in a very special way, unlike his presence anywhere else in the universe. How beautiful!

What probably did not occur to them was the fact that at this sacrificial meal of the Old Covenant, he was establishing the sacrificial meal of the New Covenant, the new and everlasting Covenant, the Sacrificial Passover Lamb that John the Baptizer had proclaimed on meeting Jesus: "Behold the Lamb of God, who will take away the sins of the whole world." Jesus had promised not to leave them orphans, including us all as well, and now he shows us how he will not leave us. He will come and be with us in a most intimate manner, in the depths of our souls, as our friend and life companion. And how many of us had that beautiful experience when we received him into our souls in Communion for the first time! That soul-moving awareness of his presence that banished all doubt expanded our minds to sense that he was with us.

It is interesting to note that at this sacred meal Judas was present. He left after receiving the body and blood of the Lord. Jesus knew Judas' heart had turned against him; he had on his soul the terrifying sin of betrayal of the Lord, yet Jesus enacted the Eucharist while Judas was still present. He did not wait until he left. That example of Jesus should speak powerfully to those who would exclude people from the Eucharist whom they judge to be sinners. If Jesus gave the Eucharist to Judas, who had already decided to betray him, how can we refuse the Eucharist to someone whom we presume in our self-righteous judgment to be a sinner? If Jesus chose to embrace sinners, who are we to say they are not worthy of his embrace?

As they were all receiving and consuming the Eucharist, what must have been their thoughts? They had celebrated this ritual year after year since their childhood. Now they celebrated it with Jesus, whom they had come to realize was the Messiah whom God had promised. But they were confused because he was always talking about dying, and the Messiah was not supposed to die.

Then their thoughts floated back a few months, and they remembered the huge crowd for whom Jesus had multiplied the seven loaves and a few fish and told them to feed the thousands of people, which they had no trouble doing. The next day, Jesus had promised his flesh and blood as the heavenly bread that came down from heaven, and the people had thought he was out of his mind and walked with him no more. He had said on that occasion that his body was real food and his blood was real drink, and that those who ate his body and drank his blood would have his life within them and would inherit eternal life. Then the flash of light: "Oh, this is the bread he was talking about in Capernaum on that day, now so far away. And this is the food for our souls which will assure for us eternal life. All of a sudden it all makes sense. This is the new sacrifice of the New Covenant in his blood. But, why does he keep talking about dying?"

Then their silent reveries on the meaning of what was taking place were shattered by an argument that suddenly sprang up, prompted no doubt by Jesus telling them that he was going to die. The next thought, then, was: Who is going to take over? Who is going to be in charge when Jesus dies? Who is the most important among them? That thought was on the minds of more than one of the apostles, as it broke out into the open and they began discussing it aloud. It was prefaced by a remark Jesus made, that "[T]he hand of the one who is to betray me is with me at this very table. But, the Son of Man must go his way as it has been decided, but woe to that man by whom he is betrayed." Then the apostles struggled over that horrible thought. "Who of us could ever do such a thing, or even think of such a thing?" And then the argument broke out as to who should be considered the greatest among them, or getting down to what was really on their minds, "Which one of us will be in charge when Jesus leaves us?" It took nerve to discuss such a matter as Jesus was sharing with them the imminent prospect of his death. But no one ever said the apostles were delicate in their manners or models of sensitivity in conversation.

During the distraction, Jesus turned to Judas and quietly told him, "Go, do what you are going to do. Do it quickly!" The others, who heard Jesus say that, did not understand what it was all about. Since Judas carried the common purse, they thought Jesus was telling him to get provisions or perhaps help some poor family and take care of some private business for Jesus. And this was all part of their meditation during those sacred moments of their First Communion in the Lord's true bread from heaven.

As shocking as it is to us now, it is probably no different from our own meditations after receiving the Lord in Communion. Think of the thoughts that go through our own minds, if we ever can manage to pull our thoughts together sufficiently to focus at least for a few minutes on the mystery of the Sacred Presence within us. So, we cannot be shocked at the eruption of such a crude discussion about who was most important among them at the Last Supper.

This discussion bothered Jesus and was a concern that he had been brooding over for months. They had had this discussion before, and Jesus had tried to chide them gently about it and held up a child as their model of true importance. But that apparently was not convincing, nor was it understood; and here, at this sacred hour, they were still caught up in the same question. Jesus felt he must again address the problem.

> "The kings of the Gentiles lord it over their subjects and those in authority over them are addressed as kind and generous patrons, but among you it must not be so. Whoever is the greatest among you must be like the youngest, and the leader among you as the servant of the others. For, who is greater, the one seated at the table or the one who serves? Is it not the one who is seated at the table? I am among you as one who serves. It is you who have stood by my side in my trial, and I confer a kingdom on you, just as my Father has conferred on me, that you may eat and drink at my table in my kingdom, and you will sit on thrones judging the twelve tribes of Israel." (Lk. 22:21–30)

And then getting up from the table, Jesus took off his outer garments, and wrapping a towel around his waste, like a slave, he poured water into a basin, fell to his knees, and began to wash the feet of his apostles. They had no idea what he was up to, and when he started to wash the feet of the first one, they were all stunned, shocked, embarrassed, and ashamed. Reluctantly, they extended their feet, as he washed each foot tenderly, and dried it. Then, finally, as he was approaching Peter, he could not find Peter's feet.

"Never, Lord, never are you going to wash my feet."

"Well, Peter, if that's the case, then you can have no part with me."

"Well, if it means that much to you, Lord, wash my hands and my head as well."

"That is not necessary, Peter, for whoever has bathed does not need to be washed all over, just his feet, for he is clean all over. So, you are clean, but not all." This was referring to Judas who was about to betray him.

Then Jesus sat back on his heels, rested his hands in his lap, and looked up into the eyes of each of the apostles. All they saw before them was the image of a slave who had just washed their feet. They lowered their eyes in shame, as Jesus said to them,

> "You call me Lord and Master, and indeed I am. If I your Lord and Master can get on my knees and wash your feet, so you should be willing to wash the feet of one another. I have given you a model to follow, so that as I have done for you, you should also do. What I say to you, I say in all truth, no slave is greater than his master, nor is any messenger greater than the one who sent him. If you understand this, fortunate are you if you put it into practice. I am not speaking of all of you. I know those I have chosen. But, so that Scripture might be fulfilled, 'The one who ate my food has raised his heel against me.' From now on I am telling you this before it happens, so that when it happens you may come to believe that I AM. And I say to you solemnly, whoever receives the one I send receives me, and whoever receives me, receives the One who sent me." (Jn. 13:4–20)

Then Jesus became very somber, and sad. The apostles knew he was deeply troubled. He spoke to them in a quiet voice: "One of you is about to betray me." The apostles looked around at one another, wondering who it could be. They could not believe what they were hearing, and each one said, "Is it I, Lord?" or "Certainly not me, Lord." Peter signaled John to ask Jesus who it was. John leaned over, for he was reclining on the couch next to Jesus, and, putting his head near Jesus, he asked him who it was who would betray him. Jesus' answer was, "He to whom I give the bread that I dip in the sauce." He then dipped the piece of matzo in the sauce and gave it to Judas. After he ate the morsel, Satan entered into him, and Jesus told him to go and do what he was going to do. Judas then left, then

John said, "And it was night." Suddenly all things turned black, with the feeling of an impending doom.

When Judas left, Jesus began his beautiful and tender farewell message to his loved ones. "Now is the Son of Man glorified, and God is glorified in him." When Jesus used the word *glorify*, it does not mean what we mean when we use that word. What Jesus meant was that God's majesty was about to be revealed in a most important event, which could include a tragic event. And he indicated that this was about to happen very soon, in a very short time.

"My children, I will be with you only a little while longer. You will look for me, and as I said to the Judeans, 'Where I go you cannot come,' so now I say it to you. I give you a new commandment, 'Love one another. As I have loved you, you also must love one another.' This is how all will know that you are my disciples, if you have love for one another."

Then Peter abruptly interrupted Jesus, and blurted out, "Master, where are you going?" "Where I am going you cannot follow me now, but you will follow me later." Then Peter continued to interrupt him, not letting him continue what he wanted so much to say to them. "But, Master, why can't I follow you now? I will lay down my life for you."

Then Jesus continued with his farewell, "Do not let your hearts be troubled. You have faith in God, have faith in me as well. I am not leaving without reason. I go to prepare a place for you in my Father's house, where there is vast space and many exciting places where you will live. I will come back and take you with me, so that where I am you also may be. And there we will be together again. So, do not be troubled that I leave. It is only for a time. And where I am going you already know the way."

Thomas then asked him, "Master, we have no idea where you are going, how can we know the way?" Jesus said to him, "I am the way, the truth and the life. No one comes to the Father except through me. If you know me you know the Father also. From now on you will know him and you have seen him." Then it was Philip's turn to interrupt Jesus. "Master, show us the Father and that will be enough for us." "Philip, have I been with you all this time and you still do not know me? How can you say, 'Show us the Father'? Do you not believe that I am in the Father, and the Father is in me? The words I speak to you are not my own. It is my Father who dwells in me who speaks through me. Believe me when I say that I am in the Father and the Father is in me, or believe because of the wonders I perform that show the Father's power coming through me. Believe me, whoever believes in me will do the works that I do, and indeed, will do greater things than these, because I am leaving and going to the Father. And whatever you ask in my name I will do, so that the Father may be glorified in the Son. If you ask anything in my name, I will do it.

"If you love me you will keep my commandments, and I will ask the Father and he will give you another Advocate to be with you always, the Spirit of truth, which the world cannot accept, because it neither sees nor knows it. But you know it because it remains with you, and will be in you. I will not leave you orphans. I will come to you. In a little while the world will no longer see me, but you will see me because I live and you will live. On that day you will realize that I am in my Father and you are in me, and I am in you. Whoever has my commandments and observes them is like one who loves me, and whoever loves me will be loved by my Father, and I will love him and reveal my living presence within him"

Judas, not the traitor, then said to him, "Why is it you will reveal yourself to us and not the world?" What confused him was that Jesus was so reluctant to let the people know he was the Messiah. That was totally incomprehensible to all of the apostles. Jesus' answer was, "Whoever loves me keeps my word, and my Father will love him, and we will come to him and make our dwelling in him. Whoever does not love me does not keep my word; yet the word that you hear is not mine, but the word of the Father who sent me." Those who keep my word and follow me will know me by my presence revealed within them. What he is saying is, "I have proclaimed my kingdom. It is already being established, quietly, in the hearts of those who accept what I teach them, and this will spread. I have proclaimed the kingdom in my own way, and it is already planted in people's hearts like seeds in a field and it will gradually grow on its own and spread till the kingdom is established throughout the whole world."

"I have told you this while I am with you. The Advocate, the Holy Spirit whom the Father will send in my name, he will teach you everything, and remind you of all that I told you. Peace I leave with you; my peace I give you. Not as the world gives do I give to you (my peace is from within). Do not let your hearts be troubled or afraid. You heard me tell you, 'I am going away and I will come back to you.' If you loved me you would rejoice that I am going to the Father, for the Father is greater than I, and I am at home with my Father. And now I have told you this before it happens, so that when it does happen you may believe. I will no longer speak much with you, for the ruler of this world is coming. He has no power over me, but the world must know that I love the Father, and do just as the Father has commanded me. Now is the time, let us pick up and go." (Jn. 13:1–38; 14:1–31)

Then, after singing a psalm to end the Passover meal, they went out and across the valley to the Mount of Olives. On the way, Jesus continued giving them last-minute counsel and instructions for the future. "This night your faith in me will be shaken. It is written, 'I will strike the shepherd, and the sheep of the flock will be dispersed.' But, after I have been raised up, I shall go before you into Galilee." Peter said to him, "Though all may have their faith shaken, mine will never be shaken." Jesus said to him, "I say to you in all honesty, this very night before the cock crows you will deny me three times." Peter still protested, "Even though I should have to die for you, I will never deny you. And all the disciples said likewise." (Mk 14:27–31)

As they continued their walk from the upper room, through the city, passing through the Temple and along Solomon's Porch and out through the Susa gate down into the Kidron Valley on their way to Gethsemane, Jesus continued talking all along the way. The walk from the upper room to Gethsemane was perhaps a thousand feet. As Jesus was in a very sad mood at the realization that his mission from his Father was coming to such a frightfully tragic end, he had many things to tell his apostles before he would be arrested and dragged away from them.

"I am the true vine and my Father is the vine grower. He takes away every branch in me that does not bear fruit, and every one that does, he prunes so it will bear more fruit. You are already pruned because of the word I have spoken to you. Remain in me as I remain in you. Just as a branch cannot bear fruit unless it remains on the vine, so neither can you unless you remain in me. I am the vine, you are the branches. Whoever remains in me and I in him will bear much fruit, because without me you can do nothing. Anyone who does not remain in me will be thrown out like a branch and wither. People will gather them together and throw them into a fire to be burned. If you remain in me and my words remain in you, ask for whatever you want and it will be done for you. By this is my Father glorified, that you bear much fruit and become my disciples. As the Father loves me, so I love you. Remain in my love. If you keep my commandments you will remain in my love, just as I have kept my Father's commandments and remain in his love.

"I have told you this so that my joy may be in you and your joy may be complete. This is my commandment, that you love one another as I have loved you. There is no one who has greater love than one who is willing to lay down one's life for one's friends. You are my friends if you do what I command you. I no longer call you slaves, because a slave does not know what his master is doing. I have called you friends, because I have told you everything I have heard from my Father. It was not you who chose me. It was I who chose you and appointed you to go and bear fruit that will last, so that whatever you ask the Father in my name He will grant you. This I command you, that you love one another.

"If the world hates you, know that it has hated me before you. If you belonged to the world, the world would love its own; but because you do not belong to the world, and I have chosen you out of the world, the world hates you. Remember the word that I have spoken to you, 'No slave is greater than his master.' If they persecuted me they will persecute you. If they kept my word they will keep yours as well. And they will do all these things on my account because they do not know the One who sent me." . . .

"When the Advocate comes whom I will send to you from the Father, the Spirit of Truth who proceeds from the Father, he will testify to me. And you also will testify to me because you have been with me from the beginning." (Jn. 15:1–27)

Jesus continued sharing with the apostles, pouring out his heart about the things that they would experience after he left them, and the opposition they would face from those who would refuse to accept the messages they would deliver. But the Holy Spirit would be with them always, reminding them of all the things that Jesus had taught them. All during this long soliloquy, you can feel the painful emotion Jesus was experiencing as he expressed his tender good-bye to his friends. He was aware that in a few minutes they would all run away from him when he was arrested. But he told them that he understood. Then he ended by telling them that they had no reason to fear, because he had conquered the world, and their teaching and their message would not be frustrated, but would win out as thousands would embrace their teachings and whole nations would come to the Lord.

By this time Jesus and his small group probably had reached the Garden of Gethsemane. Jesus then began to talk to his Father, as he raised his eyes to Heaven.

> "Father, the hour has come. Give glory to your Son, so your Son may give glory to you. Just as you gave him authority over all people, so that he may give eternal life to all you gave him. Now this is eternal life, that they should know you, the only true God, and the one whom you sent, Jesus the Christ. I glorified you on earth by accomplishing all that you have given me to do. Now glorify me again, Father, with the glory I had before the world began."

Then, continuing, he prayed for the apostles that they would have the faith and the courage to continue his mission to the world. And he prayed that they would learn to work together and that his Father would keep them from the Evil One. He asked his Father to bless them and to consecrate them in the truth, so they would always be faithful to his message and preserve its integrity.

> "And I pray not only for them, but also for those who believe in me through their word, so that they may all be one, as you, Father, are in me and I in them, that they also may be one in us, that the world may believe that you sent me. And I pray also, Father, that they may be one with me, that they may see my glory that you gave me, because you loved me before the foundation of the world." (Jn. 16:1–33; 17:1–26)

40

JESUS' STRUGGLE TO ACCEPT HIS FATHER'S WILL

The Garden of Gethsemane is even today a large grove of olive trees, some of them over two thousand years old, and on many occasions when Jesus was in Jerusalem, they sheltered him and his companions. I have so often pictured Jesus camping out there when visiting the City, and I once painted a large picture for a church with Jesus and Peter sitting against olive trees having lunch, with a loaf of bread and a flask of wine between them. Through a large opening between an odd-shaped trunk and a thick branch, the brilliant Temple on the distant hill across the valley was perfectly framed. That spot was a favorite resting place for Jesus when he was in Jerusalem. If those ancient trees that are still there could talk, they could tell us everything that took place on that fateful night after the Last Supper.

No sooner had Jesus arrived than he told the apostles, "Pray that you may not undergo the test," and of course they had no idea what he was talking about. He knew that their faith in him as the Messiah would be sorely tried in just a few moments when they witnessed what was about to take place. This, however, still eluded their imaginations, and we wonder if they even felt a need to pray. They were tired. Jesus then told Peter, James, and John to come with him, as he moved farther into the grove to pray, and then became troubled and deeply distressed. "My soul is sorrowful even unto death. Stay and watch with me." Then he walked deeper into the grove of trees, and fell to the ground and prayed that if it were possible this hour might pass. One can almost feel the sense of terror that was gripping his inner spirit.

In order to understand what Jesus was praying about and why he was so deeply troubled, we have to understand the way Jesus was structured. As the God-man he had a divine nature and a human nature, a divine mind and a human mind, a divine will and a human will. Ordinarily Jesus chose to function on a human level. He decided to become one of us and to share with us what it meant to be human. "He was like us in all things except sin," as Saint Paul expresses it.

He lived daily with all the limitations of being human. He had come from heaven to preach the good news to God's children, to preach a message of salvation. It was his burning desire to turn the hearts of all God's children to their Father in heaven. With all his divine power and ability available to pressure people's wills, he chose not to use that power but to allow the huge crowds who came to listen to him to use their own free will in deciding to believe him or reject him. That was a real test of his respect for the freedom that God has given to all of us. He chose to allow himself to be rejected and to know the terrible feeling of failure. The chief priests and the scribes and Pharisees were his Father's own magisterium, the teaching authority charged with the responsibility of teaching the Jewish people about the Messiah and to welcome him when he came. When Jesus came as the Messiah, they became his bitterest enemies, determined to eliminate him. He could have annihilated this greatest obstruction to the accomplishment of his mission. In fact, they allowed themselves to become the tools of Satan himself in destroying the mission and purpose of the Messiah's coming, to establish the rule of God on earth and launch the thousand years of the Messianic reign. He chose not to use his divine power to destroy this obstacle to that awesome dream.

What would happen in the Garden of Gethsemane would be the fulfillment of his commitment at his baptism by John in the Jordan, when Jesus, as the Son of God in human flesh, took upon himself the sins of the whole human race. In that moment he also chose to accept the punishment due for the totality of human sin from the beginning of time to the end of our existence. In the Garden, his divine will had already decided to endure whatever was involved in satisfying the demands of justice to atone for our sins, but if he was to stand in our place, the human part of Jesus had to agree to accept what was involved in being the sacrifice for our total debt to God. The awareness of what this meant Jesus kept for the most part hidden from his human consciousness and human imagination. It only began to show after he left Galilee for the last time and he began to drop hints about his impending sufferings, as he allowed his human consciousness to gradually become aware of what would eventually take place. This explains why we can see Jesus becoming more absorbed in the thought of his impending Passion.

In the Garden, Jesus allowed his imagination to experience more completely what was to take place, so he could as a man be aware of what he was taking upon himself as the price for our sins. This awareness was so graphic, so real, that there was little difference between this mental experience and the reality that would soon happen. As his human imagination experienced the events about to unfold, it shrank in horror from the thought. His whole being recoiled from it in terror. This explains Jesus' struggle in the Garden and the intense stress on the tiny blood vessels that caused the blood to effuse through the pores of his skin. In his divine nature Jesus had already decided to undergo what had to be done. Now in his human nature he was struggling with this decision.

What Jesus experienced is something none of us will ever have to experience, and that is knowing beforehand so graphically what is going to happen to us. What if, for example, we had a dream or a revelation that tomorrow morning we were going to get up and begin the day normally, but when we left the house and were crossing the street, a trailer truck would come and hit us, and although we would not die, we would be crippled all our life, and suffer excruciating pain. Would we have the courage the next morning to cross that street? That was the decision that Jesus had to make in his human will in the Garden that night, and the terror involved in forcing himself to agree to make that decision was so frightening that he literally sweat blood.

What Jesus experienced during that hour of the power of darkness was all that he was to undergo, beginning in just a few minutes: the traitor's kiss by Judas; the arrest by his own Temple guards; his being dragged before his own chief priests, and his face slapped by the high priest's lackeys for disrespecting the high priest; his conviction and condemnation for blasphemy; and their endorsement of his death sentence. He could see the cold prison cell where he would spend the night, while waiting to be dragged before the Roman governor at dawn the next morning, and the rabble crying for his condemnation and crucifixion. He could feel the whip lashing as if it was tearing the strips of flesh from his body, and the crowning with thorns, and his pathetic death march through the streets of the City on his way to Calvary. And he could see the look on his mother's face as he would pass her standing along the way, looking at him, silently, with a broken heart. Finally, he experienced being stripped naked before the laughing crowd of his own creatures, and the piercing of his hands and feet as he was being nailed to the cross. He could feel the anguish of the humiliation of being jeered at by all those he loved, and the ultimate pain of his own divinity slowly separating from his humanity, leaving him totally desolate and naked before his enemies, as he cried out to his Father in heaven to forgive them, for they know not what they do. The feeling of abandonment by God was more painful than his physical torture. And as these visions crowded through his mind, the question kept haunting him, "Do you consent to accept this chalice of suffering?"

During all this time, his dearest friends, at a time when he needed them most for comfort and support, had fallen sound asleep. "My soul is sorrowful even unto death," he said, and he told the apostles Peter, James, and John to "remain here and keep watch with me." He walked a little deeper into the Garden and fell to his knees and prayed, "Abba, dear Father, if it is possible, let this cup pass from me; yet not my will but your will be done." Returning to the apostles, he found them fast asleep. They could not bear witnessing Jesus' struggle, and recoiled from it and fell asleep, though they had not the slightest idea of the drama that was taking place in the Master's mind. The imminent tragedy was playing out for him, and it was the moment when our salvation hung on his final decision to accept or reject it. The most dramatic moment in the history of the world, which they were to play a part in, and they were sleeping through it. He said to Peter, "You could not watch with me for one hour? Watch and pray that you will not succumb to the test. The spirit is willing, the flesh is weak." Walking back to pray again, he prayed a second time, "Dear Father, if it is not possible that this cup pass without my drinking it, your will be done!" He then made his decision to die for us all and reconcile us to the Father. At that point Luke mentions that an angel came to comfort him. Then he returned again and they were still sleeping, for they could not keep their eyes open. He left them and returned to pray a third time, saying the same as before. Then he returned to his disciples and said to them, "Are you still sleeping and taking your rest? Behold, the hour is at hand for the Son of Man to be handed over to sinners. Get up, let us go. Look, my betrayer has already arrived."

At this time Judas and a contingent of Temple guards and a troop of Roman legionaries had arrived. This place was not unknown to Judas, as Jesus and his disciples often camped there. It was late into the night. Being Passover, the moon must have been bright unless there was a cloud covering. The group approached carrying lanterns, torches, swords, and clubs. It is also possible that Jesus and the apostles had started a fire when they first arrived at the Garden to warm themselves, so it would have been bright enough to identify people. Judas stepped forward and without any hesitation boldly walked up to Jesus, saying, "Hail, Rabbi," and kissed him, the sign he had agreed on with the officer. Jesus looked into his eyes and merely said, "Judas, my friend, you betray the Son of Man with a kiss?" The soldiers immediately came up to Jesus to arrest him.

The apostles were terrified and, realizing what was about to happen, asked Jesus if they should put up a resistance. But Peter, not waiting for an answer, pulled out his sword and struck the high priest's servant, cutting off his ear. Seeing this, Jesus said, "Put back the sword; those who live by the sword will perish by the sword. Do you not think that I can call upon my Father and he would provide me with twelve legions of angels. But, then, how would Scripture be fulfilled which says that it must happen this way?" Jesus then reached over and healed the wounded man.

Standing there as they were securing him, Jesus looked at the crowd and said to them, "You come out to me as against a robber, with swords and clubs to seize me. Daily I taught in the Temple, yet you did not arrest me. This is all happening in fulfillment of the prophets' predictions. I tell you, this is your hour, the time for the power of darkness."

Jesus realized that they had come to arrest him and, concerned about his apostles, said to the tribune, "For whom are you looking?" He answered, "Jesus, the Nazarean." Jesus, in a deep majestic voice that sent chills through the Jewish guards surrounding him, answered, "I AM." They were the same words God used on Sinai. The Jewish guards who previously had been sent to arrest Jesus were impressed with something sacred about Jesus; this time they were awed at Jesus' statement and, in shock, almost fainted. "Maybe there *is* something sacred about this man. Maybe he *is* the one sent by Yahweh" must have gone through their minds. Momentarily stunned at the majesty of Jesus and the solemn way he spoke out "I AM," they fell backward and possibly tripped over one another. John merely says that they fell to the ground. But Jesus then said a second time, "For whom are you looking?" And they gave the same answer. Jesus then said, "I told you that I AM. So, if you are looking for me, let these men go. They have done nothing wrong." And so the prophecy was fulfilled, "I have not lost any of those you gave me."

At that point the apostles all fled, and Saint Mark says something startling. "Now a young man followed him [Jesus] wearing nothing but a linen cloth about his body. When a soldier seized him, he left the cloth behind and ran off naked." Only Mark relates this incident, and how would Mark have known if he was not that person? This is why it seems clear that Mark most probably was at the Last Supper with Jesus and the others, or at least was living there, perhaps in his father's house, and had followed Jesus and the apostles after the supper, even if he was not invited. (Mk. 14:32–52; Mt. 26:36–56; Lk. 22:39–53; Jn. 18:1–14)

They then brought Jesus to Annas, the father-in-law of Caiaphas, who was the high priest that year. It was Caiaphas who had made the remark that it was necessary that one man die rather than the whole nation suffer.

41

THE TRIAL

The religious authorities were so thrilled that they had finally accomplished their long-awaited goal, the arrest of their Messiah, that they all gave up their plans for the celebration of the sacred feast of Passover to gather the whole Sanhedrin together for a special meeting, a trial, an illegal trial at that, because they were in such a rush to convict and condemn this man and get rid of him overnight if possible.

The trial was illegal for a number of reasons. Night trials were forbidden. The pretext was that it was a rehearsal. In the morning, a two-minute trial would make it formal and legal. There was no time for the accused to contact witnesses. Trials by Jewish law were very humane, structured to protect the accused until he could be proved guilty. In fact the trials were supposed to be in favor of the accused, and it was the court's responsibility to find reasons to acquit the accused. This trial and the one that was to follow lacked those safeguards for the accused. This one was structured to convict him without any evidence, or believable witnesses. The whole setup was illegal. The only witnesses on whose testimony the trial was based gave contradictory statements, and the case should have been dismissed on that alone. Finally two dubious witnesses came forward and made statements acceptable to the authorities. But the authorities were so determined to kill Jesus, they made a farce of their justice system and decided to question him themselves and attempt to convict him on his own words. I wonder if someday, a competent court would ever consider a retrial with the possibility of exonerating Jesus. But for now we will follow step by step what happened that fateful night and the next day.

"Those who had arrested Jesus led him away to the high priest [actually the former high priest, Annas], where the scribes and elders were already assembled." It is hard to imagine the high priest would have notified Nicodemus and Gamaliel and Joseph of Arimathea of this session. They would have protested, as Nicodemus already had on another occasion. John, the apostle who was known to the high priest and had connections with his family, entered the courtyard accompanying Jesus. Peter, however, who had been with John, stayed outside the gate, until John spoke to the gatekeeper and brought Peter inside. Then the maid who was the gatekeeper said to Peter, "You are not one of this man's disciples, are you?" Peter said, "I am not." John seems to have gone into the area where Annas was about to question Jesus. The way this was all taking place makes it apparent that Annas still wielded great influence and seems to have been the mastermind behind Jesus' arrest, requesting a contingent of Roman troops to accompany the Temple guards to arrest Jesus, and upon his delivery, dismissed them, as if he did not want them around to witness what was to take place.

The slaves and Temple guards in the courtyard were standing around the charcoal fire warming themselves. Peter was standing with them. Inside, Annas was questioning Jesus about his teachings and about his disciples. Jesus answered him, "I have spoken openly in the Temple and in the synagogues to the crowds. Nothing has been secret. Why ask me? Ask those who heard me, your own people. They know what I said." When Jesus said this, one of the guards standing nearby struck Jesus in the face and said, "Is this the way you talk to the high priest?" Jesus said, "If I have spoken wrongly, tell me what was wrong, but if what I said was right, why did you strike me?" Then Annas sent Jesus, still bound, to the high priest.

This time it was Caiaphas, the standing high priest who presided, and the entire Sanhedrin kept trying to get testimony against Jesus in order to put him to death, but they found none, though many false witnesses came forward. Finally two came forward who stated, "This man said, 'I can destroy the Temple of God and within three days rebuild it.' " The high priest rose and addressed him, "Have you no answer? What are these men testifying against you?" But Jesus was silent. Then the high priest, obviously unimpressed and embarrassed over the witnesses' flawed testimony, especially since they contradicted one another, demanded that Jesus make a statement under oath if he was the Messiah, the Son of God. Jesus, unwilling to deny his own Father before the court, answered, "You have said so. But, I tell you, from now on you will see the Son of Man seated at the right hand of the Power and coming on the clouds of heaven."

Then the high priest, in a hypocritical gesture of indignation, tore his robe as a mock gesture of shock at hearing such a blasphemous statement and declared, "He has blasphemed! What further need do we have of witnesses? You have heard the blasphemy. What do you think?" They said in reply, "He deserves to die." Then Jesus was remanded to the custody of the guards, who led him out through the courtyard. If the high priest was sincere, he should have had to prove that Jesus was not the Son of God. There certainly were enough signs performed by Jesus testifying to his divine lineage.

Peter in the meantime was being questioned by the guards as he was still standing by the fire warming himself. They said to him, "Certainly, you must be one of his disciples; your Galilean dialect betrays you." Peter denied knowing Jesus. And another, a relative of the man whose ear Peter had cut off in the Garden, said to him, "Did I not see you in the Garden with him?" Peter then began to curse and swear he did not even know him. Immediately, the cock crowed. And the cock crowed a second time, and Peter remembered the words of Jesus, "Before the cock crows twice you will have denied me three times."

At that point the guards were leading Jesus through the courtyard. As they marched past Peter, Jesus looked at Peter, and seeing the hurt look in Jesus' eyes, Peter went out and wept bitterly.

The pain of Peter's denial, I am sure, hurt Jesus more than anything the high priests could have said or done to him. They meant nothing to Jesus, but Peter was his best friend. He had appointed Peter to take his place when he should leave. The denial of Peter was a sin of monstrous dimensions and the type of sin we hope that we would never commit. And Peter committed this sin shortly after making his First Communion at the Last Supper. And the thought cannot help but cross your mind: Were Peter and Jesus still friends? We were always taught that if you commit a mortal sin you are cut off from God, and destroy the bond of love between yourself and God, and if you were to die at that moment you would go straight to hell. So, the question naturally arises. Was Peter still Jesus' friend? Were they still friends? Was the beautiful bond of love between the two of them broken? And all one can say realistically is that they were *still* friends. Both their hearts were broken over Peter's denial, but they still loved each other. But now Jesus knew for certain that he had a coward for a friend, and Peter knew for the first time in his life how much of a coward he was, that he could betray the one person he had loved more than anything or anyone else on earth, even life itself. It was too much for him to bear and he went out and cried his heart out. One of the early Fathers of the Church wrote that as Peter grew older, furrows had developed down his cheeks from all the tears he had shed every time he remembered the hurt look of Jesus as he was being led through the courtyard that night.

Betrayal by a friend or a colleague always hurts. We usually suffer such things in little, insignificant ways compared to the heartbreaking denial of Peter. On an occasion when I was pastor at a certain parish, the bishop had closed a number of schools in the city. Our school was one of them, to the deep resentment of the parishioners. As a result the students from those schools had to go to the one parish school in the city that was still open. Our parish, which was the poorest parish in the city, had the most children going to our school. My parishioners were very poor. The total annual Sunday collection amounted to twenty-five thousand dollars. The expenses for the year for the three buildings and the employees had been close to seventy thousand dollars.

The parish the students now had to attend was a wealthy parish, and it became even wealthier when the state reimbursed it with a million dollars for demolishing the school to build a highway. That parish, however, was able to buy a closed public school in excellent condition for a little over twenty thousand dollars.

The bishop told all the parishes whose schools were closed that they had to pay for their students' tuition at the open school. I was told to pay twenty-five thousand dollars to the diocesan school office. The other parishes were each assessed about a tenth of that. One priest, who was dean of the county at the time, called me and said that he had met with the other pastors and they had agreed that they could not afford it, and asked if I would support their decision. I told them I would, as there was no way I could possibly pay the amount our parish had been assessed.

The chancellor called a meeting at one of the rectories, which the seven pastors attended. He asked for everyone's cooperation. He asked each one personally, and one by one they all promised their loyalty and cooperation with the diocese. Then the chancellor looked at the pastor who'd called me and asked him. His response was, "Well, Father, our parish has always done our share and we would be happy to cooperate this time." My heart sank. Then the chancellor looked at me and asked, "What about you?" All I could say was, "My conscience doesn't change that easily. I still cannot in conscience give away that money." It was not the most difficult situation in my life, but the repercussions went on for years. I felt set up and betrayed. Compared to Jesus' broken heart that night over Peter's denial, my experience was petty, but it hurt and I paid dearly.

After Jesus was remanded to the custody of the guard, he was led to the cell where he was to spend the night. It was nothing but a ten-by-ten hole in the floor of a corridor, covered by an iron grill. It was more like a cage for an animal. The prisoner was lowered into the cell, and the grill was slammed shut. Before putting Jesus in this cage, they made a fool of him, by blindfolding him and mocking him. "Tell us who slapped you; you're supposed to be a prophet." And they kept ridiculing him. Then they took turns beating him, and when they got tired, they threw him into the hole. It is painful to watch God allowing Himself to be treated so shamefully by his insignificant creatures. Looking down into that hole when I took my parents to visit the Holy Land, my heart cried to think that that was where they'd put God the night before they condemned Him to death. I had a difficult struggle when we left the place, as it made me realize in the most graphic way the rough, rude way we so often treat God in our daily lives, and He just takes it from us, as if He expects it.

When we think of how easily we are offended at the simplest, often unintended slights to our feelings on the part of others, the humility of God becomes incomprehensible. How can God be so humble to allow Himself to be treated so rudely? There is nothing or no one greater than God, and if humility is "knowing one's place," then God's humility is even more impossible to comprehend. Yet, Jesus says to us, "Come to me, all of you who labor and are heavily burdened, and I will give you rest, for I am meek and humble of heart." The only reasoning that can make sense of this was Jesus saying, "Come to me, I am one of you now. Do not be afraid. I experience your pain. I know your loneliness. I understand your feeling of failure. I experience your weakness. Come to me, for I have chosen to become one of you. I now know what it is to be humbled by our human limitations and what we all suffer as humans."

A few hours later, at first dawn, they pulled him up out of the hole and led him before the council of elders, which consisted of the chief priests and scribes, and they brought him to the Sanhedrin. This trial was merely a formality to make legal the informal unofficial trial of the night before, which had been held to make sure everything would go smoothly and nothing could go wrong when they held the real trial. The exact same scene as before was played out again, and Jesus was formally condemned to death. However, they had a problem. Rome reserved the death penalty to itself and only the Roman governor could issue the order for an execution, so they had to take Jesus before Pilate. This had already been arranged the night before, and the governor was waiting for them at a surprising time, at dawn.

When they arrived at Pontius Pilate's palace, they stayed outside, as it was against their law to enter the residence of a Gentile. Pilate took Jesus into the praetorium, and the chief priests and elders brought the charges against Jesus. "We have found this man misleading the people. He opposes the paying of taxes to Caesar, and maintains he is the Messiah, a king." Pilate then asked Jesus, "Are you the king of the Jews?" Jesus responded, "As you say." Pilate then addressed the assembly, "I find this man not guilty." But the crowd, stirred up by the chief priests and the elders, insisted, "He is inciting the people with his teaching throughout all Judea, from Galilee where he started all the way here."

Hearing the word *Galilee,* Pilate found a way out of his predicament, or so he thought. It was clear to him that the accused was a victim of jealousy and envy over his influence with the common people. Pilate was not stupid. He was shrewd and cunning. He knew all about this preacher, who had been moving around healing the handicapped and sick and giving sight to the blind. Pilate had been receiving reports about Jesus for months. He knew the whereabouts of every known preacher and activist in his territory from the network of spies he had positioned in every neighborhood. There was no way he wanted to be part of this internal squabble among Jews, especially over a man who went about daily showing goodness toward everyone. So, when he heard of Jesus being from Galilee, he immediately realized that he would be Herod's problem. So, he ordered that Jesus be taken to Herod. Even though Pilate and Herod could not stand each other, this move would make it look like the governor was showing deference to the king, or the tetrarch, as was Herod's proper title.

So, Jesus was brought to Herod, who was in town at that time, having recently come down from the Machaerus, his mountaintop palace. It was a particularly exciting experience for him to spend Passover in Jerusalem, where he could take pride in seeing the Temple built by his father, so popular that people flowed in from every known country, many of the people not even Jews.

Jesus was put on show before Herod, and that is what it was—an exhibition, as Herod was curious about Jesus and had been eager for a long time to witness some of his tricks, or miracles, or signs, as the Jews called them.

Now that Judas realized that Jesus had no intention of evading his enemies as he done in the past, he was filled with guilt and regretted what he had done. He returned the thirty pieces of silver to the chief priests and elders, telling them, "I have sinned in betraying innocent blood." They cynically remarked, "What is that to us? That's your problem." Then, flinging the money into the Temple, he left and went out and hanged himself. The chief priests, thinking nothing about putting their Messiah to death, were squeamish about accepting blood money. They could have left it there, and let someone else pick it up, but their love of money was too much for them to do that. So, they got on their knees and greedily picked up the coins and, to cover their guilt, remarked, "It is not lawful for us to put this into the Temple treasury, since it is the price of blood." So they agreed to buy the potter's field as a burial place for strangers and foreigners, in fulfillment of a veiled prophecy spoken by Jeremiah.

Herod questioned Jesus about many things, but Jesus said not one word in response. The Jewish officials had also followed the troops escorting Jesus to Herod's palace. The chief priests and important community leaders accused Jesus viciously, in response to which Jesus again said nothing. Then, bored with their own incompetence, they turned on Jesus and made sport of him. They put an outlandish robe on him and ridiculed him, making fun of him and treating him like a fool. Still he said nothing. Then, feeling like fools, seeing Jesus showed a total lack of concern for their antics, Herod sent him back to Pilate. Luke writes that from that time, Herod and Pilate became friends, whereas they had been enemies.

Pilate was upset seeing Jesus being returned to him, as he was hoping to free him, especially since his wife had had a dream the night before about Jesus, and had told her husband to have nothing to do with this holy man, who was innocent of any crime.

Pilate called in the chief priests, the rulers, and the people standing around, and tried to work out a compromise. "You brought this man to me, accusing him of inciting the people to revolt. I have conducted my investigation in your presence and have not found the man guilty of the charges you proffer against him, nor did Herod, for he sent him back to us. So, no capital crime has been committed. I shall therefore have him flogged and then release him."

Pilate intended to turn him over to the chief priests and the rulers to judge Jesus according to their own Law, since he could not find him in violation of any Roman laws. But the high priests said they did not have the authority to execute anyone. Then Pilate went back into the praetorium and summoned Jesus. He questioned him, "Are you the king of the Jews?" Jesus answered, "Do you say this on your own, or have others told you about me?"

"Am I a Jew? Your own people and the chief priests handed you over to me. What have you done?"

Jesus answered, "My kingdom is not of this world. If my kingdom did belong to this world my subjects would be fighting to keep me from being handed over to the Jews. But, my kingdom is not in this world."

Pilate then said, "Then you are a king?"

"You say that I am a king. For this I was born and came into this world, to testify to the truth. Everyone who is loyal to the truth listens to my voice."

Pilate said, "What is truth?"

Pilate then went out to the Jews and told them, "I find no guilt in this man. But, you have a custom that I release one prisoner to you at Passover. Do you want me to release to you the king of the Jews?" And they all cried out, "Not this one, but Barabbas." Barabbas was a revolutionary in prison for murder and for inciting a riot against Rome.

Pilate either miscalculated or was being just a cynical politician. He should have known that Jesus had been turned over to him because of their hatred and under no circumstances would they have agreed to Jesus' release. Or he naively thought that if the Jews had an option they would rather have Jesus released than a troublemaker who would get them into more trouble later on. Pilate misjudged what a threat Jesus was to their religious authority, and to their control over the religion and all its monetary assets, and that to protect that they had to get rid of Jesus. When the chief priests and the people demanded Barabbas, Pilate was checkmated.

He had only one other chance. If he had Jesus scourged and lashed within an inch of his life, then he might be able to appeal to their pity. So, he turned Jesus over to the soldiers with orders to scourge him at their own pleasure, which they did. The scourge was done with a cat-o-nine-tails with sharp metal strips at the end of each thong. Each lash would rip nine pieces of flesh from the victim's body. Analysis of the shroud of Turin indicates that the soldier who did the scourging was left-handed, and the body was shredded by the hundreds of lashes. Many people would have died from that torture alone, but Jesus survived it.

When they finished, they sat Jesus down and, after weaving a crown made of branches from a thick thornbush, placed this crown on Jesus' head and put a purple military cloak on him. Mocking him, they knelt before him and said, "Hail, King of the Jews." And they struck him repeatedly with a lictor's iron rods and spat on him.

Pilate, then, thinking to appeal to the people's sense of pity, presented Jesus to them. "Look, I am bringing him out to you to show you that I find no guilt in him." Then Jesus came out, dressed in the purple cloak, and wearing the crown of thorns. Pilate said to them, "Behold the man!"

When the chief priests and the guards saw him, they cried out, "Crucify him! Crucify him!" Pilate, seeing that a riot was breaking out, took water and washed his hands in sight of the crowd, saying, "I am innocent of this man's blood. See to it yourselves." The crowd responded, "His blood be upon us and upon our children."

Pilate, frustrated and knowing he was defeated, hopelessly pleaded, "Why, what evil has he done?" And they cried out all the more. So, Pilate said to them, "Take him yourselves and crucify him. I find no guilt in him."

The Jews answered, "We have a law and according to that law he ought to die because he made himself the Son of God."

When Pilate heard this he was terrified, because of the Roman superstitions about their gods coming down and appearing in human form. Pilate then went back into the praetorium and questioned Jesus again, "Where are you from?", to which Jesus remained silent.

"You do not speak to me? Do you not realize that I have the power to release you or to crucify you?"

"You would have no power over me if it were not given to you from above. For this reason the one who handed me over to you has the greater sin." Consequently, Pilate tried again to release Jesus, but the Jews cried out, "If you release him, you are no friend of Caesar. Everyone who makes himself a king is an enemy of Caesar."

The chief priests knew Pilate was a cowardly politician, and they knew this trump card would seal their demand. So, hearing this threat, Pilate had Jesus brought out and seated him in the judge's bench in the place called the Stone Pavement, or in Greek, Lithostratos, in Hebrew, Gabbatha. It was preparation day for the Passover, and about noon. Pilate said to the Jews, "Behold your king." They cried out, "Take him away, take him away and crucify him."

Pilate said, "What, shall I crucify your king?" To which the chief priests answered, "We have no king but Caesar." Pilate knew that in their hearts they hated Caesar, but hated Jesus even more, so he handed Jesus over to them to be crucified. They took Jesus and, carrying the cross himself, he went out to what is called the Place of the Skull, in Hebrew Golgotha. (Mt. 27:1–31; Jn. 18:28, 19:1–16; Lk. 23:1–25; Mk. 15:11–20)

In trying to reflect on what had been taking place since early dawn, one of the first questions that comes to mind is who the elders were. They had not been mentioned previously in the Gospels, so it seems that they may have been highly influential members of the Jerusalem community who could be counted on by the chief priest to do the Sanhedrin's bidding and present a powerful front to the Roman authority. The second question is, where did the common people come from? And that question is more difficult to answer. The chief priests needed a mob, a rabble to intimidate the Roman governor, who could be easily rattled politically if the right pressure was applied. A screaming rabble would intimidate any weak politician. Since most of the Jewish people loved Jesus and would have defended him, the whole court proceeding had to be done while people were still asleep. Then, it seems obvious where the rabble came from— those lowlifers roaming the streets after carousing most of the night. The chief priests could easily bribe these people with a sum of money to do their bidding at the trial. These people certainly did not represent or stand in for the masses of decent people, who would never have allowed this to happen if it took place later in the day. That was why everything was rehearsed late at night and formalized at first dawn, and transferred to Pilate's court first thing in the morning while people were still asleep or at home. The chief priests were probably panicky when they were still in Pilate's court at noontime. To their thinking it should have all been over much earlier and the crucifixion well on its way.

What is so difficult to comprehend is the vicious coldheartedness of the religious leaders who could have the impudence to destroy a person whom they had overwhelming reason to believe was their long-awaited Messiah. But greed and hatred can so blind a conscience that even murdering God can be rationalized.

42

THE WAY OF THE CROSS

After the soldiers finished with Jesus, they took off the purple cloak and put on him his own clothes, then led him out into the street to begin the march to his crucifixion. Jesus was considerably weakened by the brutal lashing, which left him bleeding profusely and in agony from the open wounds. As he walked along, he staggered rather than walked, and began to stumble and fall. After he fell, the soldiers, concerned that he might not make it through the now crowded city streets to the place of crucifixion, which was outside the city walls, as Jesus had prophesied, pressed a sturdy-looking man, named Simon, from Cyrene, to help Jesus carry his cross. Mark notes that this man was coming in from the country. He was the father of Alexander and Rufus, who probably by the time Mark wrote his Gospel had already become Christians and were obviously known to the young community of Jesus' followers. Luke mentions that the soldiers thrust the cross on Simon and had him walk behind Jesus. John writes that Jesus was carrying the cross himself. What probably took place was that Jesus carried the cross for most of the journey, then after he fell a number of times under the weight of the cross, the soldiers had Simon carry it the rest of the way to Calvary, or Golgotha, the Place of the Skull.

By the time the death march took place, the streets were already flooded with people doing their last-minute shopping for Passover, which would begin in a few hours at sundown. We can be sure that many of Jesus' followers and supporters, by this time, would have heard about the evil thing their cowardly leaders had perpetrated overnight, too craven and spineless to do it in open daylight. Jesus would have recognized these people along the way and, even though nothing was said between them and Jesus, their presence alone would have been a comfort to him. He knew they were not there out of curiosity but out of love for him and compassion, though there was nothing they could do for him.

Tradition tells us that there was one woman there along the way who braved the brutality of the troops and pushed her way to Jesus, holding out a towel for him to press against his face and wipe the blood from his eyes. He looked at her in gratitude and continued on. When the woman looked at the bloodstained towel she saw Jesus' image on it. Tradition maintains that that towel is still preserved in a church in Italy. Recently, a German Jesuit professor at the Gregorian University in Rome maintained that he found in a monastery in Manopello, Italy, what he feels is the authentic Veronica's Veil. It may never be proved one way or another as to whether this veil is authentic. In either case, it is not a matter for belief, but an expression of piety on the part of some.

Farther along the way, Jesus met a group of women, mourning and lamenting his agony. He turned and looked at them and said, "Daughters of Jerusalem, do not weep for me. Weep for yourselves and for your children, for, I tell you, the days will come when people will say, 'Blessed are the barren and the wombs that never bore, and the breasts that never nursed.' At that time, people will say to the mountains, 'Fall upon us,' and to the hills, 'Cover us!' for if these things are done when the wood is green, what will happen when it is dry?" Jesus was trying to warn them that if this was happening at a time that was relatively peaceful, imagine what it would be like shortly, when the country would be involved in such a catastrophic tumult that people would wish they were dead, and wish they had never had offspring who must suffer such anguish.

When they arrived at the place of execution, there were two others to be crucified with Jesus. The three were crucified together, Jesus in the middle, and the other two on either side. The soldiers had totally stripped Jesus before the whole mob, including his enemies, there to ridicule and scoff, and make fun of him as he was being continually tortured. It is hard to imagine religious people manifesting such naked hatred. But were they really religious? True, they were in love with religion, and the trappings of religion. They performed their rituals with scrupulous attention to details, like their being so careful not to break any rules leading up to the Passover feast lest they be considered unfit to offer worship on this most sacred day. They were very conscious of those religious details while they were in the process of killing God's Holy One, the Messiah. One wonders if they ever had a pang of conscience for their insensitivity to the needs of people and their ruthless excommunications of people unable to live up to their unreasonable religious demands. It seems not.

It reminds one of some righteous Christians today who are opposed to abortion, which is proper, but are in the forefront of those demanding execution for capital crimes, and refusing financial aid to mothers who have babies, who with their meager salaries cannot provide adequate care for the children whose fathers have been delinquent, or are long gone. It is not uncommon to hear remarks from these people who say quite unashamedly that they have never seen a genuinely poor person, just people too lazy to work, or on drugs or alcohol—poor excuses as to why they feel absolved from Jesus' command to care for the poor. Clearly they have never lived in a neighborhood where there are decent, hardworking poor people who cannot afford to pay for shelter and food, and are forced to make a decision as to which they could survive on, food, or a place to live, because they could not have both. Yes, there are people today who are like the scribes and Pharisees. One thing they have in common is greed and an obsessive love of money, and resentment at having to share their wealth with others or even pay taxes.

As a priest I have seen this often. I will never forget one situation. A father asked if I could possibly help him. He had a family, a wife and four children. He had been laid off and had fallen behind in his mortgage payments. I could help him with a few payments, as I had very little myself at the time, with a 250 dollars a month salary. The man had a brother who was very wealthy. He was a good man, went to church regularly, and had a nice family. I asked him if he could help his brother. He told me he was aware of his situation, but unfortunately was not in a position to help him at that time, as the stock market was dropping and he would have to sell some of his stocks at a loss. I could not believe what I was hearing, as I knew he had millions of dollars in the stock market, and even if he covered his brother's mortgage for a year, it would be a measly pittance, and hardly a sacrifice. I often wondered if it bothered him when his brother and his family lost their home.

When Isaiah spoke of the Messiah as an innocent lamb being led to the slaughter, it was all so clear in Jesus' humble and meek manner as they were destroying him. The religious people gathered around in glee, enjoying every pain and twinge of anguish. "Look at him now," you can hear them say. "He said he was God's Son. It seems God doesn't want him. If he was God's Son, He would never let this happen to His Son. Well, we're finally rid of him. Now maybe we'll have some peace around here."

When the soldiers stripped Jesus, they threw him down upon the cross and stretched out his arms as a soldier held his hand fast to the wood and another soldier hammered an iron spike through the wrist. The wrist was the only place that could hold the weight of the hanging body. Did Jesus let out a scream of unbearable pain, or did he just cry silently for his Father's help? And then the same with the other wrist, and then they stretched his body and nailed the feet to the cross.

What was going through his mother's soul at that most horrible moment? Simeon had told her, "Your own soul a sword will pierce as the thoughts of many will be revealed." Did that really mean, "as the evil in people's hearts is revealed?" That seems to be the meaning of the sword piercing her heart as Simeon relates it to what is in people's hearts. Now she knew fully what that holy priest had meant. Seeing her Son suffering such shame and humiliating torture must have been like a sword piercing her soul. In spite of her anguish, she had to be strong for him. To see pain on her face would only have added to his anguish. She knew her son would be glancing at her occasionally, and she would have tried not to show her own pain, as a mother would, though her heart was beyond breaking. It is a wonder it did not burst from the stress. If Jesus' stress from the night before could cause him to sweat blood, his mother, who suffered whatever he suffered, he being flesh of her flesh, and of the same spirit and nature, felt his pain. While he was suffering his Passion, she suffered the same in her compassion.

How can Christians not have a reverence, and at least feel warmth and pity for, this awesome woman, whose whole existence was, as no other creature, so intimately embraced by God, having been overshadowed by the Holy Spirit as she received the Divine Son of the Eternal Father? Never before had a human been so intimately drawn into the family of God's being and raised to such sublime heights, and into such intimate relationship with the Trinity. And such will never happen again.

And yet here she is, this queen of angels, daughter of God, mother of His divine Son, crushed under the weight of such shame and degradation being heaped upon her son, caused by God's own priests and magisterium.

When we see the mother and the son suffering this awesome agony together, it is not hard to understand the bond of love that joined the two so closely. Their souls were in such perfect harmony that they thought as one and felt as one, an ideal we struggle for in our own efforts to think like Jesus and love like him. Only the Father in heaven, seeing those two as so much a part of Himself, could understand their pain, their anguish, and must also have felt in whatever way God feels the sorrow and grief that they were suffering. His Son had freely chosen to take upon himself this burden of human sin to heal the wound inflicted upon the Father, and restore the bond between the Father and his human family.

Then as the cross was lifted into the air and dropped into the hole that had been dug to receive it, all Jesus' joints were pulled apart in further agony. As he looked across the crowd of jeering enemies, viewing his naked, torn body, his first thought as he hung there was the realization that he had atoned for all humanity's sins against his Father, and now he must beg his Father to forgive the sins against His Son. "Father, forgive them, for they know not what they do." And all the wounds we had inflicted upon God were forgiven, as the innocent Lamb was sacrificed for our deliverance, our salvation.

Beneath the cross, the soldiers were arguing about who among them would take Jesus' clothes. They divided them into four parts, but his tunic was special since it was seamless, woven in one piece from top to bottom. This they decided not to tear and divide among them. Instead they cast lots to see who would win it, thus fulfilling the prophecy in Psalm 22, "They divided my garments among them and for my vesture they cast lots."

The crowd—some, curious onlookers; some, foreigners visiting for the feast; some, priests and scribes and Pharisees—stood there looking on. No doubt some were deeply moved and conscience-struck over the part they'd played in the tragedy of this clearly good and innocent holy man, who had never harmed anyone, and who went about doing good. Others, members of the Sanhedrin, callous right to the end, laughed and jeered at the humiliation of their tortured enemy, a perceived threat to their personal material paradise on this earth. "He saved others; let him save himself if he is the chosen one, the Messiah of God." Some of the soldiers also made fun of him, offering him a coarse wine, and taking up the priests' chant, "Yea, if you're the King of the Jews, save yourself," for above his head was the sign, "Jesus of Nazareth, King of the Jews."

The two criminals who were crucified with Jesus joined the crowd in yelling out. One of them ridiculed Jesus. "You're the Messiah, aren't you? Well, do your thing. Save yourself and us." The other, shocked at the man's audacity, rebuked him, "Have you no fear of God? We are under the same condemnation, but justly so for crimes we have committed, but this man has done nothing criminal." Then he said to Jesus, "Jesus, remember me when you come into your kingdom." Jesus answered him immediately, "This day you will be with me in Paradise."

In the meantime, the chief priests were furious when they saw the inscription Pilate had had the soldiers nail to the cross: "This is Jesus of Nazareth, the King of the Jews." And to make it worse, he'd had it written in Hebrew, Greek, and Latin, so every passerby visiting Jerusalem could read it. This was his revenge against the Sanhedrin for humiliating him by bullying him into condemning an innocent man. The chief priests went back to Pilate and told him to change it from "King of the Jews" to "He said, 'I am the King of the Jews.' " Pilate's abrupt response was, "What I have written, I have written."

As Jesus and the two criminals were hanging in agony, the sky suddenly became dark and the sun was so obliterated, it became like night. Beneath the cross stood Jesus' mother, her soul transfixed by that sword that Simeon had prophesied so long ago, that prophecy that had haunted this gentle mother of God's Son all her life, wondering how that prophecy would unfold. Now she was living that nightmare in its deepest meaning, as her dying, crucified son looked down on her. Seeing her broken heart, he said to her as he looked at his disciple John, standing by her side, "Mother, behold your son," as if to say, "I don't want you to be alone. John will take care of you." Then he said to John, "Son, behold your mother."

Those words were mystical in so many ways. Jesus, the Lord of the Universe, was returning to the Father, to assume his role within the Godhead, sitting at the right hand of the Father. In doing this he was leaving his earthly mother, this sacred temple created specially for him by his

Father. Her whole existence was for him, her life totally centered on him. In truth she existed only for him. Her anguish now was not only at losing a son, but at losing the intimacy of his divine presence. No human could ever understand the loss that Mary felt at that moment. It was akin to the feeling of Jesus when he cried out to his Father, "My God, my God, why have you abandoned me?" Losing this presence struck Mary as very real when Jesus gave her to his disciple to care for her. "My son is giving me to another. He is leaving me. I have lost my son" was all that those words meant. But, as time went on, those words would have another meaning for her, and for John.

In the Book of Revelation, John will describe the vision he had of Mary, in an apotheosis of supreme glory, far short of divinity, but as the Woman of the Universe, crowned with stars, standing on the moon, and as the mother of Jesus' worldwide family, the Church. All those children baptized into Jesus and sharing his life as members of his mystical body are her children, whom Satan is trying to destroy. That was the vision the Holy Spirit revealed to John. It became clear then that in those words from the cross, Jesus made his mother the mother of the Church, the mystical body of Jesus, and the mother of us all, symbolized by the person of John, her new son. I think this is a mystical concept that many Christians do not understand. Though it is mystical, it is still very real.

When we are baptized we are given a share in Jesus' life. Our incorporation into Jesus is not just an adoption. We really share the divine life of Jesus. As Saint Peter writes in his second letter, by virtue of our baptism we become partakers of the divine nature, the life of God. Thus, having Jesus' life within us, we are incorporated into Jesus, thereby becoming part of the mystical body of Jesus. Saint Paul expands on this when he talks about the gifts and the ministries of each of the members of Jesus' body. Like the hands and feet and eyes and heart of the human body, each of us is a member of Jesus' mystical body, with special functions to contribute to the health and growth of the body of Christ. Jesus is the head; we are the members. As Mary is the mother of Jesus, so she is the mother of the mystical body of Jesus, the Church. That is why we call her the mother of the Church. In Saint John's revelation, he sees Mary's mystical role in the life of the Church and her cosmic role in Jesus' cosmic mission to bring all creation together in himself as the Alpha and Omega of all creation. John symbolizes this role of Mary in his description of her with the crown of stars and the moon under her feet, being stalked by Satan to destroy her offspring, the children of the mystical body of Jesus, the Church.

It was from that moment beneath the cross that John took Mary into his life and into his home and cared for her.

Standing beneath the cross with Mary and John were Mary's sister, Mary the wife of Cleopas; and Mary Magdalen. As the drama was unfolding, strange things begin to take place. Not only had the whole earth become like night, due either to an eclipse of the sun or to deep cloud cover, which lasted for three hours, but the huge veil in the Temple separating the Holy Place from the Holy of Holies was torn down the middle. Jesus, then cried out in a loud voice, *"Eloi, Eloi, lema sabachthani,"* which is translated, "My God, my God, why have you abandoned me?" Some thought he was calling Elijah.

Did Jesus really feel he had been abandoned by his Father? Father Hans Urs Von Balthasar thinks that at that moment, Jesus felt as if in his humanity he was abandoned by his own divinity, and felt a desolation like no human could possibly experience or understand. Or was Jesus sending a powerful and dramatic message to his enemies by holding up a Scriptural mirror for them to see the horrible crime they were committing? "My God, My God, why have you abandoned me?" are the first words of the Twenty-second Psalm. It was a Messianic psalm, and the chief priests and scribes and Pharisees would have known it by heart. Those among them with any conscience left would have considered the words of that psalm, especially as some of the priests there were quoting from that psalm as they jeered at him. The psalm reads as follows:

My God, my God, why have you abandoned me? The words of my groaning do nothing to save me. My God, I call to you by day, but you do not hear me; and at night I find no let up.

Yet you, the Holy One, who make your home in the praises of Israel, in you our fathers placed their trust; they trusted you and you set them free. To you they called for help and were delivered; in you they trusted and they were not put to shame.

But, I am a worm and no man, the scorn of mankind and the contempt of my people; all who see me laugh at me. They sneer and wag their heads, "He trusted Yahweh, let Yahweh help him. Let him deliver him, since he took such delight in him."

It was you who drew me from the womb and soothed me on my mother's breast. On you I was cast from my birth; from the womb I belonged to you. Do not push me away, for I am in deep trouble, and there is no one to help me.

Many bulls are encircling me, wild bulls of Bashan closing in on me. Lions growling and roaring open their jaws at me.

My strength is trickling away; my bones are bare and disjointed; my heart is like wax melting within me. My mouth is dry as pottery; my tongue cleaves to the roof of my mouth. I am thrown down in the dust of the earth.

A pack of wild dogs surround me, a gang of evil men is closing in on me, as if to dismember me. They have pierced my hands and my feet; I can count all my bones, while they gloat and delight in my misery. They divide my garments among them, and for my robe they throw dice.

Yahweh do not stay so far from me! You are my strength, come quickly to help me; rescue my soul from the sword, the one life I have from the grasp of the dog. Save me from the lion's mouth, my poor life from the wild bulls' horns. (Ps. 22:1–21)

Then, in a hint of the resurrection, the tone changes.

I will proclaim your Name to the assembly; in the community I will praise you: "You who fear the Lord, give praise! All you descendants of Jacob, give honor; show reverence, all descendants of Israel!"

For God has not spurned the misery of this poor wretch, did not turn away from me, but heard me when I cried out. I will offer praise in the great assembly. (Ps. 22:22–25)

As soon as the first words of that psalm passed Jesus' lips, anyone with any spiritual and scriptural depth should have mentally scanned that psalm and realized that its drama was being played out before their very eyes. Perhaps it is for that reason that Luke states that as many in the crowd were going home, they were beating their breasts in shame.

It is interesting that what Jesus experienced on the cross and in the garden the night before was a phenomenon that many holy people experience as they are approaching their last days, a terrifying fear that God is abandoning them, and that God is rejecting them, and that they are not worthy of God's love, or of living in God's presence. It is a most horrifying experience that seems to have no resolution. There is nothing one can do to banish the frightful experience. Prayer does not seem to help. The soul is then attacked with doubts as to whether God is real, or just a figment the human imagination makes up to create meaning for human existence. Whereas before God was always so close and the thought of his presence so comforting, now all is dark like night, like the night on Calvary during those dreadful three hours. Will the soul ever find peace again, or will it leave the body in that dreadful terrifying state? It is very difficult to understand the spiritual psychology of this phenomenon, but it is terrifying. I think it may be the last desperate attempt of Satan to tear a soul from God, by leading it to the brink of despair.

Mother Teresa experienced this horrible nightmare later in her life, and wrote about it in her letters. Her experience is described by Brian Kolodiejchuk, M.C., editor of *Mother Teresa: Come Be My Light.*

> The condition of the poor on Calcutta's streets, rejected by all and abandoned to their pain, was, she claimed, "the true picture of my own spiritual life." She had reached the point of complete identification with "her people," with their misery, loneliness, and rejection.
>
> She too felt unwanted—not by people who needed her, but by the One who meant more to her than life, her God. She too felt unloved—not by the multitude who flocked around her, but by God, whom she loved with all the powers of her soul. She too felt unclaimed—not by the poor who found a mother in her, but by God, the child of whose love she claimed to be.

This depression and sense of abandonment she experienced right up into her later years.

Jesus, becoming weaker with each passing moment, spoke out, "I thirst," to which one of the soldiers put a sponge soaked with stale wine for him to taste. Shortly later, Jesus spoke out in a clear voice, "It is finished." The work that his Father had sent him to earth to undertake was finally accomplished. Jesus had done all his Father had asked him. He had felt over the last many months that he had failed to accomplish all that he dreamed of accomplishing for his Father, to touch the hearts of everyone he met, and reunite them in his Father's love. And after giving himself unreservedly to the Galileans and indeed to all those he had ministered to, he finally realized that his thoughts and words were on a level far above the thoughts and attitudes of the people. And when they began to walk away from him, he knew he had failed. As divine as he was, his words were always interpreted and filtered through human minds, minds that could not understand his language and the life he was promising them. It was like an alien from another planet speaking a language that no one understood.

For priests one of the most difficult aspects of our life is our need to identify with Jesus. As a Carmelite I learned to meditate and open my soul to contemplation, the object of which was to think and feel and love like Jesus, to see everything through the eyes of Jesus. In doing this we enter a world of values totally foreign to the human way of thinking. In the eyes of God, there is only one family on earth, the family of God's children. God does not see color or nationality. These are human values. God sees the world as belonging to Him. National boundaries in God's eyes are illusions, which He allows us to indulge in, as long as we are caring of our neighbors. In trying to preach sermons about war and soldiers and all those issues relevant to what happens in times of war and international conflict, Jesus' view will always be looked upon as irrelevant, and as un-American, and unpatriotic, and out of touch with reality. It is the same problem Jesus noticed he was having with the Galileans and many of the Judeans. He was out of tune with their values and their dreams, as if he was out of touch with reality. Even many Christians today think that to talk like this is irrelevant to real life. That is why the Church, if it is faithful to Jesus, will always appear to be out of step with humanity. Its values will always be countercultural, and either suspect or despised. Saint Paul made the remark that priests, as ministers of the Gospel of Jesus, will always be the off-scouring of humanity, and despised as out of sync with people's lives.

Now it was over. How did Jesus feel looking back over the past three years? Had they been good years for him? He did not accomplish all he wanted to accomplish. His battle with Satan waged continually during those years. In the end, so far, Satan had won, in the "hour of the power of darkness" as Jesus called his present conflict, though Jesus knew that in a few hours the final battle of his life would end in total victory over the Evil One, when he would rise gloriously and destroy forever Satan's grip over God's children.

The people of Jerusalem broke Jesus' heart, as he recalled how hard he had tried to gather them all together, but they would have none of him. There he was tried and condemned as a criminal when his only offense was that he was a nuisance to the priests, and a threat to the business interests of the leaders and their control over the people.

But the main purpose of his coming to earth was to save the world by ransoming us from Satan, and offering himself as the innocent Lamb of sacrifice in atonement for our sins and the sins of all humanity, and obtaining his Father's forgiveness for all our evil, and all evil from the beginning of human history until the end of human life on this earth. And he did establish a family of God, with all that it needed to grow under the guidance of the Holy Spirit, to whom he committed this little family to nurture it and protect it until the end of time. Yes, he had accomplished all his Father had asked him to do, and finally, looking up to heaven, he could say to his Father, "It is finished. Into your hands I send forth my spirit." Then he breathed forth his spirit, bowed his head, and died, just when he chose. "No one takes my life from me. I lay down my life and I take it up again," he had said months before.

That was the most dramatic moment in all of human history, considering the central figure of the drama; it was the only real, authentic death of a God. The Gospel writers try to express symbolically the enormity of the event by saying that nature itself felt the effects: "And suddenly, the veil of the Sanctuary was torn in two from top to bottom, the earth quaked, the rocks were split, the tombs opened and the bodies of many holy people rose from the dead, and these after the resurrection, came out of the tombs, entered the holy city and appeared to a number of people." (Mt. 27:51–53)

Did these things really happen, or were people's imaginations so excited that they magnified certain natural happenings, like thunder and lightning? A powerful thunder can be very earth-shaking in its violence. With regard to people coming out of the tombs, who can say, thousands of years later, what really happened? Did Matthew write these things from his own experience or did he record things that people were telling one another? The tearing of the veil of the Sanctuary can seem believable, but what caused it, if it happened? Was it an expression of the Father's reaction to what they had done to his Son? Judaism has never been the same since that day. There have been no more prophets, no more books added to the Hebrew Scriptures, those writings that spoke of the coming of a Messiah. Those prophecies suddenly came to an end. In time the Temple was destroyed and the Temple sacrifices ended. The genealogical tablets, which preserved the names of the priestly families, were destroyed with the Temple, though the Jewish people preserved in their hearts their dedication to Yahweh and to their Scriptures and worshipped Him in the honesty of their lives.

The centurion standing in front of the cross, witnessing what had been taking place, and feeling the earth shaking, commented in the hearing of Jesus' family, "This man was innocent beyond doubt. In truth he was the Son of God." When all the people who had gathered for the spectacle saw what had happened, they returned home beating their breasts. But all his acquaintances stood at a distance, including the women who had followed him from Galilee. Among them were Mary Magdalen, Mary the mother of James and Joseph, and the mother of the sons of Zebedee, and Salome. There were many other women who had come up with him from Galilee to Jerusalem.

Since it was preparation day before Passover, the body had to be disposed of immediately, as the bodies could not remain on the cross during the Sabbath, especially since this was a solemn Sabbath. The chief priests asked Pilate if the legs might be broken and the bodies taken down. Pilate gave orders to the soldiers to do just that. They then broke the legs of the two men crucified with Jesus, but when they approached Jesus' cross, they saw he was already dead, so one of the soldiers took a lance and pierced Jesus' heart. Immediately blood and water flowed out. There was a prophecy that said, "Not a bone of his body will be broken," (Ex. 12:46) and another that said, "They will look upon him whom they have pierced." (Zec. 12:10)

The centurion commanding the contingent of Roman soldiers seems to have been standing behind the women and John, who were beneath the cross. This hardened officer was either a member of a refined Roman family, or a man of some spiritual depth and extraordinary refinement. He clearly watched every detail of what was happening. Nothing eluded his penetrating gaze, as he noticed every sound, every movement, every expression of each of the crucified as they hung there, writhing in agony. He took no part in the dividing of Jesus' belongings. He noted the words of Jesus, spoken clearly and with deep meaning, especially his first words, "Father, forgive them, for they know not what they do." No Roman would have ever experienced such a noble expression of human understanding and compassion from a victim of torture for his torturers and executioners. The Roman had to be inspired by the beauty of this supposed criminal's soul. "What is it his enemies do not know? Who is this man? I have heard about him. Who hasn't? The whole world knows of him. His reputation certainly was not that of a revolutionary or a criminal. All we heard was that he had a reputation for healing people and driving evil from their hearts. His goodness must have been too much for these religious fanatics to bear. Look at him now. Even in agony he is at peace, and is concerned for others even as he dies. Who is this man, whose life is such a contradiction? The masses of the people love him. Their priests and holy men hate him. Yet he is the one who seems in truth to be holy, as those called holy seem evil. 'It is finished,' he says. What is finished? It is as if he had come from some other world sent on a mission here, and now as he dies, he knows his mission is completed. This man is a man of mystery unlike any human I have ever seen, a man of rare goodness and humanity. Yes, he is truly holy, but possessed of a holiness that seems more like the sublime holiness of a divine being. Indeed, this man must be the Son of God. Only a divine being could endure such torture and radiate such peace and serenity, and forgive us for what we have done to him. And his mother; look at her. She suffers with such grace, such dignity, not screaming like we see so often in others. She reflects the majesty of her dying son. Who are these people? She is so resigned, as if she had prepared for this moment all her life. What have we done? What have we done? Yes, Son of God, forgive me for what I have done to you and your mother." Those sentiments or similar ones had to have been what passed through the centurion's soul as he stood there contemplating the mystery unfolding before his eyes. Tradition in the Church has always maintained that that Roman centurion, Longinus, became a disciple of the Risen Son of God. He has been honored as a saint since the earliest days of Christianity.

Time passed. It was almost evening, the Jewish beginning of the next day, and Jesus was still on the cross. To take the body down from the cross took time. Who performed that work the evangelists do not say. It seems the soldiers had the responsibility to take down the bodies and dispose of them. This was not as simple a task as it might seem. It was a messy job, since the bodies may have already been mangled by whiplashing. Jesus' body was covered with blood, and the soldiers would have been careful not to bloody their uniforms and especially the leather.

While they were doing this, a man appeared on the scene, a wealthy man, and a distinguished member of the Sanhedrin, who lived a distance from Jerusalem and had not been invited to Jesus' illegal night trial nor to the session early that morning. Being the beginning of the great festival, this man, Joseph, from Arimathea, had come into the city to celebrate the feast when he heard what had happened to Jesus. This man was a disciple of Jesus. Distraught over the betrayal of his colleagues in bringing about the execution of their Messiah, Joseph went immediately to Calvary and, seeing the soldiers taking down the bodies, hurried back to the city. Being a man of high importance and known to the governor, he requested an audience with Pilate, and asked for the body of Jesus. Pilate wrote the order that the body be given to him, and Joseph immediately went back to Calvary with the governor's order and received the body of Jesus.

Nicodemus, another member of the Sanhedrin who had not been invited to the trials, also arrived at Calvary. He had already heard what had happened and came with burial spices to prepare the body for burial. Joseph of Arimathea had a tomb in the immediate vicinity that he had carved out of the rock for his own burial. John describes the event very succinctly and with helpful attention to details.

Joseph of Arimathea, secretly a disciple of Jesus for fear of the Judean officials, asked Pilate if he could remove the body of Jesus. And Pilate gave him the necessary permission and he came and took his body. Nicodemus, the one who had come first to him at night, also came, bringing a mixture of myrrh and aloes weighing about a hundred pounds. They took the body of Jesus and bound it with burial cloths along with the spices according to the Jewish burial custom. Now in the place where he had been crucified there was a garden, and in the garden a new tomb, where no one had yet been buried. So they buried Jesus there because of the Jewish preparation day, for the tomb was close by. (Jn. 20:38–42)

In burying it they placed it lengthwise on the long twelve-foot shroud, a linen shroud which Joseph of Arimathea had brought with him. They then pulled the remaining length of the shroud over the head and down to the feet and packed the covered corpse with spices. They then wrapped his head in a separate head cloth, and after reverently offering their final respects and expressions of love, they withdrew. The men then released the flat circular stone and let it roll gently down the groove till it fell into position where it automatically locked in its place. Mark wrote that Mary Magdalen and Mary the mother of Joses were there looking on. (Mk. 15:47)

While all this took place, it is possible the centurion may have assigned legionaries to oversee the burial, since it was nearby, and attest to the officials that the body had been securely buried. Matthew writes that on

the next day, following the day of preparation [which could have been early evening, since the next day begins at sunset], the chief priests and the Pharisees came to Pilate and said, "Sir, we remember this imposter while still alive said, 'After three days I will be raised up.' Give orders then that the grave be secured until the third day, lest his disciples come and steal the body and say to the people, 'He has been raised from the dead.' This last imposture will be worse than the first." Pilate said, "You can have your guard. Go, secure it as best you can." So, they went and secured the tomb by fixing a seal to the stone, and setting the guard.

The words the chief priests used in making this request are interesting. When the chief priests questioned Jesus when he drove the traders out of the Temple, they asked him by what authority he did these things.

Jesus then asked them a question and said if they answered his question he would answer theirs. They could not answer him, so he would then not answer their question, but told them, "Destroy this Temple and in three days I will rebuild it." They certainly knew what Jesus was telling them. "Destroy me and in three days I will rise." Even though they had managed to have Jesus executed, in death he still haunted them. They had to make sure that nothing would happen during those three days.

Pilate let them have their guard with orders that they seal the tomb and secure it so it could not be vandalized. This they did. After that the chief priests could in no way keep Temple intimates from learning what really occurred. When John relates in his Gospel the guards' account of what happened on that Sunday morning, it was, no doubt, information he received from his friends close to the high priestly families, who may have been priests themselves. It was not long afterward that many of the priests became disciples of the apostles.

43
_____

THE RESURRECTION OF JESUS

All four Gospels are silent after recording the death and burial. They take up the story early on Sunday morning, when they report the tales of some women that Jesus has disappeared from the tomb. John's version of the events is the most detailed and seems more precisely descriptive of what took place, though the others add items that help to fill in other details.

On the first day of the week, Mary of Magdala came to the tomb [Matthew adds that "the other Mary came to see the tomb," and Mark states that "Mary, the mother of James, and Salome came with spices so they might anoint him."], early in the morning, while it was still dark, and saw the stone removed. So, she ran and went to Simon Peter and to the other disciple whom Jesus loved, and told them, "They have taken the Lord from the tomb, and we do not know where they have put him." So Peter and the other disciple went out and came to the tomb. They both ran, but the other disciple ran faster than Peter and saw the burial cloths there, but did not go in. When Simon Peter arrived after him, he went into the tomb and saw the burial cloths there, and the cloth that had covered the head, not with the burial cloths but rolled up in a separate place. Then the other disciple also went in, the one who had arrived at the tomb first, and he saw and believed, for they did not yet understand the Scripture that he had to rise from the dead. Then the disciples returned home. (Jn. 20:1–10)

Luke's version adds other details, but unlike the other evangelists, Luke was not present on that morning. He learned stories from other sources much later on. It is possible that there were other women who also went out to the tomb that morning, but at a slightly different time and witnessed different occurrences.

But at daybreak on the first day of the week they took the spices they had prepared and went to the tomb. They found the stone rolled away from the tomb; but on entering they did not find the body of the Lord Jesus. While they were wondering what it meant, to their surprise, two men in dazzling garments appeared to them. They were terrified and bowed their faces to the ground. They said to them, "Why do you seek the living one from among the dead? He is not here. He has been raised. Remember what he said to you when he was still in Galilee that the Son of Man must be handed over to sinners and be crucified, and rise on the third day." And they remembered his words. Then they returned from the tomb and announced all these things to the eleven and to all the others. The women were Mary Magdalen, Joanna, and Mary the mother of James; the others who accompanied them also told this to the apostles, but their story seemed like nonsense and they did not believe them. But, Peter got up and went to the tomb, bent down and saw the burial cloths alone, then he went home amazed at what had happened. (Lk. 24:1–12)

Mark's account is slightly different. He mentions Salome as another woman who accompanied Mary Magdalen. He also mentions only one young man with a white robe sitting on the right side as they were enter-ing the tomb. Then there are other slight differences:

> He said to them, "Do not be frightened! You seek Jesus of Nazareth, the crucified. He has been raised; he is not here. Behold the place where they placed him. But go and tell his disciples, and Peter, 'He is going before you into Galilee; there you will see him, as he told you.' " Then they went out and fled from the tomb; they were so seized with trembling and confusion. They said nothing to anyone, for they were afraid. (Mk. 16:1–8)

Matthew adds other fascinating details. After writing about Mary Magdalen and the other Mary at the tomb, he mentions that there was a great earthquake. This is surprising because we might think that that would have been so consequential that the other evangelists would have felt it important to mention it. Perhaps it was just a shaking of the ground near the tomb, which may have had something to do with the stone fall-ing away from the entrance. But then he mentions "an angel of the Lord descended from heaven, approached and rolled back the stone, and sat upon it. His appearance was like lightning and his clothing was white as snow." But Matthew, who was with the apostles in Jerusalem, provides details not mentioned by the others. The guards were shaken with fear of the angel and became like dead men. Then the angel said to the women in reply,

> "Do not be afraid! I know that you are seeking Jesus the crucified. He is not here. He has been raised just as he said. Come and see the place where he lay. Then go quickly and tell his disciples, 'He has been raised from the dead, and he is going before you to Galilee. There you will see him.' Behold I have told you."

Then they left and ran to tell the disciples. On the way Jesus met them and greeted them. They fell down and embraced his feet, and did him homage, as he told them not to be afraid, but "Go and tell my brothers to go to Galilee, and there they will see me." What does seem to be fac-tual about Matthew's account is that the women were at the tomb and the guards were still there, and they all witnessed something sensational. Was there an angel there, or was it something the women perceived but not with their eyes, something the guards may not have seen. The guards still would have been impressed by the empty tomb. How did the body disappear while the tomb was sealed? The soldiers "sealed" the tomb, whatever that meant.

Matthew then tells the story of the guards stationed at the tomb.

> While they [the women] were going, some of the guard went into the city and told the chief priests all that had happened. They assembled with the elders and took counsel, and gave the guards a large sum of money, telling them, "This is what you are to say. 'His disciples came by night and stole him away while we were asleep.' And if it gets to the ears of the governor, we will assure him and keep you out of trouble." The soldiers took the money and did as they were told. And this story has spread among the Jews to the present day. (Mt. 28:1–15)

The Gospel accounts of that Easter Sunday morning vary in significant details. It would be much more satisfying if they all reinforced one another, but they do not, so we are left with different stories. The earthquake and the angel or angels, while interesting, may or may not have occurred. Neither is necessary to support the authenticity of what happened, and the Gospel accounts other than Matthew mention neither the angels nor the earthquake, which would seem to indicate that they either attached little importance to them or did not believe they were factual. It is important, however, to realize that, whether they took place or did not take place, they are irrelevant to the substance of the resurrection story. The incidents recorded in the Gospels about Jesus' later appearance to various persons seem so fresh and genuine. And the mention of Jesus' annoyance with the apostles' persistent disbelief in the women's stories about what happened at the tomb strongly indicates an honesty in relaying of those conversations.

As you read over these texts, many questions arise. One of them is: When did Jesus really rise from the dead? Was it on Sunday morning? By then the tomb was already empty.

Saint Peter in his First Letter writes about Jesus after his burial: "and after he was brought to life, and, in the spirit, went to preach to the spirits in prison, those spirits who had been waiting for their redemption." (1 Pt. 3:19) It seems Jesus was quite busy soon after they buried him, as he went and brought the good news to all the holy people of ancient times, those saints of the Old Covenant, and those saintly Gentiles who had followed their consciences and the lights that God had given them. In this God credited their goodwill as faith, and announced the good news to them that His heavenly home would now welcome them home to be happy with God and their loved ones forever. In the Acts of the Apostles, Saint Peter says something very pertinent. It was on the occasion of his visit to the Roman centurion Cornelius. "Then Peter proceeded to speak and said, 'In truth, I see that God shows no partiality. Rather, in every nation whoever fears him and acts uprightly is acceptable to him.'" (Acts 10:34–35) These were the spirits whom the risen Jesus visited after his burial.

For those who can accept the evidence from the Shroud of Turin, especially since the latest analysis strongly indicates that it is from the first century, and is not a fabricated artifice, we can draw relevant scientific information from it. One of the things the shroud shows is that the body was still in the state of rigor mortis immediately before the body left the shroud. If rigor mortis had left the body, the body would have relaxed and the buttocks would have settled and spread on the shroud, causing the blood stains to spread. The body in the shroud was still taut. Usually rigor mortis leaves the body within a couple of hours after death. If the shroud is any evidence, then the body left the shroud and the tomb within an hour or so after its burial, which makes sense, because why would Jesus want to hang around in a dark tomb for three days? And the Gospels seem to indicate that when the tomb was shaken open by the quaking of the earth on Sunday morning, those standing around, including the Roman guard, saw that the tomb was already empty, yet they knew for a fact that Jesus was truly dead and buried, and the tomb had been sealed, and the seal was not broken until the shaking of the earth, which shook the stone from the entrance to the tomb. The women and the guards, seeing that the tomb was already empty, meant that the body must have risen through the solid rock sometime between the burial on Friday night, which was the beginning of the Sabbath for the Jews, and very early Sunday morning.

While it is difficult to know just who visited the tomb first and how many went, and whether different groups went at different times, what is believable is that some women did go to the tomb. Clearly Mary of Magdala was one, and she may have been accompanied by Joanna, and Mary the mother of James, and other unnamed women who are mentioned by Luke.

John writes that Mary of Magdala went to the tomb. Did she go alone? It is hard to imagine that a woman, especially in such threatening circumstances, would have ventured alone out on the streets as dawn was breaking, and especially to a tomb where she knew rough Roman soldiers would be guarding the area. Women are usually more circumspect and cautious. The other evangelists mention other women with Mary Magdalen, which seems more likely, as well as another group who may have also gone at a different time.

When they arrived at the tomb, their experiences differ, depending on the Gospel source. Mary Magdalen's group just found the tomb empty, according to Mark. Distressed, they ran back to tell Peter and John, who immediately ran out to the tomb with Mary Magdalen, with nothing being said about the other women who had accompanied her to the tomb. When they arrived there and saw the body missing, they seem not to have been deeply troubled over it, and after inspecting the tomb they just left, leaving Mary Magdalen there alone. What happened to her companions who had been with her? This seems quite strange, as she was very distressed over the body having been taken. One would think that her companions would have shown some concern for her. She had all kinds of questions and concerns—who took the body, and what have they done with it? It did not even occur to her that he had risen. The apostles, if they had concerns, certainly did not show it. John says that Peter entered the tomb first and then he entered. John notes that "he saw and believed." Did he at that time, really? Then the two of them just left and went back to their hideout.

The question immediately arises: What did John believe—that Jesus rose from the dead, or what Mary Magdalen had told them? And it is interesting that he did not say that Peter believed, but that *he* believed. I know it is not nice to be cynical about the apostles, but I cannot help but feel that whoever wrote John's Gospel, even if John himself wrote it, some sixty, seventy years later—whoever wrote it put only John in a good light, that he believed. And where was the Blessed Mother at this time? She could have been in a separate part of the house where they were all staying. John was supposed to be taking care of her. Some Fathers of the Church say that Jesus appeared to his mother first, before anyone else, to reassure and comfort her. Most probably, knowing what she knew about her son, she was the only one who would have believed him when he said that on the third day he would rise from the dead. She had no reason to go to the tomb. She would have known he would not be there.

Back at the grave, Peter and John had just left. Mary Magdalen stayed there outside the tomb, weeping. As she wept, she bent down and looked into the tomb. There she saw two angels. They asked her why she was crying. "Because they have taken away my Lord, and I don't know where they have put him." When she said this she turned around and saw Jesus there but did not recognize him. He asked her, "Why are you weeping? Who are you looking for?" She thought it was the gardener, and said to him, "Sir, if you have taken him, tell me where you have put him, and I will take him away."

Then Jesus finally said to her, "Mary!" She then turned to him and said to him in Hebrew, "Rabbouni"—"My dear Teacher"—as she reached to embrace him. Then he said to her, "Stop holding on to me, for I still must go to my Father. But, you go to my brothers and tell them, 'I am going to my Father and to your Father, to my God and to your God.'"

She then went and announced to the disciples, "I have seen the Lord," and told them what he had told her.

What is interesting is that Jesus must have been present near the tomb just a few minutes before, when Peter and John were there, but did not make his presence known to them. He waited until they had left. Was he upset with them as well as with the other apostles for their lack of faith? It seems so, as we will see later on.

Matthew tells about this appearance of Jesus, and mentions the earthquake and the angel of the Lord descending from heaven, and rolling back the stone and sitting on it. He mentions that the guards were terrified. Matthew also mentions that when the women went to tell the apostles, Jesus appeared to them on the way and told the women to tell the apostles that he would see them again in Galilee. (Mt. 28:1–10)

The whole day went by and Jesus still ignored the apostles. Later in the afternoon, two of the disciples, who had been staying with the apostles, had left to go back to Emmaus (now El-Quibeybeh). As they were walking along, discussing and arguing about all that had been happening, Jesus was walking down an adjoining road. As they met, he began to walk with them, but they did not recognize him. He asked them what they were discussing and why they looked so sad. They were shocked, and Cleopas said to him, "Are you the only visitor in Jerusalem who has not heard of what has been taking place there these days?" "What kind of things?" he asked them.

> "Those things about Jesus of Nazareth, a prophet mighty in word and deed before God and all the people, and how our chief priests turned him over to a sentence of death and crucified him. We had been hoping that he would be the one who would redeem Israel. And besides this, it is now the third day since this took place. Some women of our group, however, astounded us. They had been at the tomb early in the morning and did not find his body. They came back and reported that they had indeed seen a vision of angels who announced that he was alive. Then some of those with us went to the tomb and found things just as the women had said, but him they did not see."
>
> Then Jesus, after listening to their story, said to them, "How foolish you are, and so slow to believe all that the prophets have said! Was it not necessary that the Messiah must suffer these things and then enter into his glory?" Then, beginning with Moses and all the prophets, he interpreted to them what referred to him in all the Scriptures. As they approached the village to which they were headed, he gave them the impression that he was going farther on, but they urged him, "Stay with us, for it is almost evening and the day is almost spent." So, he went in to stay with them. And it happened that while he was at table with them, he took bread, said the blessing, broke it, and gave it to them. With that their eyes were opened and they recognized him, and he vanished from their sight.
>
> Then they started saying to each other, "Were our hearts not burning within us when he was speaking to us along the way and opened the Scriptures to us?" (Jn. 24:13–32)

Now trying to read between the lines and analyzing these various appearances, it seems Jesus was enjoying this new glorified body. He seems to have been enjoying surprising his friends all of a sudden. But he still had not visited the apostles; other disciples were going back to the upper room to tell them that they had seen Jesus. And it seems that that was what Jesus intended. He seemed disappointed that, after all the preparation he had given them about his Passion and death and the promise that he would rise again, they were so dense that it never got through to them. Now that he'd met Cleopas and his companion, who no doubt was his wife, as they were together in Jerusalem with the disciples, Jesus knew they would be rushing back to Jerusalem, the whole seven miles, to tell the apostles that they had just seen Jesus, increasing their wonder as to why Jesus was not visiting them.

But, something did happen before Cleopas and his wife got there. It seems that Peter either was out on an errand, or was in the upper room alone while the others were out, and at that time, Jesus did appear to Peter. So, when the couple arrived there, they found gathered together the eleven and those with them, who were saying, "The Lord has been truly raised up, and has appeared to Simon." Then the two recounted what had happened to them along the way, and how he was made known to them in the breaking of the bread. (Lk. 24:13–35) Mark says that the apostles did not believe them either. (Mk. 16:12–13)

Finally, while they were all still talking, Jesus appeared again. You can tell he was having fun with this new-found body that could move at will instantly to any place he wished to be. One might think that he would have quietly knocked at the door, and even though the disciples might have been momentarily frightened, he could have reassured them that it was he. But, no, he had to shock the nightlights out of them by walking through the wall into the room, which was only dimly lighted with oil lamps. Naturally, they were beside themselves and in a panic jumped up with their mouths open, unable to say a word because they were so terrified.

"Well, just don't stand there with your mouths open as if you are seeing a ghost. Look at my hands and my feet, and see that it is I. Touch me and see; a ghost does not have flesh and bones as you can see I have." And he showed them his hands and his feet. While they were still looking at him as if stupefied, he asked them, "Have you anything to eat?"

They gave him a piece of baked fish, which he took and ate it in front of them. (Lk. 24:36–43)

Mark, in recounting this appearance of Jesus, says that "he rebuked them for their unbelief and their hardness of heart because they had not believed those who saw him after he had been raised." Then he commissioned them to go out into the whole world and proclaim the Gospel to every creature. (Mk. 16:14–15)

Luke and John are much gentler in describing Jesus' handling of the situation. Luke has him saying,

> "These are my words that I spoke to you while I was still with you, that everything written about me in the Law of Moses and in the prophets and psalms must be fulfilled." Then he opened their minds to understand the Scriptures. And he said to them, "Thus it is written that the Messiah would suffer and rise from the dead on the third day and that repentance for the forgiveness of sins would be preached throughout the whole world, beginning at Jerusalem. You are witnesses to these things." (Lk. 24:48)

John's account is much more substantial. He must have had a prodigious memory for the words that Jesus spoke. He alone quotes Jesus so beautifully as he reveals Jesus' mind.

> On the evening of that first day of the week, when the doors were locked for fear of the Jews, Jesus came and stood in their midst and said to them, "Peace be with you." When he had said this, he showed them his hands and his side. The disciples rejoiced when they saw the Lord. Jesus said to them, "Peace be with you. As the Father has sent me, I send you." And when he had said this, he breathed on them and said to them, "Receive the Holy Spirit. Whose sins you shall forgive, they are forgiven them, and whose sins you shall retain, they are retained." (Jn. 20:19–23)

John then goes on to tell the story about Thomas, who was not there the night of Jesus' appearance to the others. When Thomas had returned and was with the others, they told him that they had seen the Lord. He did not believe it. "Unless I see the nail holes in his hands and put my finger into the nail holes, and put my hand into his side, I will not believe." Eight days later, they were all gathered in the house, and Thomas was with them. The doors were closed. Jesus came and stood among them. "Peace be with you," he said, then to Thomas he said, "Put your finger here into my hands. Give me your hand, and put it into my side. From now on do not be so unbelieving, but believe." Thomas replied, "My Lord and My God!" Jesus said, "You believe because you have seen me. Blessed are they who believe and have not seen." (Jn. 20:24–29)

John, in a special epilogue, tells of Jesus appearing again to the disciples. This time it is in Galilee, by the Sea of Tiberias. There was Simon Peter, with Thomas called the Twin, Nathaniel from Cana in Galilee, the sons of Zebedee, and two more of the disciples. Simon said, "I'm going fishing." They replied, "We'll come with you." They all got into the boat and pulled out into the sea. They had been out all night and caught nothing.

At early dawn, a man was standing on the shore. It was Jesus, but the disciples did not recognize him. Jesus called out, "Men, did you catch anything?" They answered, "No." Now, I stop and think for a minute. The apostles had been out all night. It was late spring. It was damp on the lake. There were probably insects and mosquitoes in abundance following the boat. Most likely the disciples were not particularly happy, and it is hard to imagine that all they said was, "No." It would have been more likely that at least Peter would have said something a lot more colorful. He was in the habit of using colorful language when he was excited. I would love to have heard the exact response, and Jesus would have hardly been shocked. He was used to Peter. All Jesus said was, "Throw the net over the starboard side and you'll find something." They did, and the catch of fish they caught was so great they had a hard time pulling it in. Then John said to Peter, "It is the Lord." Peter immediately tied his outer garment around him, for he was naked, and jumped into the water. The other disciples came on in with the boat, towing the net with the fish, for they were only about three hundred feet from the shore.

As soon as they got out of the boat, they saw a round of bread and a fish cooking over a charcoal fire. Jesus said, "Bring some of the fish you have just caught." Peter went to the boat and dragged the net ashore, full of big fish, 153 of them, and in spite of the great number of fish, the net did not break. Jesus said, "Come and have breakfast." No one dared to ask, "Who are you?" They were certain it was Jesus, although this appearance was such a shock. Jesus then walked over and offered them bread and then the fish. This was the third time Jesus had revealed himself to his disciples after rising from the dead.

"When they had finished eating, Jesus called Peter aside and said to him, 'Simon, son of John, do you love me more than these others do?' He answered, 'Yes, Lord, you know that I love you.' 'Feed my lambs,' Jesus then said to him. A second time, he said to him, 'Simon, son of John, do you love me?' To which Peter replied, 'Lord, you know that I love you.' 'Take care of my sheep.' Then, he said to him a third time, 'Simon, son of John, do you love me?' Peter was now hurt that Jesus should ask him a third time, 'Do you love me?' He said, 'Lord, you know everything. You know that I love you.' And Jesus said to him, 'Feed my sheep. And I tell you, Simon, in all seriousness, when you were young, you put on your own belt and walked where you liked. But, when you grow old, you will stretch out your hands and someone else will put a belt around you, and take you where you would rather not go.'"

In saying this, Jesus was indicating the kind of death by which Peter would give glory to God. After this he said, "Come, follow me."

Peter turned and saw John following them, and said to Jesus, "And what about him?" To which Jesus answered, "What is that to you? If I should want him to remain until I return, what business is it of yours? You are to follow me." From Jesus' comment, the rumor spread among the brothers that this disciple, John, would not die. Yet, Jesus did not say, "He will not die," but, "If I want him to stay behind until I come."

This is an interesting sideline; it again points up the competition for Jesus' favor. John must have been eavesdropping when Jesus was talking with Peter, because he is the one who quotes word for word what Jesus said to Peter, even the prophecy about Peter's future manner of dying, which was none of John's business. So when Peter turned and caught John nearby, he was upset. And he immediately put Jesus on the spot by asking him about how John was going to die. Jesus bluntly told Peter it was none of his business.

Then, John says at the end that he is the one who has written down these things so that he could vouch for what Jesus said and did, though not all, because as he says, "I think that the whole world could not contain all the books that would have to be written." (Jn. 21:1–25)

This is a beautiful event, showing such tenderness in Jesus' relationship with these dear friends he had left, and showing that he still missed their former togetherness. He also showed some of his old playfulness, shocking them by his abrupt appearance on the shore, while waiting for them to finish with their fishing. The thought crosses my mind, "Did Jesus prevent them from catching any fish all night, just so he could show them this nice gesture, with all the big fish?" He knew they probably were short of funds and had to bring the fish to market so they could pay some bills. It is so beautiful seeing Jesus on the shore cooking breakfast for them all, though I cannot help but wonder where he got the charcoal, and how he started the fire, and where he got the fish that were cooking on the fire and the loaf of bread. And why did they not recognize Jesus on the shore? Could it be they were all nearsighted? Three hundred feet is quite a distance if one is nearsighted. Or perhaps there was a light fog or mist over the lake that early in the morning.

John mentions that Peter pulled the net ashore. The seven of them had a hard time pulling the net with that huge catch of fish. Yet, Peter pulled that net full of fish onto the land by himself. Think about that! There were 153 fish. "Large fish," John says. Judging by the size of the fish there today, each fish weighed perhaps two or two and a half pounds. Add the weight of the heavy, water-soaked net, weighing another two hundred pounds, and you get a total weight of close to six hundred pounds. Peter must have been one bull of a man. I never forgot what I learned about Peter when I went to the Vatican a few years ago. We went into the excavations underneath Saint Peter's Basilica, and toured the ancient Roman cemetery along the row of ancient mausoleums built for wealthy Romans. They were like little cottages, with a table and chair and frescoes on the walls. The tomb of Saint Peter was as the end of the pathway, directly under the main altar in the basilica above. The remains of Saint Peter were contained in just a simple burial cask on a flat slab. Next to his tomb was another tomb holding the remains of another Christian. On it were the words, "Holy Peter, pray for our father who is resting next to you."

But what was important for me was the report of the doctor who ana-lyzed the bones of Peter, and concluded that he was not very tall and also quite wide, and all I could think of was that he was built like a little bull. He obviously was strong enough to pull that wet six-hundred-pound net full of fish, by himself.

But that little episode with Jesus on the shore of the lake was not just a warm meeting of friends. There was a very important purpose in Jesus meeting the disciples that morning. He had some unfinished business with Peter. And he needed the witnesses to be present at the time. Peter had denied three times even knowing Jesus. There had to be closure to that incident. It obviously still troubled Jesus, and it was still painful for Peter, who would never forget what he had done, and in front of Jesus' enemies. Jesus had to clear up that whole painful incident. "Simon, do you love me?" Imagine men talking like this? But it shows the tenderness of Jesus' relationship with these gruff but gentle friends of his. "Lord, you know that I love you." "Feed my lambs," the little sheep in the flock. "Si-mon, do you love me more than these others here?" "Lord, you know that I love you." "Care for my sheep." Then, a third time, "Simon, do you love me?" "Lord, you know all things. You know that I love you." "Feed my sheep," the whole flock, the little lambs, the big sheep, and all the others in the flock. You are responsible for them all. I am turning my whole flock over to you. It is interesting that Jesus did not call him "Rock" or "Peter," because that would be his title as head of the Church. It was not Peter the Rock on which Jesus was to build his Church who denied Jesus, but the weak human being named Simon, the son of John, who was denying he'd ever known Jesus.

So, in that brief encounter between the two, Jesus gave Peter a chance to make up for the three denials, and on the solid foundation of a most painfully humbling recognition of his dreadful human weakness, Jesus bestowed on Peter the awesome responsibility to oversee and care for his whole flock, as the good shepherd to take the place of the Good Shep-herd. Imagine God placing the awesome responsibility for the future of his mission of human redemption in the hands of a human being who had just recently denied he ever knew him. By bonding this transfer of divine authority with the reminder of Simon's tragic human weakness, Jesus is telling him, "While you exercise my authority over my flock, always be mindful of your own sinfulness, and care for them with humility." God seems to be the only one who can recognize the potential value of a sinner and not decide he must be banished from society or socially destroyed, rather than helped and allowed to continue to use his talents for the good of others. This is not the only example in Scripture of God using sinners as instruments for good. Moses had murdered an Egyptian soldier, and later he was made by God the greatest lawgiver of civilization. Saul had persecuted and had hunted down Jesus' disciples and, fighting against God's grace, was responsible for their imprisonment and execution. Yet, God still made him a "vessel of election" by consecrating him as the apostle to the Gentiles. King David had committed adultery and murder, yet God called him, for his sincere repentance and genuine holiness, a "man after my own heart." Today with our self-righteous society, we would judge them to be unfit for any kind of public responsibility.

With these incidents recorded, the evangelists end their recounting of Jesus' life by saying that over the forty days after his resurrection, Jesus was seen by some five hundred of his disciples, and after taking his disciples with him to a place on the Mount of Olives, not far from Bethany, Luke says in his Gospel and in the beginning of the Acts of the Apostles,

Now having met together, they asked him, "Lord, has the time come for you to restore the kingdom of Israel?" He replied, "It is not for you to know the times or the dates that the Father has decided by his own authority, but you will receive the power of the Holy Spirit which will come upon you, and then you will be my witnesses not only in Jerusalem but throughout Judea and Samaria, and in truth to the very ends of the earth."

And he was lifted up while they were looking on, and a cloud took him from their sight. They were still staring into the sky as he went, when suddenly two men in white were standing beside them, and they said, "Men of Galilee, why are you standing there looking up to the sky? This Jesus who has been taken from you into heaven will come back again in the same way as you have seen him leave."

So, from the Mount of Olives, as it is called, they went back to Jerusalem, a short distance away, no more than a Sabbath day's walk. When they reached the city, they went to the upper room where they were staying. Among the group there were Peter and John, James and

Andrew, Philip and Thomas, Bartholomew and Matthew, James the son of Alphaeus and Simon the Zealot, and Jude the son of James. With one heart all these joined constantly in prayer, together with some women, including Mary the mother of Jesus, and with his brothers. (Acts 1:1–14)

This might seem to be a good time to end the story of Jesus' life on earth, among all his earthly friends and the close-knit family he had gathered around him, but his life with them is not really ended, as we begin to see.

44

I WILL NOT LEAVE YOU ORPHANS. I WILL SEND THE HOLY SPIRIT

It is surprising to see Jesus' little community, so devastated and burdened with such grief over the departure of their beloved Master, whom they are now beginning to understand in a new light. They have experienced many years of mystery and struggle over their inscrutable and nagging question, "Who is this man?" And they began to ponder among themselves. "Now light is dawning as to some of that mystery. He is a special revelation of Yahweh's relationship with Israel, and if he is the Messiah, he is a different kind of Messiah than we had expected. Yet, he has all the signs of a Messiah, and John said that he is 'the one who is to come.' But, he wasn't supposed to die, and he did die, but then he also rose from the dead, and like Elijah and Moses and Enoch, he was taken up to heaven in our very sight. And we witnessed everything. And now we must carry on what he taught us. He promised that he would not leave us orphans. We know he is still with us, and we must carry on the mission he entrusted to us." These, I am sure, are the thoughts that went through their minds.

With that attitude they recuperated from their recent trauma in a surprisingly short time. We see Peter, the Rock, taking charge immediately after the Ascension. In a gathering of the community, consisting of roughly 120 people, Peter stood up and said to them,

> Brothers, the passage of Scripture had to be fulfilled in which the Holy Spirit, speaking through David, foretells the fate of Judas, who acted as guide to the men who arrested Jesus, after being one of our company and sharing our ministry. As you know, he bought a plot of land with the money he was paid for his crime. He fell headlong and burst open, and all his entrails poured out. Everyone in Jerusalem heard about it and the plot is now called the "Bloody Acre," Hakeldama in Hebrew.
>
> "Now in the Book of Psalms it says, 'Reduce his encampment to ruin, and leave his tent unoccupied.' And again, 'Let someone else take over his office.' " (Acts 2:15–20)

Peter showed an enlightened prudence in his decision to replace Judas. He knew it was Jesus' wish that there be twelve members in his chosen band of apostles, representing the twelve tribes of Israel. He also made a wise decision when he decided that this person who would take Judas' place should be a person who had been with them from the beginning of their relationship with Jesus, from the time John was baptizing up to the very day when Jesus was taken up. And this person must serve as a witness to his resurrection. There were two persons who were picked as candidates, Barnabas and Matthias. After deliberation and prayer, they drew lots, and the lot fell to Matthias. From then on he was considered one of the Twelve Apostles.

For the most part the community stayed indoors, for fear of arrest or even worse. The apostles as well stayed behind locked doors for the same reason; they were too afraid to even let anyone know they were still in town. The upper room where they were staying was a prominent home in Jerusalem, and anyone moving freely from that place could easily be noticed. The twelve were still bound by fear, no different than before Jesus was arrested. Now they were without him and the feeling of security he provided for them. Many people in Jerusalem would recognize them as having been Jesus' constant companions, and they did not want word of their presence to get back to the scribes and Pharisees and the chief priests. So, they laid low for as long as they could, though they knew they had to start carrying out the mission Jesus had given them. When and how they could begin was a pressing question, especially since they were already suspect. Jesus had told them that they should wait for the Holy Spirit to come upon them. That gave them time to prepare, and this they did by meeting quietly and spending the time in prayer. A great comfort to them was the presence of Jesus' mother in their midst continually, as she shared with them details of Jesus' life and became for them the spiritual bond between themselves and her departed son.

The festival of Pentecost was another important feast among the Israelites. Depending on whether the people followed the Pharisees' or the Sadducees' reckoning, it was to begin on either the fiftieth or the fifty-first day after the Sabbath in Passover. It was to be a one-day festival, and on that day, two wheat loaves made with leaven were to be brought to the priests in the Temple and waved before the Lord. The feast was a reminder of their slavery in Egypt, from which they had been freed. There were also other sacrificial offerings that had to be brought to the Temple. Lee Smith, in his *Old Doctrines, New Light,* available on the Internet, has valuable information about this feast and its relevance to Christianity.

Since this was a joyful and popular festival, there were many Gentiles who celebrated, as well, which created concern for the Pharisees, because they might be contaminated if they encountered any of these uncircumcised pagans. To protect themselves from this casual contamination, they had permission from the Roman authorities to erect a clearly visible placard between the Court of the Gentiles and the Court of the Women, warning Gentiles, "No stranger is to enter within the balustrade around the Temple and enclosure. Whoever is caught is responsible to himself for his death, which will ensue." Interestingly, this placard was found in an excavated area about 140 years ago by a French archaeologist by the name of Clermont-Ganneau. This information one can also find on Lee Smith's website.

The Pentecost we are concerned about, involving the first community of Jesus' followers, probably took place on that Sabbath when Pentecost was being celebrated in Jerusalem. The city was flooded with Israelites and Gentiles from many foreign countries. In the Acts of the Apostles, Luke describes the event.

When Pentecost came around they had all met together, when suddenly there came from heaven a sound as of a violent wind, which filled the entire house where they were sitting. There appeared to them tongues as of fire. These tongues separated and came to rest on the head of each of them. They were all filled with the Holy Spirit and began to speak different languages as the Spirit gave them the power to express themselves.

Now there were devout men living in Jerusalem from every nation under heaven, and at the sound they all came together and all were beside themselves at hearing these men speaking in their own language. Completely astonished, they said, "It is evident that these men are all Galileans. How is it that we are all hearing them in our own native language? Parthians, Medes, Elamites, people from Mesopotamia, Judea, Cappadocia, Pontus and Asia, Phrygia and Pamphylia, Egypt and the parts of Libya round Cyrene, residents of Rome, Jews and proselytes alike, Cretans and Arabs, we hear them preaching in our own language about the wonders of God." Everyone was amazed and mystified, and asked others what it all meant. Some just laughed. "They've had too much new wine to drink," they said. (Acts 2:1–13)

Then Peter stood up with the Eleven and addressed them in a loud voice: "Men of Judea, and all you who live in Jerusalem, make no mistake about this, but listen carefully to what I have to say. These men are not drunk, as you think; it is only the third hour of the day. On the contrary, this what the prophet was talking about: In the final days—the Lord declares—I shall pour out my Spirit on all humanity. Your sons and daughters shall prophesy, your young people shall see visions, your old people shall dream dreams. Even on the slaves, men and women, I shall pour out my Spirit. I shall show signs in the sky above and cryptic messages on the earth below. The sun will be turned into darkness and the moon into blood before the day of the Lord comes, the great and terrible day. And all who call upon the name of the Lord will be saved." (Acts 2:14–21; Jl 3:1–5)

What is remarkable about the apostles after that event is that they showed none of the fear of being arrested that had kept them locked up in their dwelling. Emboldened by their anointing by the Holy Spirit, they courageously went outside their dwelling and spoke to the vast crowd that had gathered. Peter immediately took his place as the spokesman and spoke fearlessly what had to be said, defending the others from the scoffing of a few hecklers, and telling the crowd bluntly that what they were witnessing was the overwhelming power of God, come to warn them. Peter expressed himself in words that would never have occurred to him before. Remember, he was not educated, but suddenly he spoke as one knowledgeable in the Scriptures, quoting passages relatively obscure to most people but that described precisely what was happening at that moment.

> "Men of Israel, listen to what I have to say to you. Jesus the Nazarene was a man commended to you by God by the miracles and signs that God worked through him when he was among you as you all well know. This man, who was put into your power by the deliberate intention and foreknowledge of God, you took and had crucified and killed by men outside the Law. But, God raised him to life, freeing him for the pangs of the netherworld; for it was impossible for him to be held in its power since, as David says of him, 'I have kept the Lord before my sight always, for with him at my right hand nothing can shake me. So, my heart rejoiced and my tongue delighted; my body too will rest secure for you will not abandon me to the world of the dead or allow your holy one to see corruption. You have taught me the way of life, you will fill me with joy in your presence.' " (Acts 2:22–28; Ps. 16:8–11)

This is the original speaking in tongues. Apparently, in the beginning, when the apostles went out to the crowd that had gathered, the apostles broke up and were speaking to various parts of the crowd, and then Peter stood up and addressed them all. When he spoke, he spoke in his own language, but all the people there understood him in the language of the country they came from. That was what speaking in tongues was all about. It was a divinely originated phenomenon for God to communicate messages to people, messages they could understand.

Today at prayer gatherings, people start speaking in sounds that nobody understands, and in every place I have been where this occurred, the sounds are always the same, as if they had passed those sounds on from one group to another. And no one understands anything that is said. That just is not the way God works. God is highly efficient, and when he inspires such a phenomenon it is to teach something. People learn nothing from the sounds that people utter today that they call speaking in tongues. In the early Church if someone did speak in a language no one understood, there was usually a person there who had the gift of understanding and could interpret the language, and the group benefited from what was taught. But even that support is lacking in those happenings today.

In continuing with Peter's address to the huge gathering on that first Pentecost Sabbath, he continues telling them,

> "Brothers, no one can deny that the patriarch David himself is dead and buried; his tomb is still with us. But, since he was a prophet, and knew that God had sworn to him an oath, 'to make one of his descendants succeed him on the throne,' he spoke with foreknowledge about the resurrection of the Christ; he is the one who was 'not abandoned to the netherworld,' and 'whose body did not see corruption.' God raised this man Jesus to life, and of that we are all witnesses. Now raised to the heights by God's right hand, he received from the Father the Holy Spirit, who was promised, and what you see and hear is the outpouring of that Spirit. For David himself never went up to heaven, but yet he said, 'The Lord said to my Lord, take your seat at my right hand, till I have made your enemies your footstool.'
>
> "For this reason the whole House of Israel can be certain that the Lord and Christ whom God has made is this Jesus whom you crucified."

The fruit of Peter's talk inspired by the Holy Spirit was awesome. A large number of people in that gathering were touched deeply and asked what they must do, and after Peter told them that they should repent and be baptized, they baptized about three thousand souls that day, and the Church was greatly increased. These remained faithful to the teaching of the apostles, to the brotherhood, to the breaking of bread and to the prayers.

The apostle continued to work many miracles and signs. The people in their fervor gave up many of their possessions to help the poor and they learned to share with one another, as everything was held in common, so no one remained in need. Every day they went together to the Temple to pray, but met in their houses for the breaking of bread, and on those occasions those who came with much food shared generously with those who had less. The wider community had great respect for this new community of Jesus' disciples. And every day new converts continued to swell their numbers. (Acts 2:29–47)

It now becomes even clearer that Jesus' story did not end with his Ascension into heaven, as he is still alive in the ministry of salvation that he had come to initiate. The apostles were wondering when the kingdom that Jesus had talked about would be established, but it was already established and growing at a miraculous pace. We cannot consider the drama of his life and work ended, until we see how his apostles carried out his ministry of redemption in the years that followed. That drama reached its peak when the disciples finally realized after much bitter controversy that Jesus was the divine Son of God, and that the Holy Spirit was God, and that together with the Father they constituted the three persons of the Triune God.

The Holy Spirit sent by Jesus had begun to make Jesus' presence more deeply felt than when he was with them in the body. He was now within them, present in a way that was intimate, the dwelling of the Godhead within, guiding and directing their lives. He was made real to people as the apostles preached the story of his life and touched the hearts of those who would not follow him when he was in the flesh. He also became more vividly present as Peter reached out to heal the crippled and the sick as he encountered them each day. When the people saw the apostles, it was not the human instruments they accepted and embraced. It was the living Jesus they saw in them whom they embraced, the Jesus they saw radiating through the simple, dedicated lives of these holy apostles, through whom Jesus chose to make his presence real throughout the world. Yes, Jesus still lives and is very much alive in this process of redemption that he won for us.

One day Peter and John were going to the Temple for prayers at the ninth hour. That was three o'clock in the afternoon. They encountered a crippled man being carried along. This was a daily happening, as his family or friends brought him to the Beautiful Gate so he could sit there and beg as the people filed through. This man recognized Peter and John, as their reputation was growing among the Temple worshippers. The man put out his hand, asking them for money. Peter and John looked into his eyes and said, "Look at us!" He turned and looked at them, expecting something, but Peter said, "Gold and silver we have not, but what I do have I will give you. In the name of Jesus Christ, the Nazarene, get up and walk!" Peter then took him by the hand and helped him up. When his feet and ankles began to grow strong, and he felt secure, he jumped up, stood there, and then began to walk, following Peter and John into the Temple. The crowd standing around saw him and recognized him as the crippled beggar, who was now jumping up and down, praising God. The people were astonished and overwhelmed by the realization of what had just happened. Peter and John's reputation grew even more that day.

The people had been used to seeing Jesus perform such signs, but not his disciples. Now Jesus had been taken away, and his disciples were manifesting the same powers that Jesus had so powerfully exhibited. What would naturally cross their minds was, "What is the connection? How did these men get this power to work such awesome signs?" They now began to see Peter as the continuation, the extension of Jesus' life, carrying on the ministry that Jesus had dedicated his life to. There is something very supernatural about this mission. Jesus did speak of a kingdom, even though it may not have been the kingdom that people were expecting. He talked about the kingdom of heaven being in people's hearts. With Jesus' demise, that kingdom, whatever it was, was now very much alive and growing each day. That was what the people saw. That miracle performed on a crippled man was a powerful endorsement from on high.

Immediately an excited crowd gathered around Peter and John. The healed man was clinging to Peter and John. As the crowd surrounded them, Peter began to speak.

"Men of Israel, why are you surprised at this? Why are you staring at us as if we made the man walk through out own power or holiness? It is the God of Abraham, Isaac, and Jacob, the God of our ancestors, who has glorified his servant Jesus, whom you handed over, and then disowned in the presence of Pilate after he had given his verdict to release him. It is you who accused the Holy and Righteous One, you who demanded that a murderer be released to you while you killed the prince of life. God, however, raised him from the dead, and to that fact we are witnesses, and it is in the name of Jesus which through faith in him, has brought back the strength of this man whom you see here and who is well known to you. It is faith in him that has restored this man to health, as you can all see.

"Now I know, brothers, that neither you nor your leaders had any idea what you were really doing, but this is the way God carried out what he had foretold when he said through all the prophets that his Christ would suffer. Now you must repent and turn to God so that your sins may be wiped out and that the Lord may bless your life with peace and comfort. Then he will send you the Christ he has predestined, that is Jesus, whom heaven must keep until the day when all things will be restored which God proclaimed through the prophets. As Moses said, 'From among your brothers the Lord God will raise up for you a prophet like me; you will listen to whatever he tells you. Anyone who refuses to listen to that prophet will be cut off from the people.' (Dt. 18:15–19) In fact all the prophets who have ever spoken, from Samuel on, have prophesied what has been happening in these days.

"You are the heirs of the prophets, the heirs of the covenant God made with your ancestors when he told Abraham, 'All the nations of the earth will be blessed in your descendants.' (Gn. 22:18) It was for you in the first place that God raised up his servant and sent him to bless you as every one of you turns from his wicked ways." (Acts 3:11–26)

What is astonishing here is not just the fearlessness of Peter and John, having no trace of their previous anxiety over the possibility of arrest, but with their sudden, uncanny knowledge of Scripture. These men were not trained in the Scriptures. They had no scrolls they could take out and read in their free time. They were simple fishermen, and knew only what they had been taught by their local itinerant Pharisees or scribes, or what they had learned from Jesus, which surely was substantial. But much of this on-the-spot, spontaneous Scriptural knowledge, which fit so perfectly the situations in which they found themselves, is surprising. Jesus had told them not to worry about what they should say, and that it would be given them from above how they needed to respond. And on this occasion, it was clear that God was with them, and that the Spirit was speaking through Peter.

As bold as John and Peter were in proclaiming the risen Jesus, it did not take long before gossip reached the ears of the priests, who immediately called the captain of the Temple guard and the Sadducees, and confronted Peter and John for preaching the resurrection of Jesus. It was the one thing they did not want to be spread around Jerusalem, and for good reason. Jesus had appeared to various groups of people, judicious persons of sound judgment, who could be trusted for their common sense. The number of these people was in the vicinity of five hundred, if not more. That could become a powerful basis for a credible rumor. As this news spread like a wildfire around the city, it understandably made the authorities panicky. They had heard from the Roman legionaries at the tomb what really happened, and though they bribed them to make up a tale that Jesus' body was stolen, word was already spreading that this was not true, thus making the conversion of such a large number of people, including a considerable number of priests, relatively easy, especially now that Jesus' apostles had his power to heal serious maladies.

So, the priests had Peter and John arrested. It is interesting that the priests, many of whom were Sadducees who did not believe a resurrection after death, brought Sadducees with them, when they heard that Peter was talking about the resurrection of Jesus. Pharisees, on the other hand, believed in the resurrection of the body after death, though they had no idea what would happen to it or where it would go after it was reunited with the soul. The guard locked up Peter and John until the next day, as it was already late and there was no time to gather judges for a hearing.

The next day, the hearing convened, with Annas, the high priest, and Caiaphas, Alexander and Jonathan, and members of the high priestly families. It was an impressive gathering, the whole upper echelon of the Temple elite, intended to intimidate the two prisoners. But the apostles were now changed persons. They knew they had God on their side, and no human beings could intimidate them.

They were made to stand before this august panel like common criminals. Then the interrogation began: "By what power or on whose authority do you do these things?" Then Peter, as it says in the Acts of the Apostles,

Filled with the power of the Holy Spirit, spoke out, "Rulers of the people and elders! If you are questioning us today about an act of compassion to a cripple, and how he was healed, then, you must know, all of you, and the whole people of Israel, that it is by the name of Jesus Christ the Nazarene, whom you crucified, and God has raised from the dead, by this name and by no other this man stands before you curéd. This is 'the stone which you the builders rejected but which has become the cornerstone.' (Ps. 118:22) Only in him is there salvation, for of all the names in this world given to men, this is the only one by which we can be saved."

The judges, taken aback by the boldness of Peter and John, as they knew that they were uneducated, were at a loss as to what they should do next, especially as the crippled man, whom all Jerusalem knew, was standing there in front of them. What more proof did Peter need?

The scene reminds me of a story that a very distinguished judge told a group of us one day. This man had a very deep and powerful voice that, together with his imposing stature, intimidated a lot of people who appeared in his courtroom. One day, a young teenaged girl who had grown up in the streets was brought before this judge. It was her first time in court, and it was on a rather light charge, for which the girl thought she was innocent. The judge, in his most solemn, deep voice, spoke to her very seriously. "Young lady, you are standing before this court after having been charged with a serious crime, and this court is not going to take what you did lightly." Before he got the last word out, the young girl spoke out, "Get off it, man! You don't impress me one bit with that deep voice and that funny robe you're wearing. You may frighten your wife, but you don't frighten me. So, give me one good reason why I am even here in the first place."

The judge told us that he was so flabbergasted that he literally did not know what to say next. So, in embarrassment, he adjourned the court to his chambers and settled the matter in a very informal way. "After that incident," he told us, "every time I used my deep, solemn voice in court I thought of that girl and had to smile to myself."

I think that is what happened to that high-powered court that tried to overwhelm this simple, supposedly ignorant fisherman. With Jesus, they knew they were dealing with a mind that far exceeded their most brilliant scholars. None of them could best him, either in debate or their daily strategies. Their accusations against him for violating the Law were met with such stinging rebuttal that it made their legal prohibitions appear laughable.

But these simple men, what had they done that was so wrong? All they did was show compassion for a man crippled from birth, and through God's blessing healed the fellow. How can anyone consider that a crime? And it wasn't even on the Sabbath. And with the healed man standing there in front of everyone, the whole affair looked like a farce.

Checkmated, the judges ordered Peter and John outside the room while they deliberated among themselves. "The whole city knows what has happened to this beggar; there's no way we can deny it." So, they decided to dismiss the two with the warning that they not talk about Jesus to anyone.

They then called in Peter and John and gave them a strict warning not to teach in the name of Jesus. But Peter and John spoke up boldly, "You be the judge. Do we obey you or do we obey God? What we have seen and heard is true, and we cannot refuse to tell the truth of what we have seen and heard with our own eyes and ears." So, the court repeated its threat and released them. It was afraid of the people who had witnessed the miracle. As the news spread all over Jerusalem the people were loudly praising God for the miraculous signs taking place. (Acts 4:1–22)

As soon as they were released they went to the disciples and they all expressed their delight that they were found worthy to suffer for Jesus. Life among them was much the same as it had been when Jesus was with them. They were united in heart and soul. No one made an issue of private ownership of material goods, as everything was owned in common. The apostles preached the kingdom of God just as Jesus had done before and as he had taught them, and they were held in high esteem. Although there were poor among them, no one was in want as everyone shared.

As the apostles continued to preach the risen Jesus, the chief priests were incensed at their refusal to obey the orders of their court, so again and again they were arrested. On occasion, they were freed from the prison cell by the intervention of an angel. It baffled the court when it was reported that they were not in their cells, though the cell doors were still locked. While the full court of the Sanhedrin was meeting, a highly respected Pharisee named Gamaliel arose to speak. "Men of Israel, listen to what I have to say. Have nothing to do with these men. If their work is of human origin, it will eventually die out as have all the others. If, however, their work is from God, there is no way to stop it, and you may find yourselves fighting the Almighty." So, this holy man, who was a teacher of Saint Paul as a young man, was successful in persuading the Sanhedrin to release the apostles, again with the warning not to talk about Jesus, or his resurrection.

It was about this time that a very large number of priests as well as Pharisees went over to Jesus' teachings and became disciples. This is significant. When the chief priests were convening the Sanhedrin, Luke mentions that they called the Sadducees to the sessions. It seems obvious that they did not want the Pharisees present, and for good reason. The Pharisees believed that God will one day raise the dead to life, and the Pharisees would be a divisive force at meetings because the Sadducees did not believe in life after death, which explains why the chief priests and the Sanhedrin were so frustrated with the apostles' insistence on preaching the resurrection of Jesus all throughout Jerusalem. It was particularly maddening that they were preaching, just like Jesus, right under the noses of the religious authorities, in the Temple precincts, in the various porticoes where the Temple scholars also held their sessions. It was a particular affront to their authority that the apostles just ignored their court order and boldly preached Jesus to the large crowds of worshipers who came to the Temple daily.

People kept joining the young community of Jesus' disciples daily. What was particularly sensational was seeing the priests and Pharisees coming into the Christian community in such large numbers, making one wonder why this was happening so soon after Jesus' resurrection. One theory is that the authentic report of the Roman legionaries sent to guard the tomb was beginning to circulate among the inner circle of the Temple priests and Pharisees, that Jesus had risen. How could they have kept that original report a secret, a report that could only have said that, when the sealed tomb opened after daybreak, the body was already gone, as if it just passed through the solid rock during the night? And this is what the Fathers of the Church will write later on, that Jesus rose from the dead like a "ray of light passing through a window without breaking the glass."

Something sensational had to have happened for such a large group of priests and Pharisees to come into the Church at that one particular period. It makes good sense and is logical that these men had solid reason to accept the resurrection, because they do not seem to have been previous disciples and seem to have come to the faith well prepared beforehand.

The next question that arises is what the religious life was like among that early community. One wonders how the apostles baptized the crowd of three thousand on Pentecost, as there was no large body of water in Jerusalem where the crowd could be immersed. The answer seems to be in the apostles' own understanding of what Jesus had instructed them. There is an ancient document that dates back to the years 95–100 A.D. This document, entitled "The Didache," or "The Teaching of the Twelve Apostles," concerned the daily administration of the Church and how the simple rituals were to be performed. This book was originally listed in the canon of sacred Scripture, but was later dropped when the canon was set in its final permanent form, as we have it today. But it was still a most important handbook for the early Church. The following are some of the rules for the administering of the sacraments.

1. And concerning baptism, baptize this way: After reviewing all of this teaching, baptize in the Name of the Father, Son, and Holy Spirit, in living [running] water.
2. But if living water is not available, then baptize into other water; and cold is preferred, but if not available in warm.
3. But if neither is available, pour water three times upon the head in the Name of the Father, Son, and Holy Spirit.
4. But before the baptism, let the overseer fast, and also the one being baptized, and all others who are able; be sure to instruct the one being baptized to fast one or two days before. ("The Didache," Ch. 7)

Another issue concerned who was to be baptized. Everyone who confessed Jesus, young and old, men and women, and infants as well were to be baptized. The early fathers give us the answers to that question. One of these is Origen. "The Church received from the apostles the tradition of giving baptism to infants. The apostles, to whom were committed the secrets of the divine sacraments, knew there are in everyone innate strains of [original] sin, which must be washed away through water and the Spirit." (Origen, "Commentaries on Romans 5:9") Origen lived from 185 to 254 A.D.

Saint Hippolytus also gives testimony to the early Church's baptizing of infants. "The children should be baptized first. All of the children, who can answer for themselves, let them answer. If there are any children who cannot answer for themselves, let their parents answer for them, or someone else from their family." (Hippolytus, "The Apostolic Tradition," 21–4) Hippolytus lived from 170 to 236 A.D.

These two men lived in the second century and into part of the third century; their time was not that far removed from the time when John the Evangelist was still alive, and also Saint Ignatius of Antioch, who was a young boy, probably a teenager, when Jesus was alive. So, Origen and Hippolytus were testifying to long-standing customs that had been in practice in the churches since the time of the apostles.

As one reads the Acts of the Apostles, it is clear that the young community of Jesus' followers had been well trained by Jesus. Wondering what he did during those forty days after his resurrection, it seems he steered the apostles on a detailed and practical course, as there does not seem to be a lag time while the apostles had to figure out what they had to do, and how they should proceed. Baptism was in place. Eucharist, or the breaking of bread, as it was called, was done frequently, at least on Sunday evenings, and sometimes during the week. The community of Jesus' followers would go to the Temple or the synagogue on the Sabbath, and gather for the breaking of bread on Sunday. It is interesting that in gathering for the breaking of bread there was no Scripture reading, merely prayers, sharing of faith experiences, and Eucharist in the context of a simple meal, which each family would bring to the gathering. That was their official weekly worship service. It might seem strange, since Scripture is always part of our worship services, but we have to remember there were no Bibles available in those days, only scrolls of the Hebrew Scriptures, which were considered sacred and were kept in special places in the Temple and in synagogues. And as there was not a New Testament, there were no Christian Scriptures to read. So, when Paul talks about all Scripture being inspired, he is not talking about the New Testament, as there was no New Testament yet, only correspondence from apostles or other bishops to their disciples, which were not as yet considered as the inspired word of God. That would not happen until much later on, as people themselves could not certify writing as inspired. That declaration had to be made by the bishops as successors of the apostles, together with the pope as successor to Peter. Only then could it be binding on the Christian community to accept them as inspired. Until that point, people might consider them beautiful writings and feel inspired by them, but they would be under no *obligation* to use them as a divinely inspired way of life.

One of the powers Jesus bestowed on the apostles of which they at first they did not understand the ramifications was the power to receive back into the Church members who had apostatized during persecutions. When these lapsed Christians came back to the apostles and asked to be received back into the community, the apostles did know what to do, so they told the people they would look into the matter. At their meeting, Saint James suggested that they consider what Jesus had said to them at the Last Supper, "after breathing on us he gave us the Holy Spirit, and said, 'Peace be with you. Whose sins you shall forgive they are forgiven; whose sins you shall retain, they are retained.' " And the apostles remembered and for the first time they exercised that power by receiving the confession of the repentant apostates and declaring their sins forgiven and allowing them to receive the Eucharist again.

This makes sense in the real life of the early Christians. As part of the ritual of the gatherings for worship, public confession of serious sins was important. Then the apostles or bishops consecrated by them accepted their confessions, using the power Jesus had given them on that first Easter night. As far back as the "Didache," confession of sins was strongly urged. "In the congregation, confess your sins; do not come to your prayer with an evil conscience." And "On the Sabbath assembly [which took place on the Sunday], as you gather together, eat a meal, and give thanks, after first confessing your sins, that your sacrifice may be pure." The Eucharist, which in Greek means "thanksgiving," was their sacrifice of thanks, and in the earliest days of the Church was done in the context of a simple meal. ("Didache," Ch. 7:1) The Eucharist was not only a communal meal, it was a sacrifice, not separate from the sacrifice on Calvary, but a representation of that same sacrifice, offered to the Father in fulfillment of Jesus' command to do this as a living memorial of his sacrifice.

Life for the earliest Christians was not easy. They lived in constant dread of arrest and confiscation of their property, and even execution. Many could not withstand the pressures, and so they capitulated and renounced their Christian faith, only to come back after the persecution subsided and ask if they could be accepted back into the community. Saint Cyprian, writing around 250 A.D., gives testimony to the practice of confession: "I entreat you, dear brothers that each one should confess his own sins while he is still in this world—while his confession can still be received and while the satisfaction and remission made by the priests are still pleasing to the Lord." (Cyprian, quoted in Bercot, vol. 5, p. 445)* And in another place, Cyprian writes, "They do violence to His body and blood [i.e., the Eucharist] before their sin is expiated, before confession of their crime has been made! They do this before their consciences have been purged by sacrifice and by the hand of the priest!" (Cyprian, quoted in Bercot, vol. 5, p. 441)

Tertullian, probably a priest in the Church at Carthage, was a lawyer and an early witness. He wrote around 197 A.D., "Some, not able to find this peace [i.e., ecclesiastical forgiveness] in the Church, have been seeking it from the imprisoned martyrs." (Tertullian, quoted in Bercot, vol. 3, p. 693)

What was of critical importance for the earliest communities was leadership. Jesus chose twelve apostles to carry on his message of the kingdom of heaven to the whole world. The apostles had known Jesus personally, having traveled with him during his life on earth, and having been trained by him over the course of his public ministry. Their tenure on life, however, was unpredictable, and this presented a serious problem for the young Church. If anything happened to them, who would be qualified to carry on this unique ministry? They were not just chosen like a human leader would choose someone to continue his projects. Jesus knew his mission of redemption would continue until the end of time. To guarantee that, he not only chose his twelve apostles, he gave them special powers

---

* This and all following references are from *The Ante-Nicene Fathers*, Alexander Roberts and James Donaldson, eds. 1885–1887; repr. 10 vols. Peabody, Mass.: Hendrickson, 1994. The quotations used were from *A Dictionary of Early Christian Beliefs*, David W. Bercot, ed.

and authority to chose their successors and to consecrate them with the same supernatural powers Jesus had given to them.

Within only a few years after Jesus' death, James the Apostle, who presided over the Church in Jerusalem, was martyred and had to be replaced. As the apostles traveled to other places and established churches, and then moved on, it was necessary for them to appoint and consecrate leaders to take their place. Saint Paul preached in so many places, he had to train local converts to take over when he left. After training them and watching their spiritual growth, he consecrated them, placing his hands on them and calling down the Holy Spirit upon them. One of these was Timothy, who succeeded Paul as the first bishop of Ephesus. Titus was another bishop consecrated by Paul. "Bishop" became the title for these persons who were consecrated by the apostles. They shared in the same authority to teach and the same powers to consecrate at Eucharist, and reconcile repentant sinners to the community and into God's forgiving grace. "Whose sins you shall forgive they are forgiven; whose sins you shall retain, they are retained." They also had the same power to consecrate other bishops as they were needed, and to share part of their power with other men, and perhaps, at times, women, to preside and consecrate at Eucharist and reconcile sinners to God's grace, as the communities grew and spread to outlying areas.

Saint Paul laid down the qualities he wanted to see in a bishop. "This is a faithful saying: If a man desires the position of a bishop, he desires a good work. A bishop then must be blameless, the husband of one wife, temperate, sober-minded, of good behavior, hospitable, able to teach." (1 Tm. 3:1–2)

Since these people stood in the place of the apostles, the same status Jesus bestowed on the apostles applied to the bishops, as well. "If people accept you, they accept me. If people reject you, they reject me, and him who sent me." The "Didache" again lays down rules for the appointment of bishops. "Appoint, therefore, for yourselves, bishops and deacons worthy of the Lord; men who are meek, not lovers of money, truthful and tested; for they also render to you the service of prophets and teachers. Do not despise them, therefore, for they are your honored ones, together with the prophets and teachers." ("Didache," Ch. 7:381)

And Saint Ignatius of Antioch, who as a young boy was close to Jesus, warned the Christian communities around 105 A.D. to treat the bishops with respect. "I exhort you to study to do all things with a divine harmony, while your bishop presides in the place of God, and your presbyters in the place of the assembly of apostles, along with your deacons." (Ignatius, quoted in Bercot, vol. 1, p. 61)

So, it is easy to see that Jesus had trained the apostles well. As soon as they were left on their own, with the Holy Spirit guiding them, they immediately embarked on their mission of preaching the kingdom. But they were not alone. The Holy Spirit whom Jesus had promised to send to them was always present, guiding, cajoling, prodding, comforting, and strengthening. There were trouble spots occasioned by differing interpretations of the meaning of some of Jesus' directives, like the differing interpretations of how the dietary laws should pertain to the new converts and whether Jewish converts were still under the obligation to observe those laws. For the most part, everyone seemed to work smoothly with one another, and if a matter came up, it was referred to Peter, the Rock. Paul had a problem with Peter following a double standard: on the one hand, observing the dietary laws when he was dining with Jewish Christians, and then eating "unclean" food when eating with Greek Christians. Paul made an issue of that right to Peter's face, as Paul felt strongly that Jesus came to free us from all the old laws. However, Paul did worse than Peter. When Paul decided to consecrate Timothy as bishop, he had a problem. Timothy's mother was a Jew, and Timothy had never been circumcised, so to avoid shocking Jewish Christians, he circumcised Timothy, even though he was fully aware that Jesus had abrogated the law of circumcision.

And then there were the problems arising from their sharing all things in common. The apostles soon found themselves overwhelmed with the daily burdens of distribution of food and clothing and other necessities of life, like shelter for the homeless, and care of the sick. It was at that time that the apostles felt it necessary to begin a new order in their ranks, the order of deacon, which was a sharing in the powers that Jesus had given to the apostles themselves. This delegated power was to care for the poor and sick and later play an official though limited role in administering the sacraments. This was an example of how they exercised the authority Jesus gave to them when he said to Peter, "Whatever you bind on earth, I will bind in heaven." (Mt. 16:19)

45

WHO IS THIS MAN JESUS WHOM
YOU PREACH?

I t was not long after a considerable number of learned Gentiles accepted Jesus and his message that they began to ask questions along
the lines of, "Who is this Jesus you preach to us? Is he one of us or is he
a demigod, or is he God?" This was legitimate enough. Saint Peter even
encouraged that kind of questioning when he wrote, "Find a reason for
your faith." Peter was not offended by the new converts questioning. He
understood their questioning, as he had questioned his faith all his life
with Jesus, filled with doubts right to the end. So, when *his* converts had
doubts and problems with *their* faith, trying to understand this Jesus who
was supposed to be their Savior, he could empathize with them, especially those converts who were deeply into philosophy and the meaning
of life.

John also experienced the same questioning among his converts and
even among his loyal disciples. They had a need to plumb more deeply
into an understanding of who this Jesus was whom they were called to
worship. "Is he a god, as we were taught to look upon gods, or is he only
partly god, since we are told he is human like us? What kind of a god is
this?" That is the way they must have thought.

John knew his disciples. Many were Greek philosophers who were
familiar with their philosopher Heraclitus and his understanding of the
"Logos" as the source and fundamental order of the universe. John cleverly worked that philosophical concept into the beginning of his Gospel.

"In the beginning was the *Logos*, the Word, and the *Logos*, the Word,
was with God and the *Logos*, the Word, was God. All things created
came into being through him, and nothing that exists came into being
without him. What came into being through him was life, life for the

light of the human family, a light that shines in darkness, a darkness that was not able to extinguish it." (Jn. 1:1–5)

John also worked into his speaking and writing the idea of light and darkness, concepts familiar to the philosophers, which provided an easy transition from philosophy to faith in the minds of these searching wise men. Jesus was the Word, the Logos, the Word expressed by the Mind of God, giving eternal existence in reality to this thought produced from the mind of the Father, and expressed as the Word of God. This divine Word has his own identity, his own being, his own existence, a living facet of the divine nature. By the overshadowing of the Holy Spirit, he took upon himself a human nature and was born of the Virgin Mary, and lived just like us in all things but sin.

Although the apostles and their immediate disciples never used the term Holy Trinity in referring to God, they taught about each of the three divine persons. Teaching about Jesus as the Son of God was paramount in the beginning, then as their teaching of their disciples advanced they spoke of the Holy Spirit as the living Spirit of God. Irenaeus, writing around 180 A.D., said, "I have largely demonstrated that the Word, namely the Son, was always with the Father. And that Wisdom also, who is the Spirit, was present with Him before all creation. He declares this by Solomon: 'By Wisdom, God founded the earth, and by understanding He has established the heavens.' . . . There is therefore one God, who by the Word and Wisdom created and arranged all things." (Irenaeus, quoted in Bercot, vol. 1, p. 488)

Hermas, writing around 150 A.D., said, "If you be patient, the Holy Spirit who dwells in you will be pure. He will not be darkened by any evil spirit, but dwelling in a wide region, He will rejoice and be glad. . . . But, if any outburst of anger takes place, immediately the Holy Spirit, who is sensitive, is constricted. For He does not have a pure place and He seeks to depart, for He is choked by a vile spirit." (Hermas, quoted in Bercot, vol. 2, p. 23)

By the time the Fathers of the Church rose to their proper place in the life of the Christian community, the Gospel had already spread not only to most of the known Roman world, but as far east as India by Saint Thomas. Saint Mark brought the Gospel to Egypt, and other places in the region. Peter went to Antioch and then on to Rome. Paul traveled from country to country around the eastern end of the Mediterranean, up into Macedonia and other regions in the vicinity, ending up in Rome, where he was finally martyred for his faith.

The life of the kingdom of heaven which Jesus came to earth to establish was well underway, and will grow continually through good and bad times, like the rich harvest he talked about, but a harvest in which they will find weeds. It is also like the catch of fish, with wonderful fresh fish, but also, many bad fish. The kingdom of God will grow miraculously through the centuries, in spite of evil without and evil within. It will grow through prosperity and through degradation, and even after humbling and degrading moments, will become more vital and life-giving. Nothing will stop its growth, as it is the divine work of God for the salvation of the whole human race, and it will be on this earth as long as there are human beings needing redemption and salvation. All other institutions will come and go, and the Church that Jesus established will continue unto the end, because it is the living, mystical body of Jesus Christ, forever alive among us.

Thanks be to God.

ACKNOWLEDGMENTS

This manuscript could not have been written without the valuable help and suggestions of friends who painstakingly read and reread chapter after chapter to make sure the thoughts were clearly stated and expressed in a way that would make sense to readers. Jesus did not teach or speak to confuse us, but to enlighten us in understanding the important and unchanging truths necessary for us if we are to follow Him as our Way, our Truth and our Life. I am grateful to my dear friends Brad Broyles, my faithful assistant, and Richard and Elizabeth Della Ratta for their painstaking reading and rereading of the manuscript as it was being written, helping me, not only in clarifying ideas, but in polishing and refining the text itself. For that valuable help I am most grateful. Deacon Gary Riggi, a dear friend who is much more current in his knowledge of theological and Scriptural matters than I, was most helpful in his suggestions as to the interpretation of certain events in Jesus' life and how certain sayings of Jesus could be better expressed to make them more poignant to a modern audience.

I am also grateful to my agent and friend, Peter Ginsberg, for his unflagging support and encouragement in difficult times. Without his help much of my work would not have been possible. And my friends, Trace Murphy and Bill Barry and Darya Porat, who have always been ready to help smooth the way, and devise creative suggestions when the road sometimes became uncomfortable, how can I thank them for all their valuable help?

And I cannot even find words to express my admiration and gratitude to Jean Lynch, who showed heroic patience and persistent genius in polishing a manuscript with so many flaws.

Joseph F. Girzone